Angel Sanctuary™

story and art by **Kaori Yuki**
vol. 12

Angel Sanctuary

Vol. 12
Shôjo Edition

STORY AND ART BY KAORI YUKI

Translation/Alexis Kirsch
English Adaptation/Matt Segale
Touch-up & Lettering/James Hudnall
Cover, Graphics & Design/Izumi Evers
Editor/Nancy Thistlethwaite

Managing Editor/Annette Roman
Director of Production/Noboru Watanabe
Vice President of Publishing/Alvin Lu
Sr. Director of Acquisitions/Rika Inouye
VP of Sales & Marketing/Liza Coppola
Publisher/Hyoe Narita

Printed in Canada.

Published by VIZ Media, LLC
P.O. Box 77010
San Francisco, CA 94107

Shôjo Edition
10 9 8 7 6 5 4 3 2 1
First printing, January 2006

www.viz.com
store.viz.com

Angel Sanctuary ™

story and art by Kaori Yuki   vol. 12

The Story Thus Far

High school boy Setsuna Mudo's life is hellish. He's always been a troublemaker, but his worst sin was falling incestuously in love with his beautiful sister Sara. But his troubles are preordained—Setsuna is the reincarnation of the Lady Alexiel, an angel who rebelled against Heaven and led the demons of Hell in a revolt. Her punishment was to be reborn into tragic life after tragic life. This time, her life is as Setsuna.

Setsuna's body, left behind on Earth while he searched Hell for his beloved Sara's soul, has died. When Setsuna returned from Hell along the Meidou path of reincarnation, he reemerged on Earth in the body of the Angel Alexiel. Now Setsuna is determined to brave the gates of Heaven in order to retrieve his sister.

The Angel Alexiel appears before Nanatsusaya and reveals that she had made a pact with Rosiel long ago to kill him and destroy God in order to break the never-ending curse that was placed upon them. Finding she was unable to carry out the task in the past, she waited for the savior Setsuna before awakening to fight against Heaven.

Kurai tries to sacrifice herself for Setsuna, but Arachne steps in and takes her place. Setsuna is then resurrected in his own body and pledges to save Sara. The Fallen Angel Zaphikel uses Raziel to contact Setsuna in secret. He asks Setsuna to join the rebel organization and fight Sevothtarte, who is holding Sara prisoner.

Contents

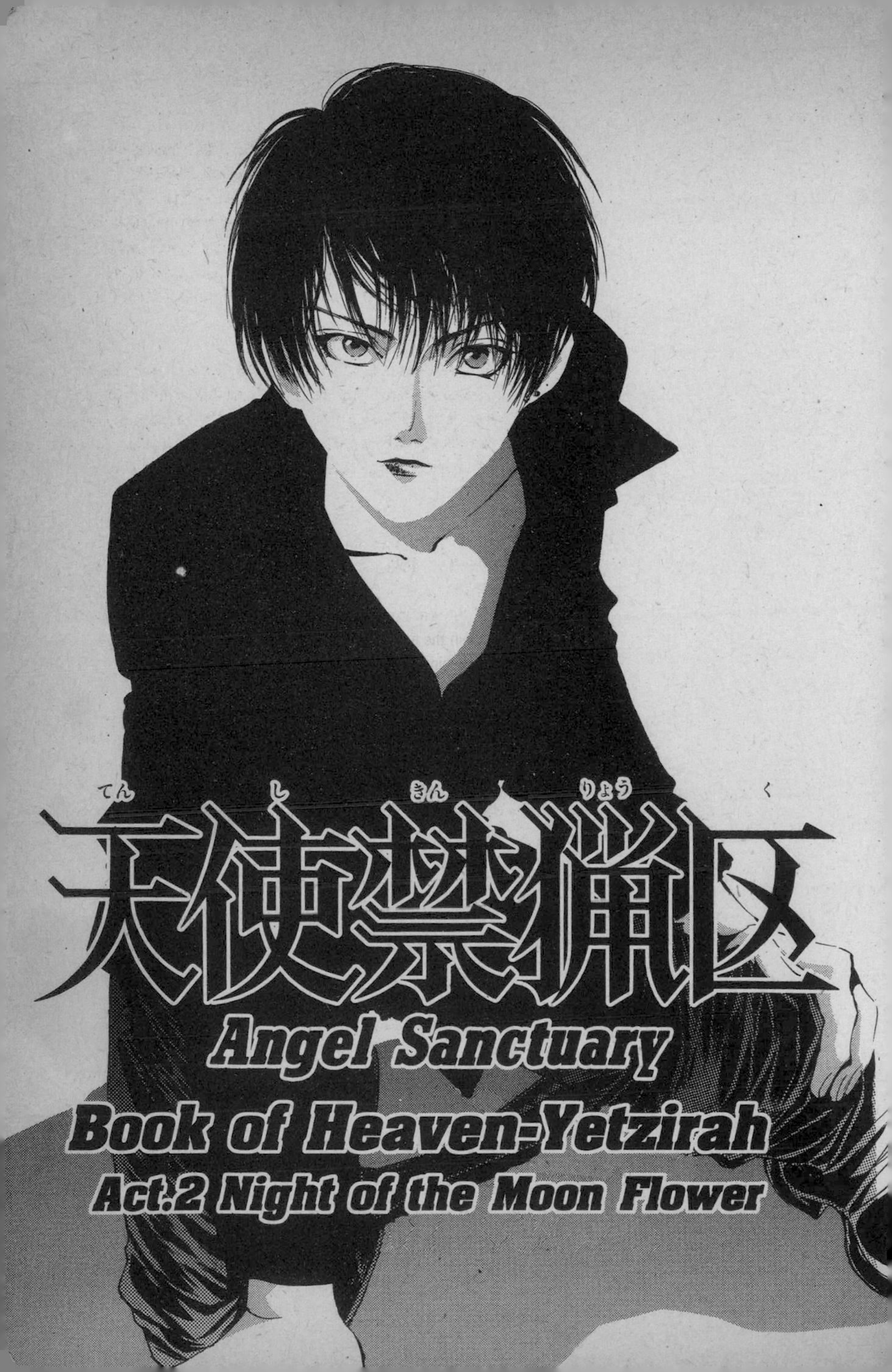

てん し きん りょう く
天使禁猟区
Angel Sanctuary
Book of Heaven-Yetzirah
Act.2 Night of the Moon Flower

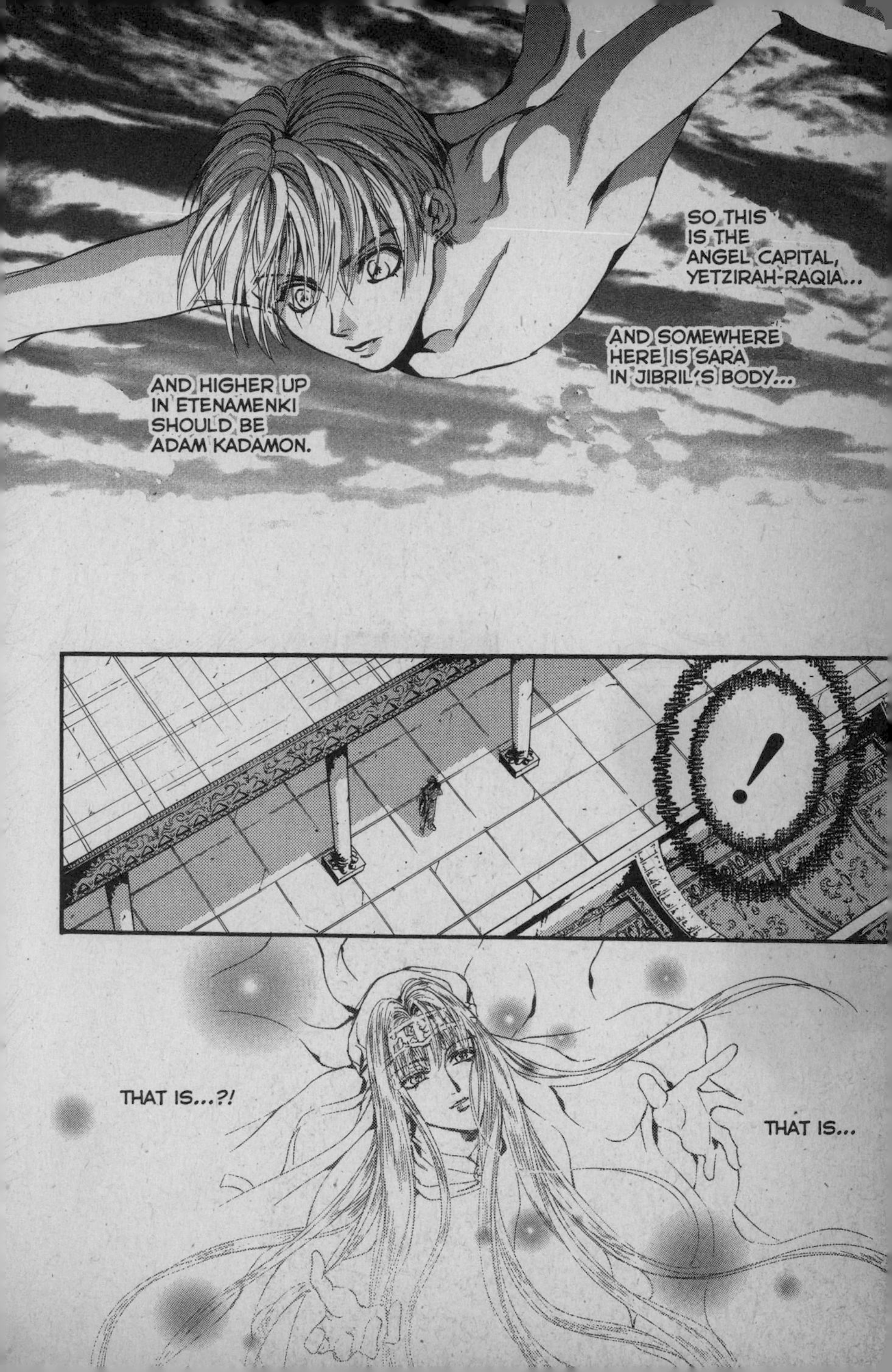
SO THIS IS THE ANGEL CAPITAL, YETZIRAH-RAQIA...
AND SOMEWHERE HERE IS SARA IN JIBRIL'S BODY...
AND HIGHER UP IN ETENAMENKI SHOULD BE ADAM KADAMON.
!
THAT IS...
THAT IS...?!

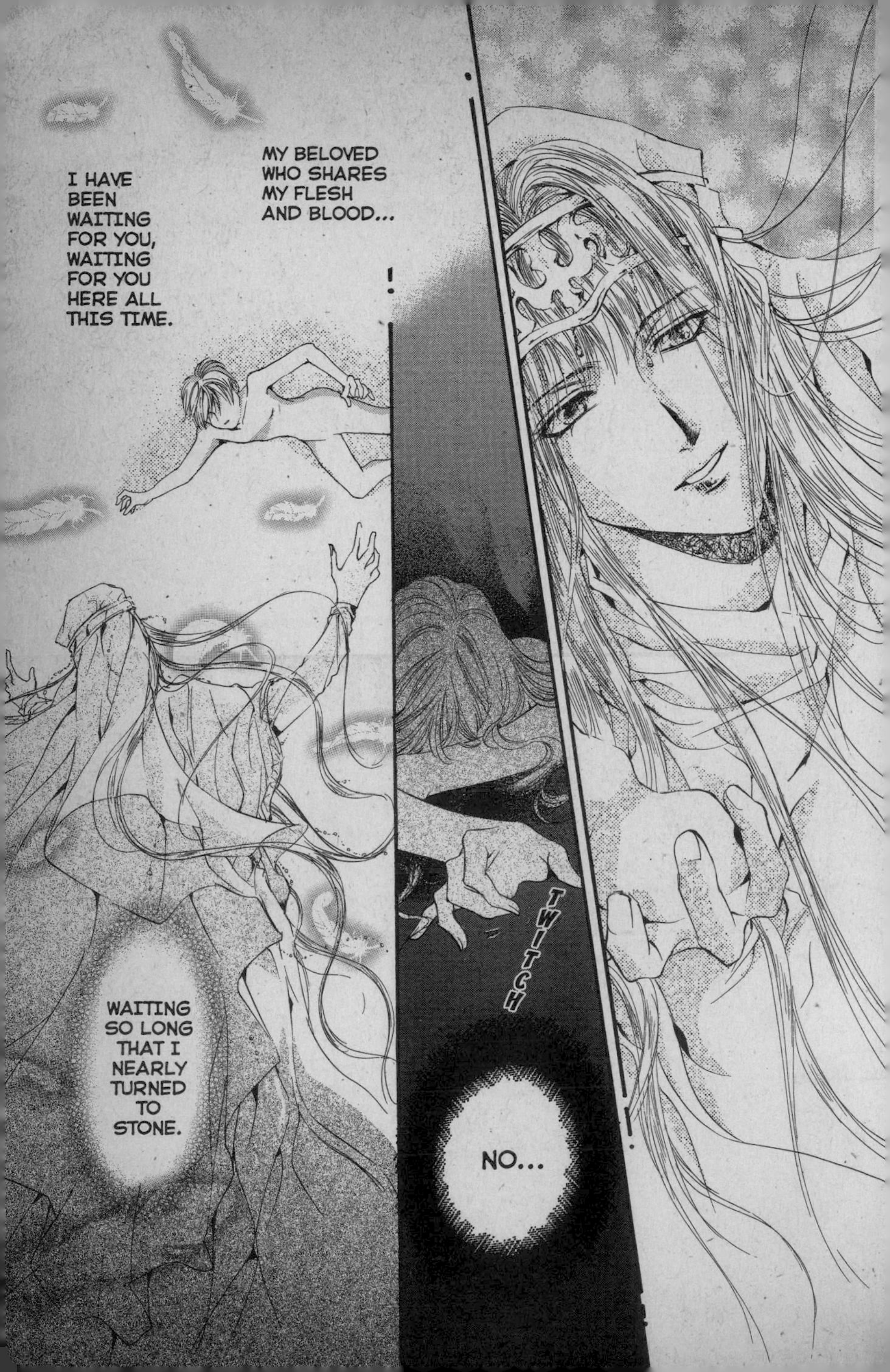
!
TWITCH
NO...
MY BELOVED WHO SHARES MY FLESH AND BLOOD...
I HAVE BEEN WAITING FOR YOU, WAITING FOR YOU HERE ALL THIS TIME.
WAITING SO LONG THAT I NEARLY TURNED TO STONE.

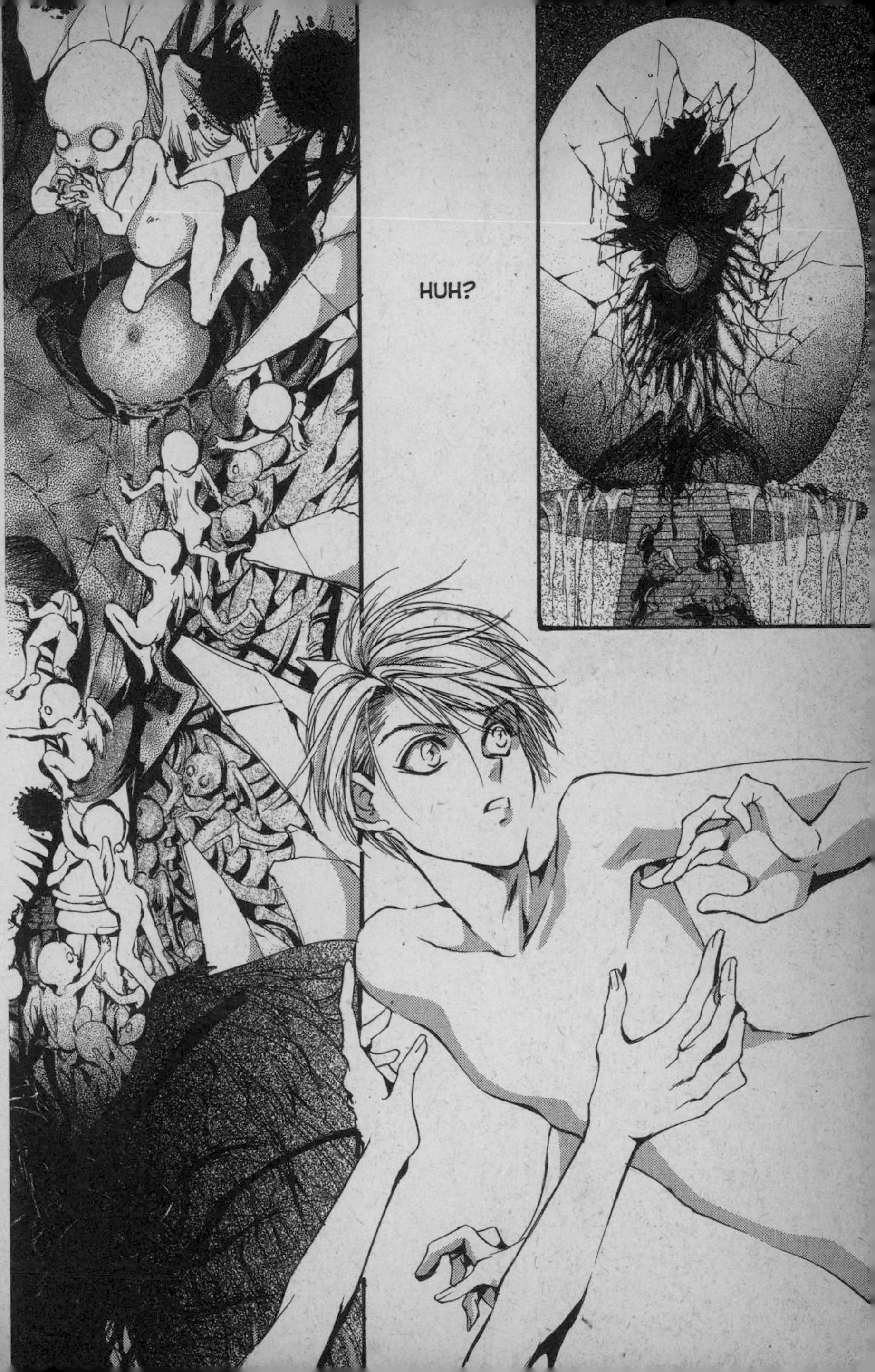
HUH?

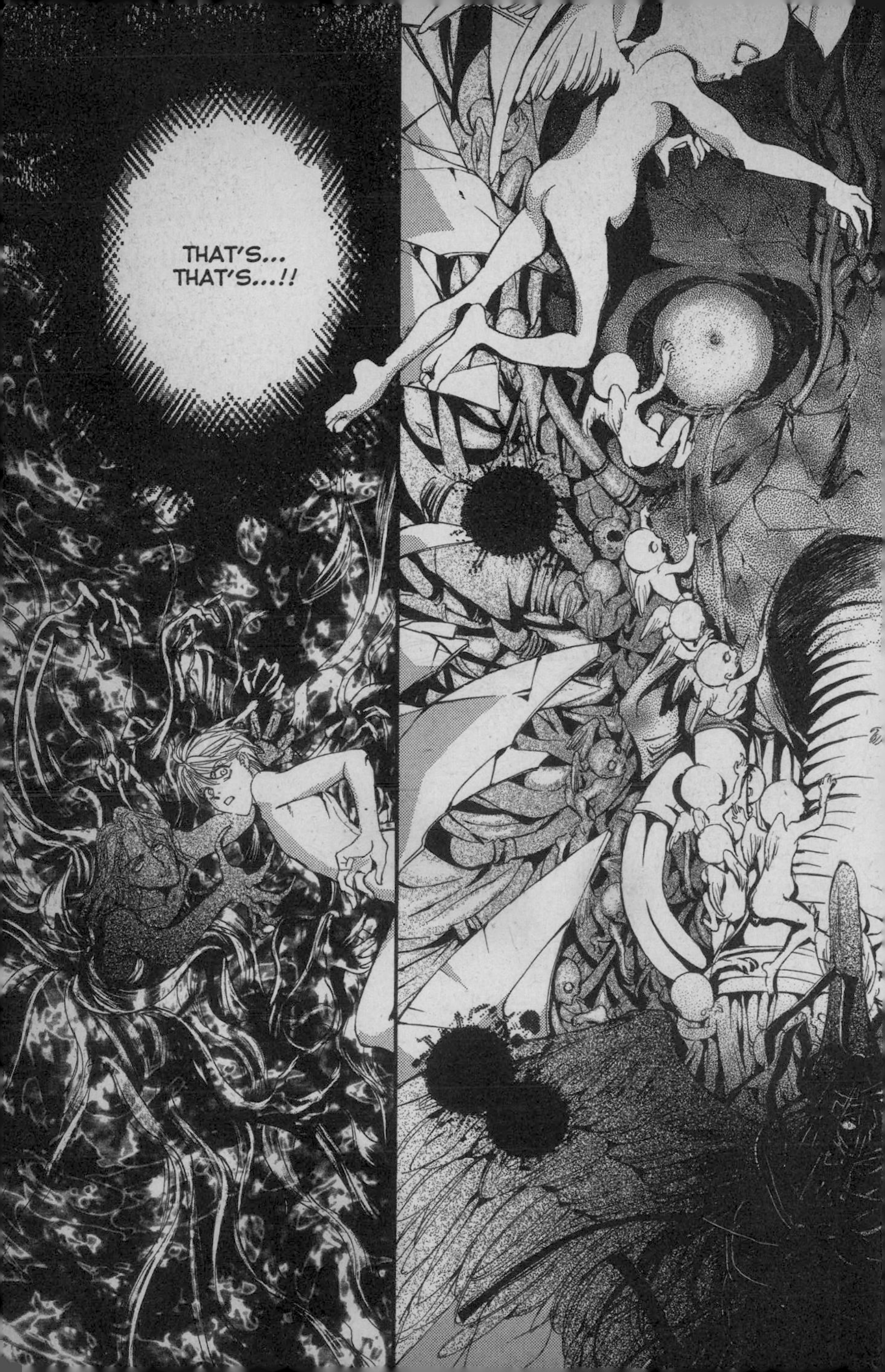
THAT'S... THAT'S...!!

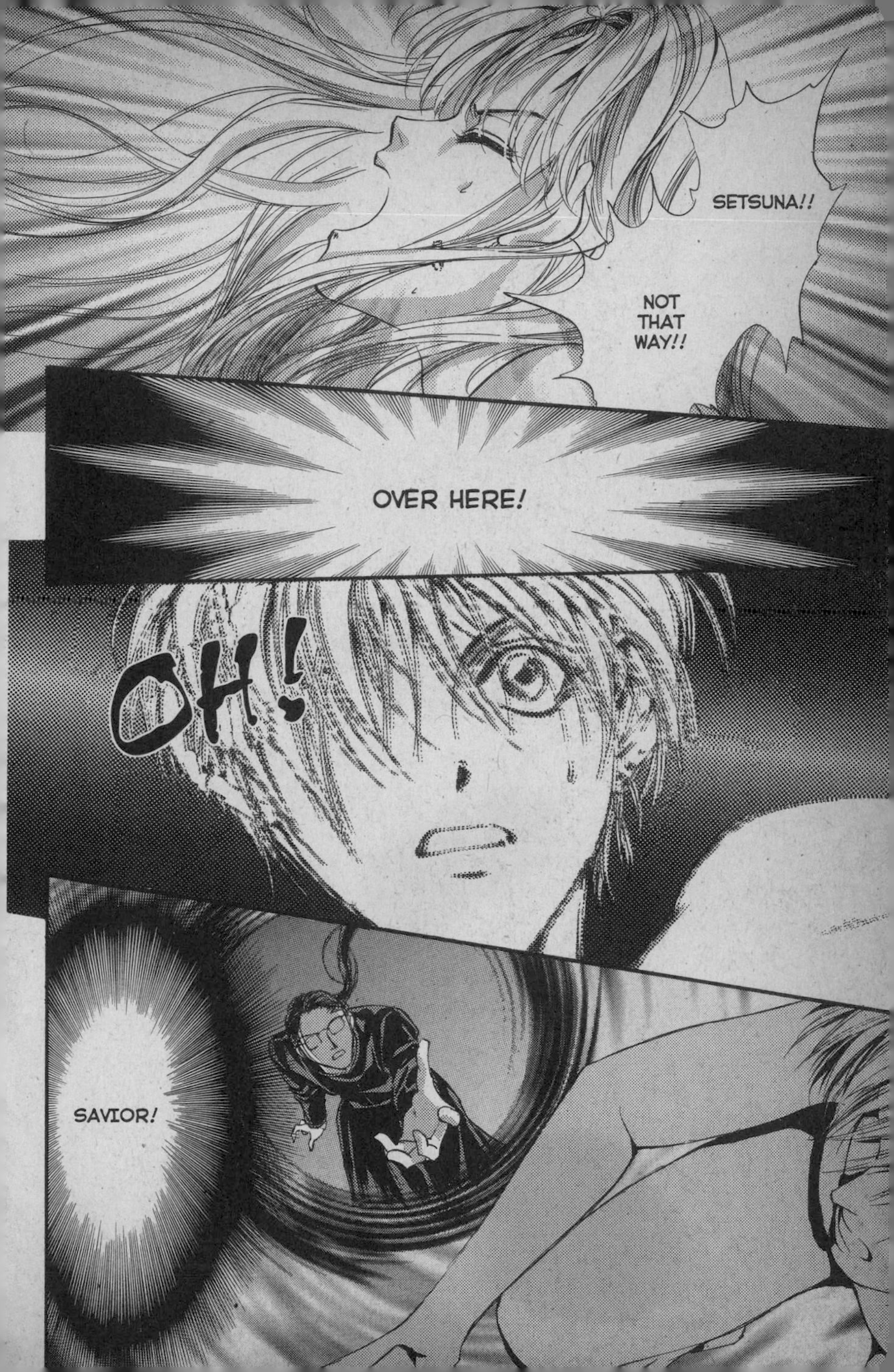
SETSUNA!!
NOT THAT WAY!!
OVER HERE!
OH!
SAVIOR!

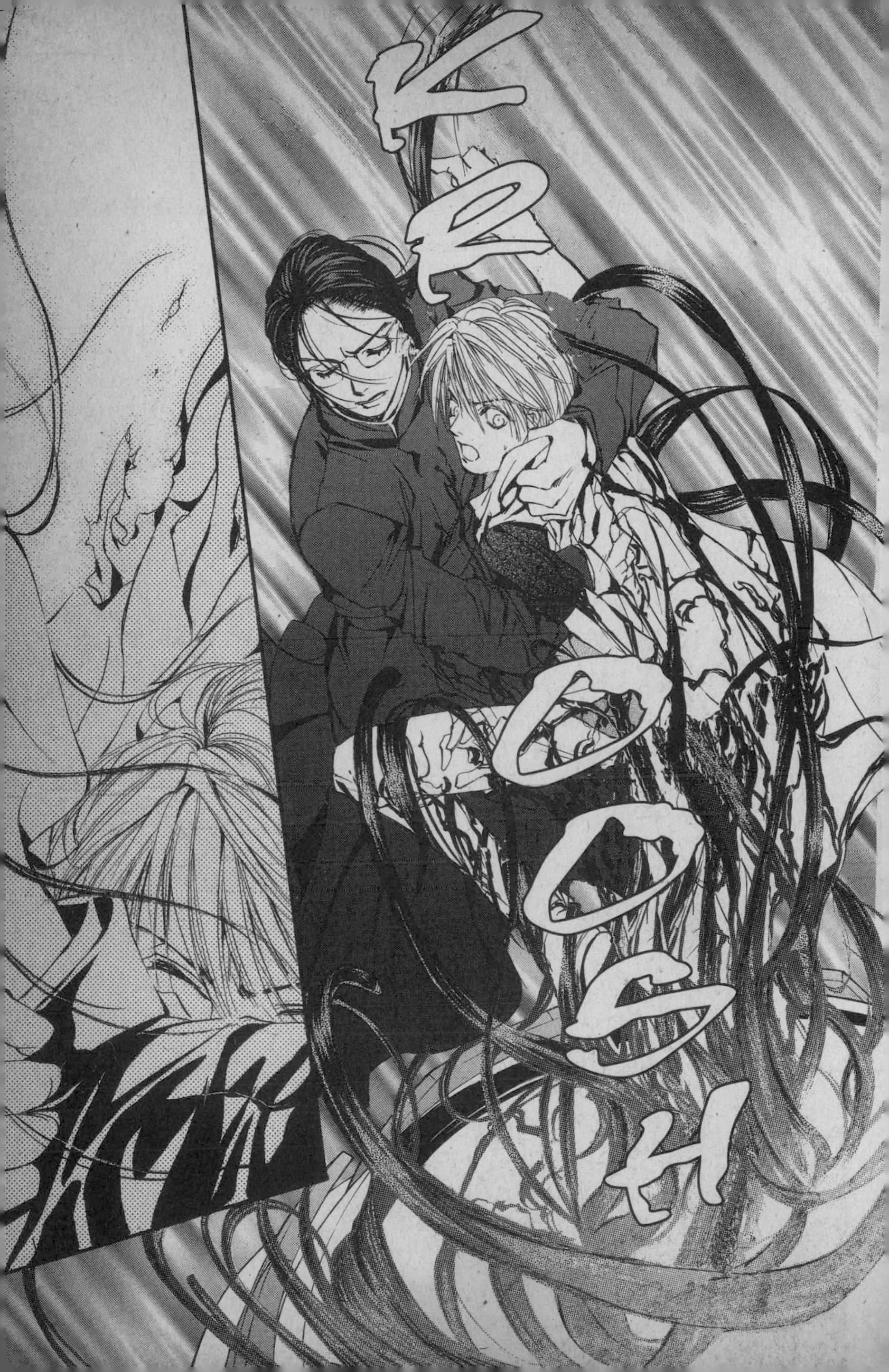
SWOOSH

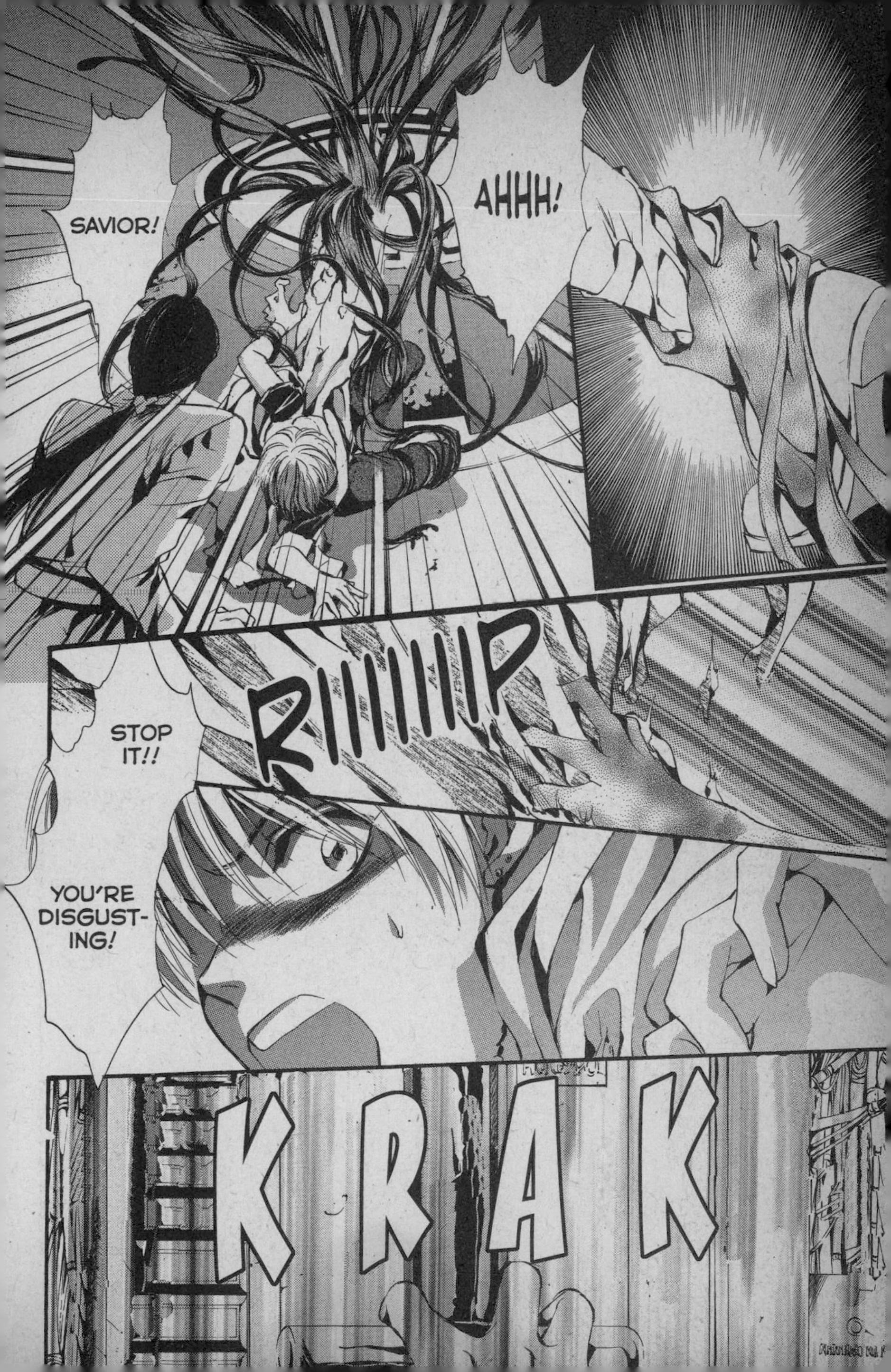
AHHH!
SAVIOR!
RIIIIIP
STOP IT!!
YOU'RE DISGUST-ING!
KRAK

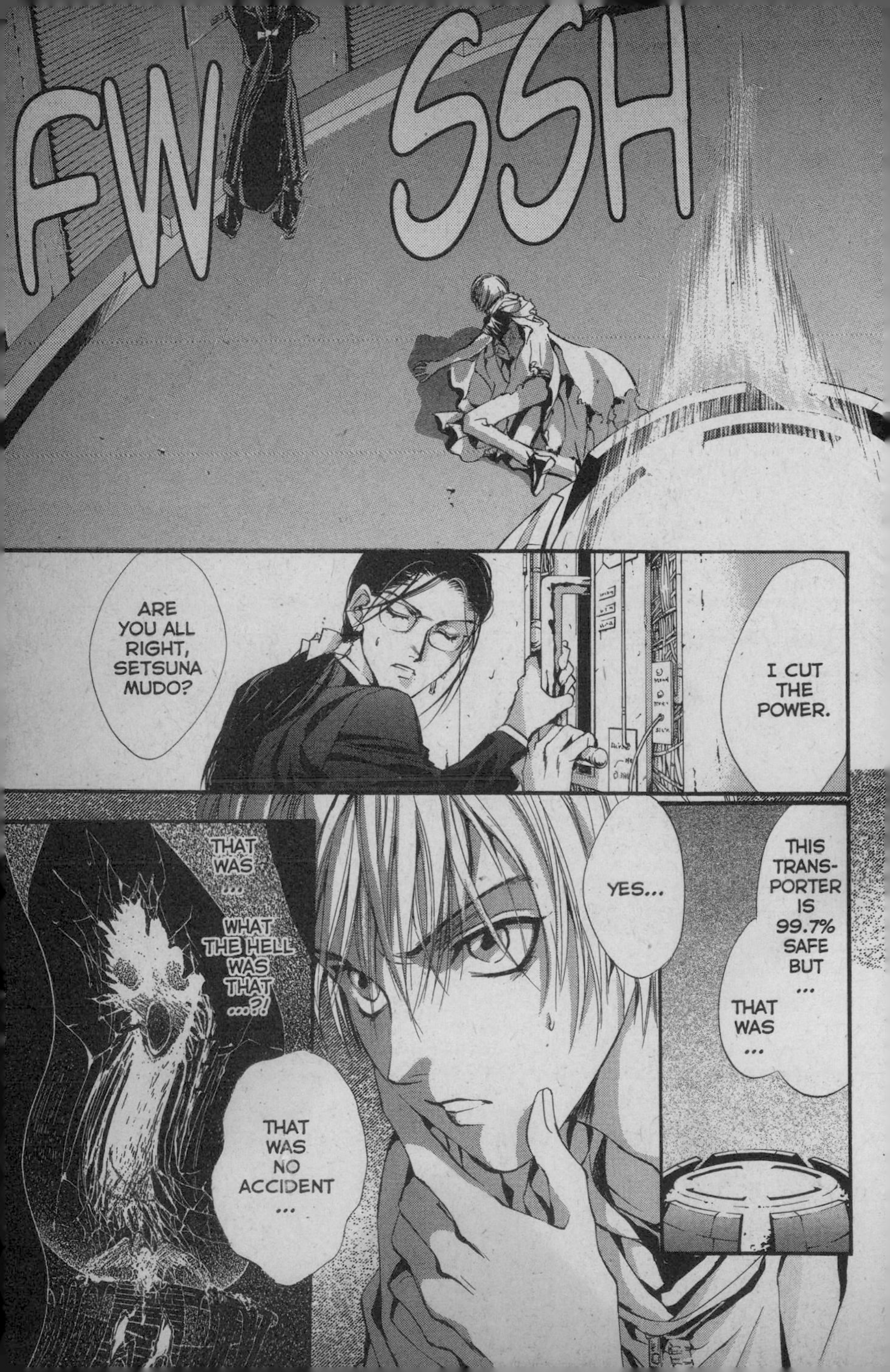
FWISSH
I CUT THE POWER.
ARE YOU ALL RIGHT, SETSUNA MUDO?
THIS TRANSPORTER IS 99.7% SAFE BUT ...
THAT WAS ...
YES...
THAT WAS ... WHAT THE HELL WAS THAT ...?!
THAT WAS NO ACCIDENT ...

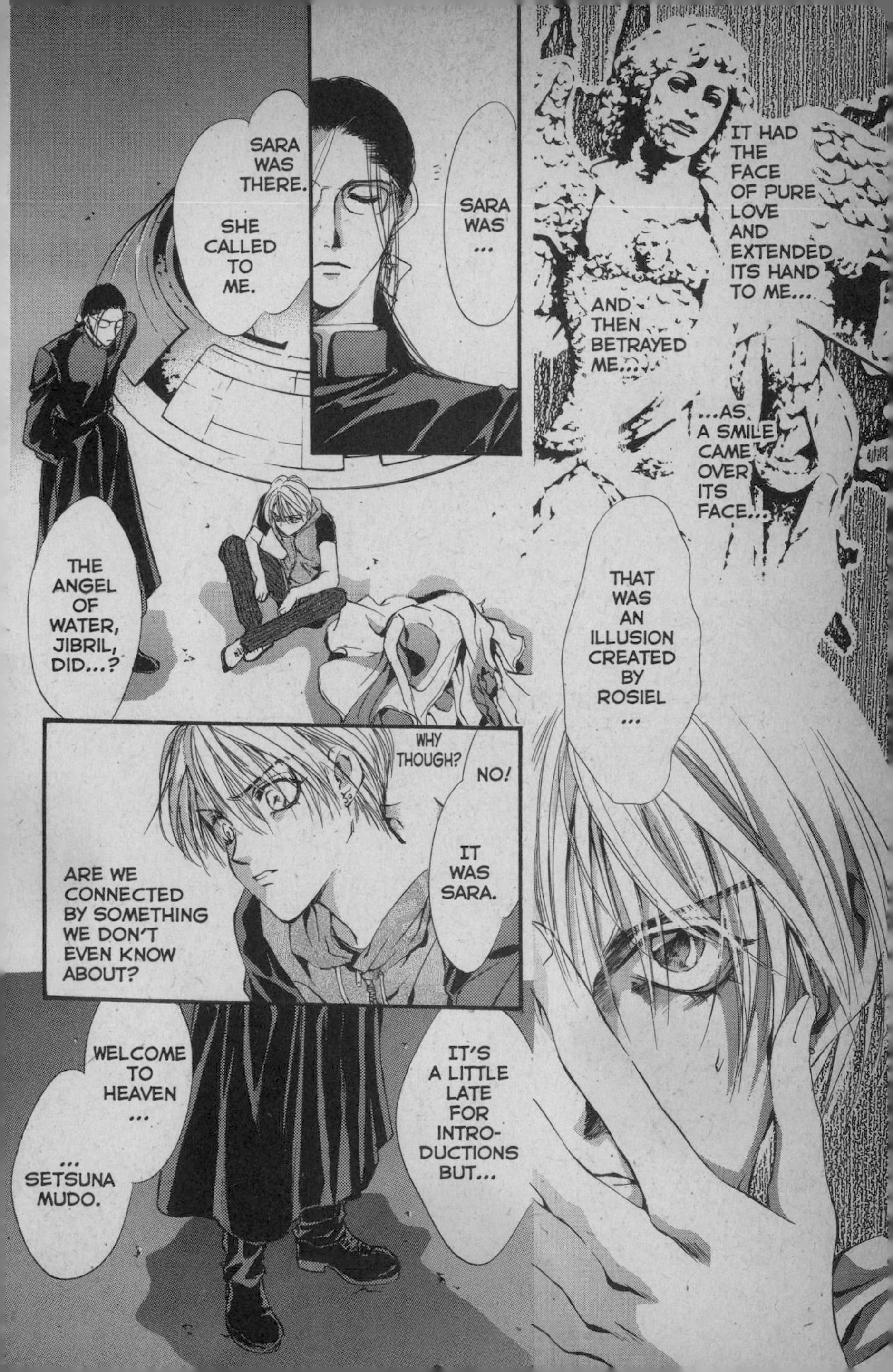
IT HAD THE FACE OF PURE LOVE AND EXTENDED ITS HAND TO ME...
AND THEN BETRAYED ME...
...AS A SMILE CAME OVER ITS FACE...
SARA WAS ...
SARA WAS THERE.
SHE CALLED TO ME.
THE ANGEL OF WATER, JIBRIL, DID...?
THAT WAS AN ILLUSION CREATED BY ROSIEL ...
NO!
IT WAS SARA.
WHY THOUGH?
ARE WE CONNECTED BY SOMETHING WE DON'T EVEN KNOW ABOUT?
IT'S A LITTLE LATE FOR INTRODUCTIONS BUT...
WELCOME TO HEAVEN ...
... SETSUNA MUDO.

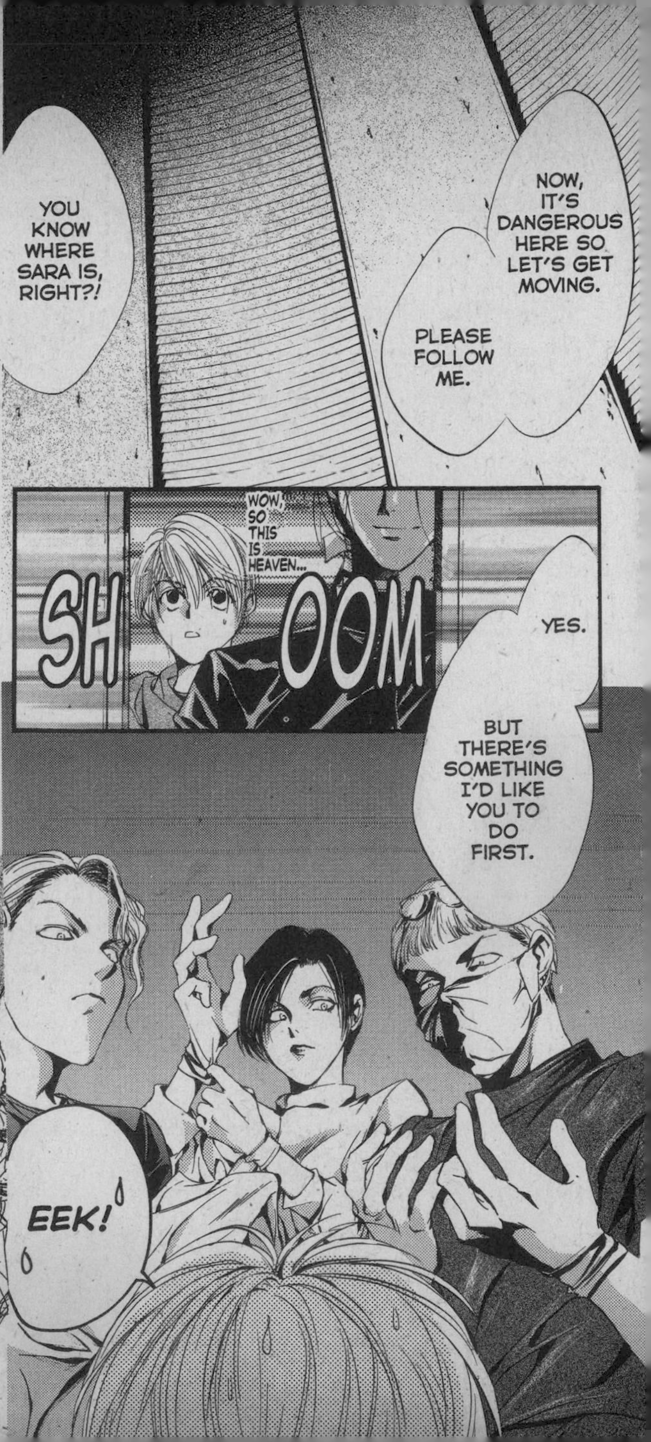
NOW, IT'S DANGEROUS HERE SO LET'S GET MOVING.
PLEASE FOLLOW ME.
YOU KNOW WHERE SARA IS, RIGHT?!
WOW, SO THIS IS HEAVEN...
SH OOM
YES.
BUT THERE'S SOMETHING I'D LIKE YOU TO DO FIRST.
EEK!

12 books. It's happened so quickly. I guess this story will probably go up to book 16 or 17, so...? Well... I don't know just yet. July 1999 would be the perfect time to end but we'll see. Don't worry, I'll end it at the appropriate place. I don't want to just have the characters act crazy and have the series drag on and on and then have everything go back to normal in the last chapter, anything but that... But when people think it's about to end I get letters like "Please don't end it!" and others like "I know you have to but...sob...." That really makes it painful.

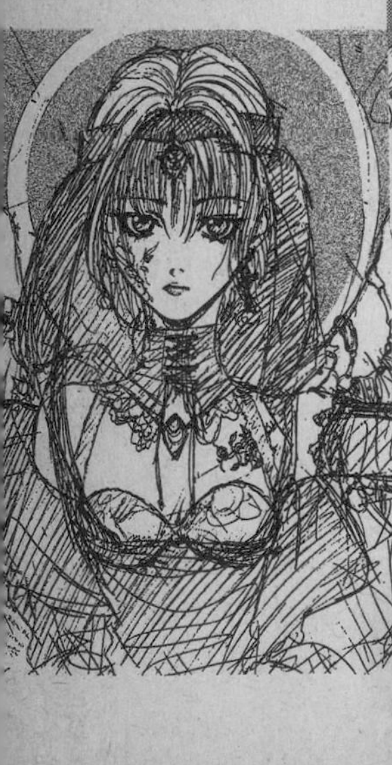

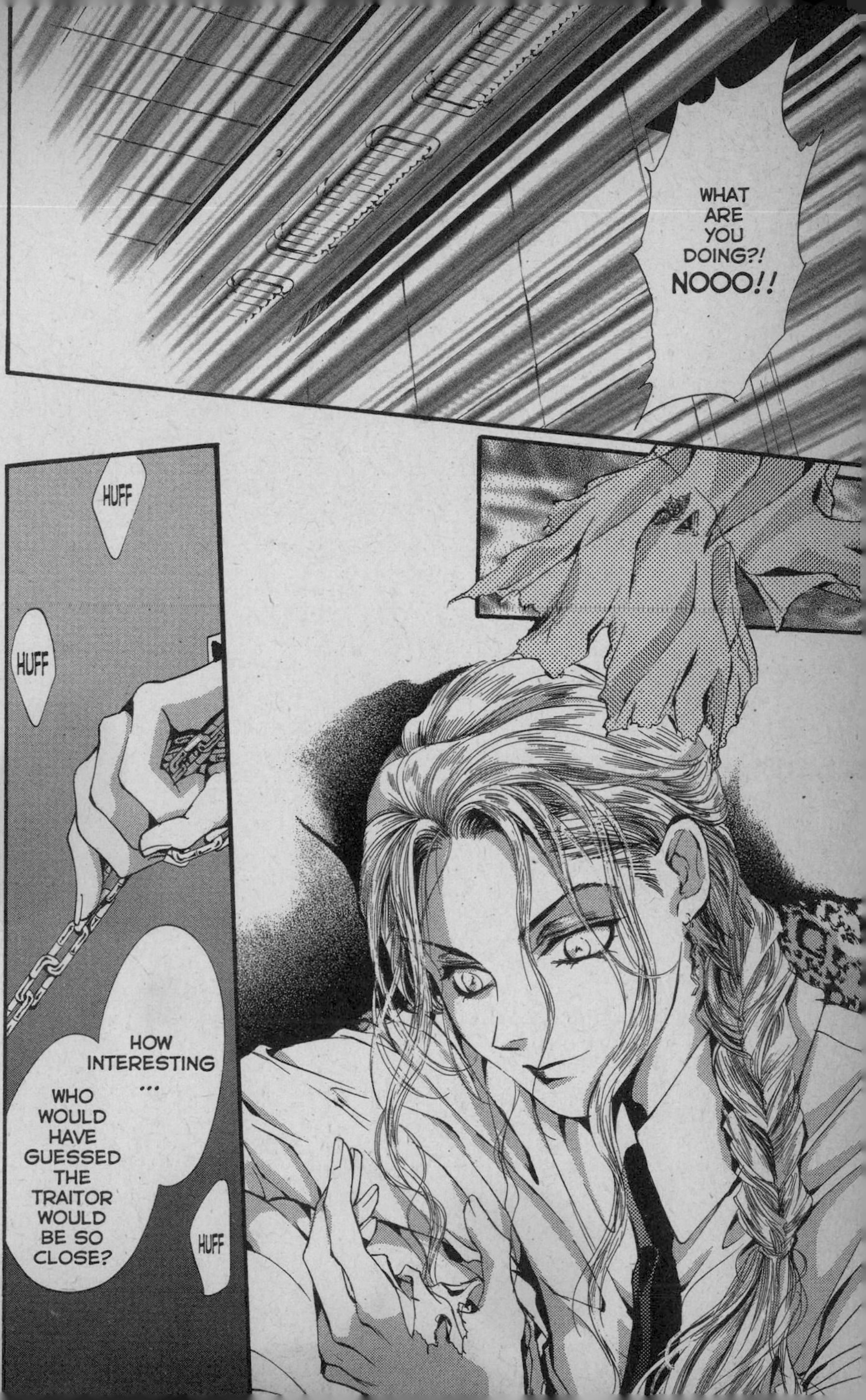
WHAT ARE YOU DOING?! NOOO!!
HUFF
HUFF
HOW INTERESTING... WHO WOULD HAVE GUESSED THE TRAITOR WOULD BE SO CLOSE?
HUFF

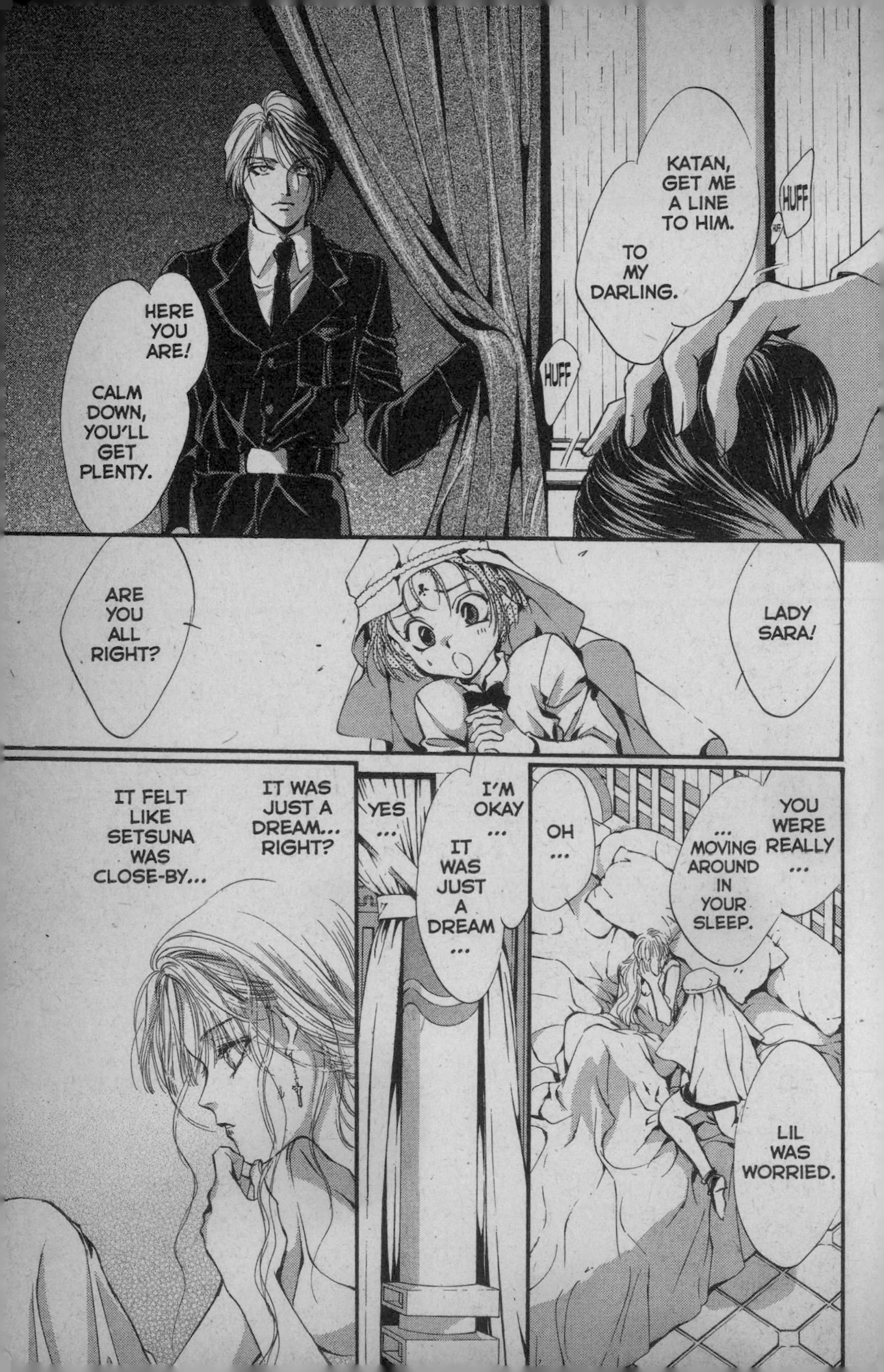

HUFF
KATAN, GET ME A LINE TO HIM.
TO MY DARLING.
HUFF
HERE YOU ARE!
CALM DOWN, YOU'LL GET PLENTY.
LADY SARA!
ARE YOU ALL RIGHT?
YOU WERE REALLY...
...MOVING AROUND IN YOUR SLEEP.
LIL WAS WORRIED.
OH...
I'M OKAY...
IT WAS JUST A DREAM...
YES...
IT WAS JUST A DREAM... RIGHT?
IT FELT LIKE SETSUNA WAS CLOSE-BY...

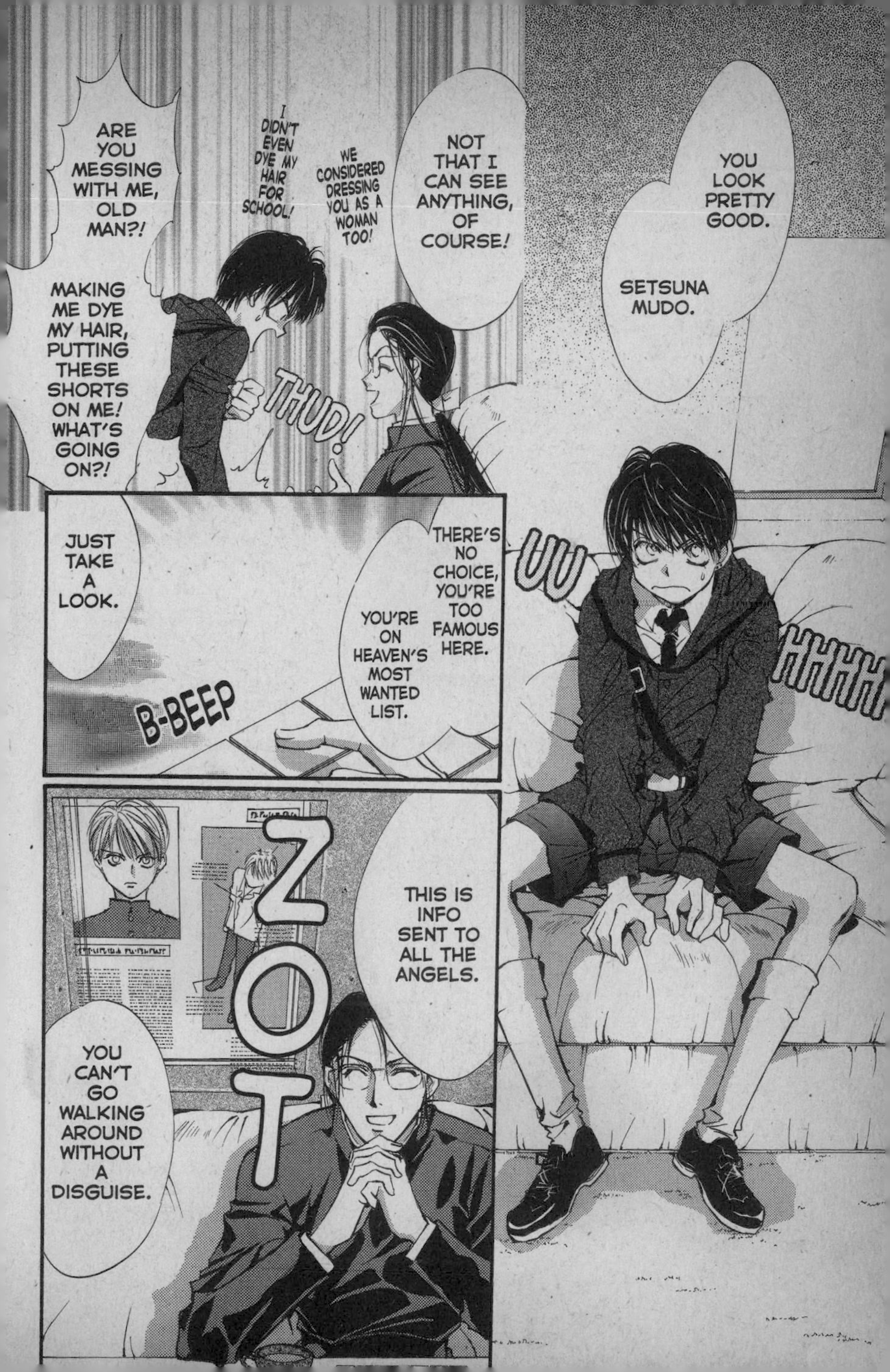
YOU LOOK PRETTY GOOD.
SETSUNA MUDO.
UUHHHHH
NOT THAT I CAN SEE ANYTHING, OF COURSE!
WE CONSIDERED DRESSING YOU AS A WOMAN TOO!
I DIDN'T EVEN DYE MY HAIR FOR SCHOOL!
THUD!
ARE YOU MESSING WITH ME, OLD MAN?!
MAKING ME DYE MY HAIR, PUTTING THESE SHORTS ON ME! WHAT'S GOING ON?!
THERE'S NO CHOICE, YOU'RE TOO FAMOUS HERE.
YOU'RE ON HEAVEN'S MOST WANTED LIST.
B-BEEP
JUST TAKE A LOOK.
THIS IS INFO SENT TO ALL THE ANGELS.
ZOT
YOU CAN'T GO WALKING AROUND WITHOUT A DISGUISE.

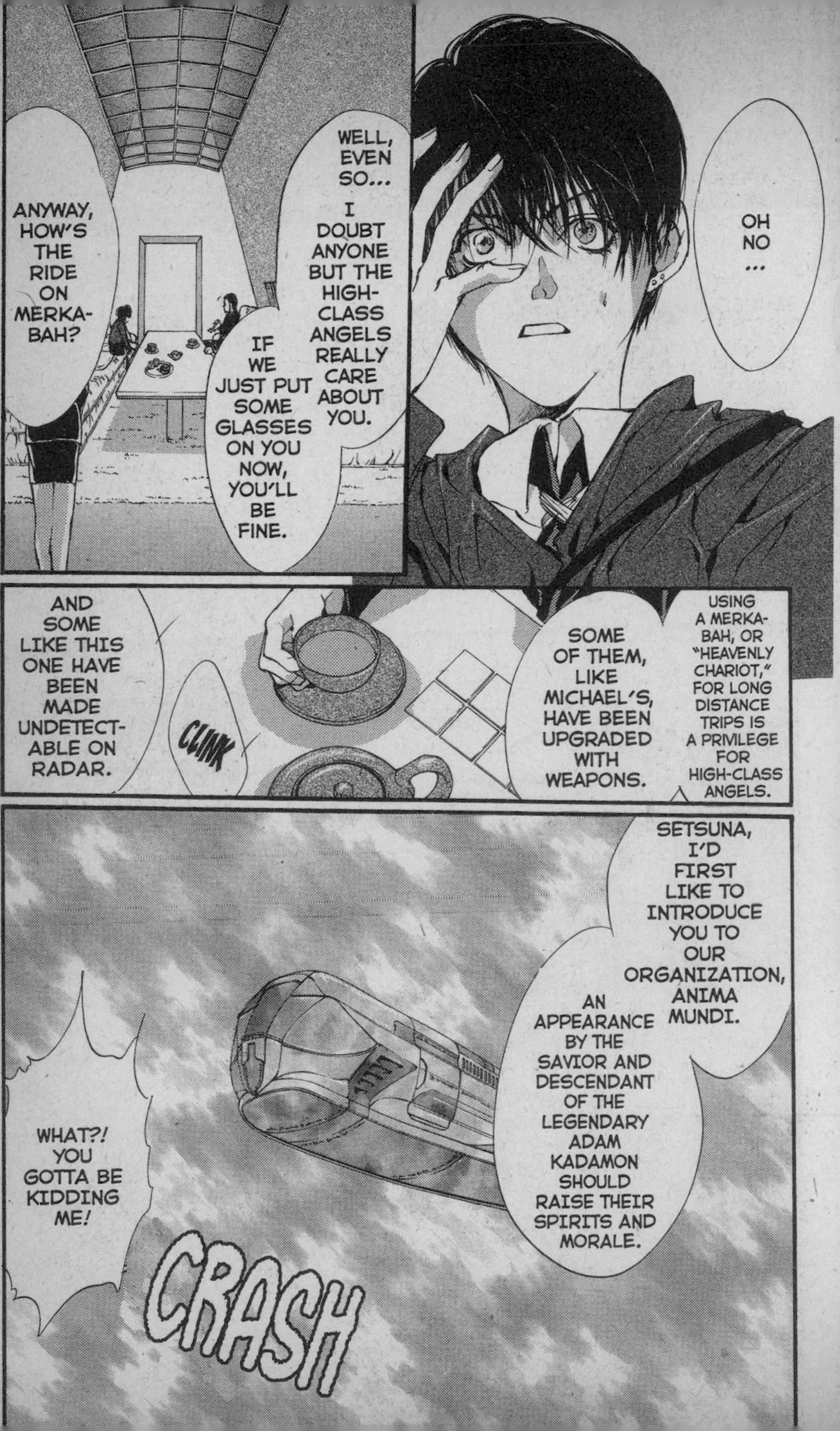
OH NO ...
WELL, EVEN SO... I DOUBT ANYONE BUT THE HIGH-CLASS ANGELS REALLY CARE ABOUT YOU.
IF WE JUST PUT SOME GLASSES ON YOU NOW, YOU'LL BE FINE.
ANYWAY, HOW'S THE RIDE ON MERKA-BAH?
USING A MERKA-BAH, OR "HEAVENLY CHARIOT," FOR LONG DISTANCE TRIPS IS A PRIVILEGE FOR HIGH-CLASS ANGELS.
SOME OF THEM, LIKE MICHAEL'S, HAVE BEEN UPGRADED WITH WEAPONS.
CLINK
AND SOME LIKE THIS ONE HAVE BEEN MADE UNDETECT-ABLE ON RADAR.
SETSUNA, I'D FIRST LIKE TO INTRODUCE YOU TO OUR ORGANIZATION, ANIMA MUNDI.
AN APPEARANCE BY THE SAVIOR AND DESCENDANT OF THE LEGENDARY ADAM KADAMON SHOULD RAISE THEIR SPIRITS AND MORALE.
CRASH
WHAT?! YOU GOTTA BE KIDDING ME!

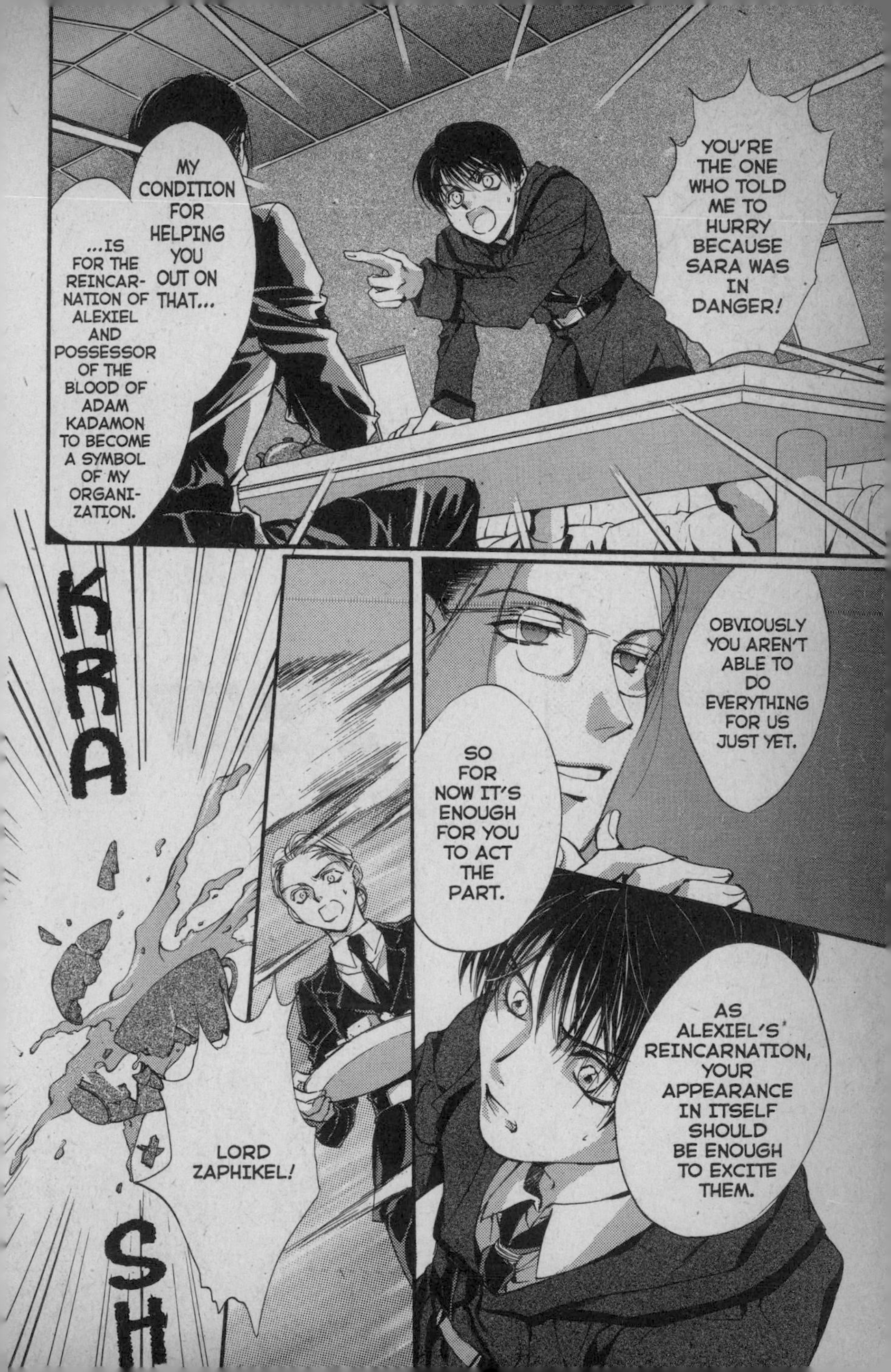
YOU'RE THE ONE WHO TOLD ME TO HURRY BECAUSE SARA WAS IN DANGER!
MY CONDITION FOR HELPING YOU OUT ON THAT...
...IS FOR THE REINCARNATION OF ALEXIEL AND POSSESSOR OF THE BLOOD OF ADAM KADAMON TO BECOME A SYMBOL OF MY ORGANIZATION.
OBVIOUSLY YOU AREN'T ABLE TO DO EVERYTHING FOR US JUST YET.
SO FOR NOW IT'S ENOUGH FOR YOU TO ACT THE PART.
AS ALEXIEL'S REINCARNATION, YOUR APPEARANCE IN ITSELF SHOULD BE ENOUGH TO EXCITE THEM.
LORD ZAPHIKEL!
KRASH

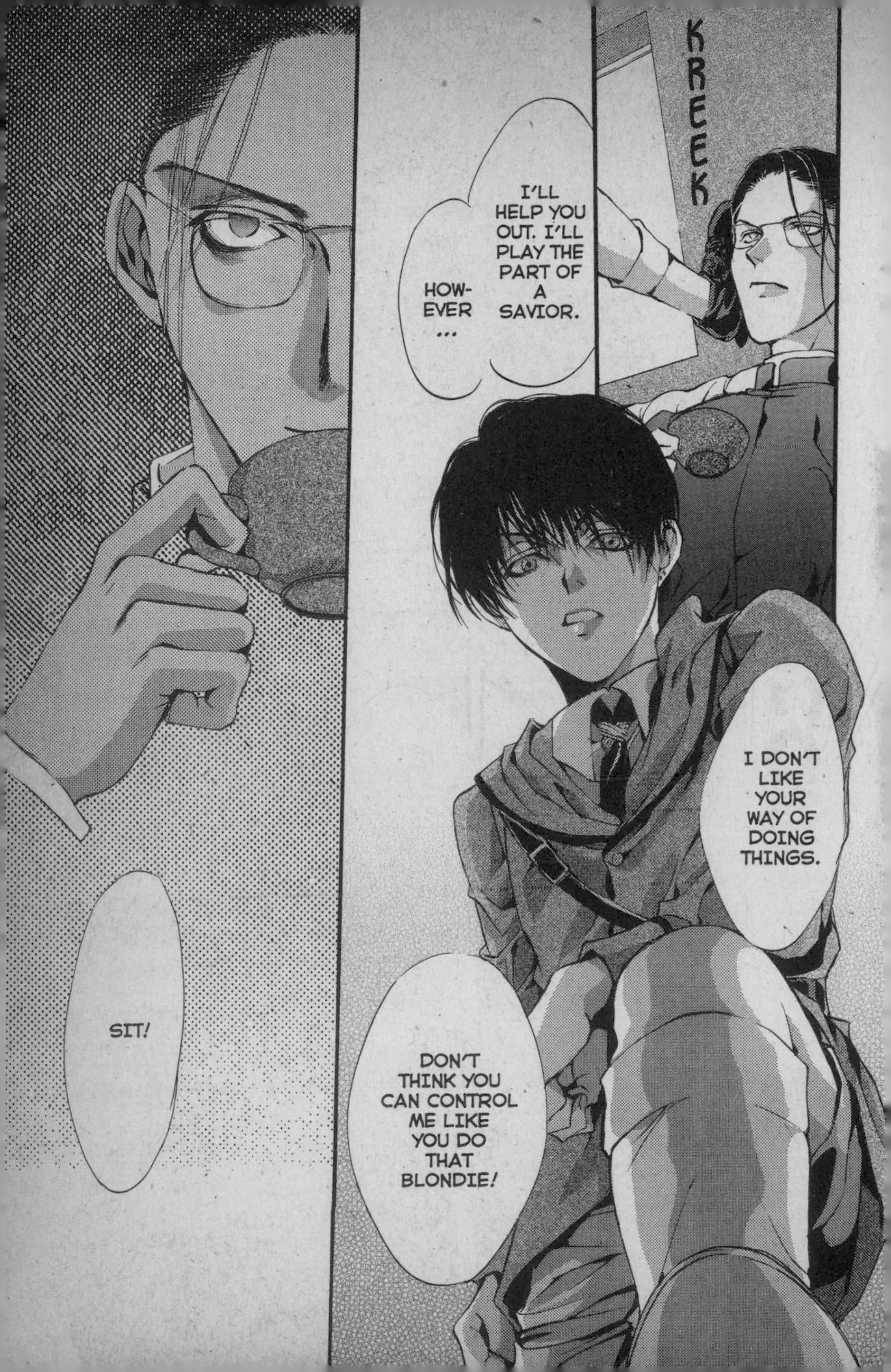
KREEK
I'LL HELP YOU OUT. I'LL PLAY THE PART OF A SAVIOR.
HOW-EVER...
I DON'T LIKE YOUR WAY OF DOING THINGS.
DON'T THINK YOU CAN CONTROL ME LIKE YOU DO THAT BLONDIE!
SIT!

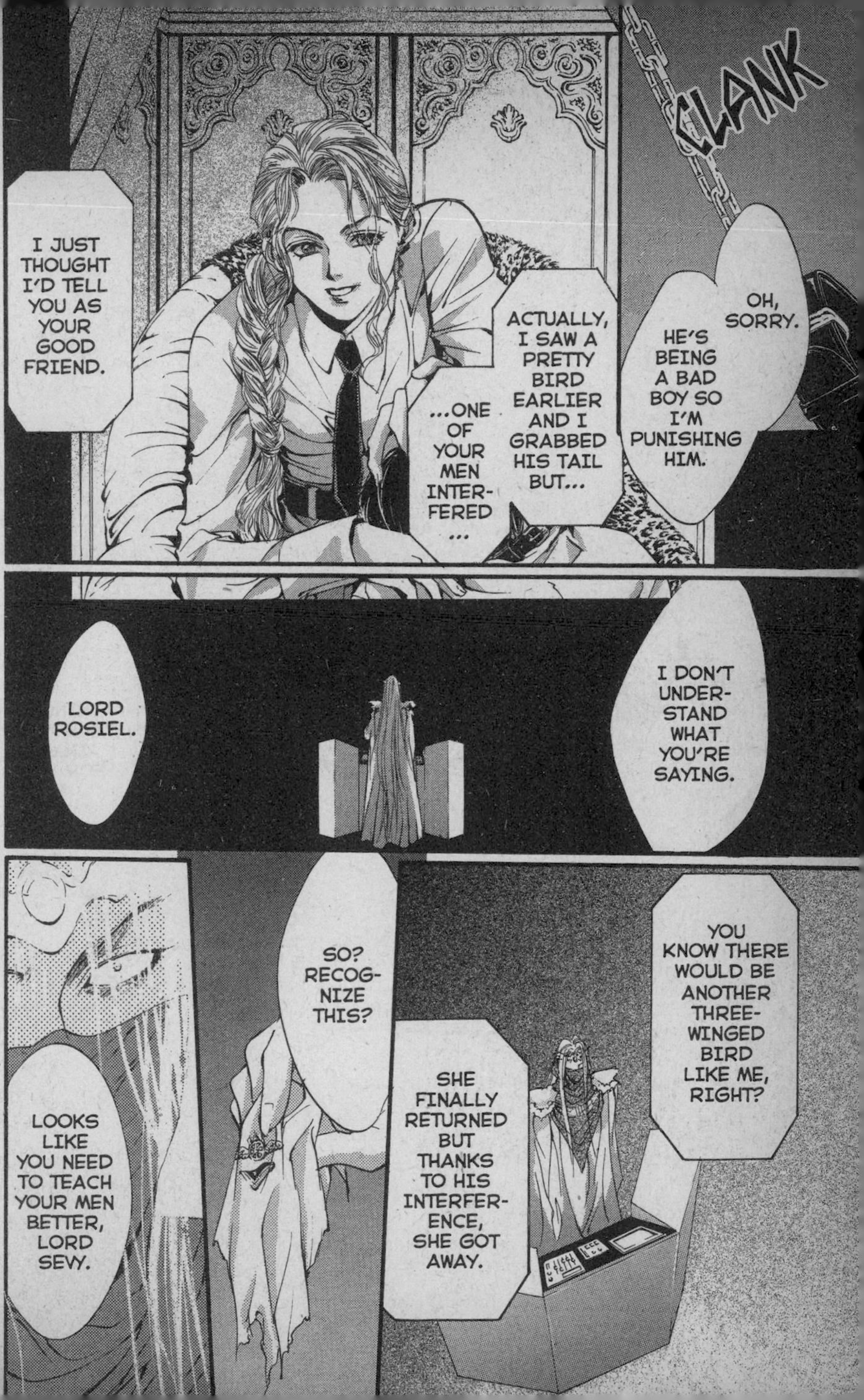
CLANK
OH, SORRY.
HE'S BEING A BAD BOY SO I'M PUNISHING HIM.
ACTUALLY, I SAW A PRETTY BIRD EARLIER AND I GRABBED HIS TAIL BUT...
...ONE OF YOUR MEN INTERFERED...
I JUST THOUGHT I'D TELL YOU AS YOUR GOOD FRIEND.
I DON'T UNDERSTAND WHAT YOU'RE SAYING.
LORD ROSIEL.
YOU KNOW THERE WOULD BE ANOTHER THREE-WINGED BIRD LIKE ME, RIGHT?
SHE FINALLY RETURNED BUT THANKS TO HIS INTERFERENCE, SHE GOT AWAY.
SO? RECOGNIZE THIS?
LOOKS LIKE YOU NEED TO TEACH YOUR MEN BETTER, LORD SEVY.

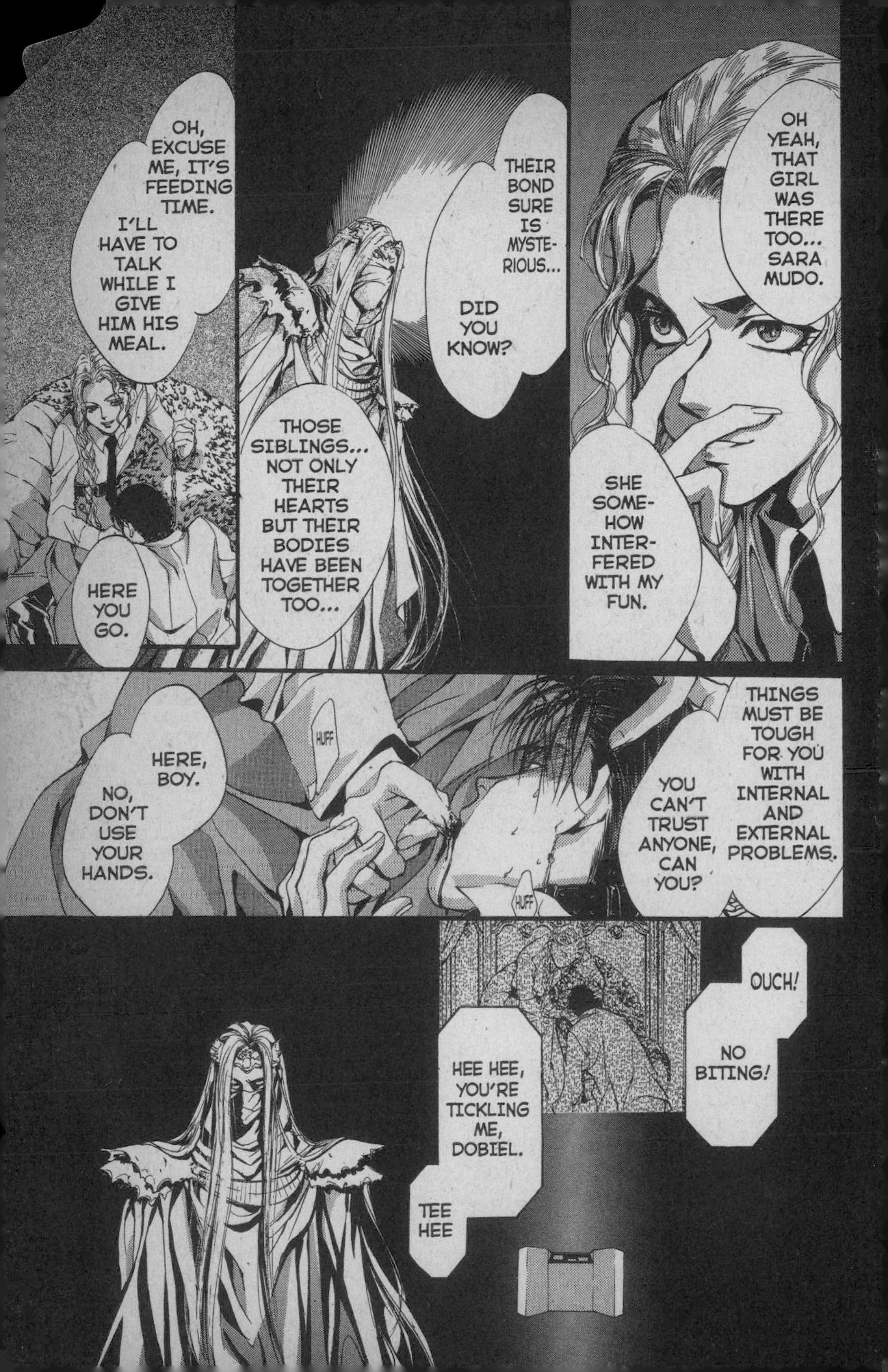
OH YEAH, THAT GIRL WAS THERE TOO... SARA MUDO.
SHE SOMEHOW INTERFERED WITH MY FUN.
THEIR BOND SURE IS MYSTERIOUS...
DID YOU KNOW?
THOSE SIBLINGS... NOT ONLY THEIR HEARTS BUT THEIR BODIES HAVE BEEN TOGETHER TOO...
OH, EXCUSE ME, IT'S FEEDING TIME.
I'LL HAVE TO TALK WHILE I GIVE HIM HIS MEAL.
HERE YOU GO.
THINGS MUST BE TOUGH FOR YOU WITH INTERNAL AND EXTERNAL PROBLEMS.
YOU CAN'T TRUST ANYONE, CAN YOU?
HUFF
HUFF
HERE, BOY.
NO, DON'T USE YOUR HANDS.
OUCH!
NO BITING!
HEE HEE, YOU'RE TICKLING ME, DOBIEL.
TEE HEE

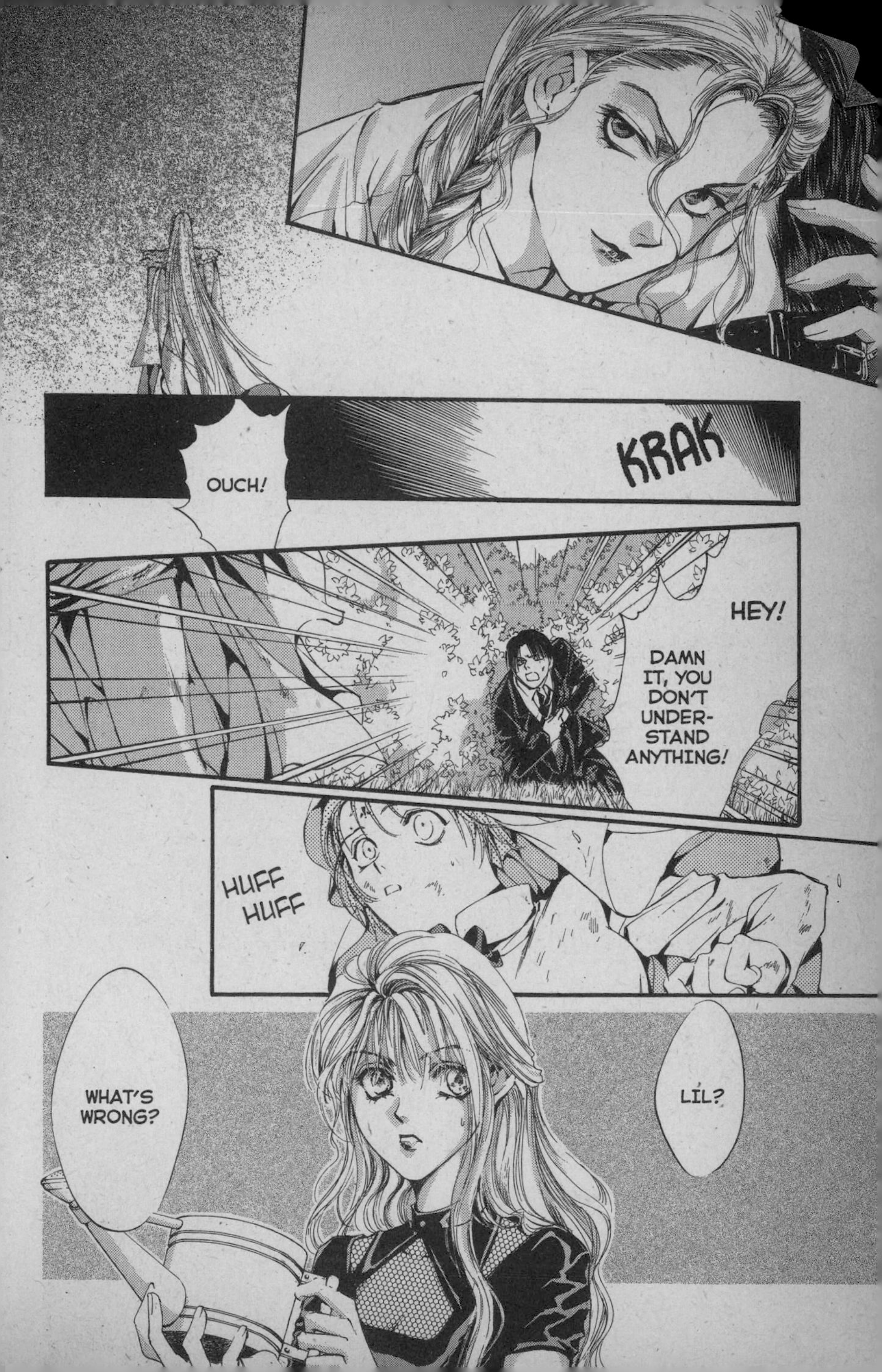
KRAK
OUCH!
HEY!
DAMN IT, YOU DON'T UNDER-STAND ANYTHING!
HUFF HUFF
LIL?
WHAT'S WRONG?

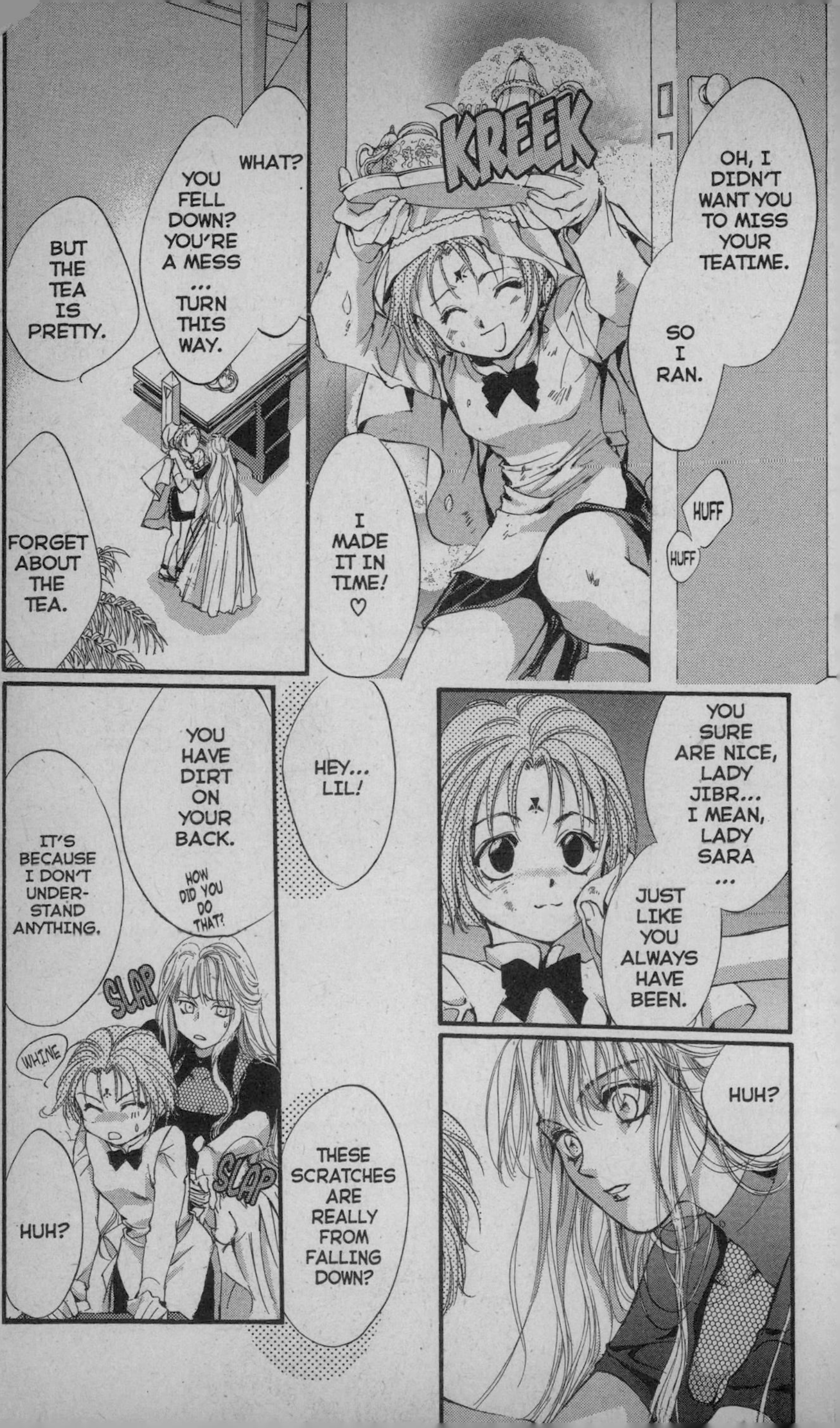
KREEK
OH, I DIDN'T WANT YOU TO MISS YOUR TEATIME.
SO I RAN.
HUFF
HUFF
I MADE IT IN TIME! ♡
WHAT?
YOU FELL DOWN? YOU'RE A MESS ... TURN THIS WAY.
BUT THE TEA IS PRETTY.
FORGET ABOUT THE TEA.
YOU SURE ARE NICE, LADY JIBR... I MEAN, LADY SARA ...
JUST LIKE YOU ALWAYS HAVE BEEN.
HUH?
HEY... LIL!
YOU HAVE DIRT ON YOUR BACK.
HOW DID YOU DO THAT?
IT'S BECAUSE I DON'T UNDER-STAND ANYTHING.
SLAP
WHINE
SLAP
THESE SCRATCHES ARE REALLY FROM FALLING DOWN?
HUH?

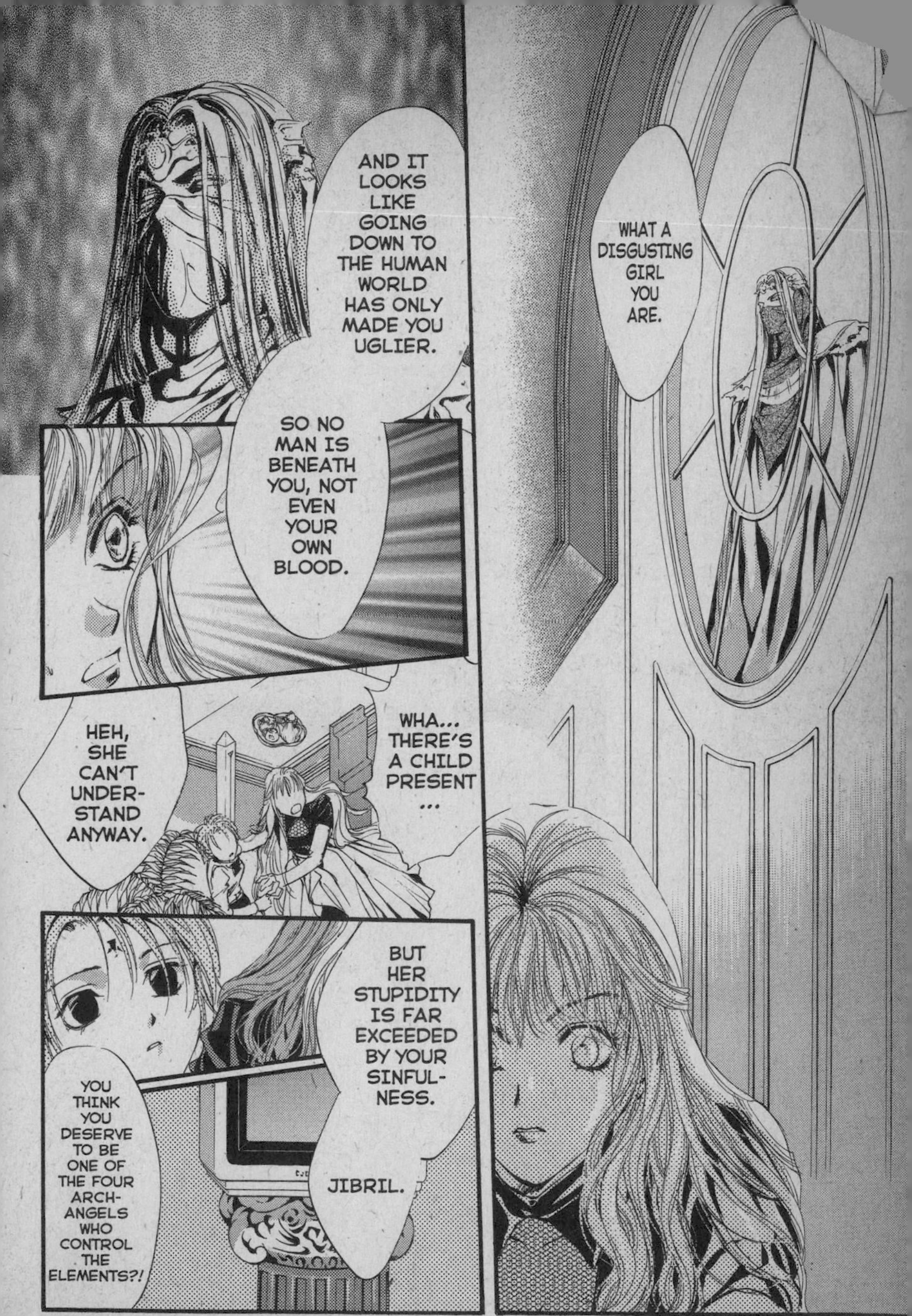
WHAT A DISGUSTING GIRL YOU ARE.
AND IT LOOKS LIKE GOING DOWN TO THE HUMAN WORLD HAS ONLY MADE YOU UGLIER.
SO NO MAN IS BENEATH YOU, NOT EVEN YOUR OWN BLOOD.
WHA... THERE'S A CHILD PRESENT...
HEH, SHE CAN'T UNDER-STAND ANYWAY.
BUT HER STUPIDITY IS FAR EXCEEDED BY YOUR SINFUL-NESS.
JIBRIL.
YOU THINK YOU DESERVE TO BE ONE OF THE FOUR ARCH-ANGELS WHO CONTROL THE ELEMENTS?!

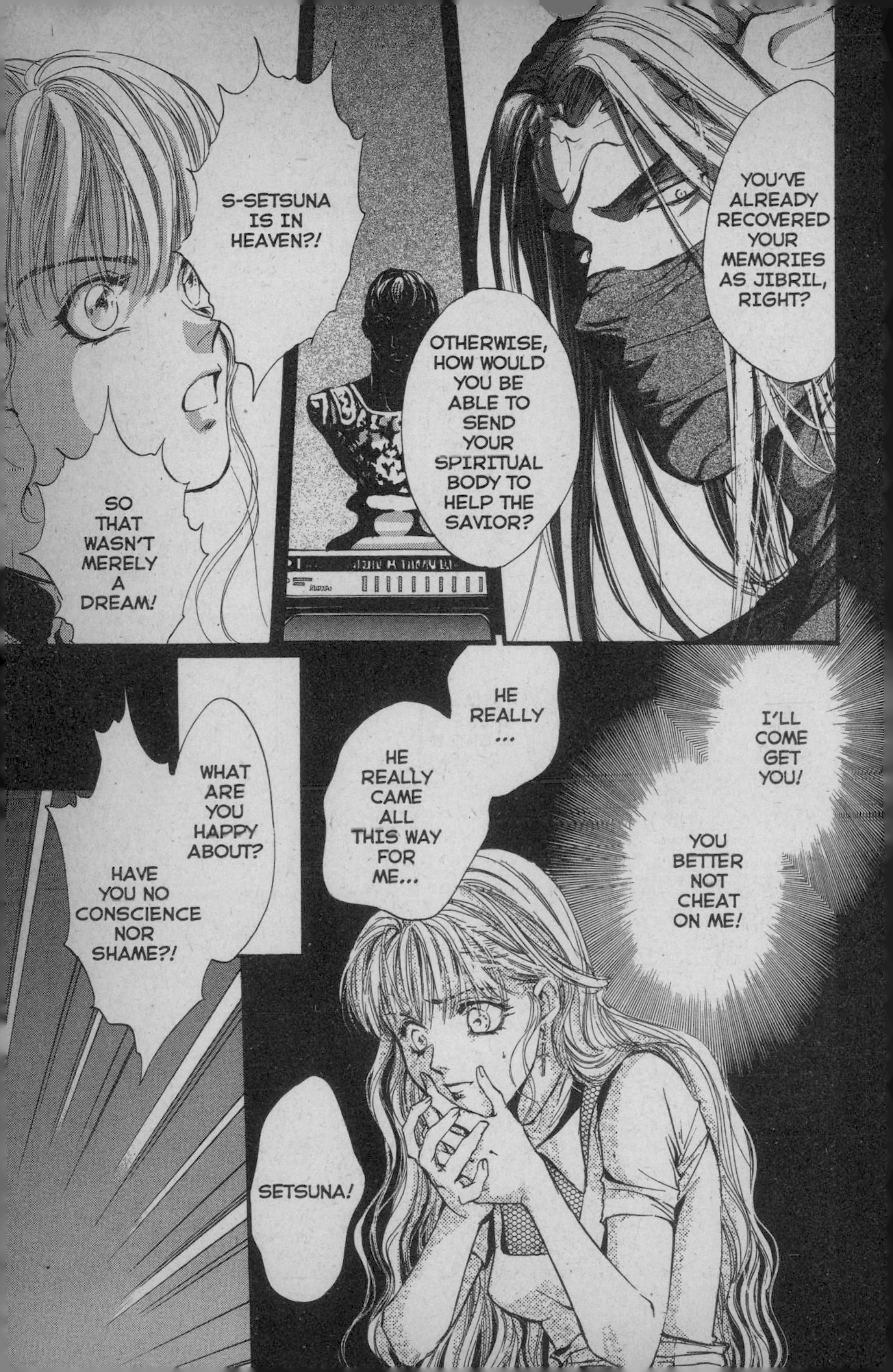
YOU'VE ALREADY RECOVERED YOUR MEMORIES AS JIBRIL, RIGHT?
OTHERWISE, HOW WOULD YOU BE ABLE TO SEND YOUR SPIRITUAL BODY TO HELP THE SAVIOR?
S-SETSUNA IS IN HEAVEN?!
SO THAT WASN'T MERELY A DREAM!
I'LL COME GET YOU!
YOU BETTER NOT CHEAT ON ME!
HE REALLY...
HE REALLY CAME ALL THIS WAY FOR ME...
SETSUNA!
WHAT ARE YOU HAPPY ABOUT?
HAVE YOU NO CONSCIENCE NOR SHAME?!

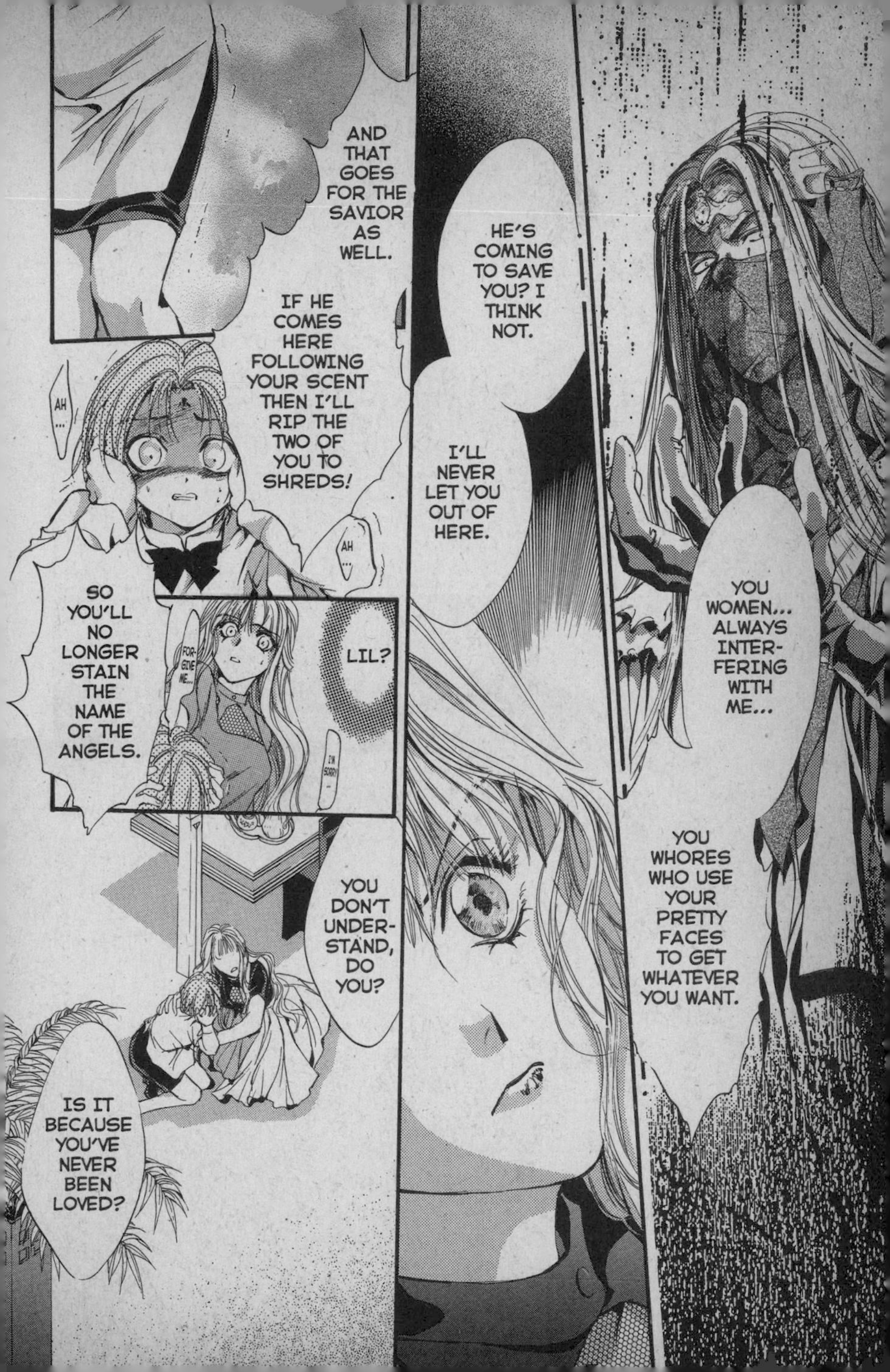
YOU WOMEN... ALWAYS INTERFERING WITH ME...
YOU WHORES WHO USE YOUR PRETTY FACES TO GET WHATEVER YOU WANT.
HE'S COMING TO SAVE YOU? I THINK NOT.
I'LL NEVER LET YOU OUT OF HERE.
AND THAT GOES FOR THE SAVIOR AS WELL.
IF HE COMES HERE FOLLOWING YOUR SCENT THEN I'LL RIP THE TWO OF YOU TO SHREDS!
AH ...
AH ...
SO YOU'LL NO LONGER STAIN THE NAME OF THE ANGELS.
LIL?
FOR-GIVE ME...
I'M SORRY ...
YOU DON'T UNDER-STAND, DO YOU?
IS IT BECAUSE YOU'VE NEVER BEEN LOVED?

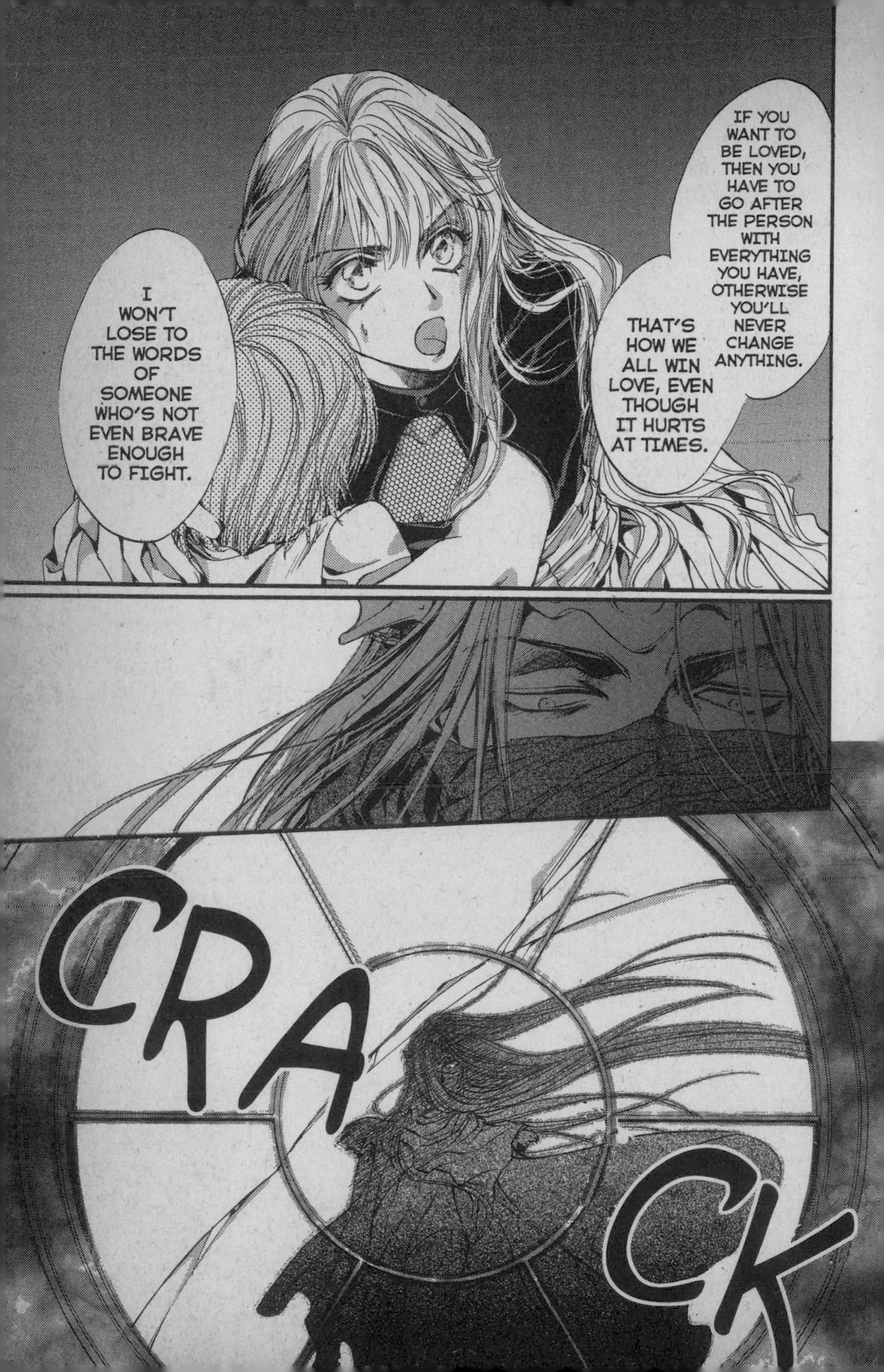
IF YOU WANT TO BE LOVED, THEN YOU HAVE TO GO AFTER THE PERSON WITH EVERYTHING YOU HAVE, OTHERWISE YOU'LL NEVER CHANGE ANYTHING.
THAT'S HOW WE ALL WIN LOVE, EVEN THOUGH IT HURTS AT TIMES.
I WON'T LOSE TO THE WORDS OF SOMEONE WHO'S NOT EVEN BRAVE ENOUGH TO FIGHT.
CRACK

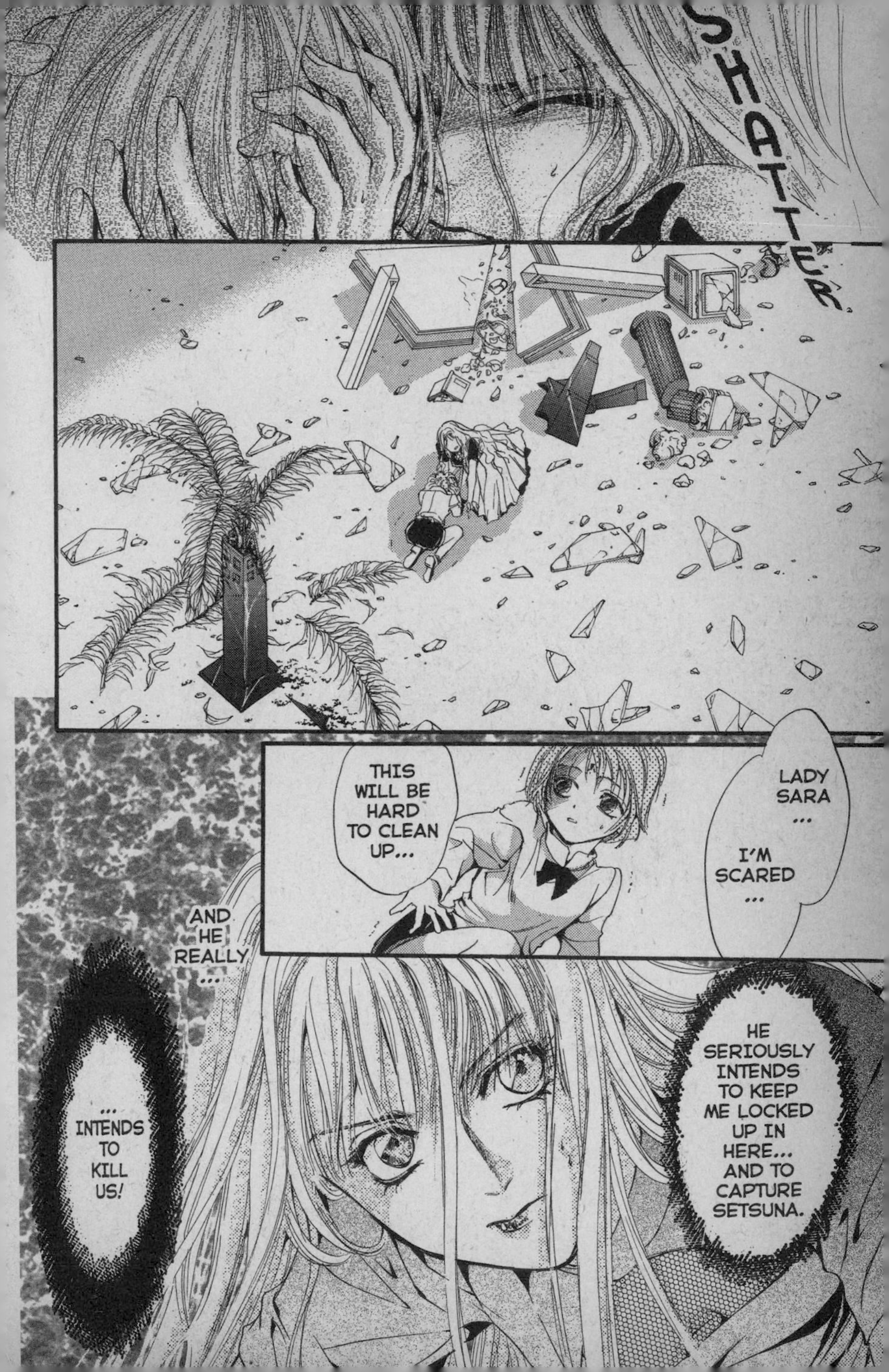
SHATTER
LADY SARA ... I'M SCARED ...
THIS WILL BE HARD TO CLEAN UP...
HE SERIOUSLY INTENDS TO KEEP ME LOCKED UP IN HERE... AND TO CAPTURE SETSUNA.
AND HE REALLY...
... INTENDS TO KILL US!

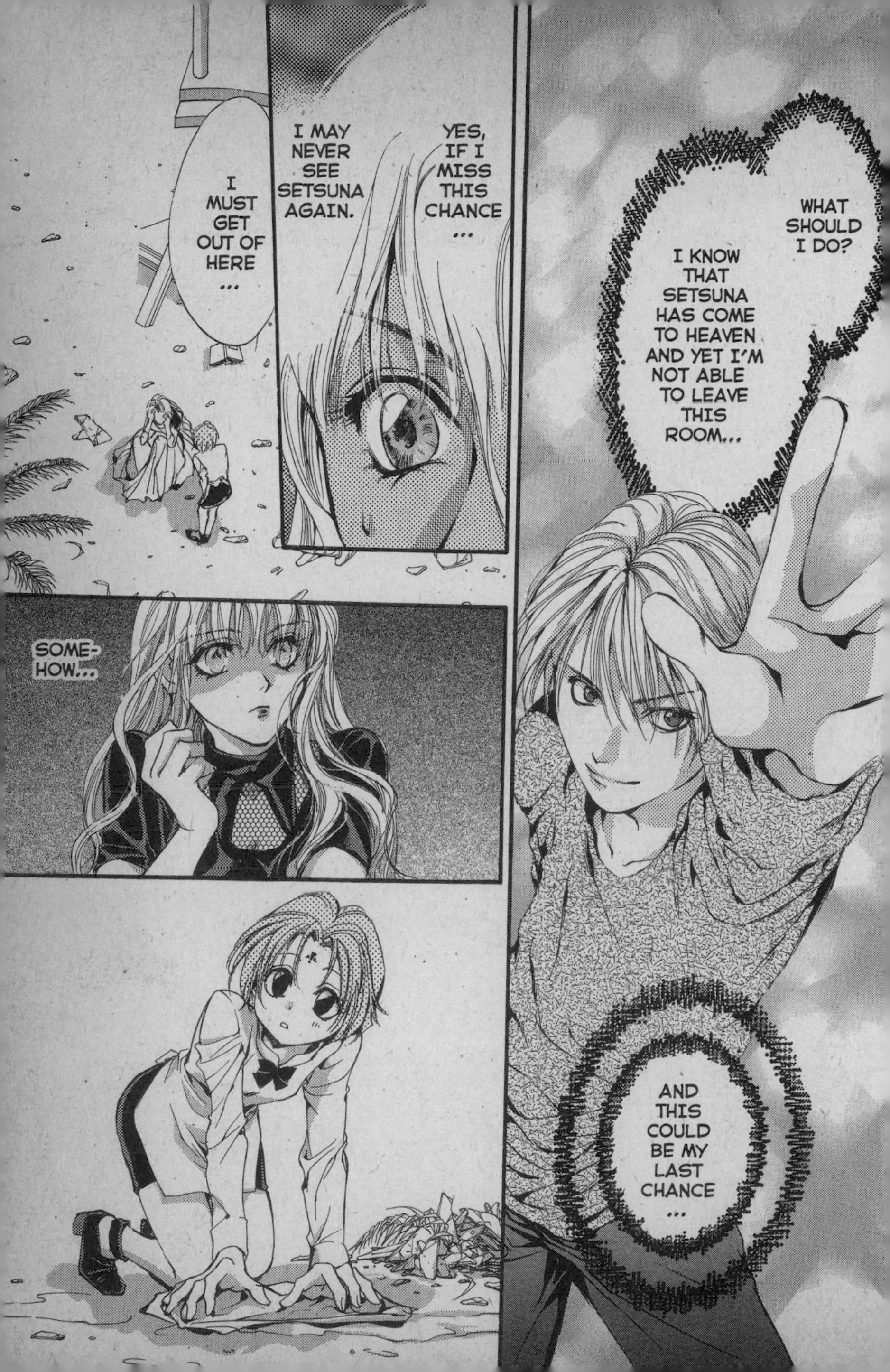
WHAT SHOULD I DO?
I KNOW THAT SETSUNA HAS COME TO HEAVEN AND YET I'M NOT ABLE TO LEAVE THIS ROOM...
AND THIS COULD BE MY LAST CHANCE...
YES, IF I MISS THIS CHANCE...
I MAY NEVER SEE SETSUNA AGAIN.
I MUST GET OUT OF HERE...
SOME-HOW...

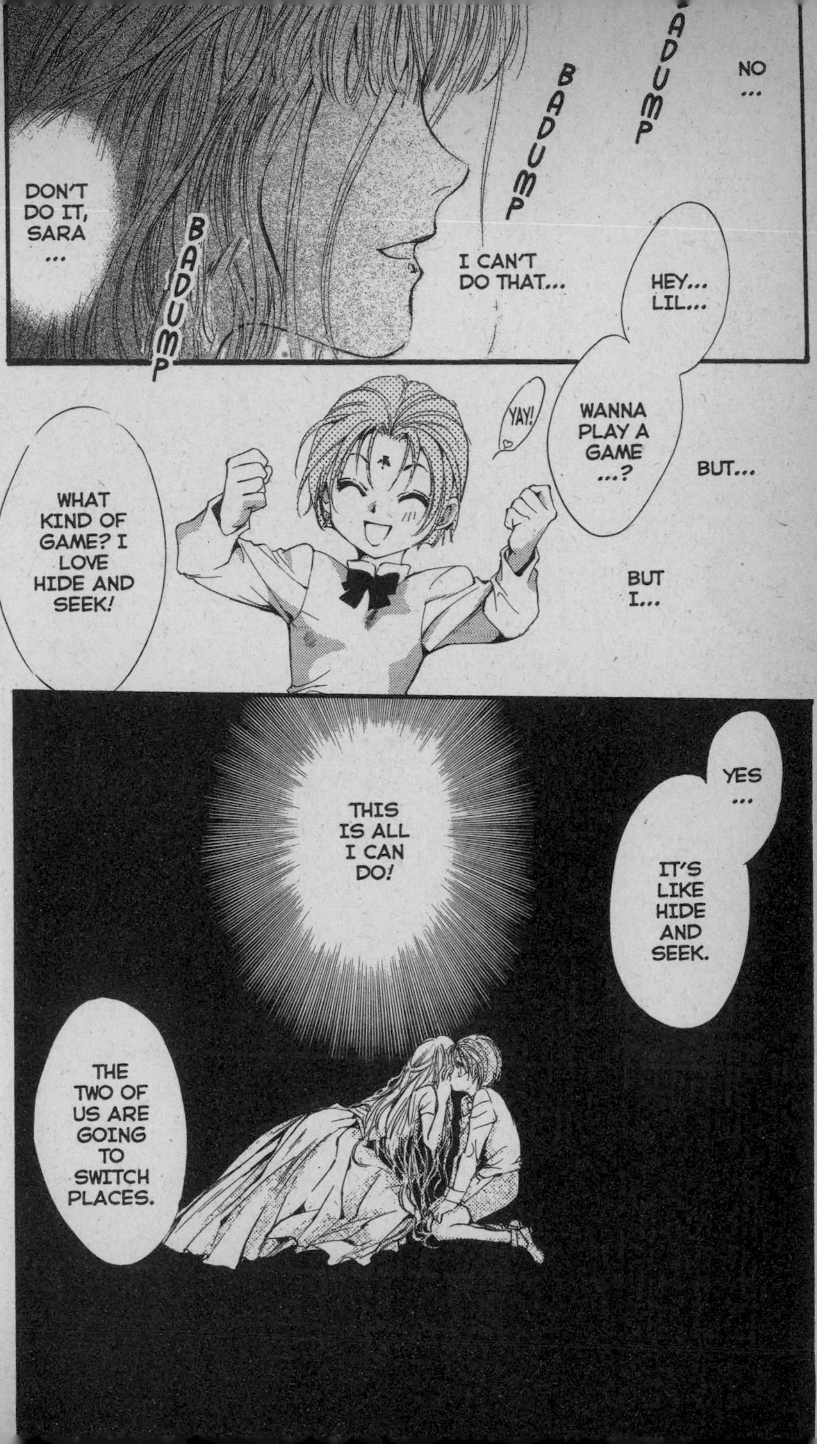
NO ...
BADUMP
BADUMP
BADUMP
BADUMP
I CAN'T DO THAT...
DON'T DO IT, SARA ...
HEY... LIL...
WANNA PLAY A GAME ...?
BUT...
BUT I...
YAY!
WHAT KIND OF GAME? I LOVE HIDE AND SEEK!
YES ...
IT'S LIKE HIDE AND SEEK.
THIS IS ALL I CAN DO!
THE TWO OF US ARE GOING TO SWITCH PLACES.

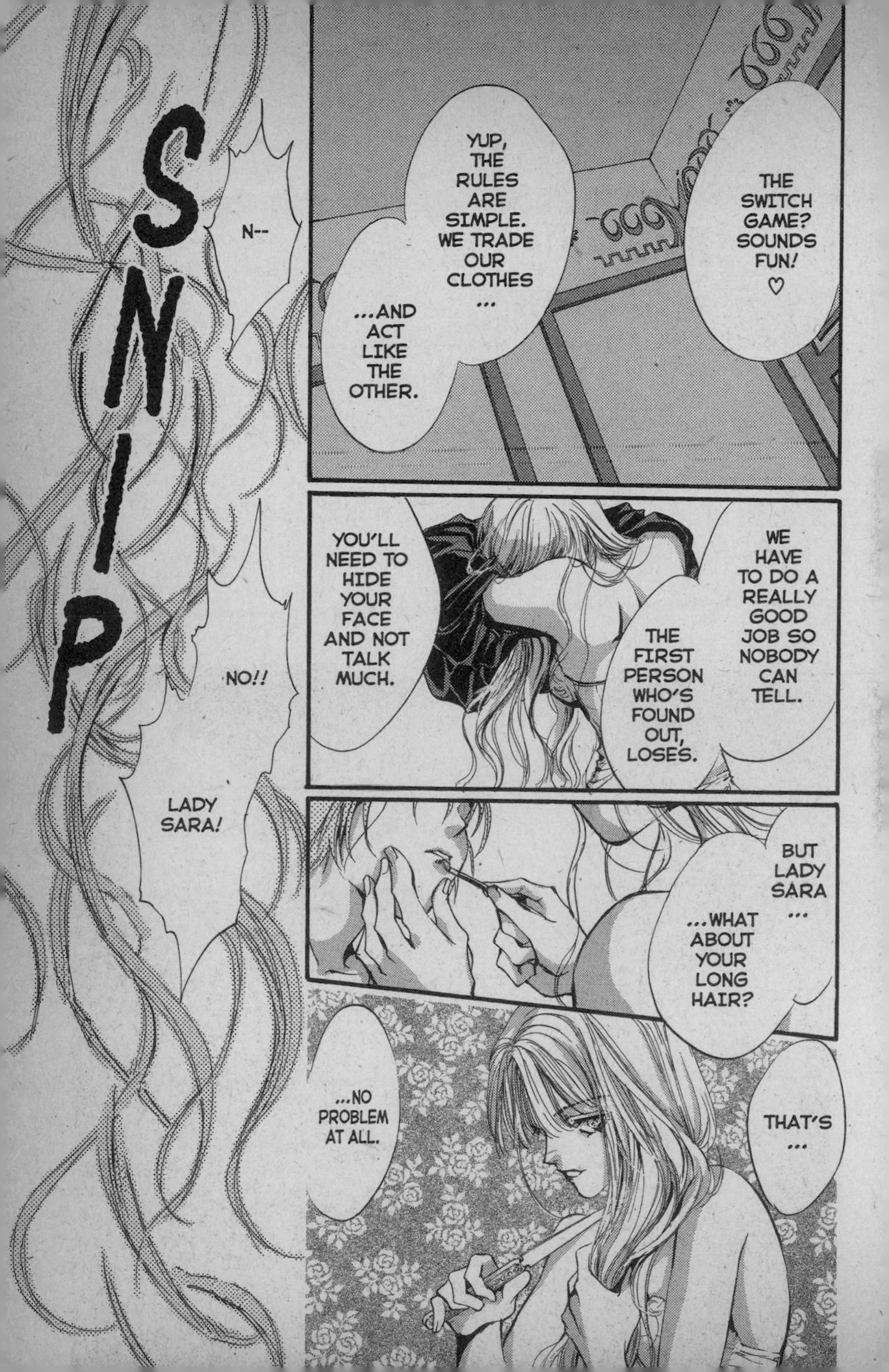
THE SWITCH GAME? SOUNDS FUN! ♡
YUP, THE RULES ARE SIMPLE. WE TRADE OUR CLOTHES...
...AND ACT LIKE THE OTHER.
WE HAVE TO DO A REALLY GOOD JOB SO NOBODY CAN TELL.
THE FIRST PERSON WHO'S FOUND OUT, LOSES.
YOU'LL NEED TO HIDE YOUR FACE AND NOT TALK MUCH.
BUT LADY SARA...
...WHAT ABOUT YOUR LONG HAIR?
THAT'S...
...NO PROBLEM AT ALL.
N--
SNIP
NO!!
LADY SARA!

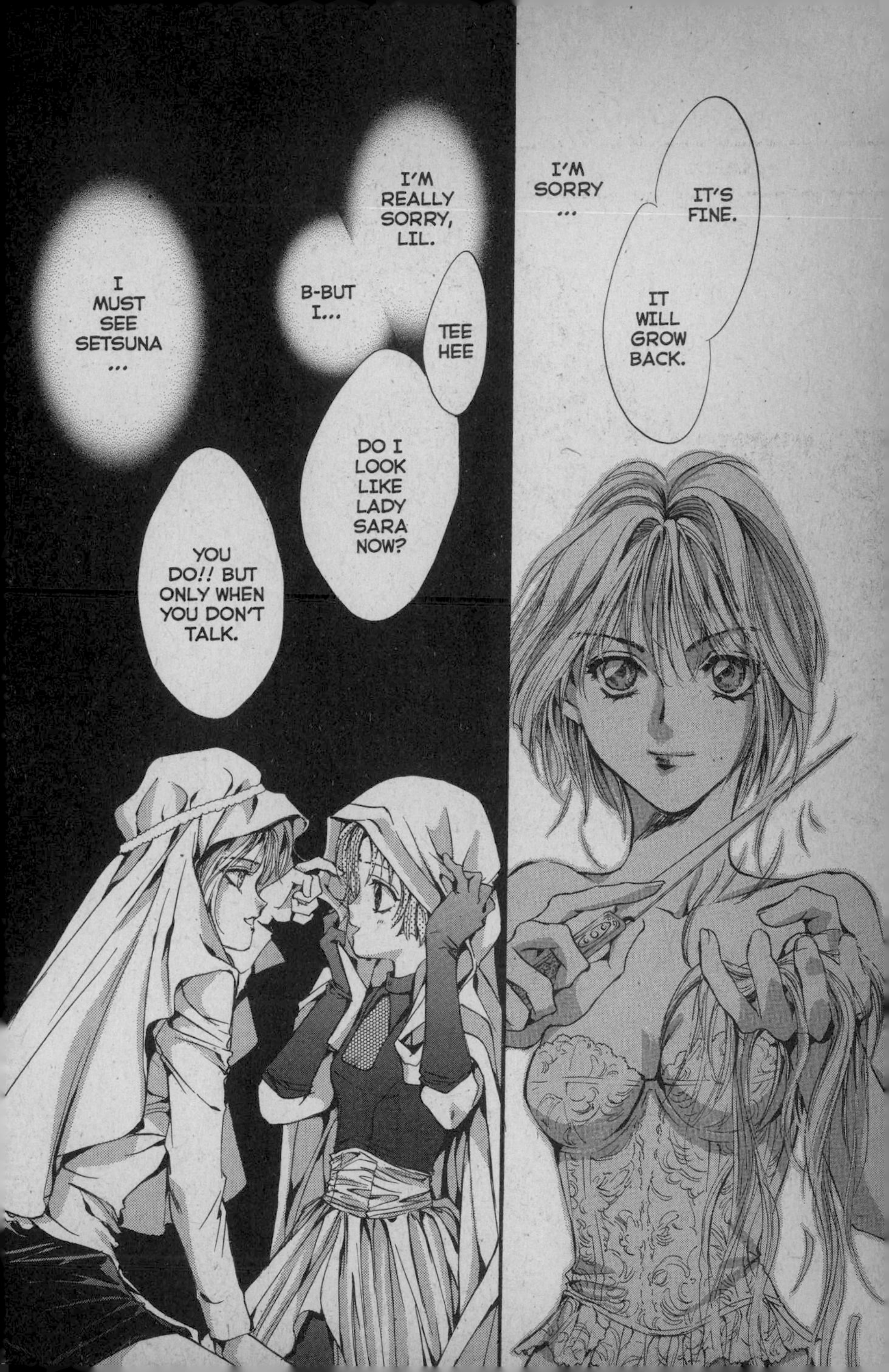
I'M SORRY...
IT'S FINE.
IT WILL GROW BACK.
I'M REALLY SORRY, LIL.
B-BUT I...
I MUST SEE SETSUNA...
TEE HEE
DO I LOOK LIKE LADY SARA NOW?
YOU DO!! BUT ONLY WHEN YOU DON'T TALK.

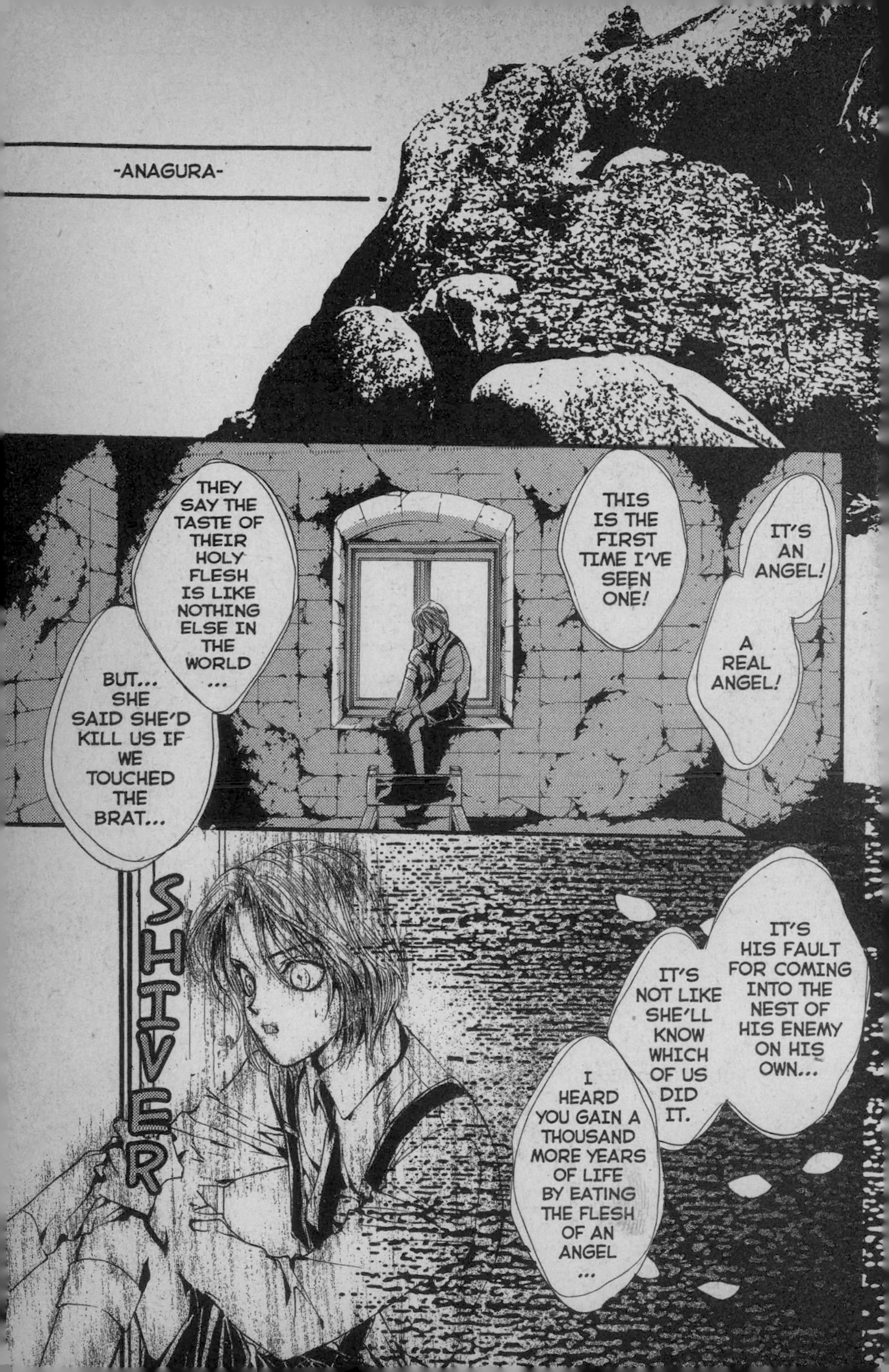
-ANAGURA-
IT'S AN ANGEL!
A REAL ANGEL!
THIS IS THE FIRST TIME I'VE SEEN ONE!
THEY SAY THE TASTE OF THEIR HOLY FLESH IS LIKE NOTHING ELSE IN THE WORLD...
BUT... SHE SAID SHE'D KILL US IF WE TOUCHED THE BRAT...
IT'S HIS FAULT FOR COMING INTO THE NEST OF HIS ENEMY ON HIS OWN...
IT'S NOT LIKE SHE'LL KNOW WHICH OF US DID IT.
I HEARD YOU GAIN A THOUSAND MORE YEARS OF LIFE BY EATING THE FLESH OF AN ANGEL...
SHIVER

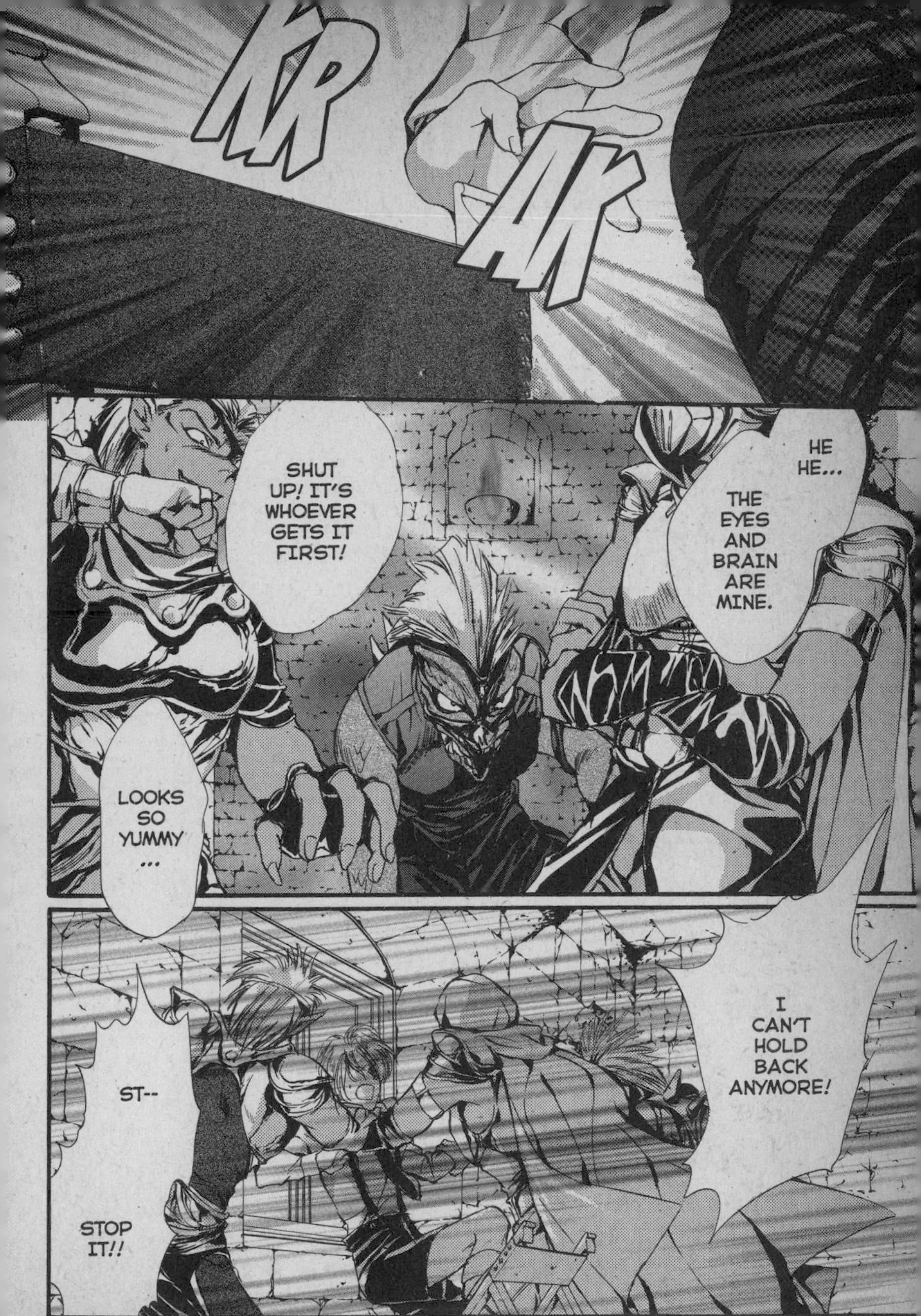
KRAK
HE HE... THE EYES AND BRAIN ARE MINE.
SHUT UP! IT'S WHOEVER GETS IT FIRST!
LOOKS SO YUMMY ...
I CAN'T HOLD BACK ANYMORE!
ST--
STOP IT!!

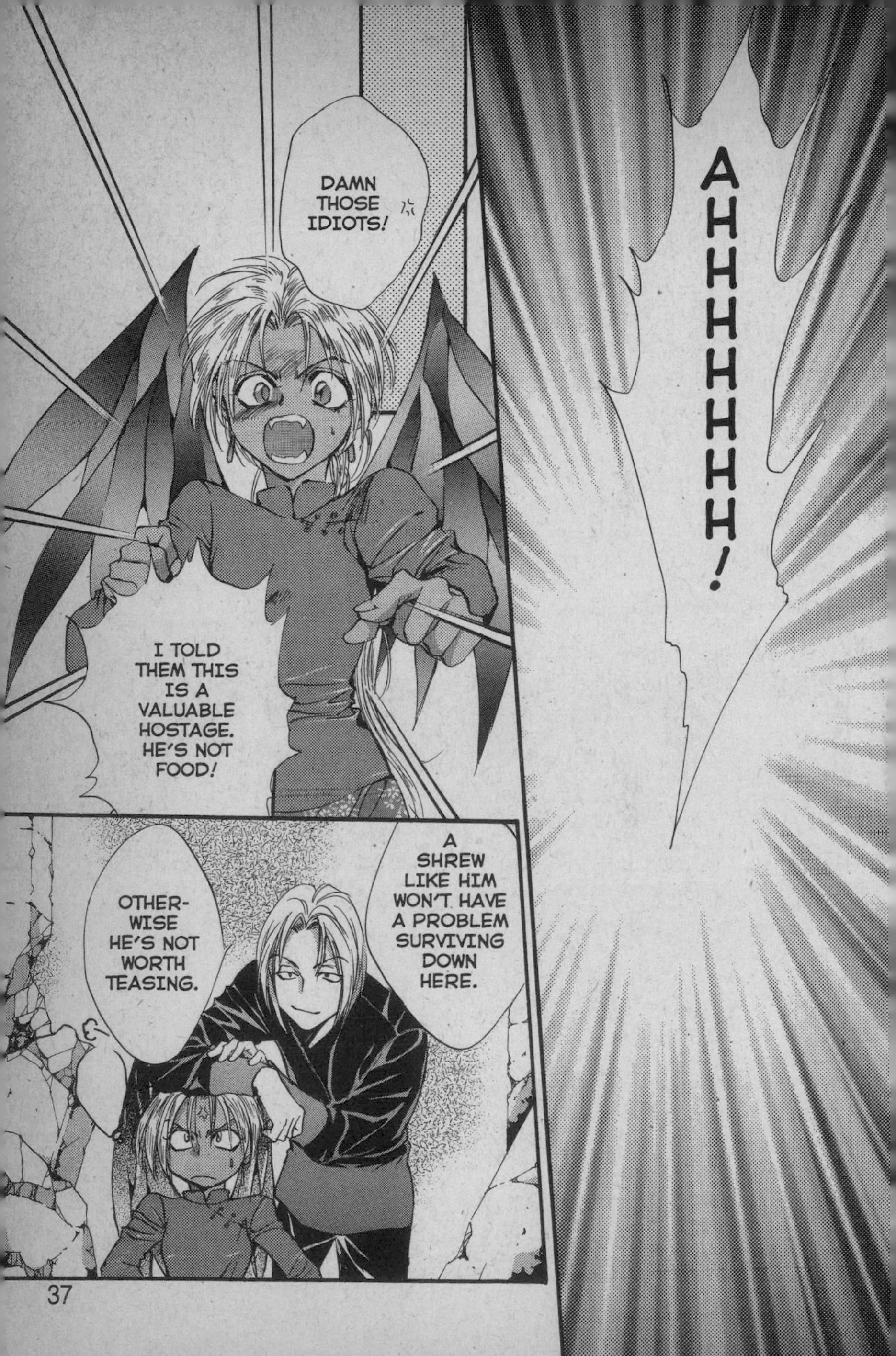
AHHHHHHH!
DAMN THOSE IDIOTS!
I TOLD THEM THIS IS A VALUABLE HOSTAGE. HE'S NOT FOOD!
A SHREW LIKE HIM WON'T HAVE A PROBLEM SURVIVING DOWN HERE.
OTHER-WISE HE'S NOT WORTH TEASING.

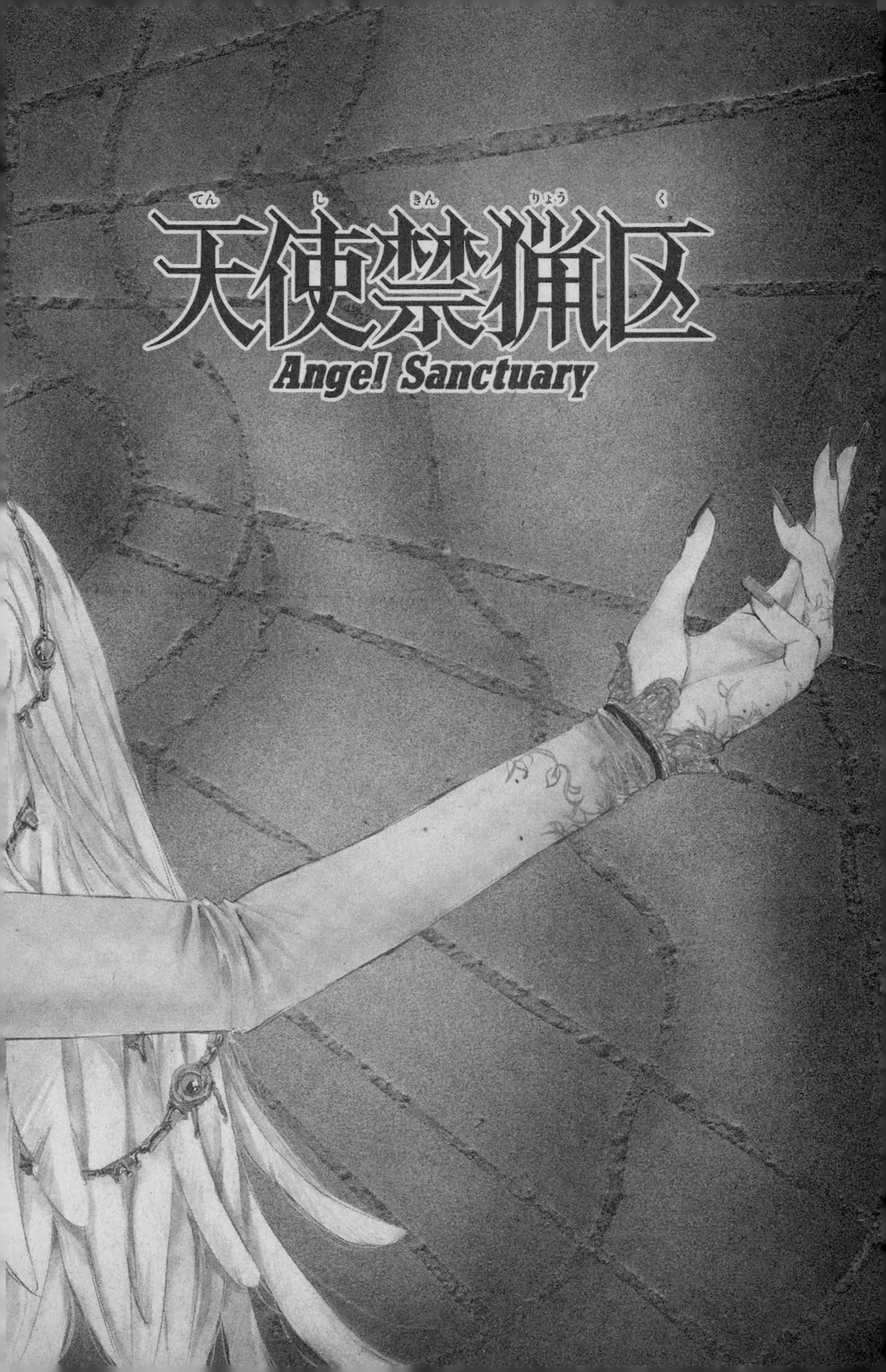
天使禁猟区
Angel Sanctuary

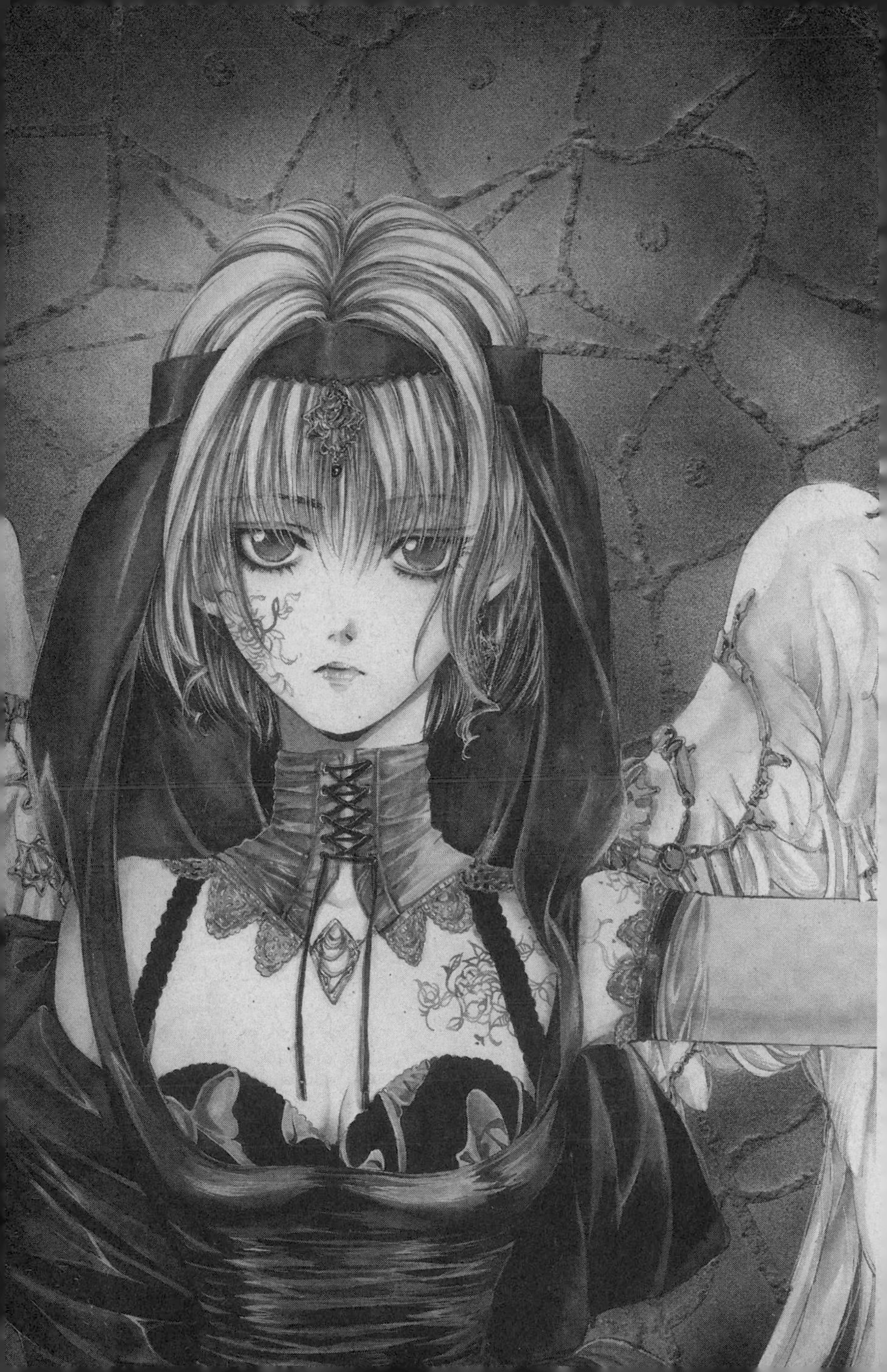

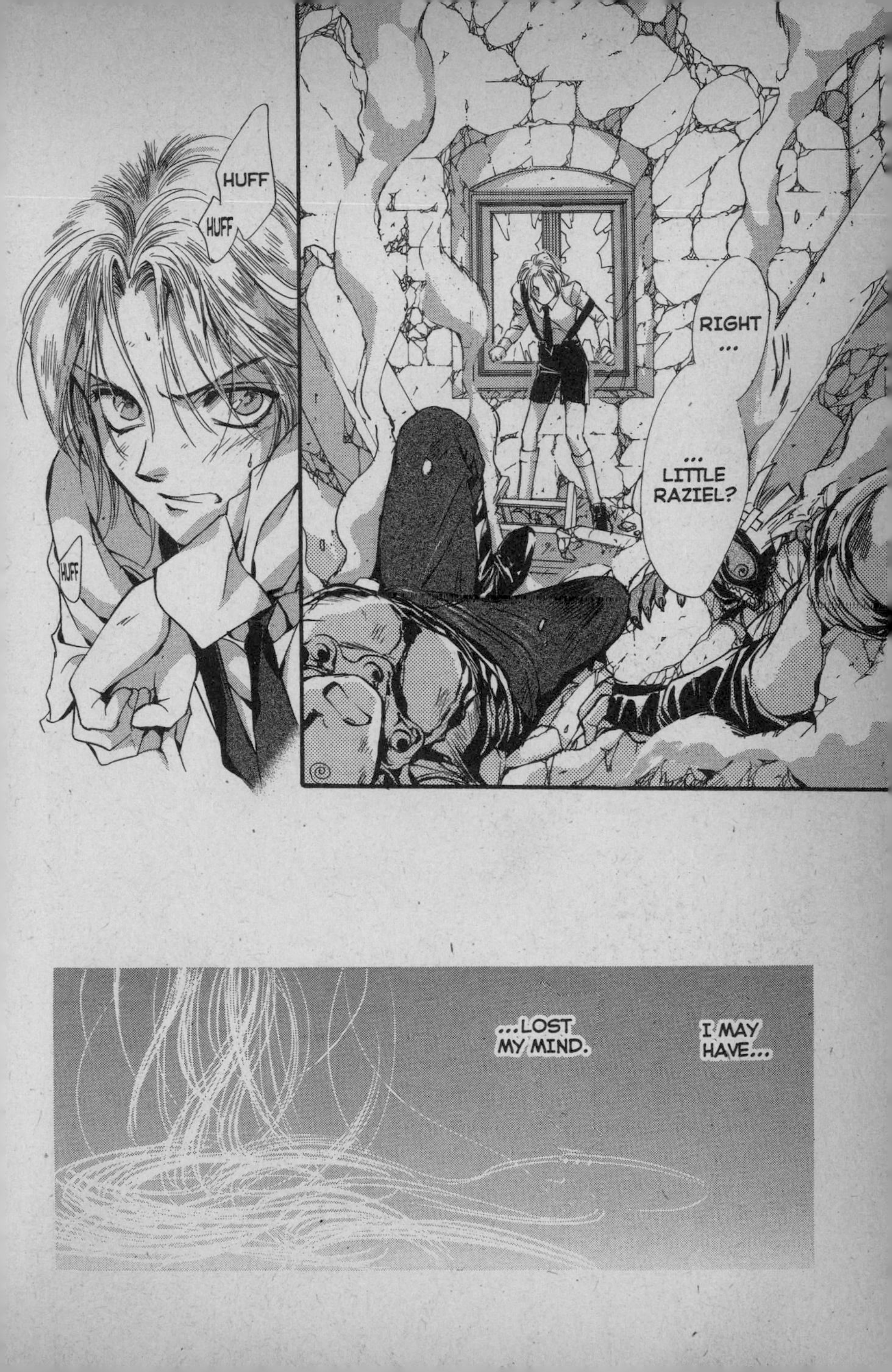
RIGHT ...
... LITTLE RAZIEL?
HUFF
HUFF
HUFF
I MAY HAVE...
...LOST MY MIND.

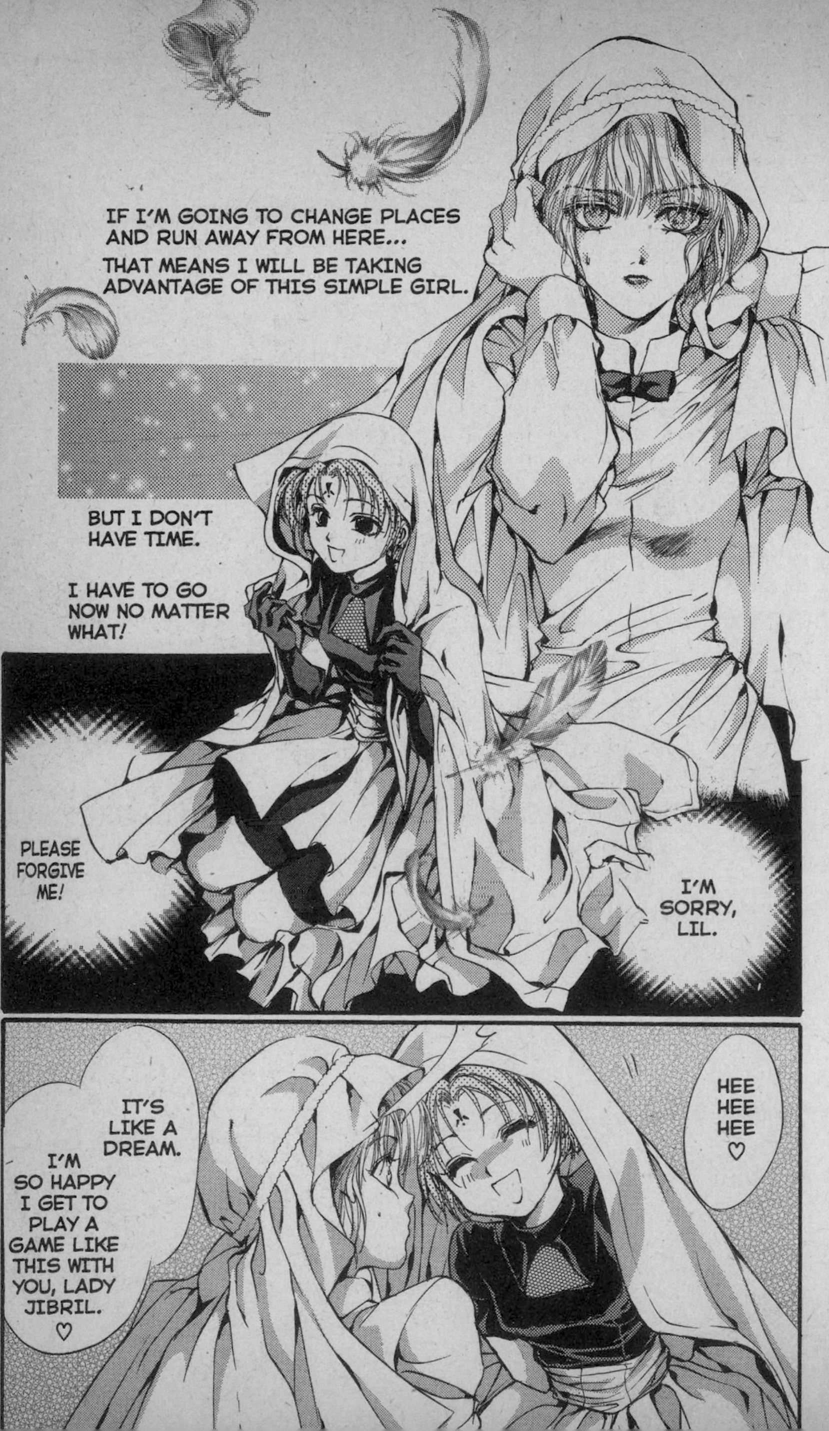
IF I'M GOING TO CHANGE PLACES AND RUN AWAY FROM HERE...
THAT MEANS I WILL BE TAKING ADVANTAGE OF THIS SIMPLE GIRL.
BUT I DON'T HAVE TIME.
I HAVE TO GO NOW NO MATTER WHAT!
I'M SORRY, LIL.
PLEASE FORGIVE ME!
HEE HEE HEE ♡
IT'S LIKE A DREAM.
I'M SO HAPPY I GET TO PLAY A GAME LIKE THIS WITH YOU, LADY JIBRIL. ♡

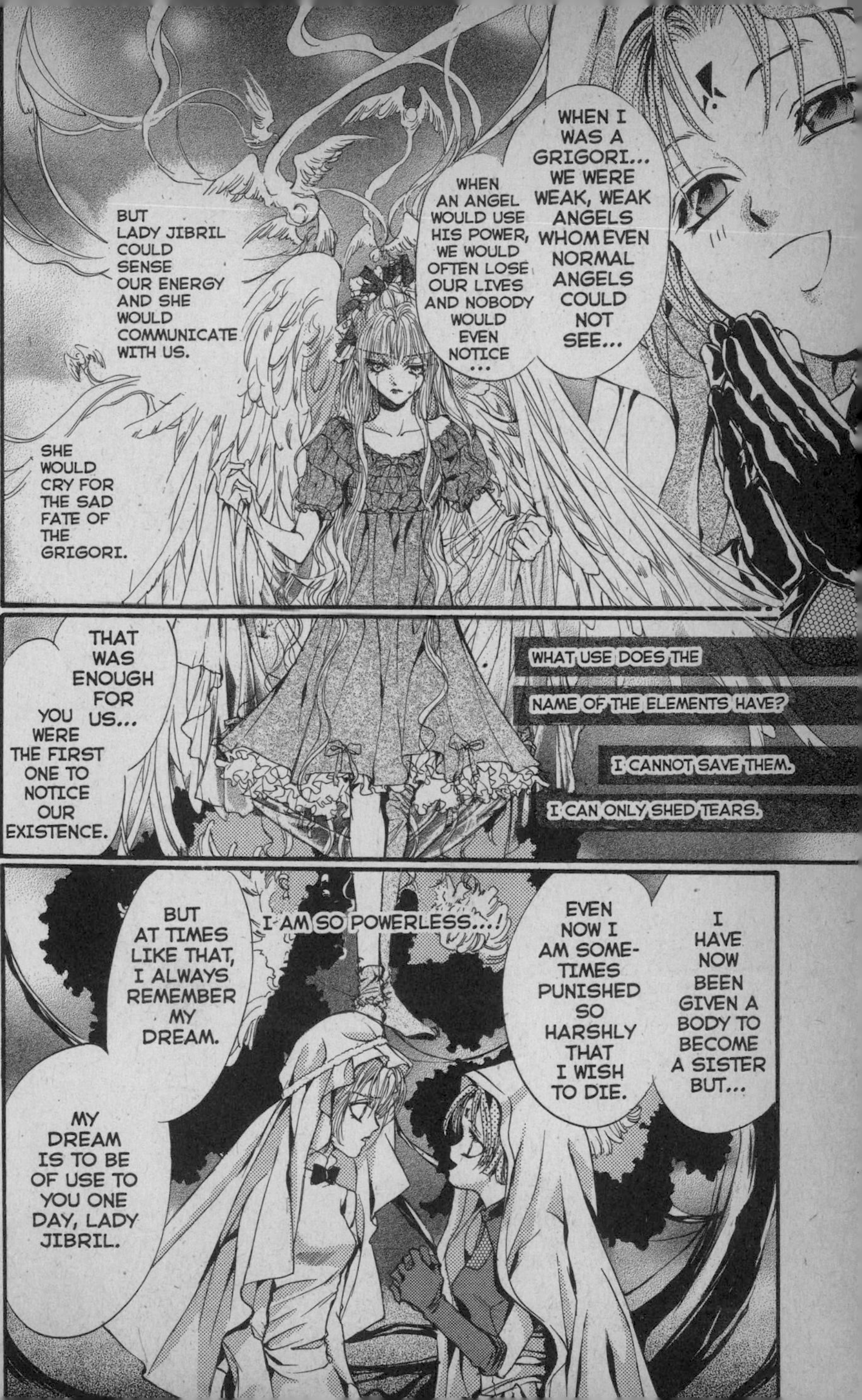
WHEN I WAS A GRIGORI... WE WERE WEAK, WEAK ANGELS WHOM EVEN NORMAL ANGELS COULD NOT SEE...
WHEN AN ANGEL WOULD USE HIS POWER, WE WOULD OFTEN LOSE OUR LIVES AND NOBODY WOULD EVEN NOTICE...
BUT LADY JIBRIL COULD SENSE OUR ENERGY AND SHE WOULD COMMUNICATE WITH US.
SHE WOULD CRY FOR THE SAD FATE OF THE GRIGORI.
WHAT USE DOES THE
NAME OF THE ELEMENTS HAVE?
I CANNOT SAVE THEM.
I CAN ONLY SHED TEARS.
THAT WAS ENOUGH FOR US...
YOU WERE THE FIRST ONE TO NOTICE OUR EXISTENCE.
I HAVE NOW BEEN GIVEN A BODY TO BECOME A SISTER BUT...
EVEN NOW I AM SOME-TIMES PUNISHED SO HARSHLY THAT I WISH TO DIE.
I AM SO POWERLESS...!
BUT AT TIMES LIKE THAT, I ALWAYS REMEMBER MY DREAM.
MY DREAM IS TO BE OF USE TO YOU ONE DAY, LADY JIBRIL.

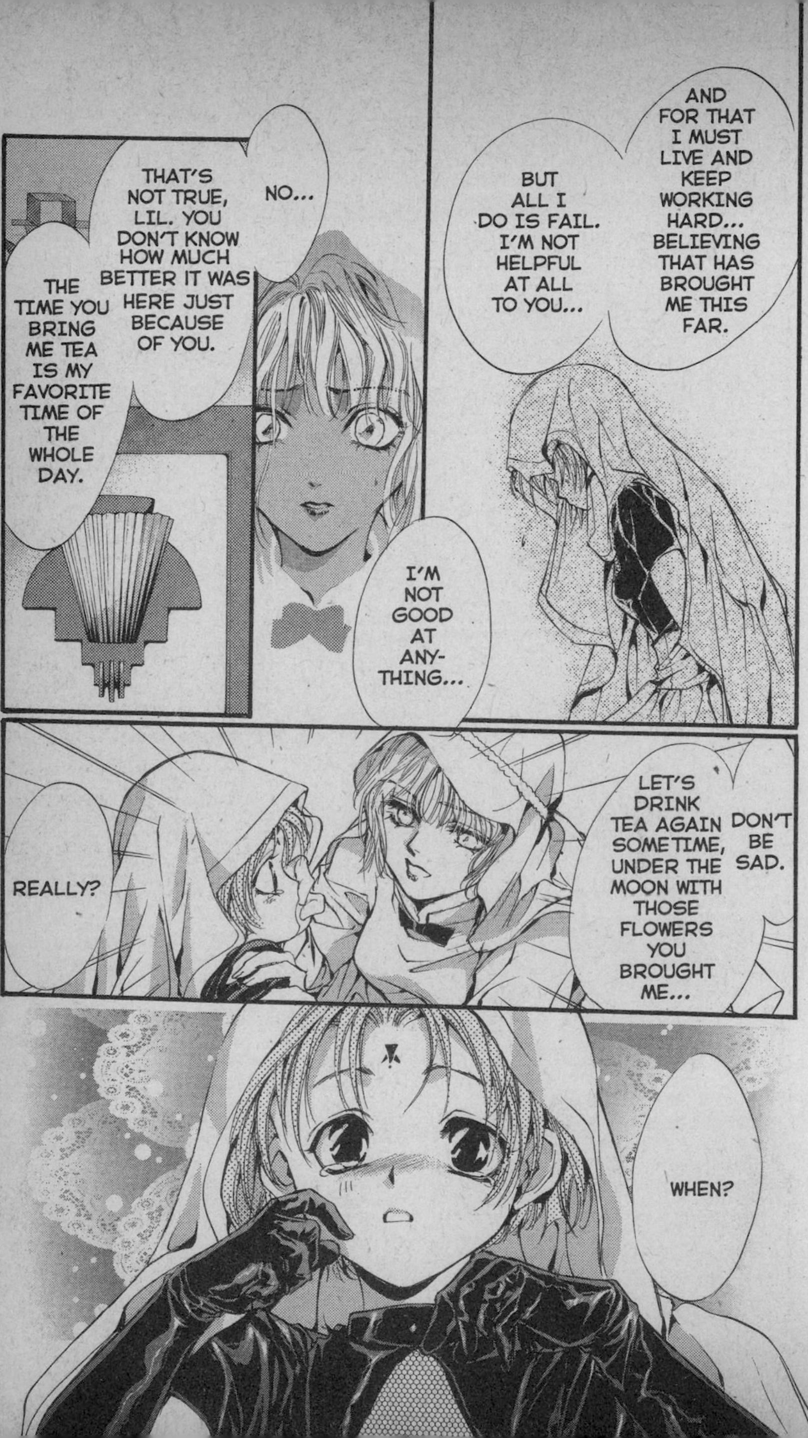
AND FOR THAT I MUST LIVE AND KEEP WORKING HARD... BELIEVING THAT HAS BROUGHT ME THIS FAR.
BUT ALL I DO IS FAIL. I'M NOT HELPFUL AT ALL TO YOU...
I'M NOT GOOD AT ANYTHING...
NO...
THAT'S NOT TRUE, LIL. YOU DON'T KNOW HOW MUCH BETTER IT WAS HERE JUST BECAUSE OF YOU.
THE TIME YOU BRING ME TEA IS MY FAVORITE TIME OF THE WHOLE DAY.
DON'T BE SAD.
LET'S DRINK TEA AGAIN SOMETIME, UNDER THE MOON WITH THOSE FLOWERS YOU BROUGHT ME...
REALLY?
WHEN?

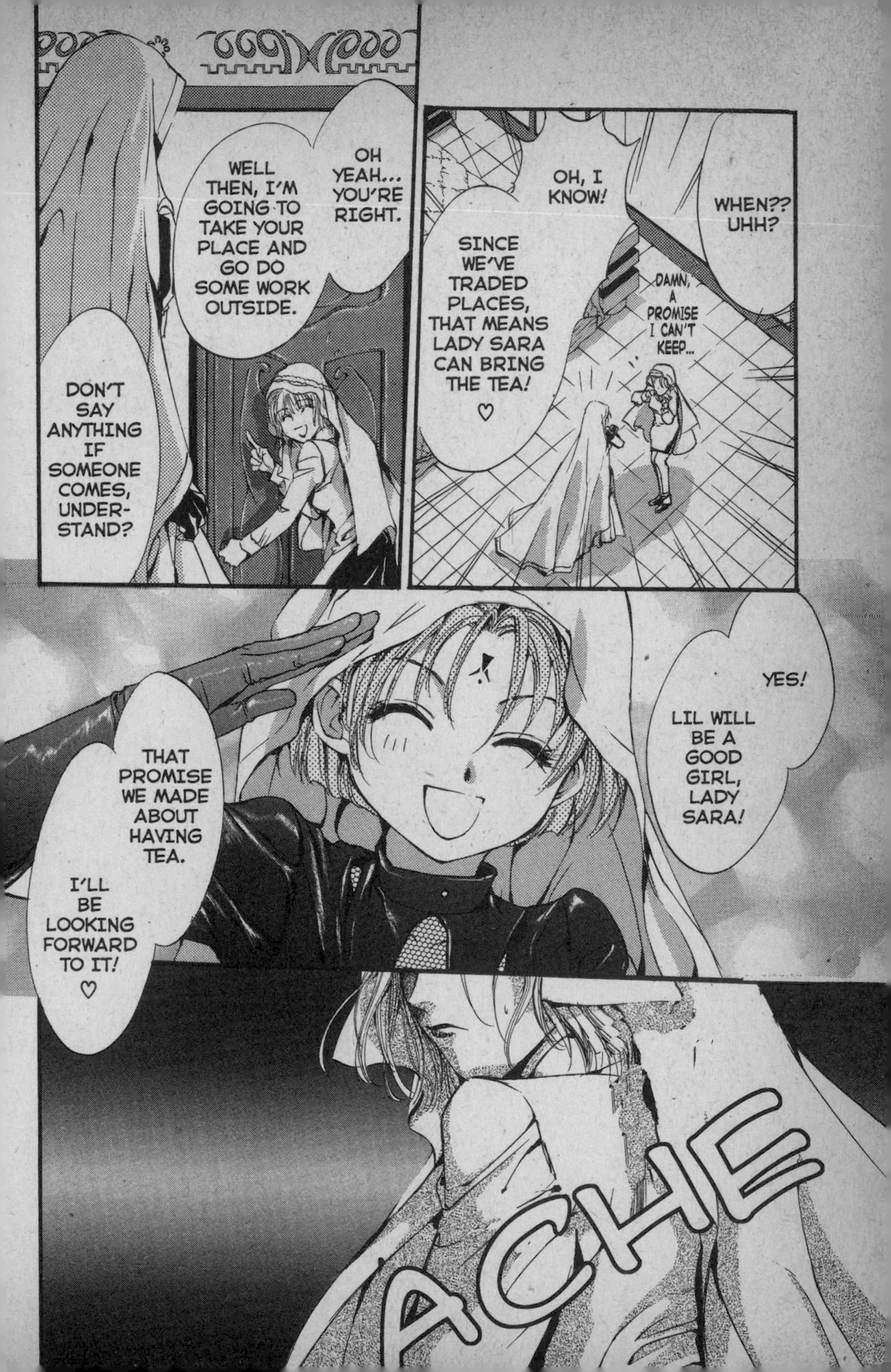
WHEN?? UHH?
OH, I KNOW!
SINCE WE'VE TRADED PLACES, THAT MEANS LADY SARA CAN BRING THE TEA! ♡
DAMN, A PROMISE I CAN'T KEEP...
OH YEAH... YOU'RE RIGHT.
WELL THEN, I'M GOING TO TAKE YOUR PLACE AND GO DO SOME WORK OUTSIDE.
DON'T SAY ANYTHING IF SOMEONE COMES, UNDERSTAND?
YES!
LIL WILL BE A GOOD GIRL, LADY SARA!
THAT PROMISE WE MADE ABOUT HAVING TEA.
I'LL BE LOOKING FORWARD TO IT! ♡
ACHE

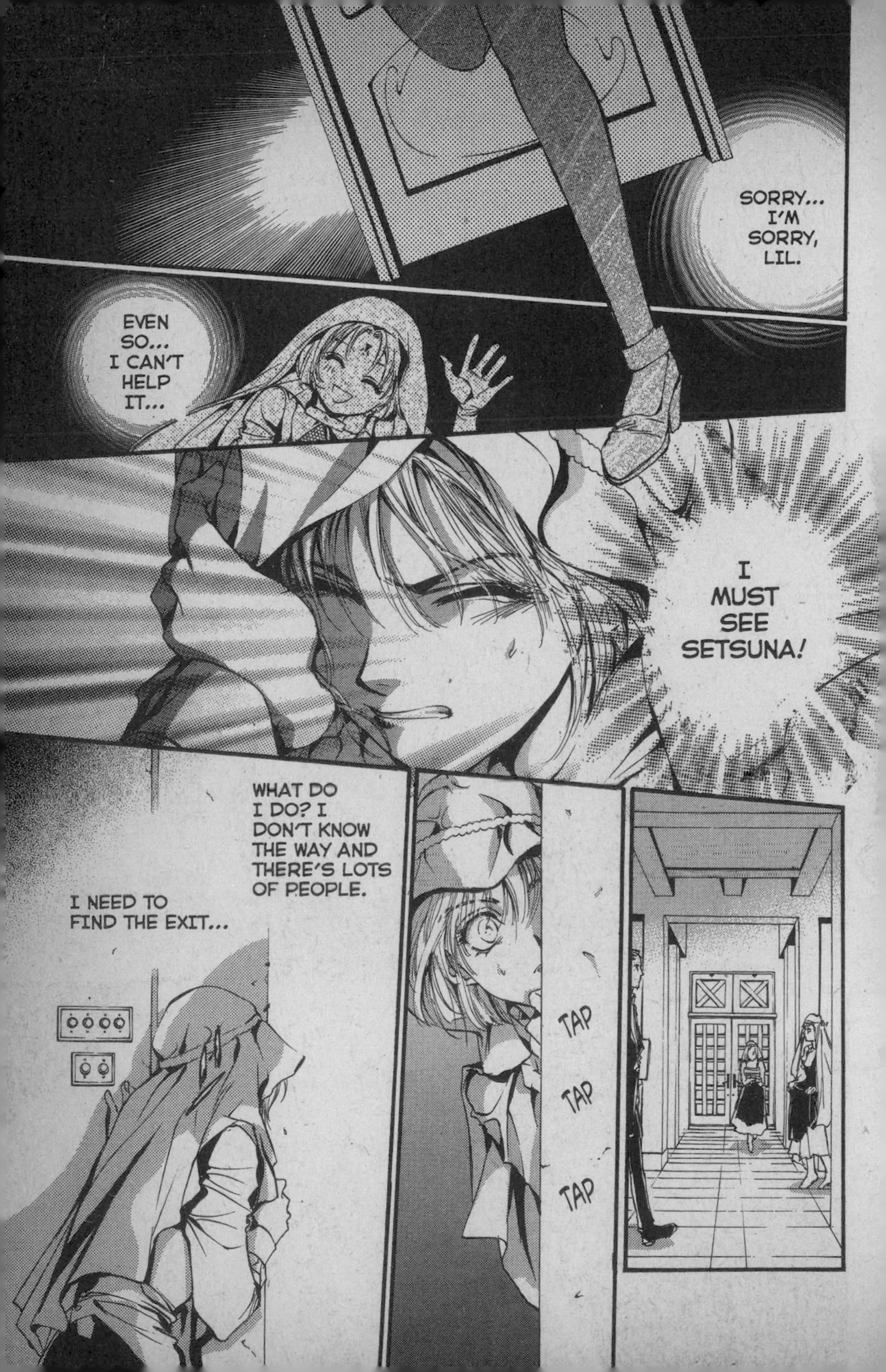
SORRY... I'M SORRY, LIL.
EVEN SO... I CAN'T HELP IT...
I MUST SEE SETSUNA!
TAP
TAP
TAP
WHAT DO I DO? I DON'T KNOW THE WAY AND THERE'S LOTS OF PEOPLE.
I NEED TO FIND THE EXIT...

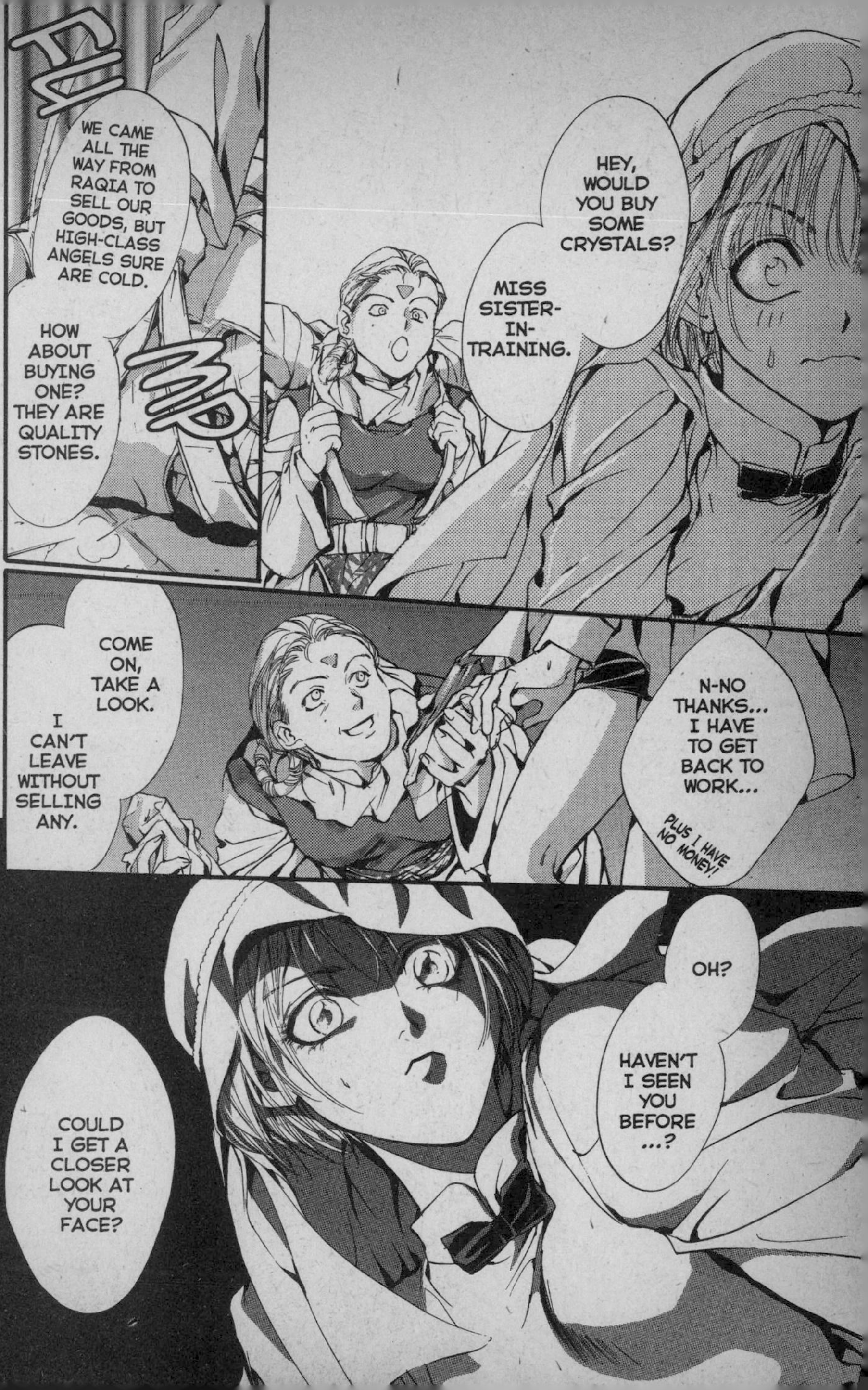
HEY, WOULD YOU BUY SOME CRYSTALS?
MISS SISTER-IN-TRAINING.
WE CAME ALL THE WAY FROM RAQIA TO SELL OUR GOODS, BUT HIGH-CLASS ANGELS SURE ARE COLD.
HOW ABOUT BUYING ONE? THEY ARE QUALITY STONES.
N-NO THANKS... I HAVE TO GET BACK TO WORK...
PLUS I HAVE NO MONEY!
COME ON, TAKE A LOOK.
I CAN'T LEAVE WITHOUT SELLING ANY.
OH?
HAVEN'T I SEEN YOU BEFORE ...?
COULD I GET A CLOSER LOOK AT YOUR FACE?

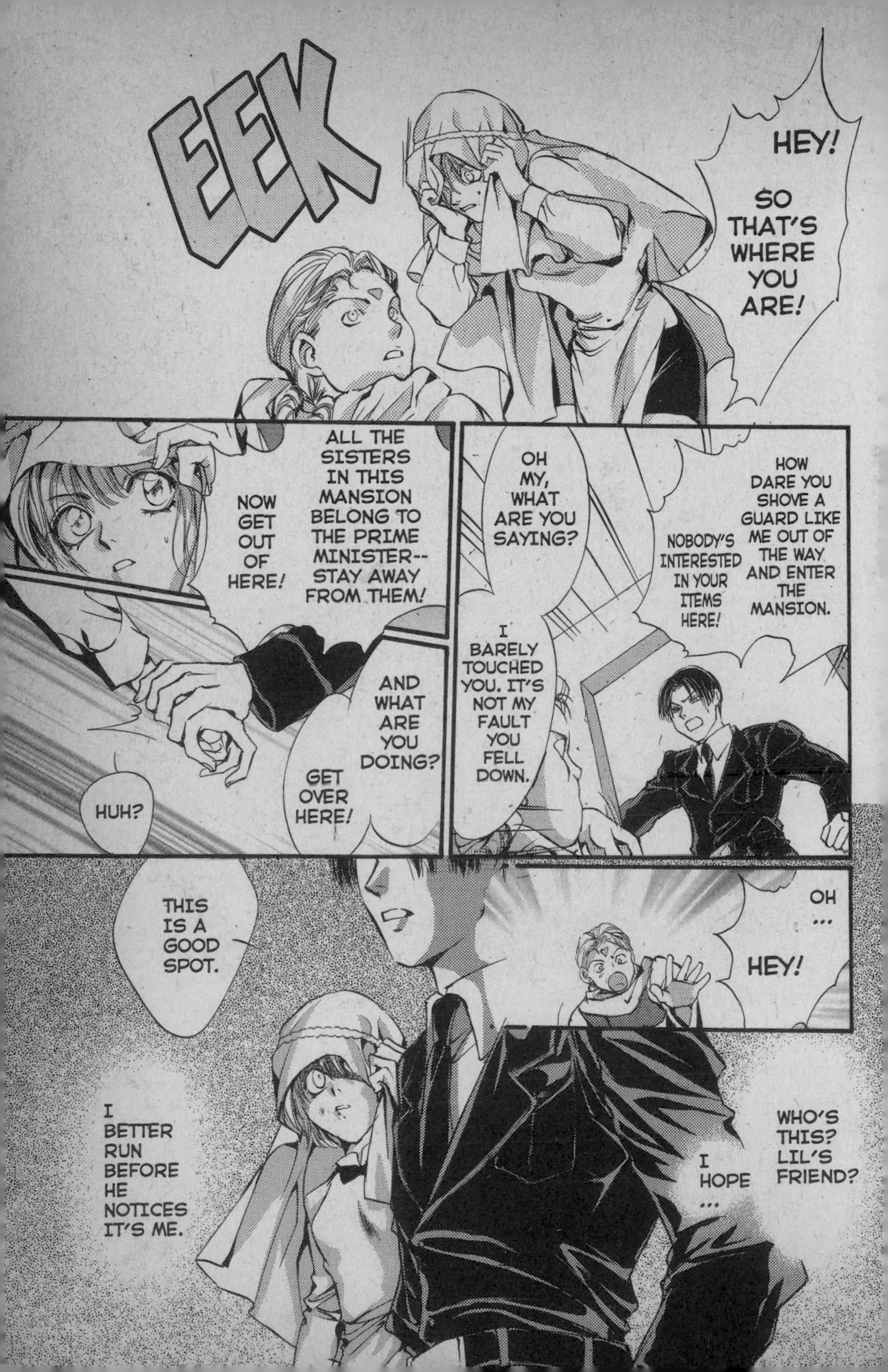
HEY!
SO THAT'S WHERE YOU ARE!
EEK
HOW DARE YOU SHOVE A GUARD LIKE ME OUT OF THE WAY AND ENTER THE MANSION.
NOBODY'S INTERESTED IN YOUR ITEMS HERE!
OH MY, WHAT ARE YOU SAYING?
I BARELY TOUCHED YOU. IT'S NOT MY FAULT YOU FELL DOWN.
ALL THE SISTERS IN THIS MANSION BELONG TO THE PRIME MINISTER--STAY AWAY FROM THEM!
NOW GET OUT OF HERE!
AND WHAT ARE YOU DOING?
GET OVER HERE!
HUH?
OH ...
HEY!
THIS IS A GOOD SPOT.
WHO'S THIS? LIL'S FRIEND?
I HOPE ...
I BETTER RUN BEFORE HE NOTICES IT'S ME.

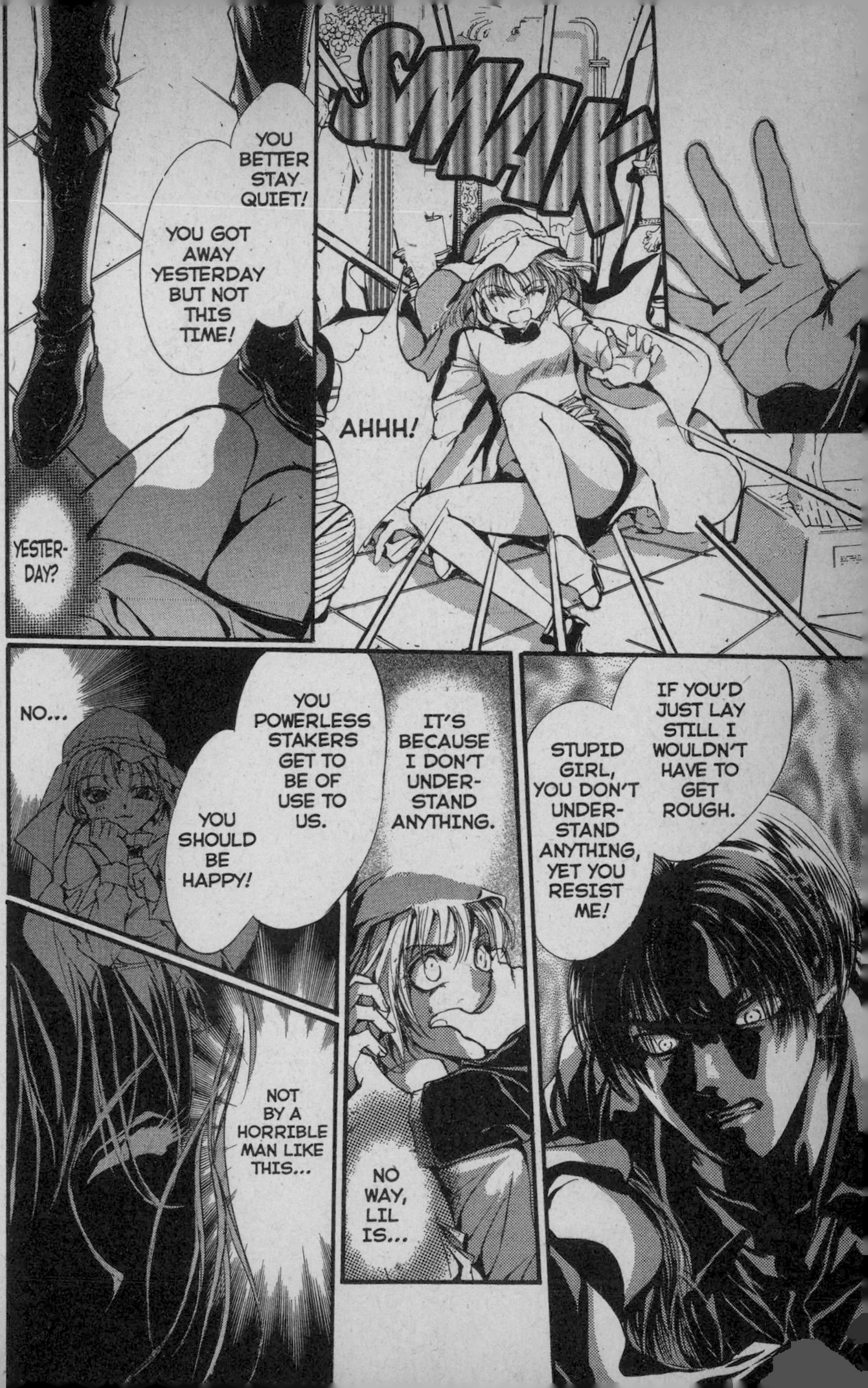
SMAK
AHHH!
YOU BETTER STAY QUIET!
YOU GOT AWAY YESTERDAY BUT NOT THIS TIME!
YESTER-DAY?
IF YOU'D JUST LAY STILL I WOULDN'T HAVE TO GET ROUGH.
STUPID GIRL, YOU DON'T UNDER-STAND ANYTHING, YET YOU RESIST ME!
IT'S BECAUSE I DON'T UNDER-STAND ANYTHING.
YOU POWERLESS STAKERS GET TO BE OF USE TO US.
YOU SHOULD BE HAPPY!
NO...
NO WAY, LIL IS...
NOT BY A HORRIBLE MAN LIKE THIS...

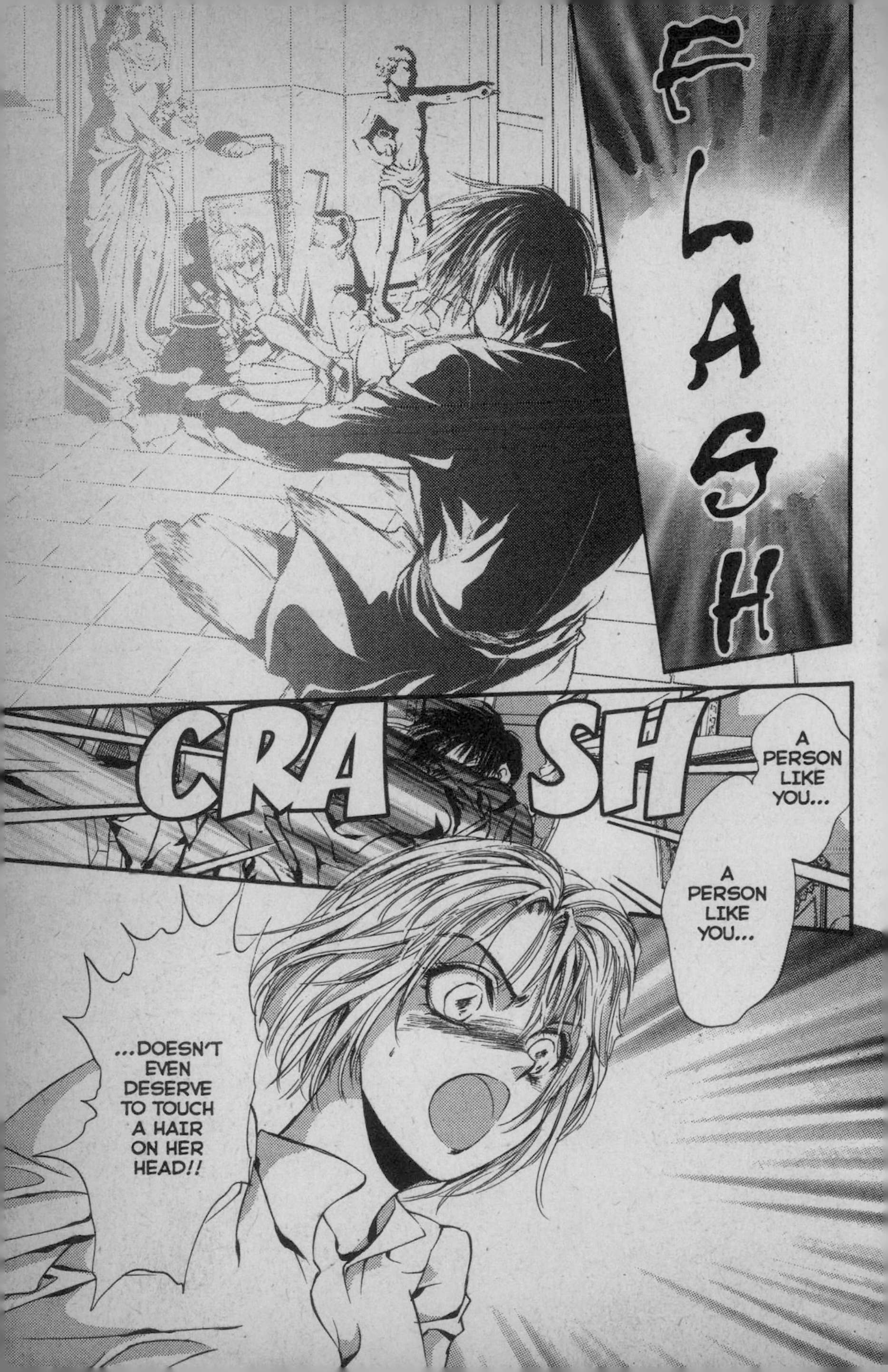
FLASH
CRASH
A PERSON LIKE YOU...
A PERSON LIKE YOU...
...DOESN'T EVEN DESERVE TO TOUCH A HAIR ON HER HEAD!!

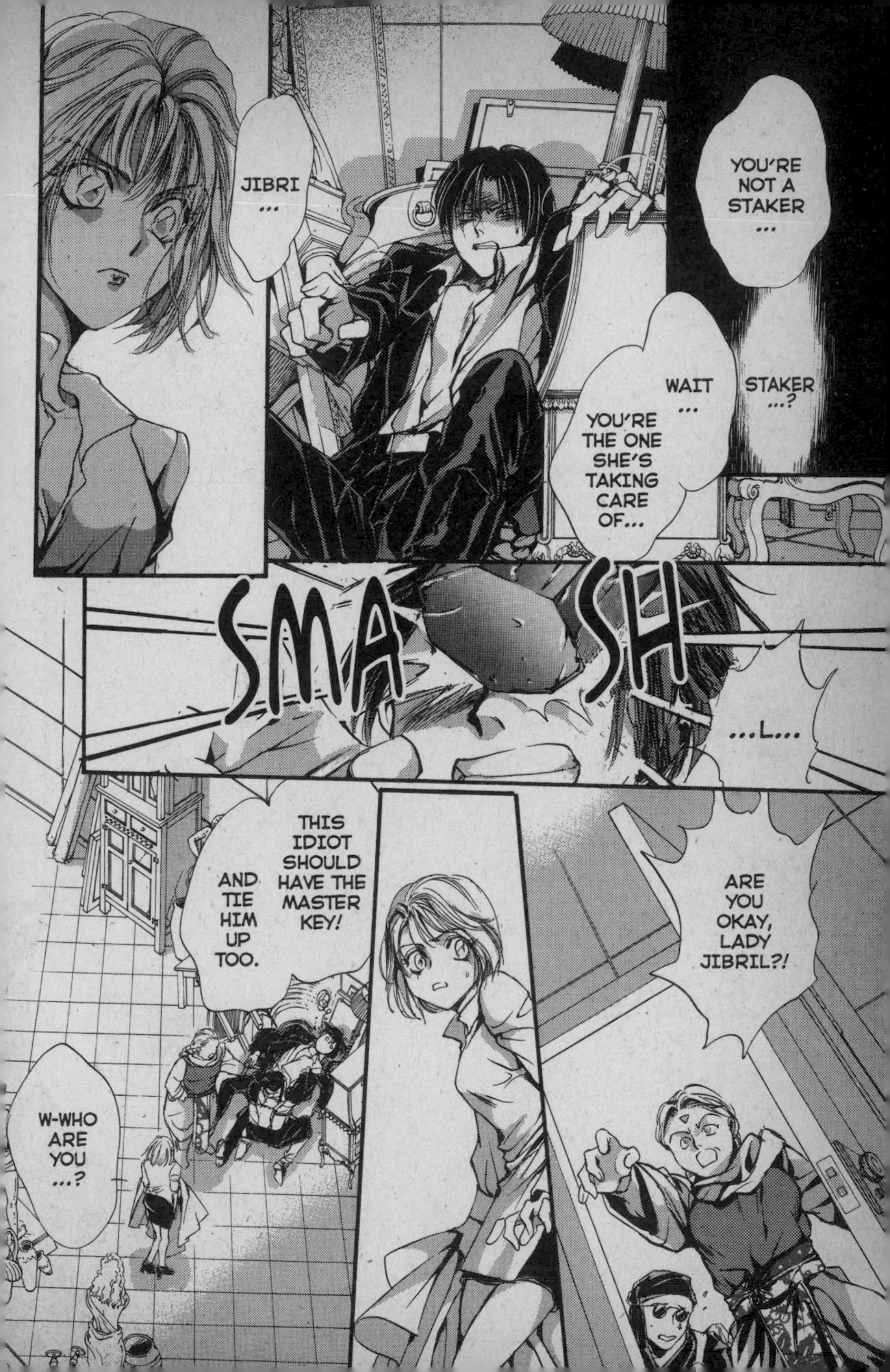

YOU'RE NOT A STAKER...
STAKER...?
WAIT...
YOU'RE THE ONE SHE'S TAKING CARE OF...
JIBRI...
SMASH
...L...
ARE YOU OKAY, LADY JIBRIL?!
THIS IDIOT SHOULD HAVE THE MASTER KEY!
AND TIE HIM UP TOO.
W-WHO ARE YOU...?

After I had Jibril cut her hair I got a letter that said... "You sure like having your characters cut their hair, like Melediana in Caine." I read that and realized it was kind of true, I do cut the character's hair a lot... Wait, that's just two characters! Plus both did it for totally different reasons. Not that I care... Since Lil Lil and Jibril are different sizes, I would think that the clothes Sara would be wearing would be really tight... But since that's hard to express in art I just neglected it. Jibril is taller and Lil Lil has a less developed body. She's maybe 13-14 in human age? Oh, and Lil Lil wasn't raped by that man...

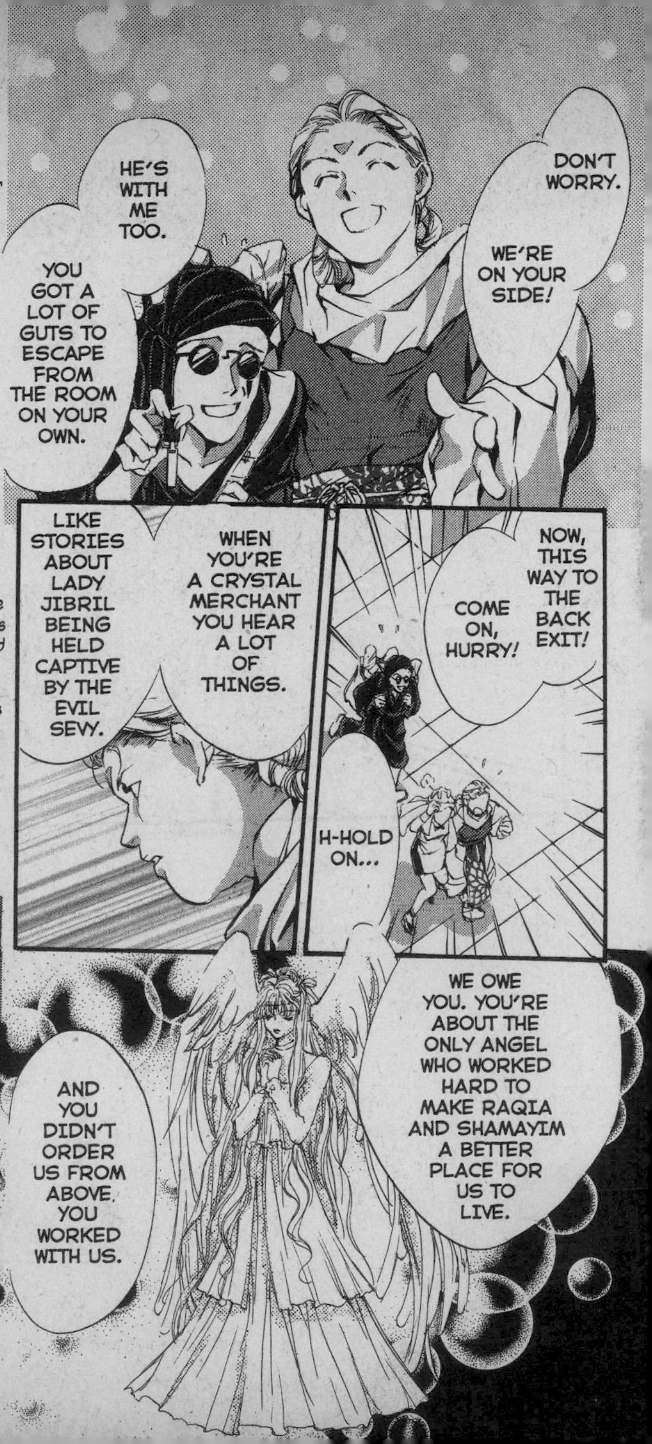
DON'T WORRY.
WE'RE ON YOUR SIDE!
HE'S WITH ME TOO.
YOU GOT A LOT OF GUTS TO ESCAPE FROM THE ROOM ON YOUR OWN.
NOW, THIS WAY TO THE BACK EXIT!
COME ON, HURRY!
H-HOLD ON...
WHEN YOU'RE A CRYSTAL MERCHANT YOU HEAR A LOT OF THINGS.
LIKE STORIES ABOUT LADY JIBRIL BEING HELD CAPTIVE BY THE EVIL SEVY.
WE OWE YOU. YOU'RE ABOUT THE ONLY ANGEL WHO WORKED HARD TO MAKE RAQIA AND SHAMAYIM A BETTER PLACE FOR US TO LIVE.
AND YOU DIDN'T ORDER US FROM ABOVE. YOU WORKED WITH US.

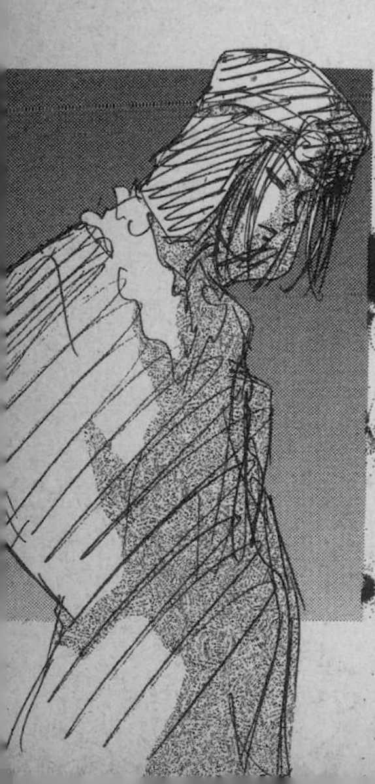

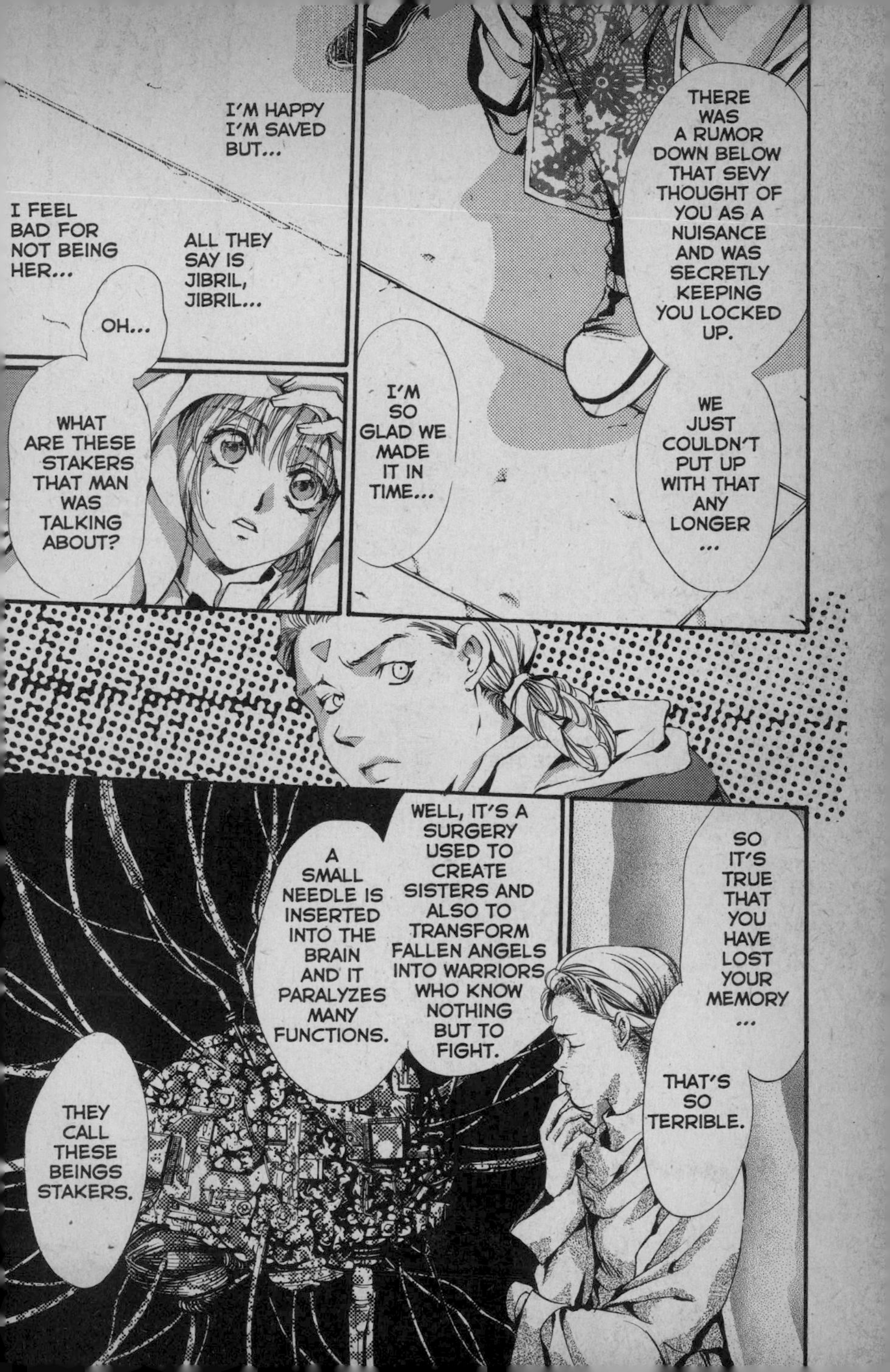
THERE WAS A RUMOR DOWN BELOW THAT SEVY THOUGHT OF YOU AS A NUISANCE AND WAS SECRETLY KEEPING YOU LOCKED UP.
WE JUST COULDN'T PUT UP WITH THAT ANY LONGER...
I'M SO GLAD WE MADE IT IN TIME...
I'M HAPPY I'M SAVED BUT...
ALL THEY SAY IS JIBRIL, JIBRIL...
I FEEL BAD FOR NOT BEING HER...
OH...
WHAT ARE THESE STAKERS THAT MAN WAS TALKING ABOUT?
SO IT'S TRUE THAT YOU HAVE LOST YOUR MEMORY...
THAT'S SO TERRIBLE.
WELL, IT'S A SURGERY USED TO CREATE SISTERS AND ALSO TO TRANSFORM FALLEN ANGELS INTO WARRIORS WHO KNOW NOTHING BUT TO FIGHT.
A SMALL NEEDLE IS INSERTED INTO THE BRAIN AND IT PARALYZES MANY FUNCTIONS.
THEY CALL THESE BEINGS STAKERS.

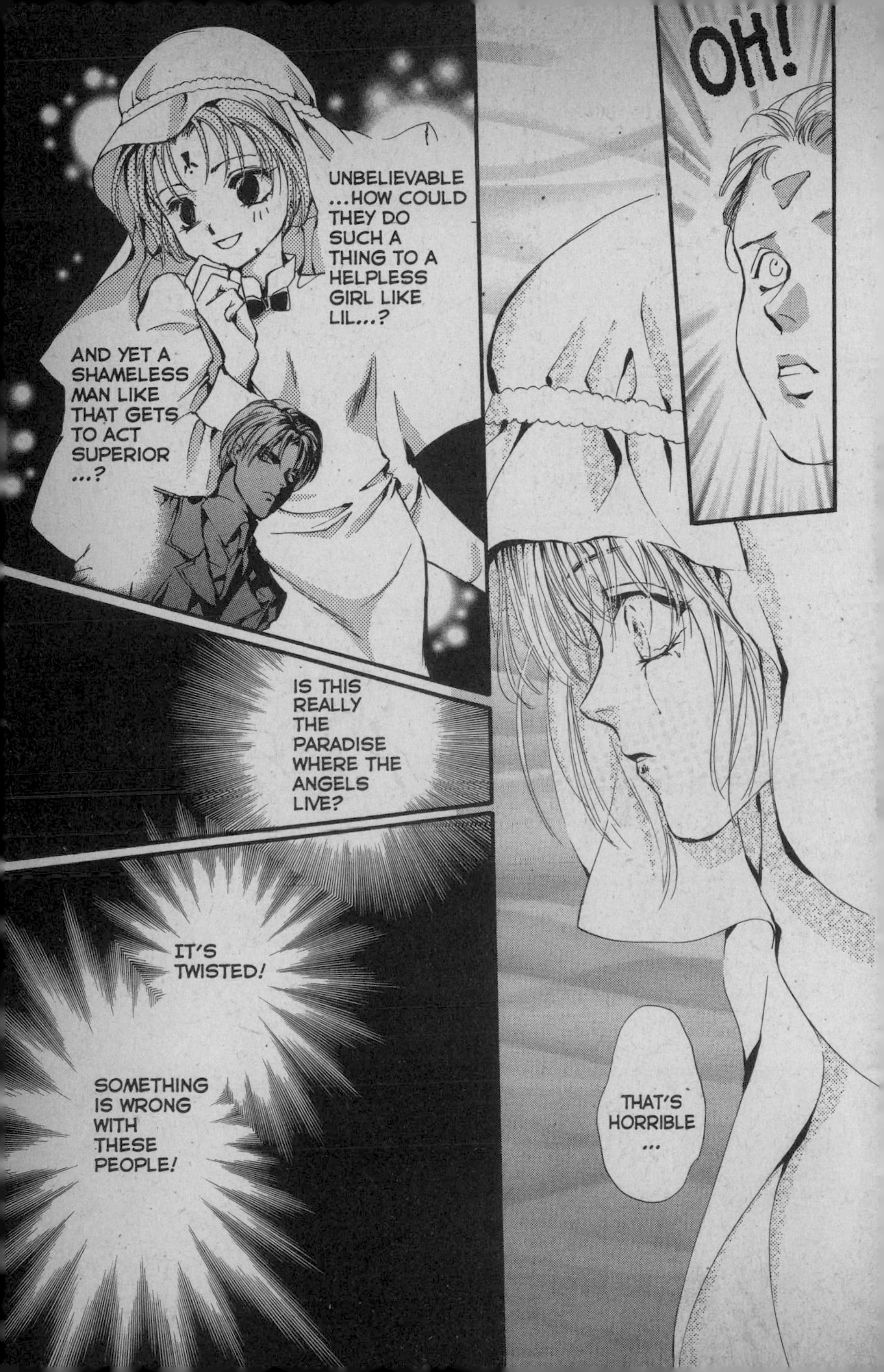
OH!
THAT'S HORRIBLE ...
UNBELIEVABLE ...HOW COULD THEY DO SUCH A THING TO A HELPLESS GIRL LIKE LIL...?
AND YET A SHAMELESS MAN LIKE THAT GETS TO ACT SUPERIOR ...?
IS THIS REALLY THE PARADISE WHERE THE ANGELS LIVE?
IT'S TWISTED!
SOMETHING IS WRONG WITH THESE PEOPLE!

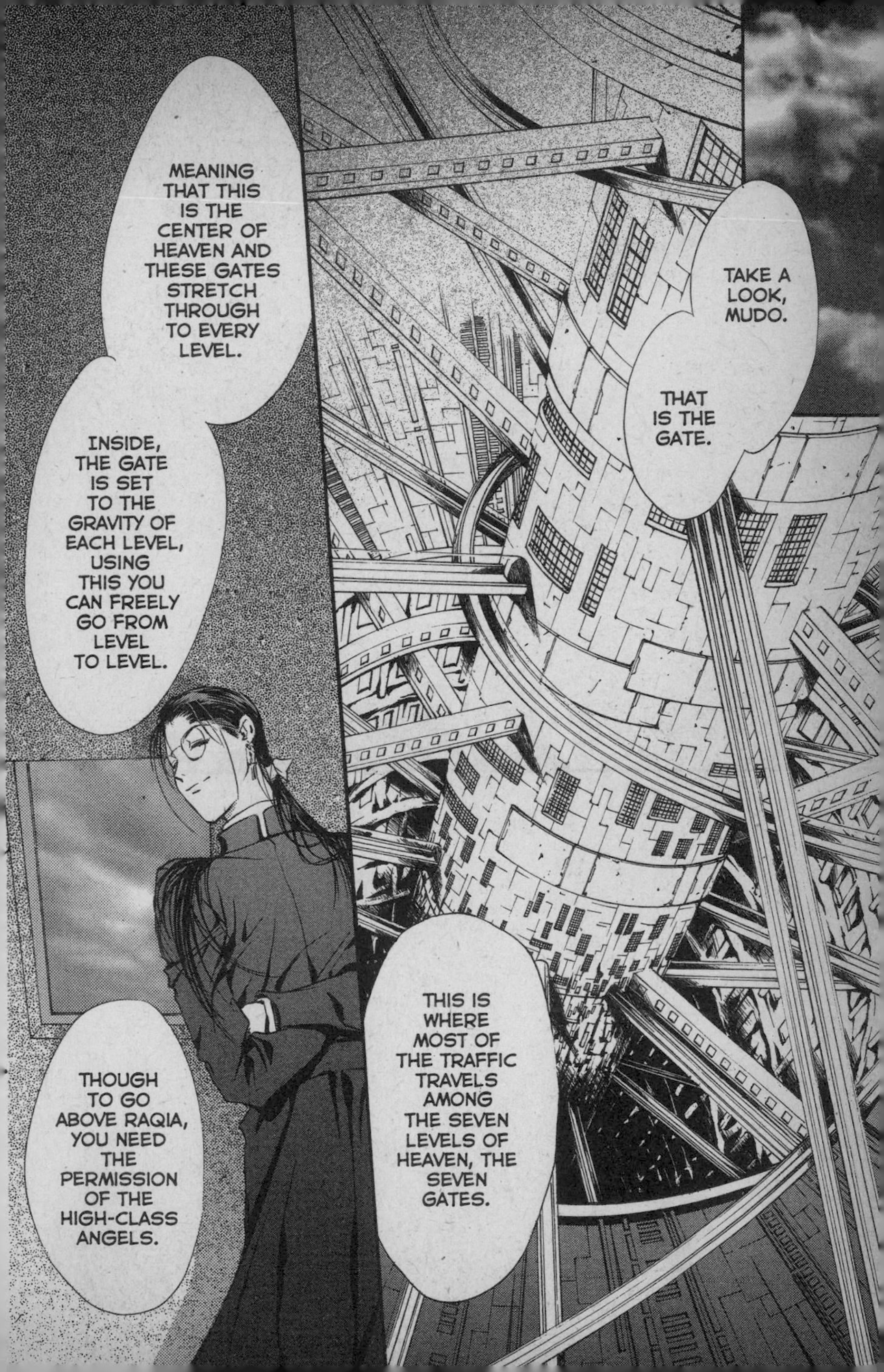
TAKE A LOOK, MUDO.
THAT IS THE GATE.
THIS IS WHERE MOST OF THE TRAFFIC TRAVELS AMONG THE SEVEN LEVELS OF HEAVEN, THE SEVEN GATES.
MEANING THAT THIS IS THE CENTER OF HEAVEN AND THESE GATES STRETCH THROUGH TO EVERY LEVEL.
INSIDE, THE GATE IS SET TO THE GRAVITY OF EACH LEVEL, USING THIS YOU CAN FREELY GO FROM LEVEL TO LEVEL.
THOUGH TO GO ABOVE RAQIA, YOU NEED THE PERMISSION OF THE HIGH-CLASS ANGELS.

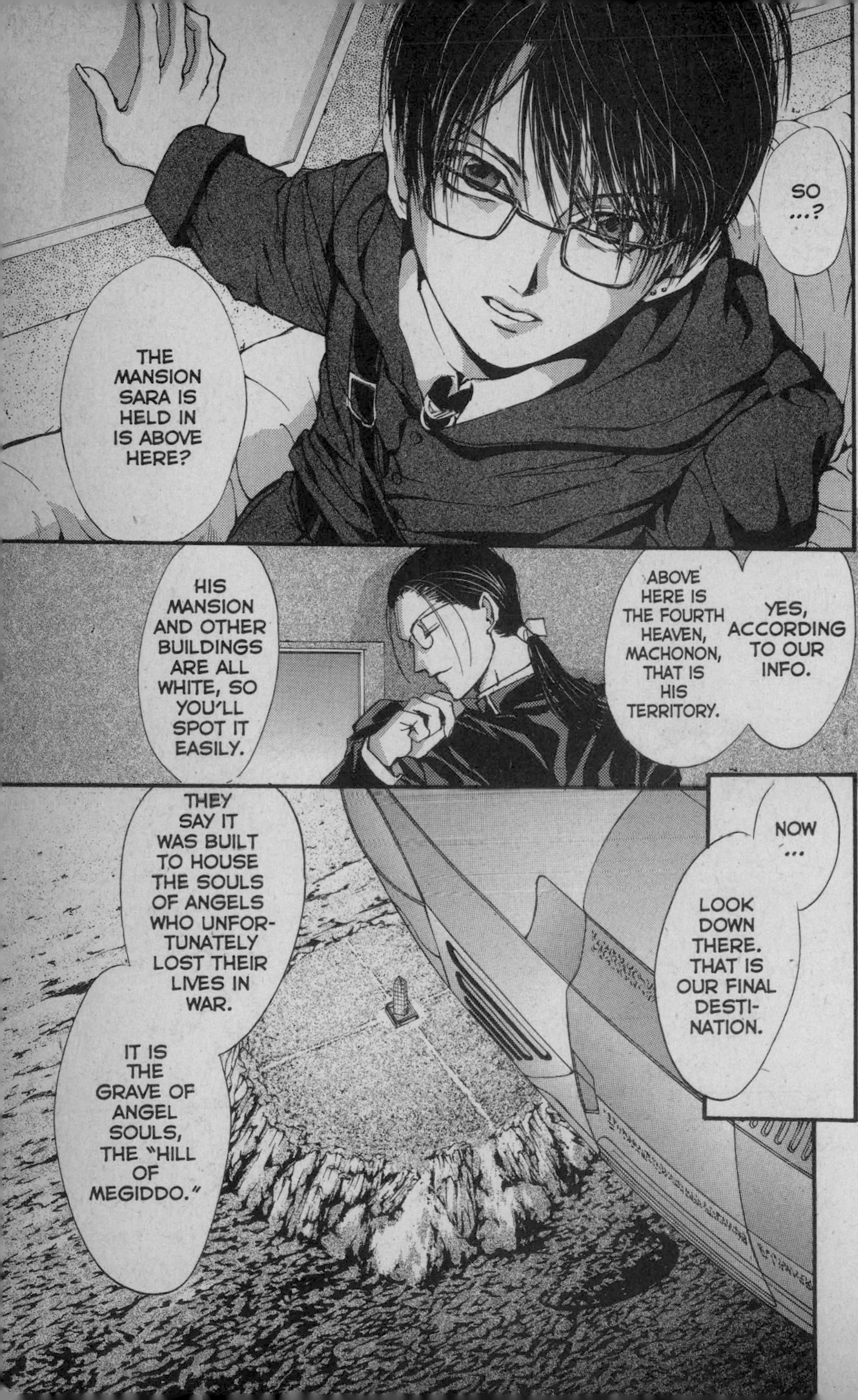
SO ...?
THE MANSION SARA IS HELD IN IS ABOVE HERE?
YES, ACCORDING TO OUR INFO.
ABOVE HERE IS THE FOURTH HEAVEN, MACHONON, THAT IS HIS TERRITORY.
HIS MANSION AND OTHER BUILDINGS ARE ALL WHITE, SO YOU'LL SPOT IT EASILY.
NOW ...
LOOK DOWN THERE. THAT IS OUR FINAL DESTI- NATION.
THEY SAY IT WAS BUILT TO HOUSE THE SOULS OF ANGELS WHO UNFOR- TUNATELY LOST THEIR LIVES IN WAR.
IT IS THE GRAVE OF ANGEL SOULS, THE "HILL OF MEGIDDO."

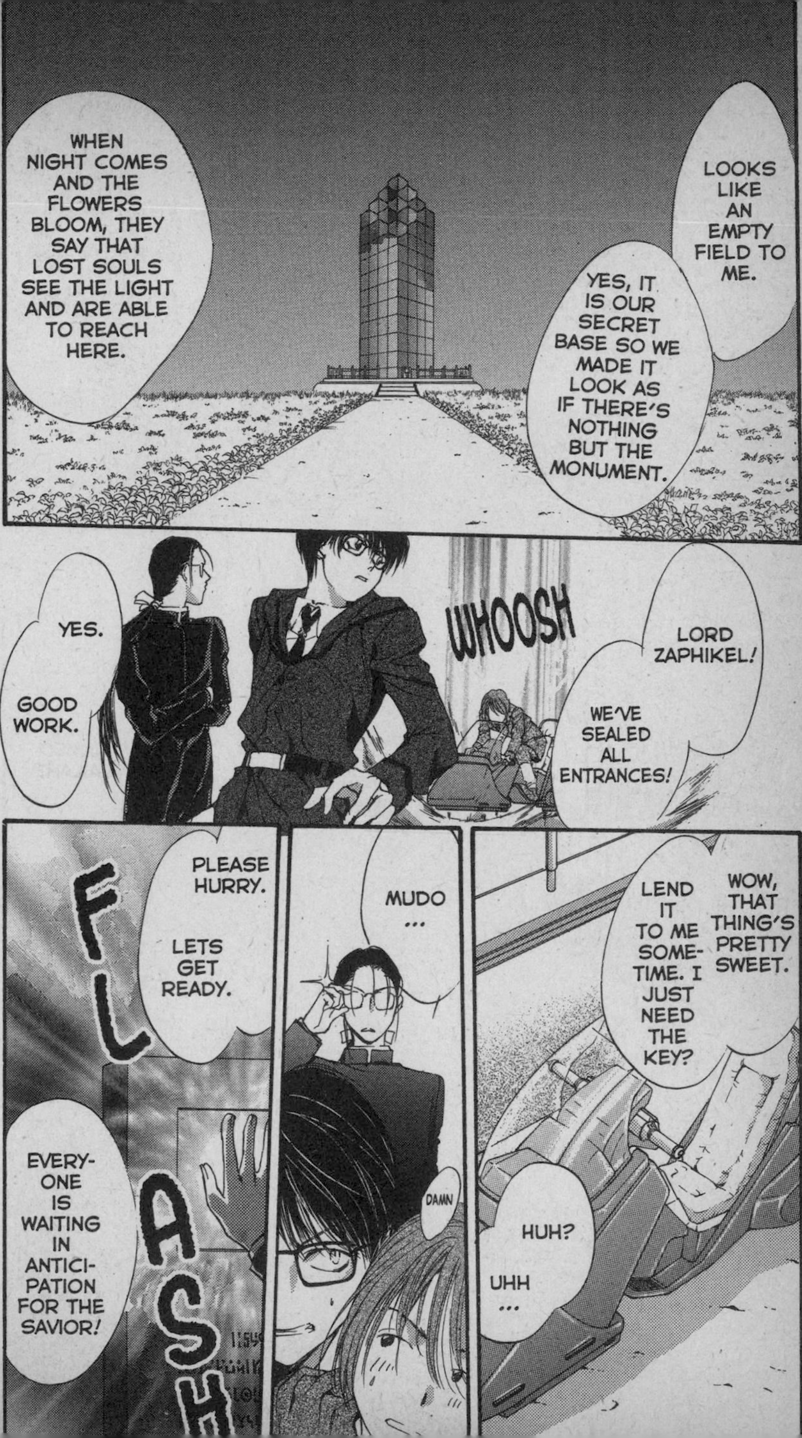

LOOKS LIKE AN EMPTY FIELD TO ME.
YES, IT IS OUR SECRET BASE SO WE MADE IT LOOK AS IF THERE'S NOTHING BUT THE MONUMENT.
WHEN NIGHT COMES AND THE FLOWERS BLOOM, THEY SAY THAT LOST SOULS SEE THE LIGHT AND ARE ABLE TO REACH HERE.
WHOOSH
LORD ZAPHIKEL!
WE'VE SEALED ALL ENTRANCES!
YES.
GOOD WORK.
WOW, THAT THING'S PRETTY SWEET.
LEND IT TO ME SOME-TIME. I JUST NEED THE KEY?
HUH?
UHH ...
MUDO ...
DAMN
PLEASE HURRY.
LETS GET READY.
FLASH
EVERY-ONE IS WAITING IN ANTICI-PATION FOR THE SAVIOR!

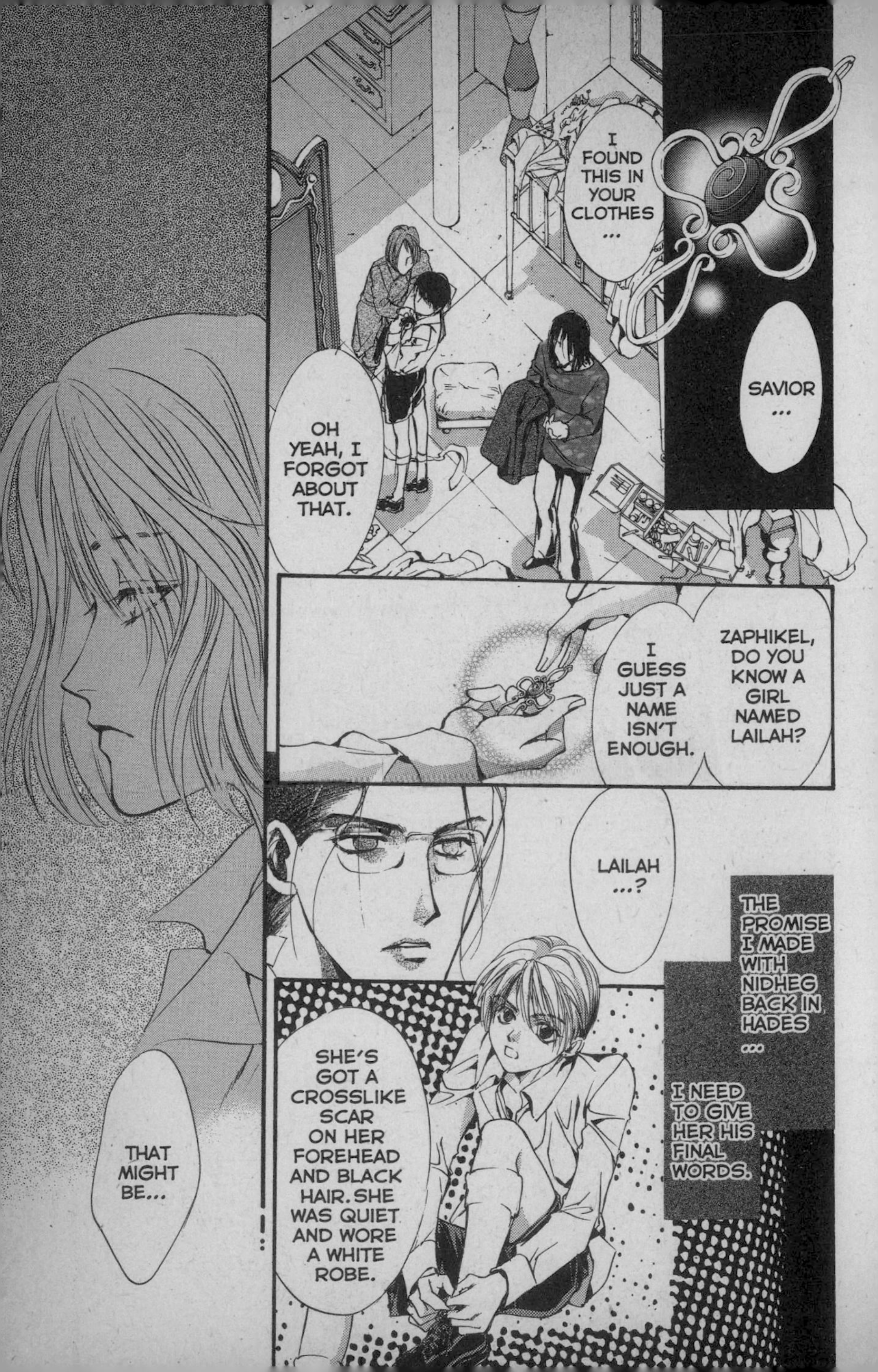
I FOUND THIS IN YOUR CLOTHES ...
SAVIOR ...
OH YEAH, I FORGOT ABOUT THAT.
ZAPHIKEL, DO YOU KNOW A GIRL NAMED LAILAH?
I GUESS JUST A NAME ISN'T ENOUGH.
LAILAH ...?
THE PROMISE I MADE WITH NIDHEG BACK IN HADES ...
SHE'S GOT A CROSSLIKE SCAR ON HER FOREHEAD AND BLACK HAIR. SHE WAS QUIET AND WORE A WHITE ROBE.
I NEED TO GIVE HER HIS FINAL WORDS.
THAT MIGHT BE...

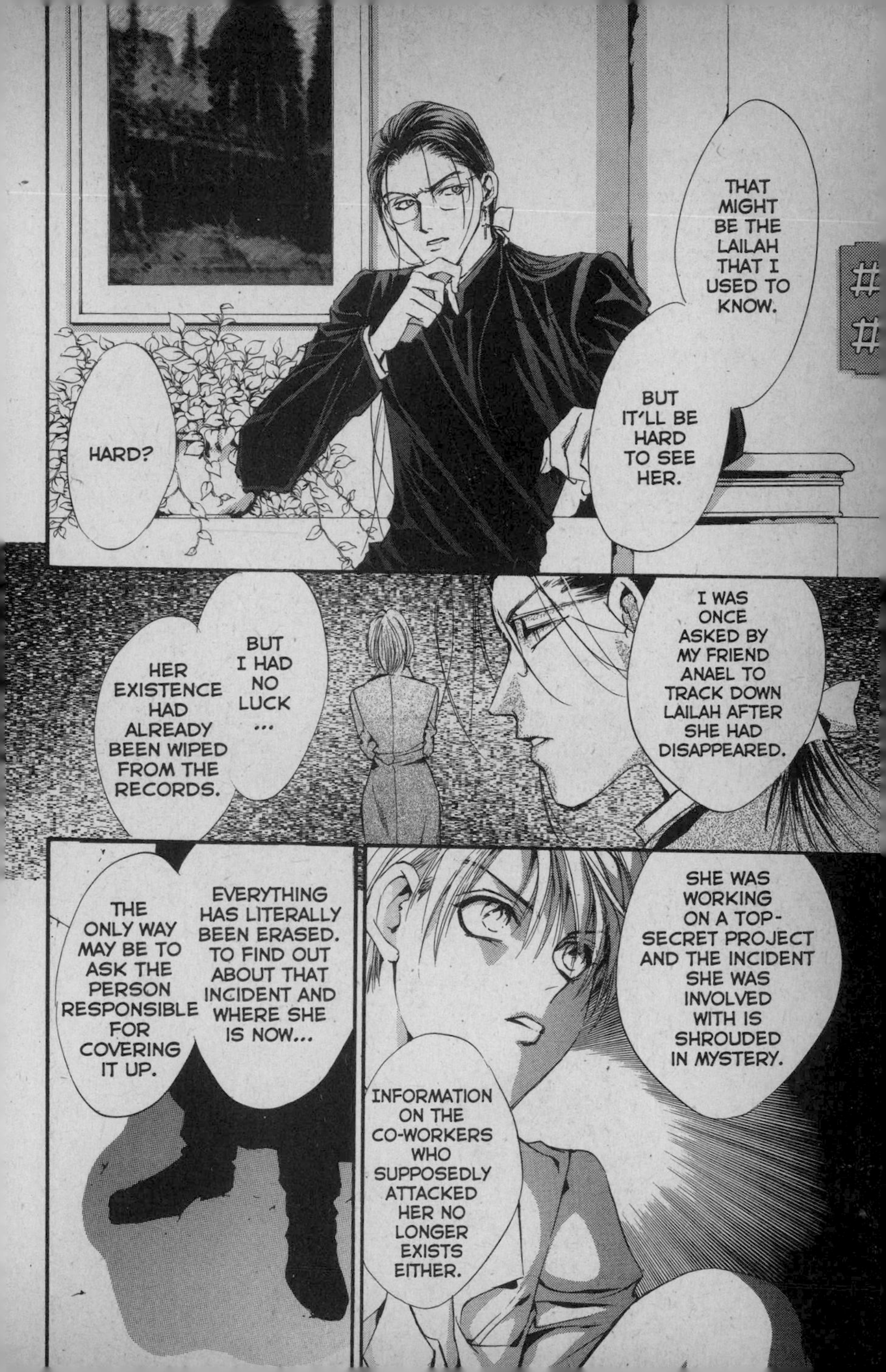
THAT MIGHT BE THE LAILAH THAT I USED TO KNOW.
BUT IT'LL BE HARD TO SEE HER.
HARD?
I WAS ONCE ASKED BY MY FRIEND ANAEL TO TRACK DOWN LAILAH AFTER SHE HAD DISAPPEARED.
BUT I HAD NO LUCK...
HER EXISTENCE HAD ALREADY BEEN WIPED FROM THE RECORDS.
SHE WAS WORKING ON A TOP-SECRET PROJECT AND THE INCIDENT SHE WAS INVOLVED WITH IS SHROUDED IN MYSTERY.
INFORMATION ON THE CO-WORKERS WHO SUPPOSEDLY ATTACKED HER NO LONGER EXISTS EITHER.
EVERYTHING HAS LITERALLY BEEN ERASED. TO FIND OUT ABOUT THAT INCIDENT AND WHERE SHE IS NOW...
THE ONLY WAY MAY BE TO ASK THE PERSON RESPONSIBLE FOR COVERING IT UP.

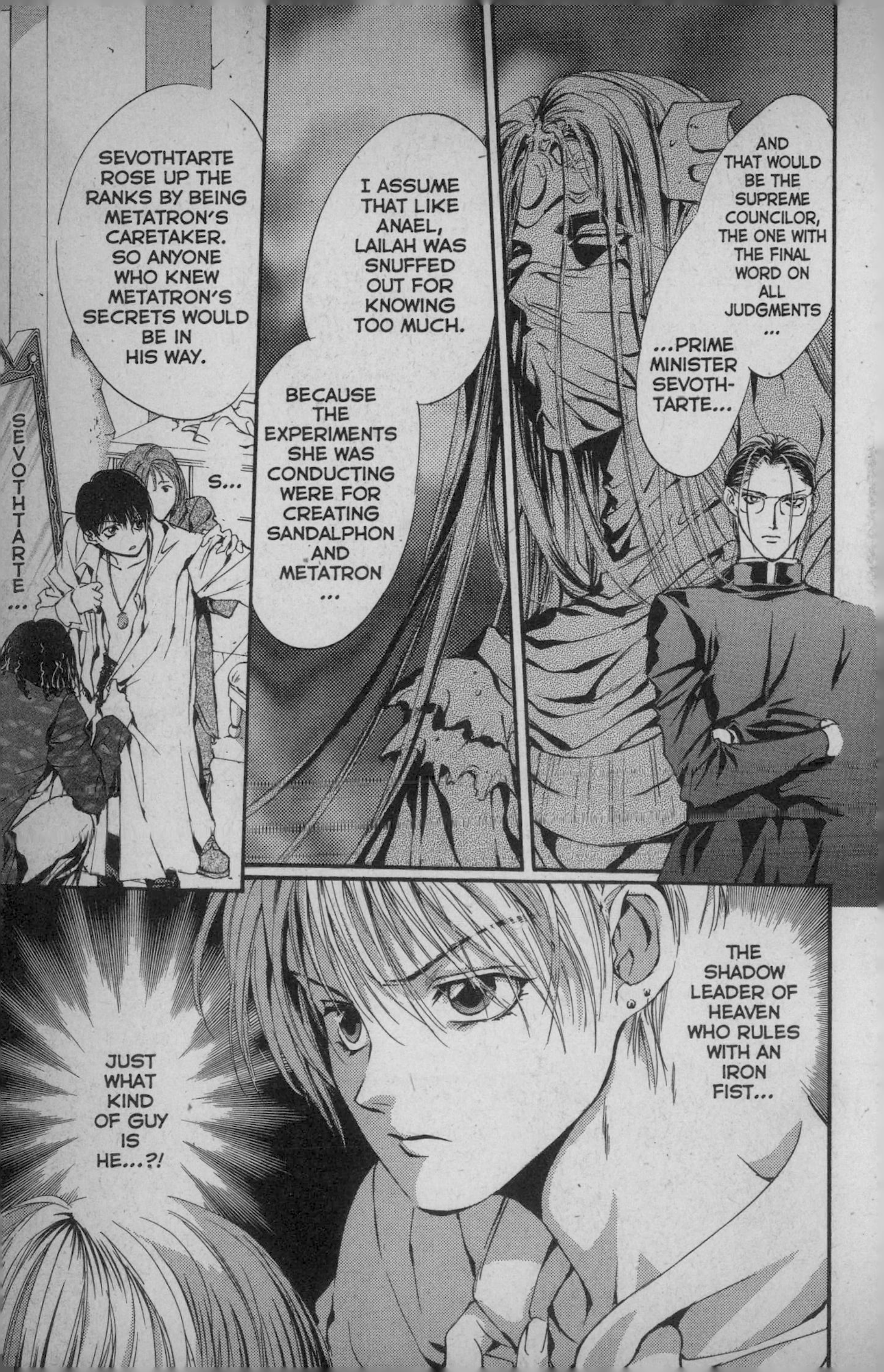
AND THAT WOULD BE THE SUPREME COUNCILOR, THE ONE WITH THE FINAL WORD ON ALL JUDGMENTS ...
...PRIME MINISTER SEVOTH-TARTE...
I ASSUME THAT LIKE ANAEL, LAILAH WAS SNUFFED OUT FOR KNOWING TOO MUCH.
BECAUSE THE EXPERIMENTS SHE WAS CONDUCTING WERE FOR CREATING SANDALPHON AND METATRON ...
SEVOTHTARTE ROSE UP THE RANKS BY BEING METATRON'S CARETAKER. SO ANYONE WHO KNEW METATRON'S SECRETS WOULD BE IN HIS WAY.
S...
SEVOTHTARTE ...
THE SHADOW LEADER OF HEAVEN WHO RULES WITH AN IRON FIST...
JUST WHAT KIND OF GUY IS HE...?!

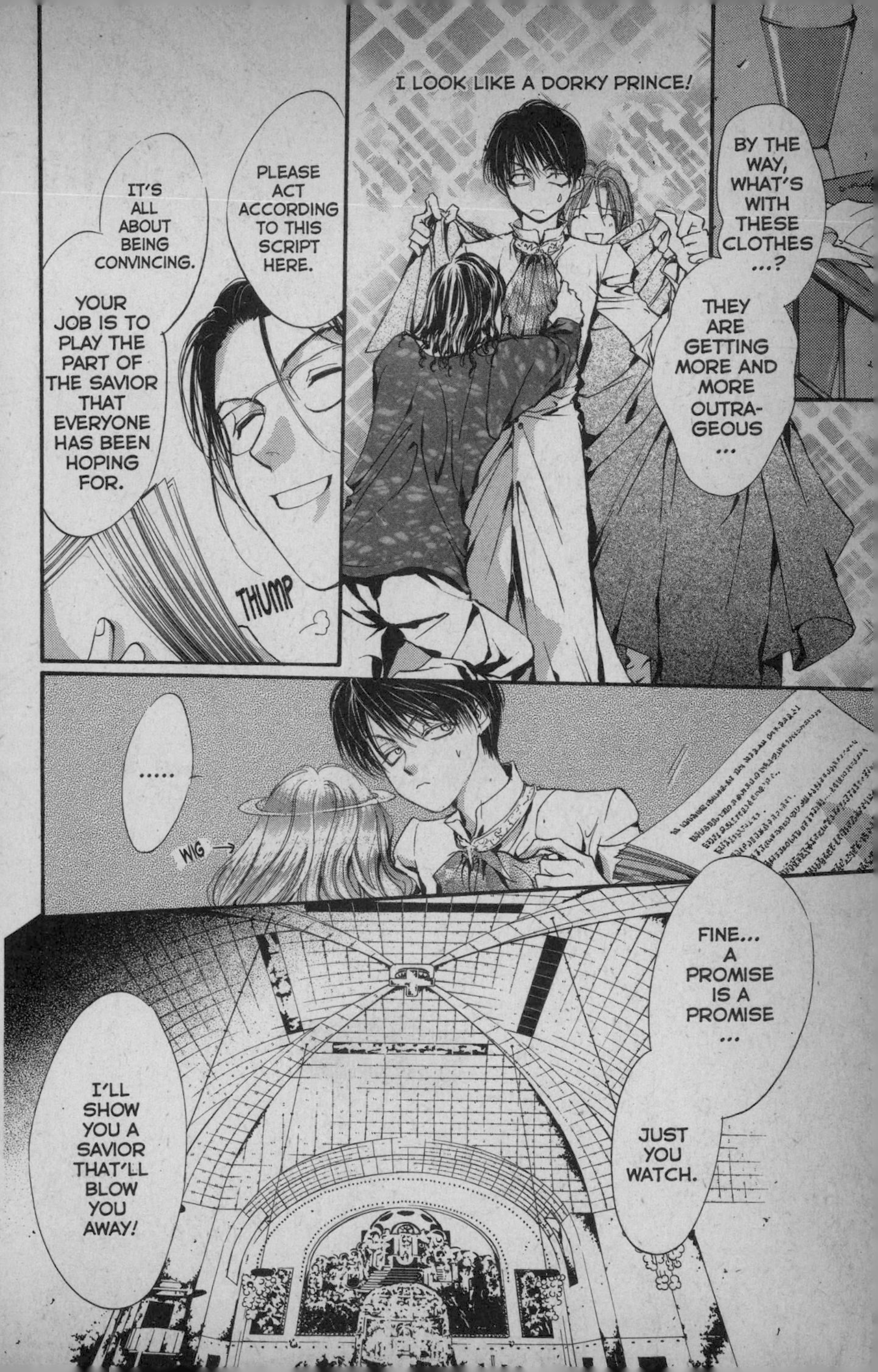
BY THE WAY, WHAT'S WITH THESE CLOTHES ...?
THEY ARE GETTING MORE AND MORE OUTRAGEOUS ...
I LOOK LIKE A DORKY PRINCE!
PLEASE ACT ACCORDING TO THIS SCRIPT HERE.
IT'S ALL ABOUT BEING CONVINCING.
YOUR JOB IS TO PLAY THE PART OF THE SAVIOR THAT EVERYONE HAS BEEN HOPING FOR.
THUMP
.....
WIG
FINE... A PROMISE IS A PROMISE ...
JUST YOU WATCH.
I'LL SHOW YOU A SAVIOR THAT'LL BLOW YOU AWAY!

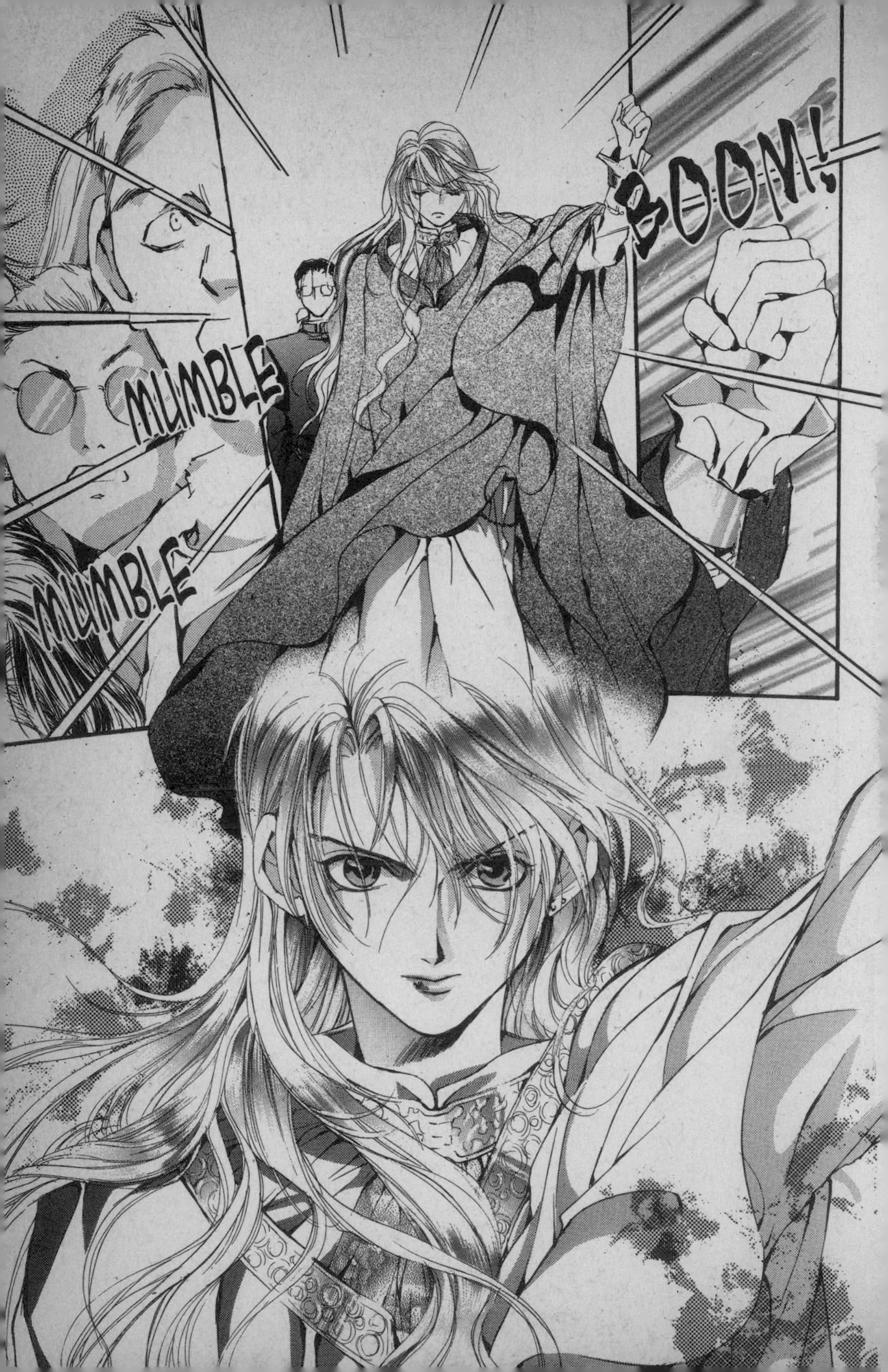
BOOM!
MUMBLE
MUMBLE

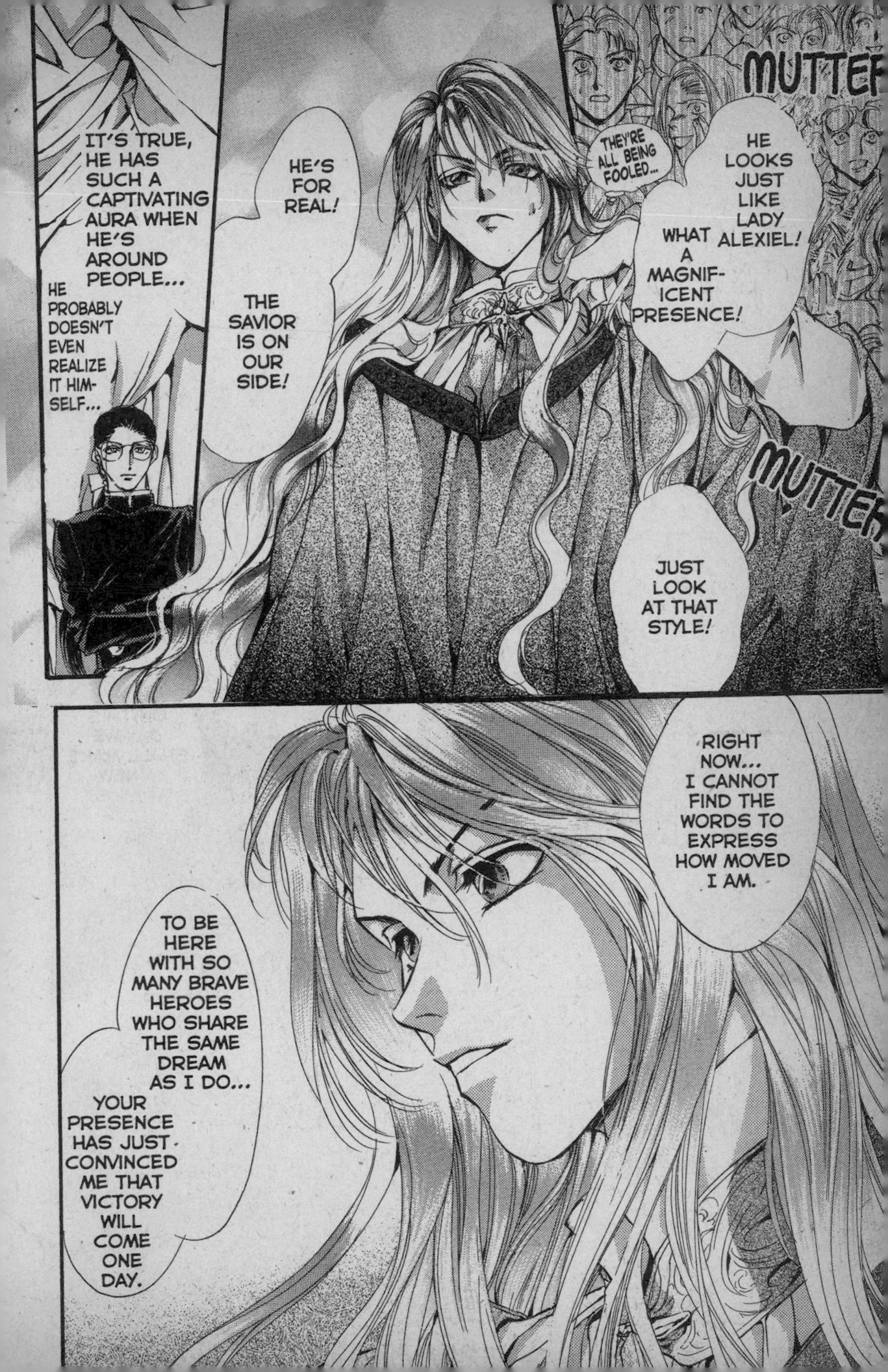
MUTTER
THEY'RE ALL BEING FOOLED...
HE LOOKS JUST LIKE LADY ALEXIEL!
WHAT A MAGNIFICENT PRESENCE!
HE'S FOR REAL!
THE SAVIOR IS ON OUR SIDE!
MUTTER
JUST LOOK AT THAT STYLE!
IT'S TRUE, HE HAS SUCH A CAPTIVATING AURA WHEN HE'S AROUND PEOPLE...
HE PROBABLY DOESN'T EVEN REALIZE IT HIMSELF...
RIGHT NOW... I CANNOT FIND THE WORDS TO EXPRESS HOW MOVED I AM.
TO BE HERE WITH SO MANY BRAVE HEROES WHO SHARE THE SAME DREAM AS I DO...
YOUR PRESENCE HAS JUST CONVINCED ME THAT VICTORY WILL COME ONE DAY.

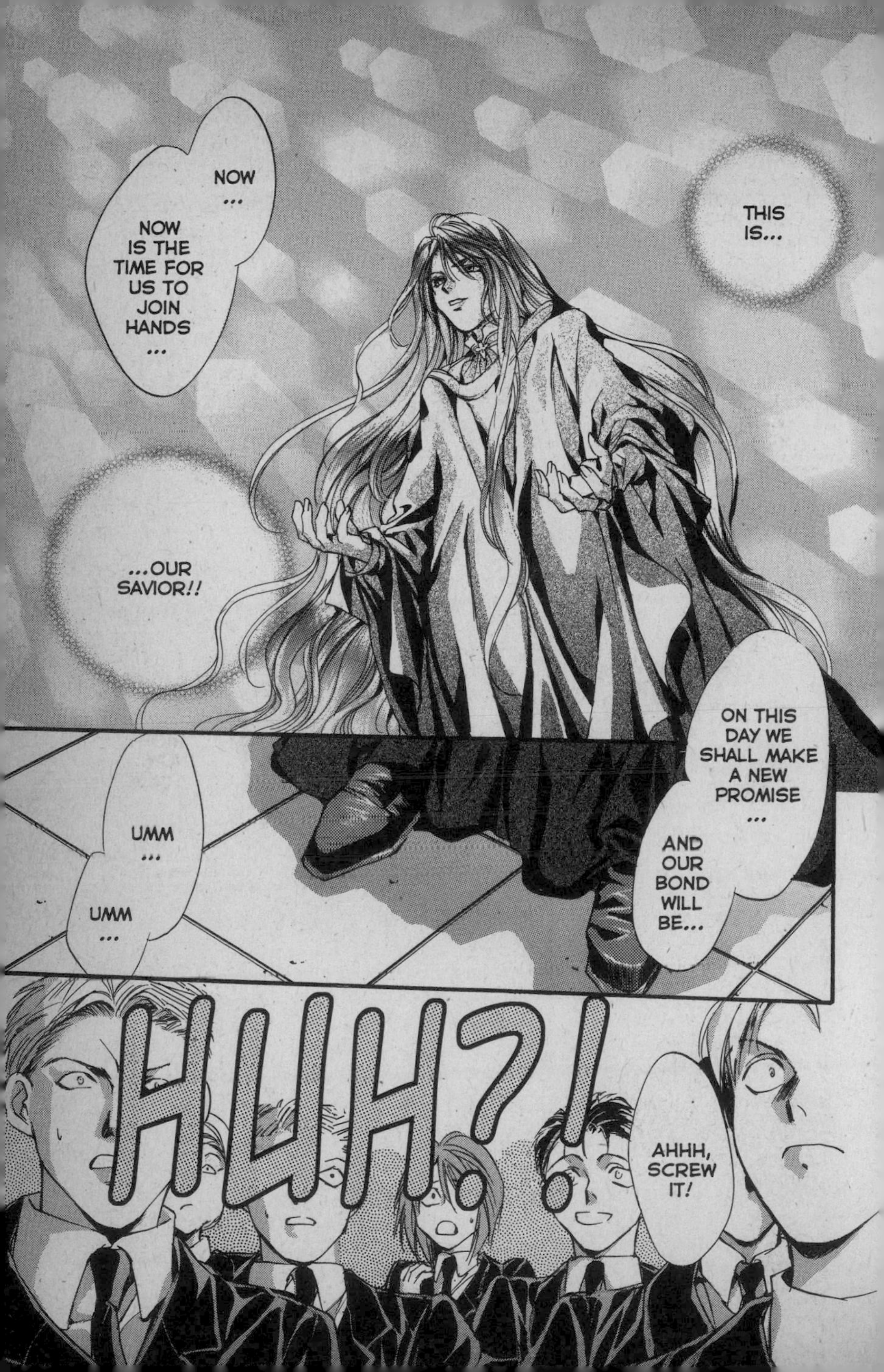
THIS IS...
NOW ... NOW IS THE TIME FOR US TO JOIN HANDS ...
...OUR SAVIOR!!
ON THIS DAY WE SHALL MAKE A NEW PROMISE ...
AND OUR BOND WILL BE...
UMM ...
UMM ...
AHHH, SCREW IT!
HUH?!

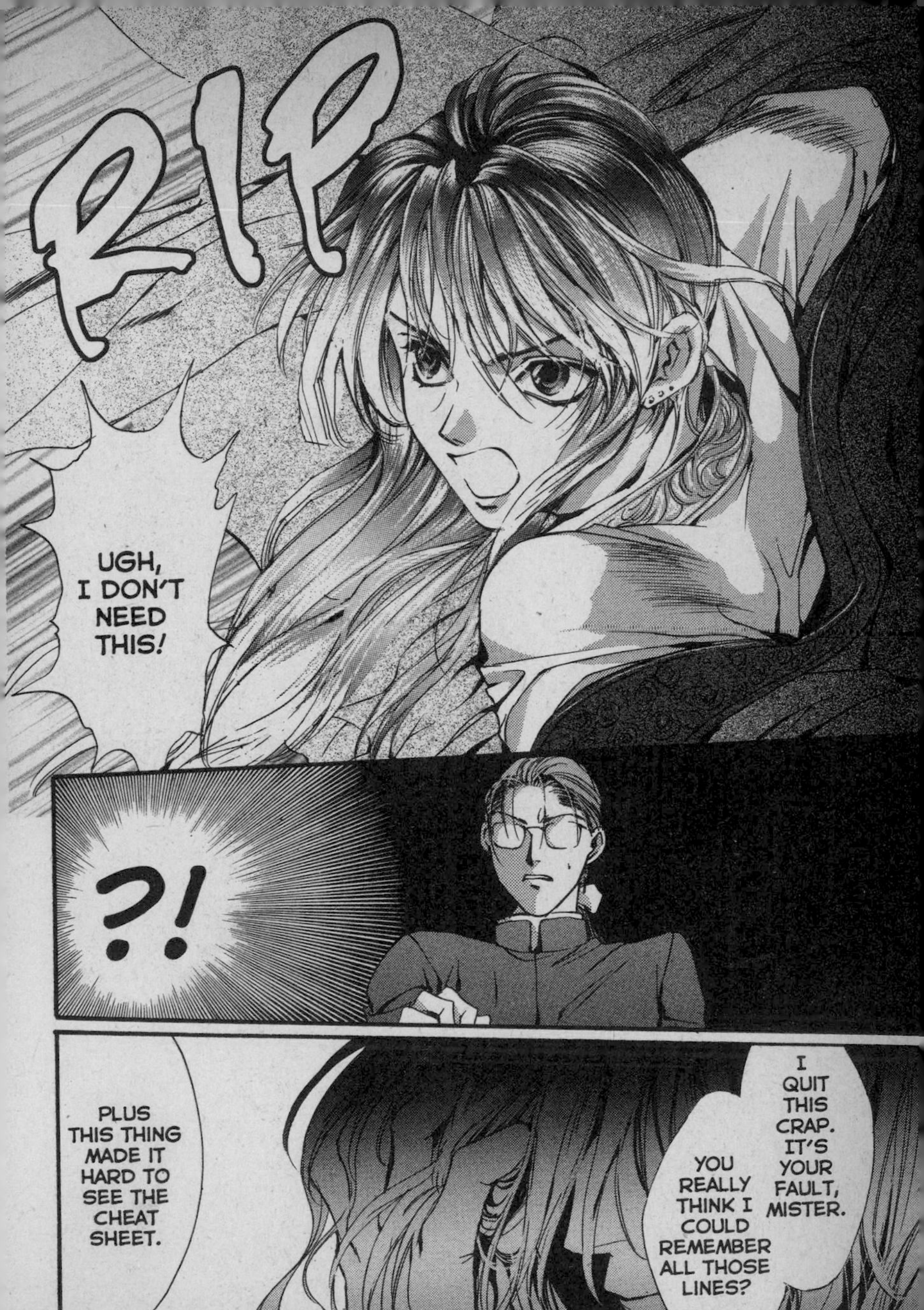
RIP
UGH, I DON'T NEED THIS!
?!
I QUIT THIS CRAP. IT'S YOUR FAULT, MISTER.
YOU REALLY THINK I COULD REMEMBER ALL THOSE LINES?
PLUS THIS THING MADE IT HARD TO SEE THE CHEAT SHEET.

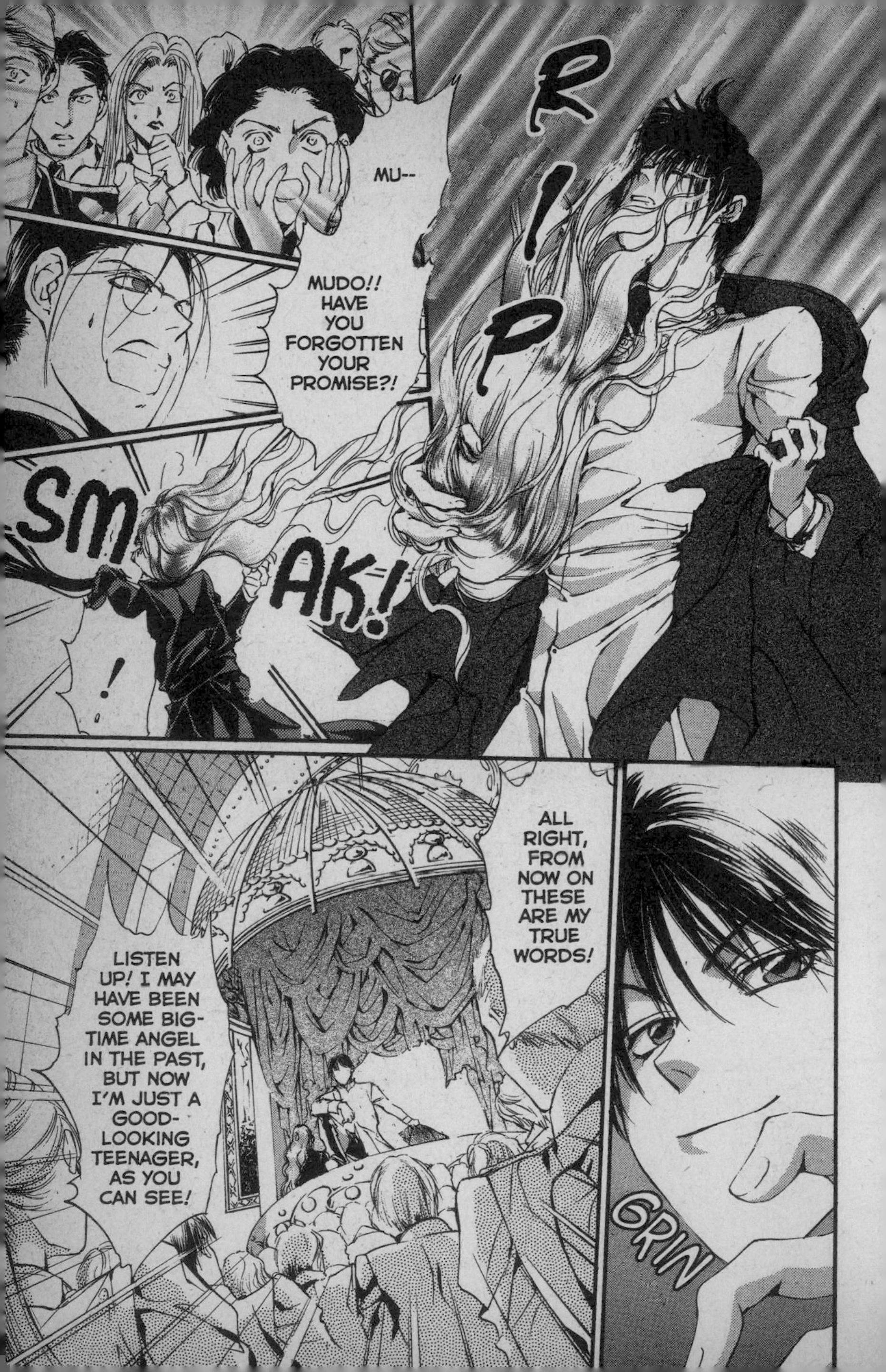
RIP
MU--
MUDO!! HAVE YOU FORGOTTEN YOUR PROMISE?!
SMAK!
!
GRIN
ALL RIGHT, FROM NOW ON THESE ARE MY TRUE WORDS!
LISTEN UP! I MAY HAVE BEEN SOME BIG-TIME ANGEL IN THE PAST, BUT NOW I'M JUST A GOOD-LOOKING TEENAGER, AS YOU CAN SEE!

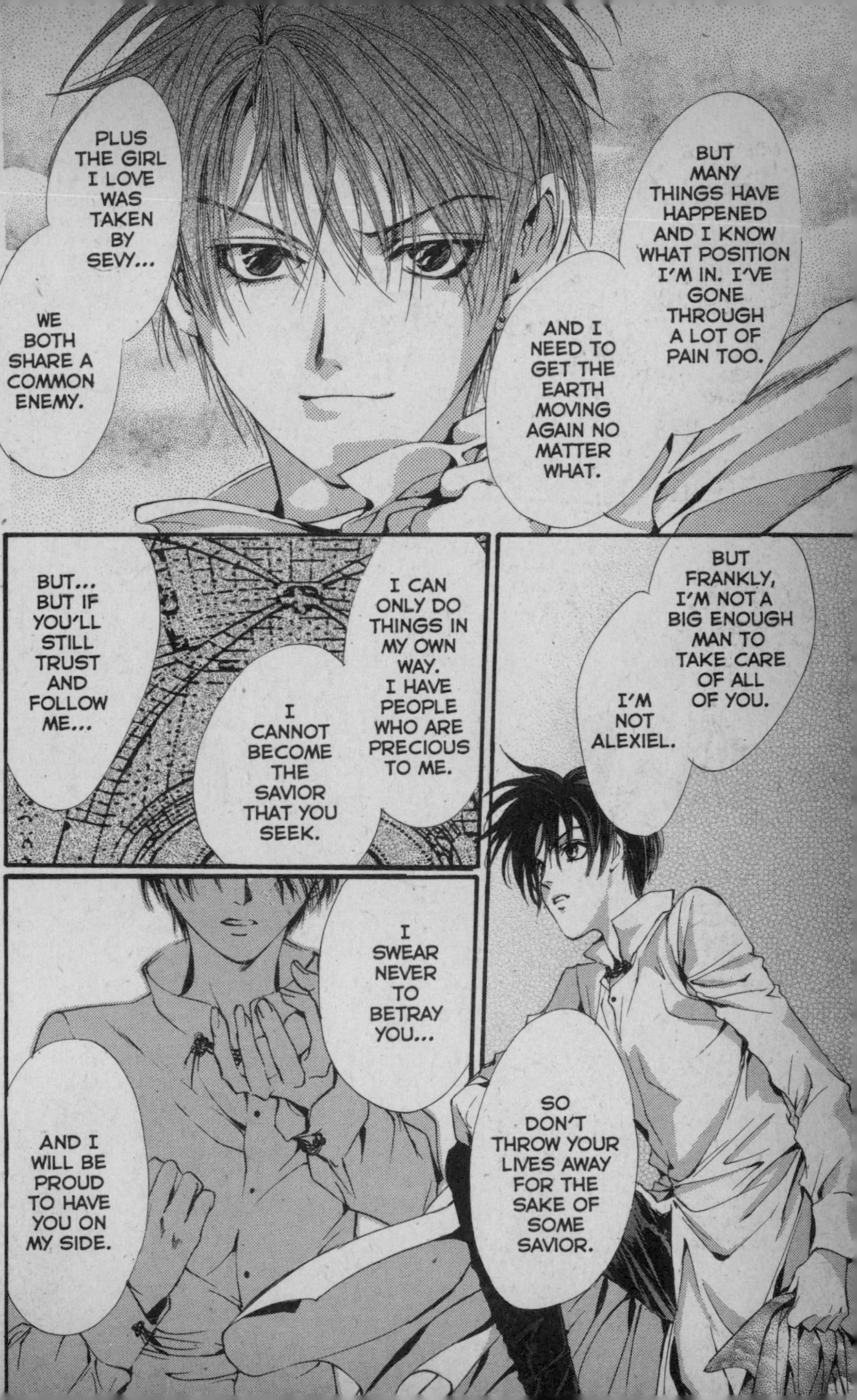
BUT MANY THINGS HAVE HAPPENED AND I KNOW WHAT POSITION I'M IN. I'VE GONE THROUGH A LOT OF PAIN TOO.
AND I NEED TO GET THE EARTH MOVING AGAIN NO MATTER WHAT.
PLUS THE GIRL I LOVE WAS TAKEN BY SEVY...
WE BOTH SHARE A COMMON ENEMY.
BUT FRANKLY, I'M NOT A BIG ENOUGH MAN TO TAKE CARE OF ALL OF YOU.
I'M NOT ALEXIEL.
SO DON'T THROW YOUR LIVES AWAY FOR THE SAKE OF SOME SAVIOR.
I CAN ONLY DO THINGS IN MY OWN WAY. I HAVE PEOPLE WHO ARE PRECIOUS TO ME.
I CANNOT BECOME THE SAVIOR THAT YOU SEEK.
BUT... BUT IF YOU'LL STILL TRUST AND FOLLOW ME...
I SWEAR NEVER TO BETRAY YOU...
AND I WILL BE PROUD TO HAVE YOU ON MY SIDE.

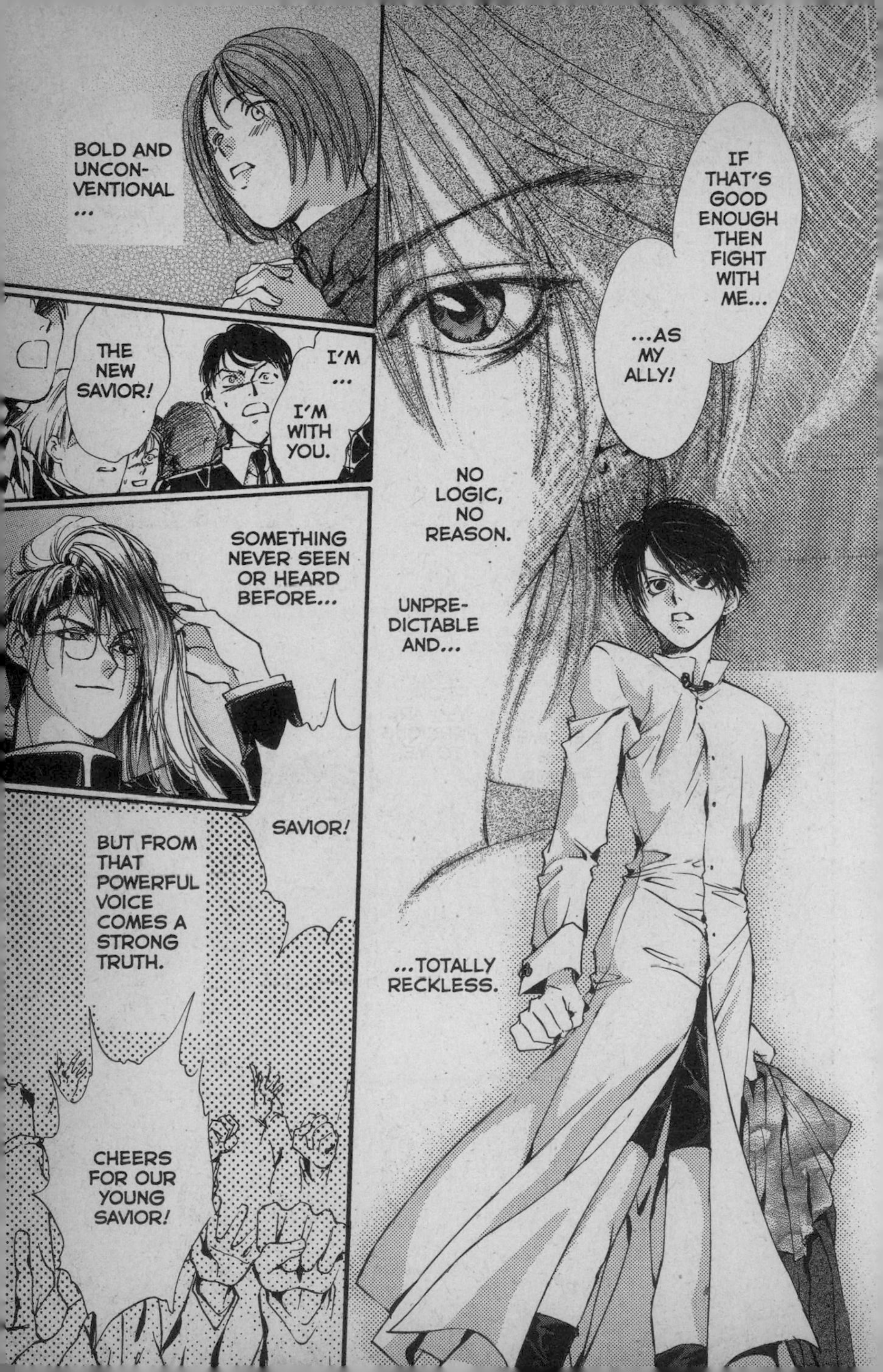
IF THAT'S GOOD ENOUGH THEN FIGHT WITH ME...
...AS MY ALLY!
NO LOGIC, NO REASON.
UNPREDICTABLE AND...
...TOTALLY RECKLESS.
BOLD AND UNCONVENTIONAL...
I'M... I'M WITH YOU.
THE NEW SAVIOR!
SOMETHING NEVER SEEN OR HEARD BEFORE...
SAVIOR!
BUT FROM THAT POWERFUL VOICE COMES A STRONG TRUTH.
CHEERS FOR OUR YOUNG SAVIOR!

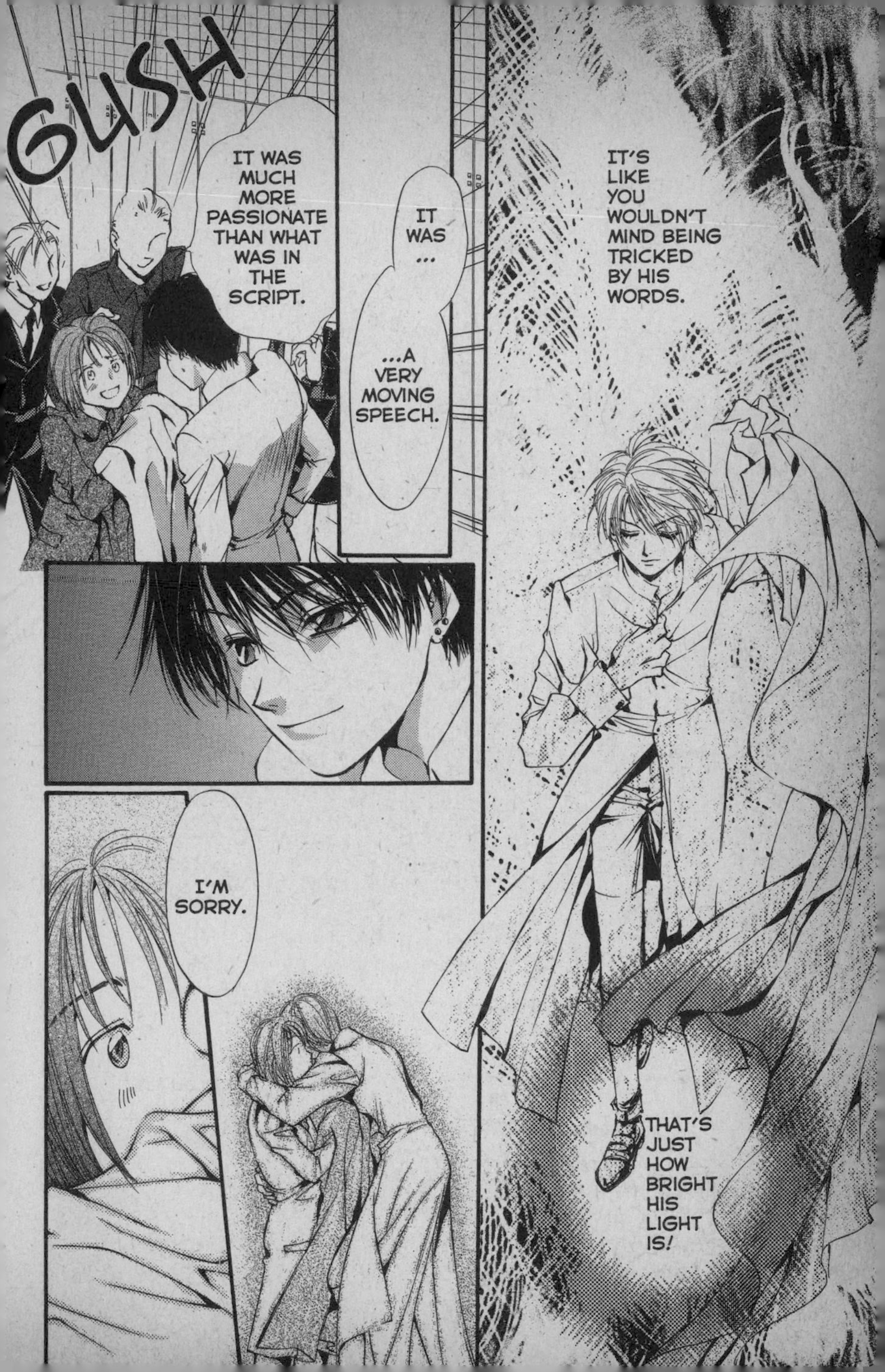
IT'S LIKE YOU WOULDN'T MIND BEING TRICKED BY HIS WORDS.
THAT'S JUST HOW BRIGHT HIS LIGHT IS!
IT WAS ...
...A VERY MOVING SPEECH.
GUSH
IT WAS MUCH MORE PASSIONATE THAN WHAT WAS IN THE SCRIPT.
I'M SORRY.

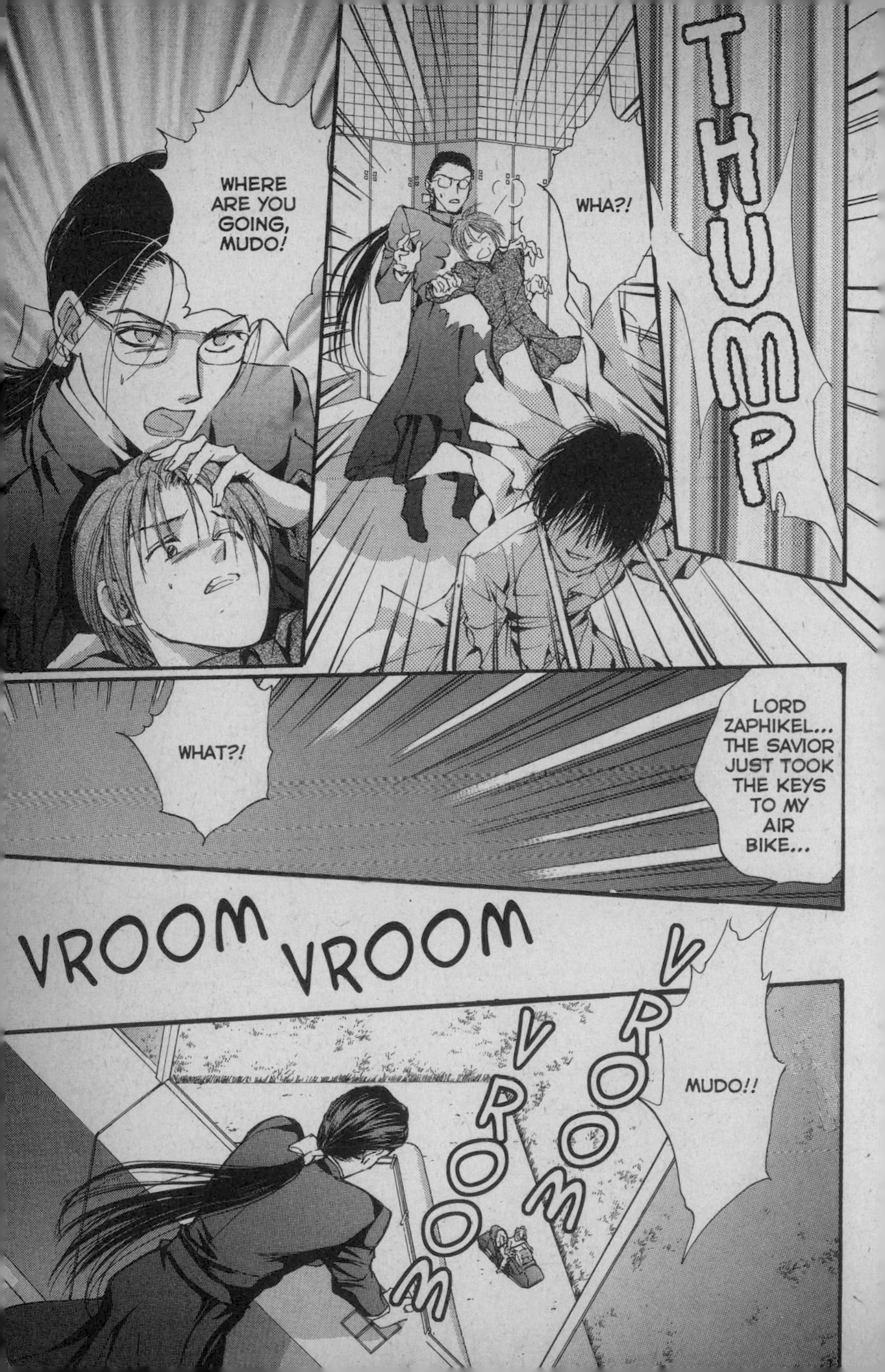
THUMP
WHA?!
WHERE ARE YOU GOING, MUDO!
LORD ZAPHIKEL... THE SAVIOR JUST TOOK THE KEYS TO MY AIR BIKE...
WHAT?!
VROOM VROOM
VROOM
MUDO!!
VROOM

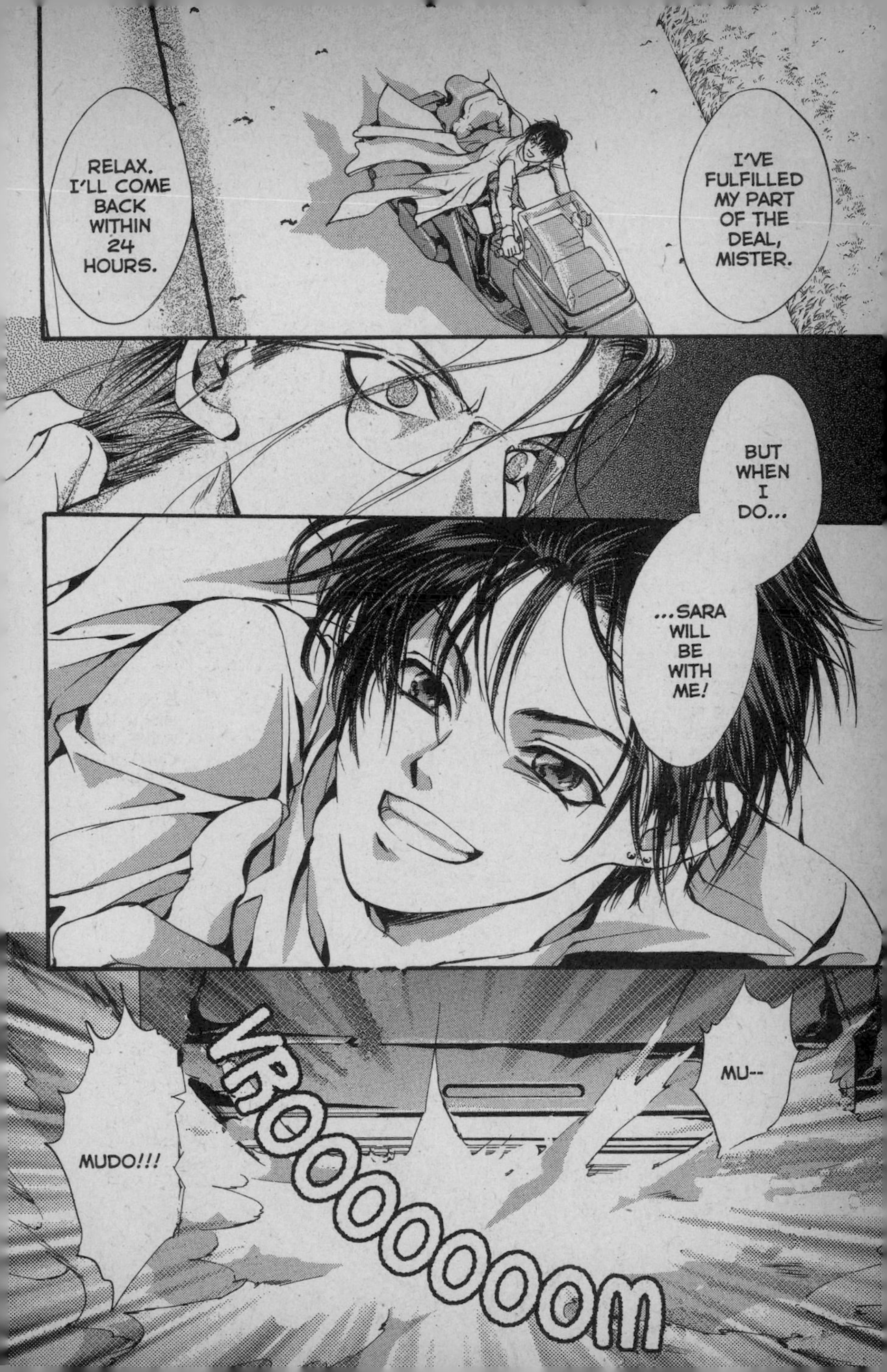
I'VE FULFILLED MY PART OF THE DEAL, MISTER.
RELAX. I'LL COME BACK WITHIN 24 HOURS.
BUT WHEN I DO...
...SARA WILL BE WITH ME!
MU--
VROOOOOOOOM
MUDO!!!

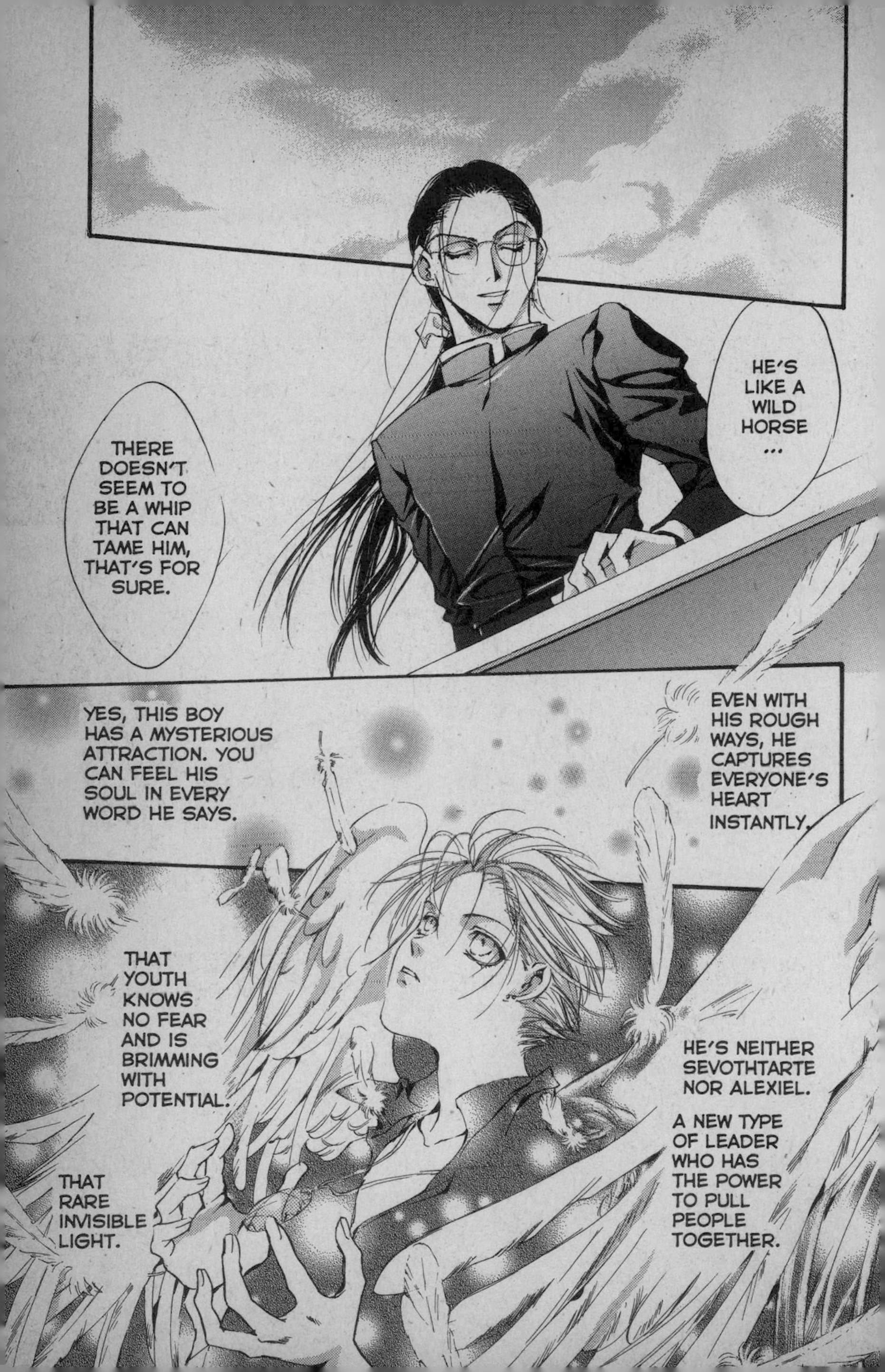
HE'S LIKE A WILD HORSE ...
THERE DOESN'T SEEM TO BE A WHIP THAT CAN TAME HIM, THAT'S FOR SURE.
EVEN WITH HIS ROUGH WAYS, HE CAPTURES EVERYONE'S HEART INSTANTLY.
YES, THIS BOY HAS A MYSTERIOUS ATTRACTION. YOU CAN FEEL HIS SOUL IN EVERY WORD HE SAYS.
HE'S NEITHER SEVOTHTARTE NOR ALEXIEL.
A NEW TYPE OF LEADER WHO HAS THE POWER TO PULL PEOPLE TOGETHER.
THAT YOUTH KNOWS NO FEAR AND IS BRIMMING WITH POTENTIAL.
THAT RARE INVISIBLE LIGHT.

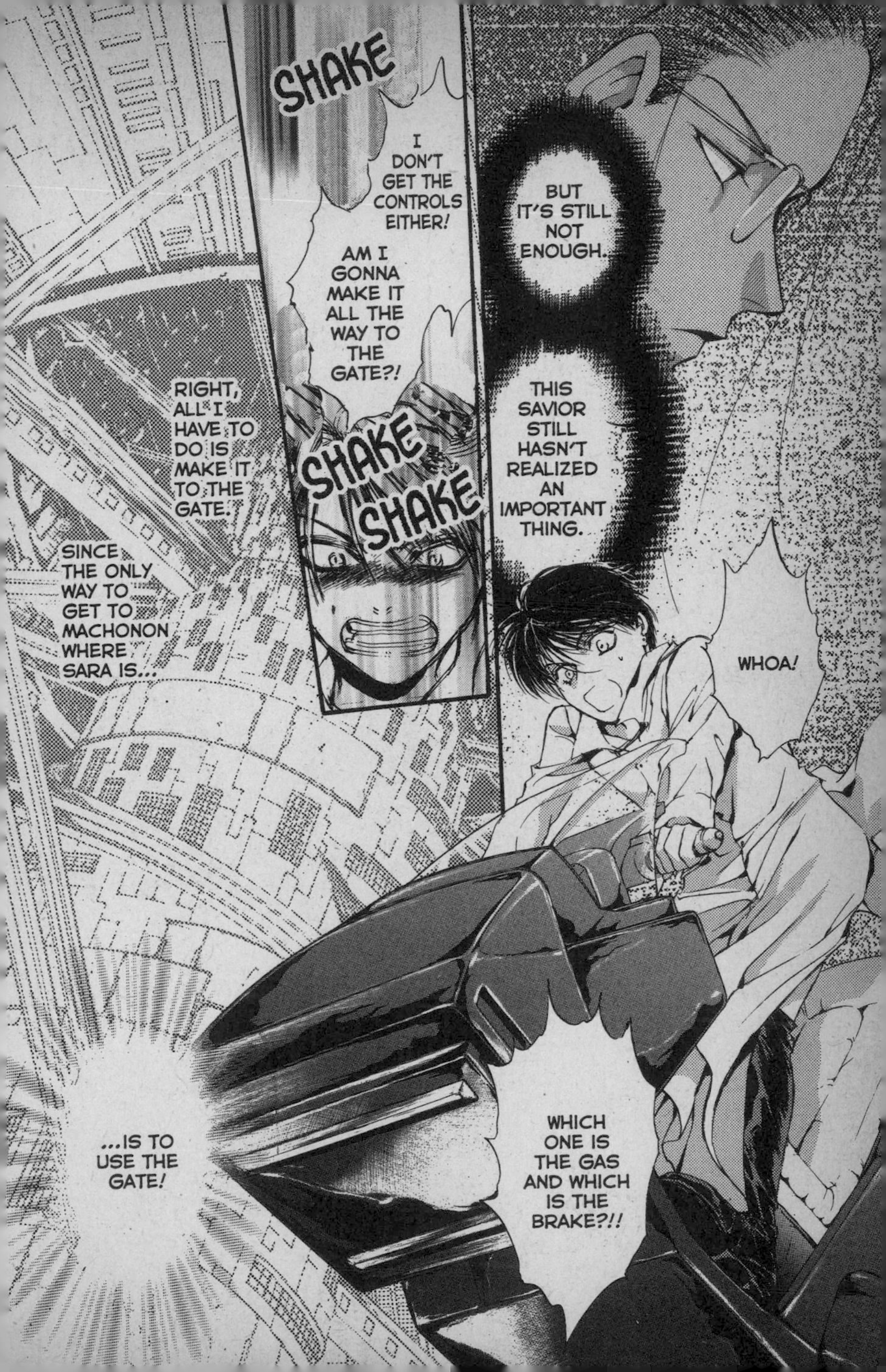
BUT IT'S STILL NOT ENOUGH.
THIS SAVIOR STILL HASN'T REALIZED AN IMPORTANT THING.
WHOA!
WHICH ONE IS THE GAS AND WHICH IS THE BRAKE?!!
SHAKE
I DON'T GET THE CONTROLS EITHER!
AM I GONNA MAKE IT ALL THE WAY TO THE GATE?!
SHAKE SHAKE
RIGHT, ALL I HAVE TO DO IS MAKE IT TO THE GATE.
SINCE THE ONLY WAY TO GET TO MACHONON WHERE SARA IS...
...IS TO USE THE GATE!

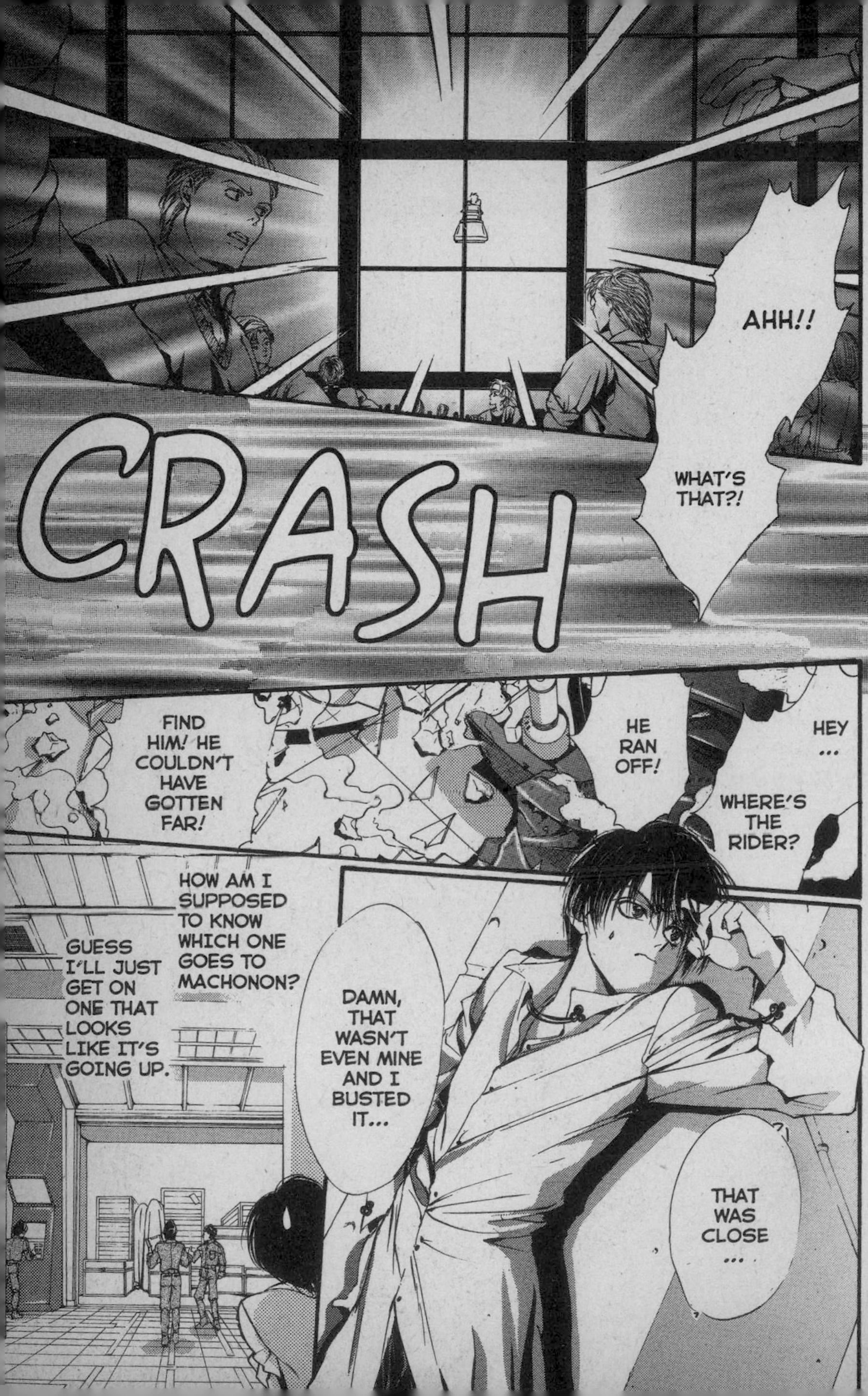
AHH!!
WHAT'S THAT?!
CRASH
HEY ... WHERE'S THE RIDER?
HE RAN OFF!
FIND HIM! HE COULDN'T HAVE GOTTEN FAR!
THAT WAS CLOSE ...
DAMN, THAT WASN'T EVEN MINE AND I BUSTED IT...
HOW AM I SUPPOSED TO KNOW WHICH ONE GOES TO MACHONON?
GUESS I'LL JUST GET ON ONE THAT LOOKS LIKE IT'S GOING UP.

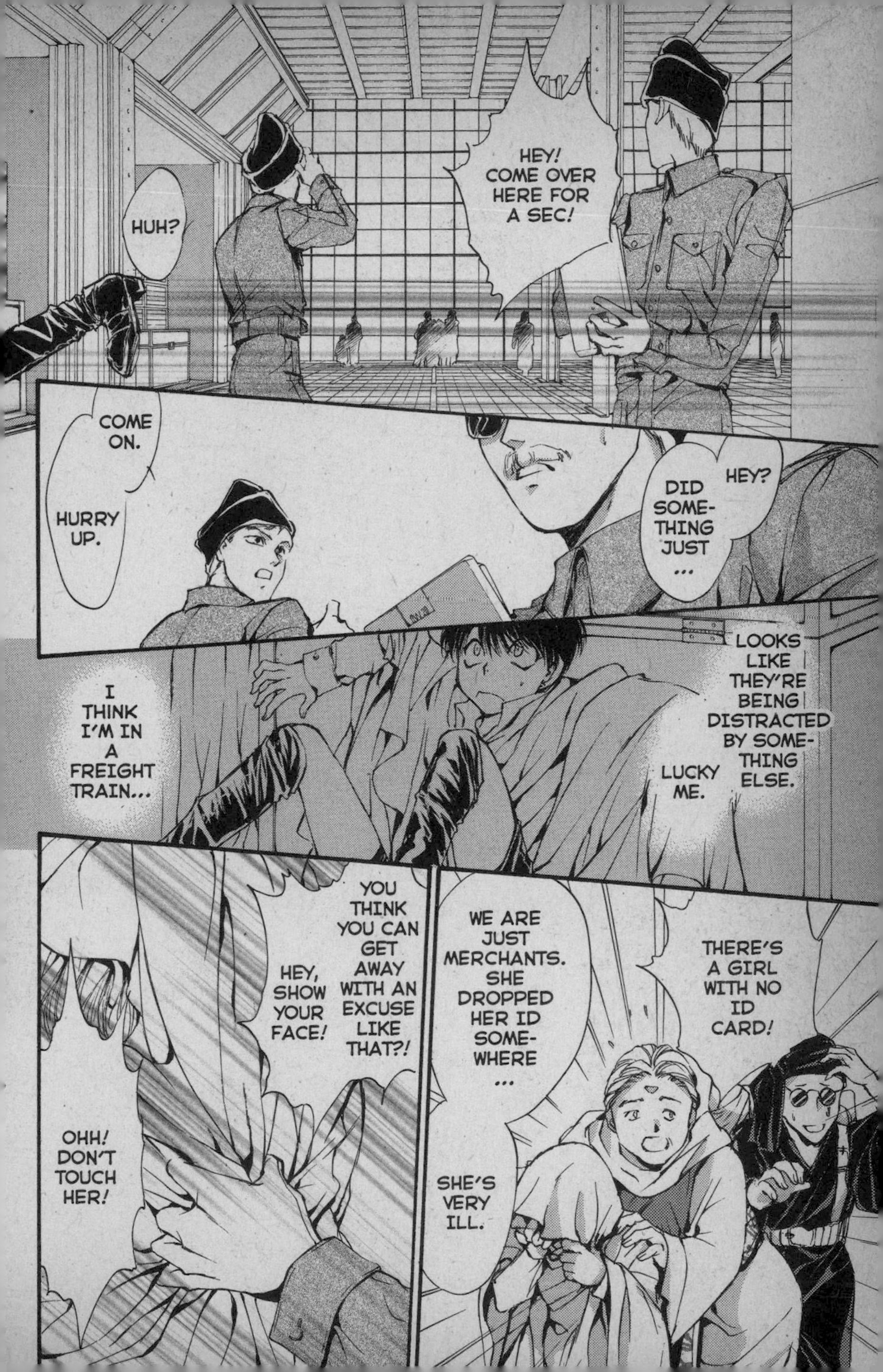
HEY! COME OVER HERE FOR A SEC!
HUH?
HEY? DID SOMETHING JUST ...
COME ON. HURRY UP.
LOOKS LIKE THEY'RE BEING DISTRACTED BY SOMETHING ELSE.
LUCKY ME.
I THINK I'M IN A FREIGHT TRAIN...
THERE'S A GIRL WITH NO ID CARD!
WE ARE JUST MERCHANTS. SHE DROPPED HER ID SOMEWHERE ...
SHE'S VERY ILL.
YOU THINK YOU CAN GET AWAY WITH AN EXCUSE LIKE THAT?!
HEY, SHOW YOUR FACE!
OHH! DON'T TOUCH HER!

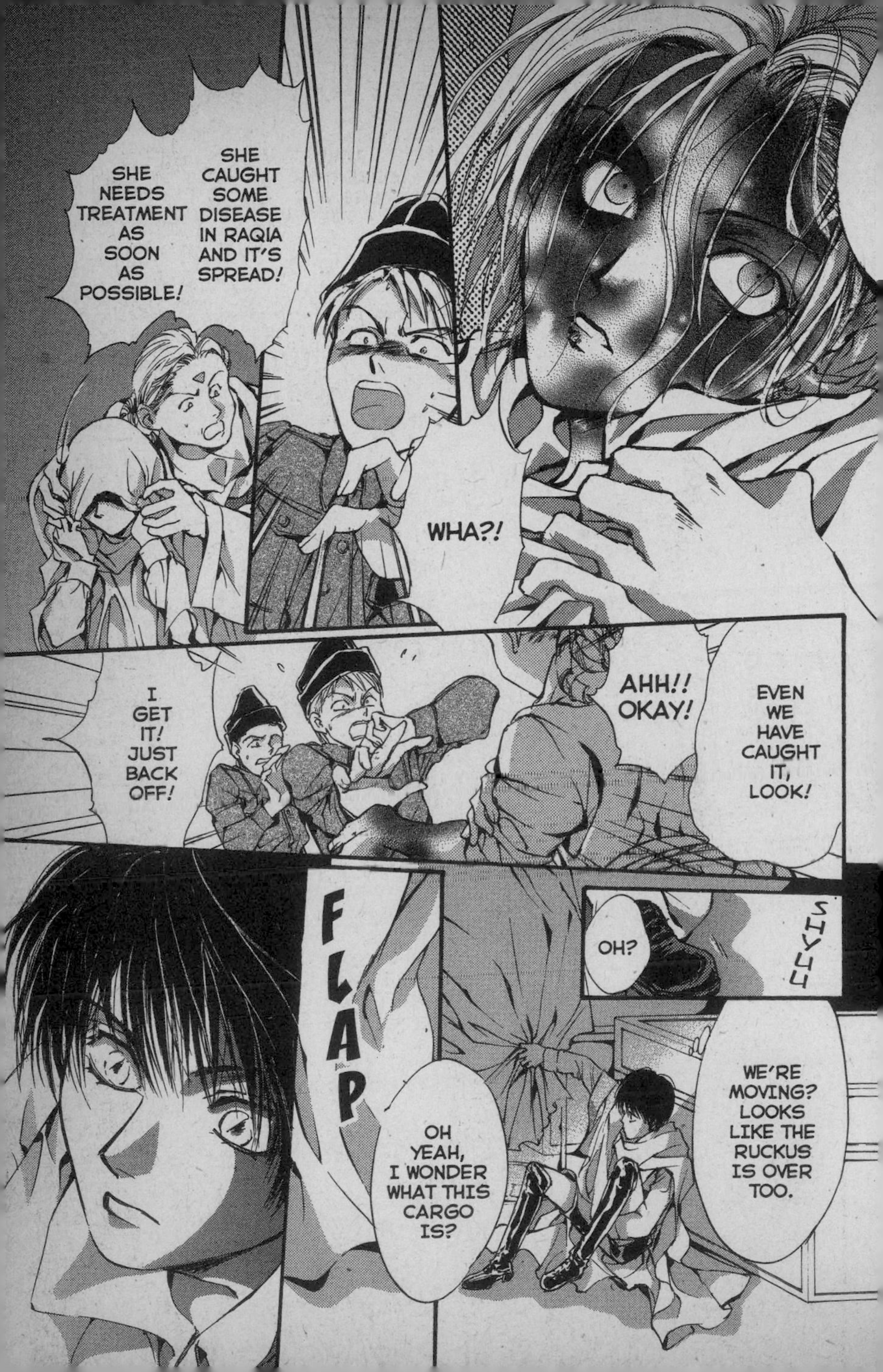
WHA?!
SHE CAUGHT SOME DISEASE IN RAQIA AND IT'S SPREAD!
SHE NEEDS TREATMENT AS SOON AS POSSIBLE!
EVEN WE HAVE CAUGHT IT, LOOK!
AHH!! OKAY!
I GET IT! JUST BACK OFF!
SHYUU
OH?
WE'RE MOVING? LOOKS LIKE THE RUCKUS IS OVER TOO.
OH YEAH, I WONDER WHAT THIS CARGO IS?
FLAP

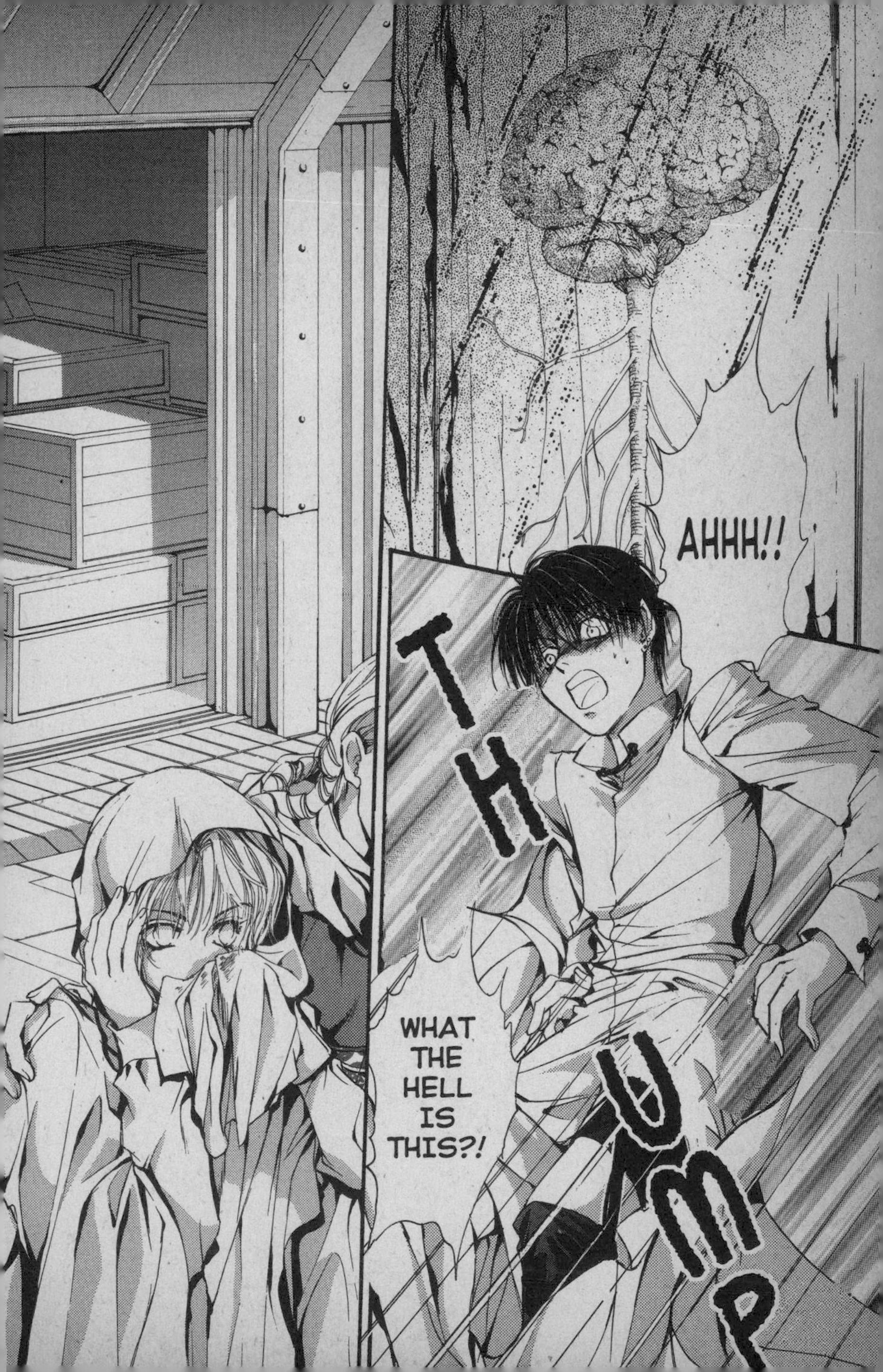
AHHH!!
THUMP
WHAT THE HELL IS THIS?!

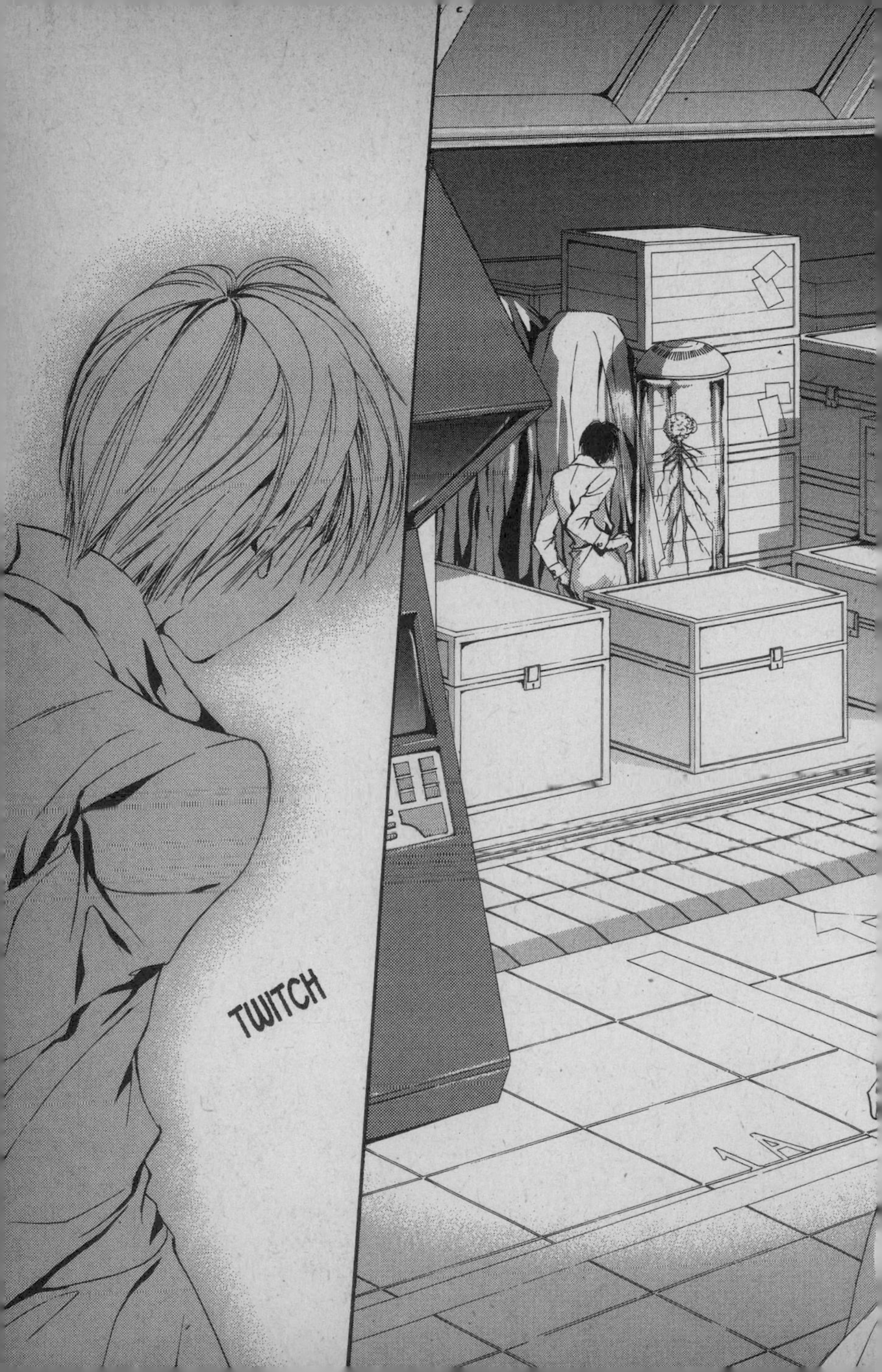
TWITCH

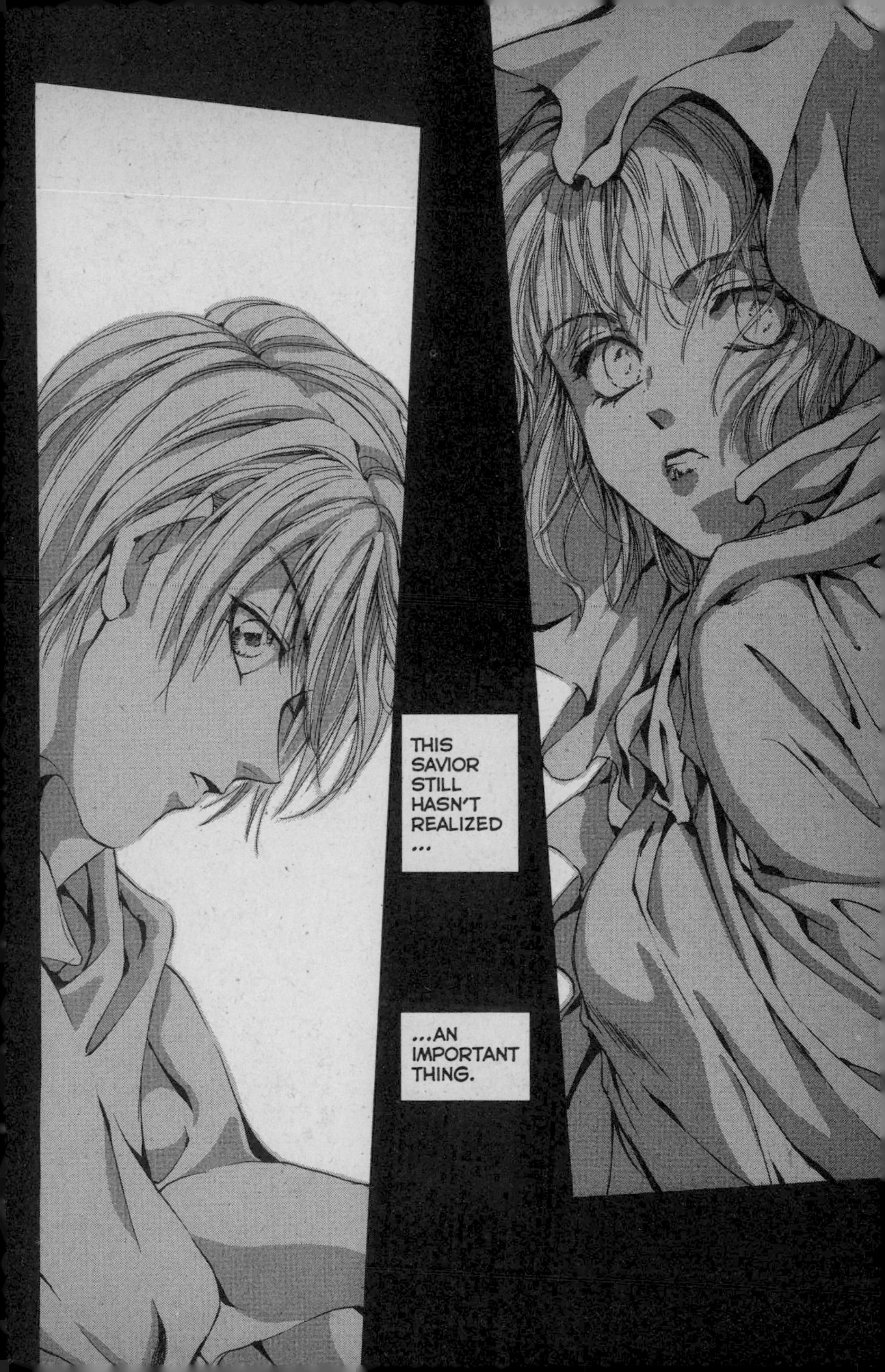
THIS SAVIOR STILL HASN'T REALIZED ...
...AN IMPORTANT THING.

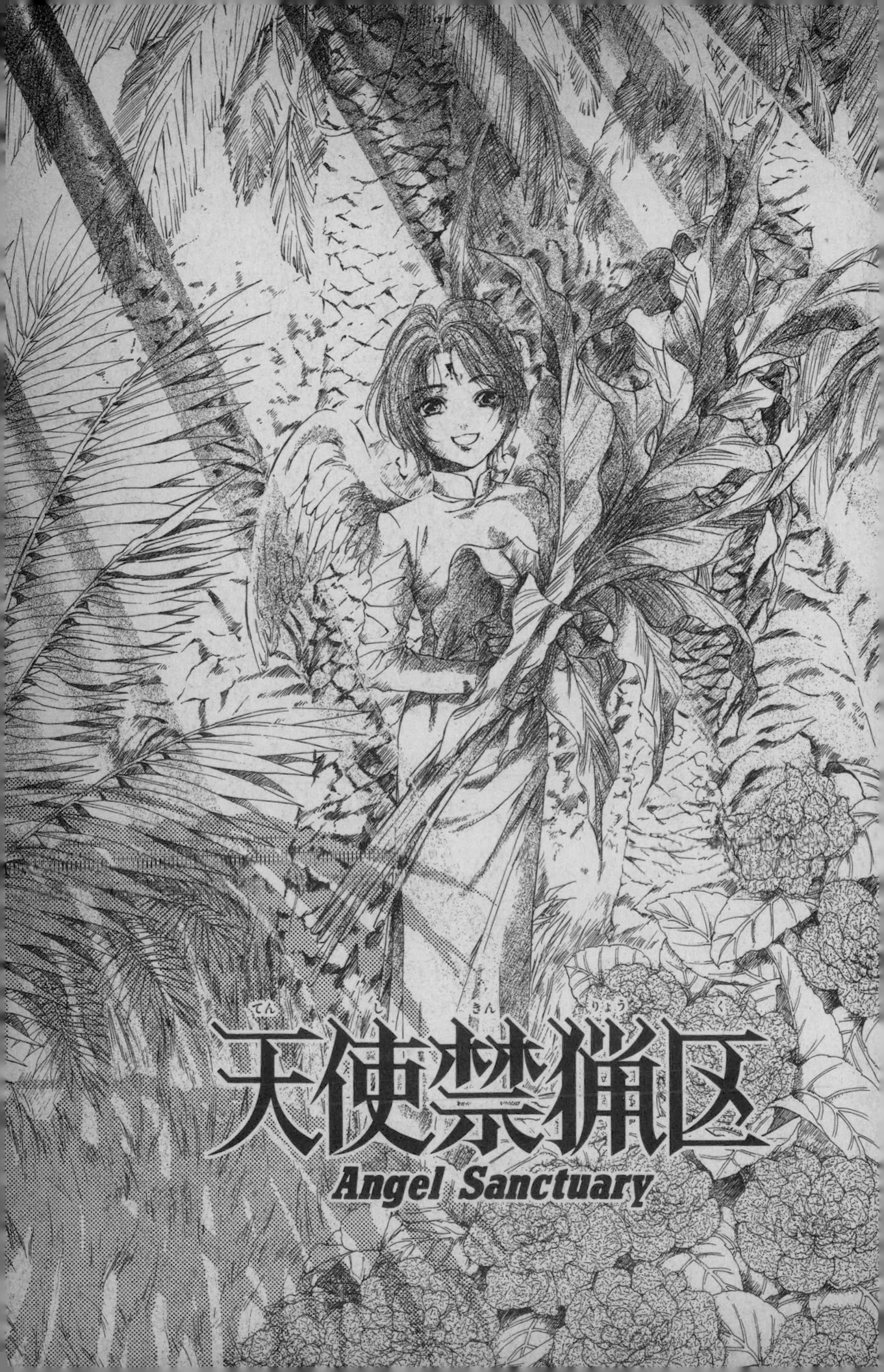

天使禁猟区
Angel Sanctuary

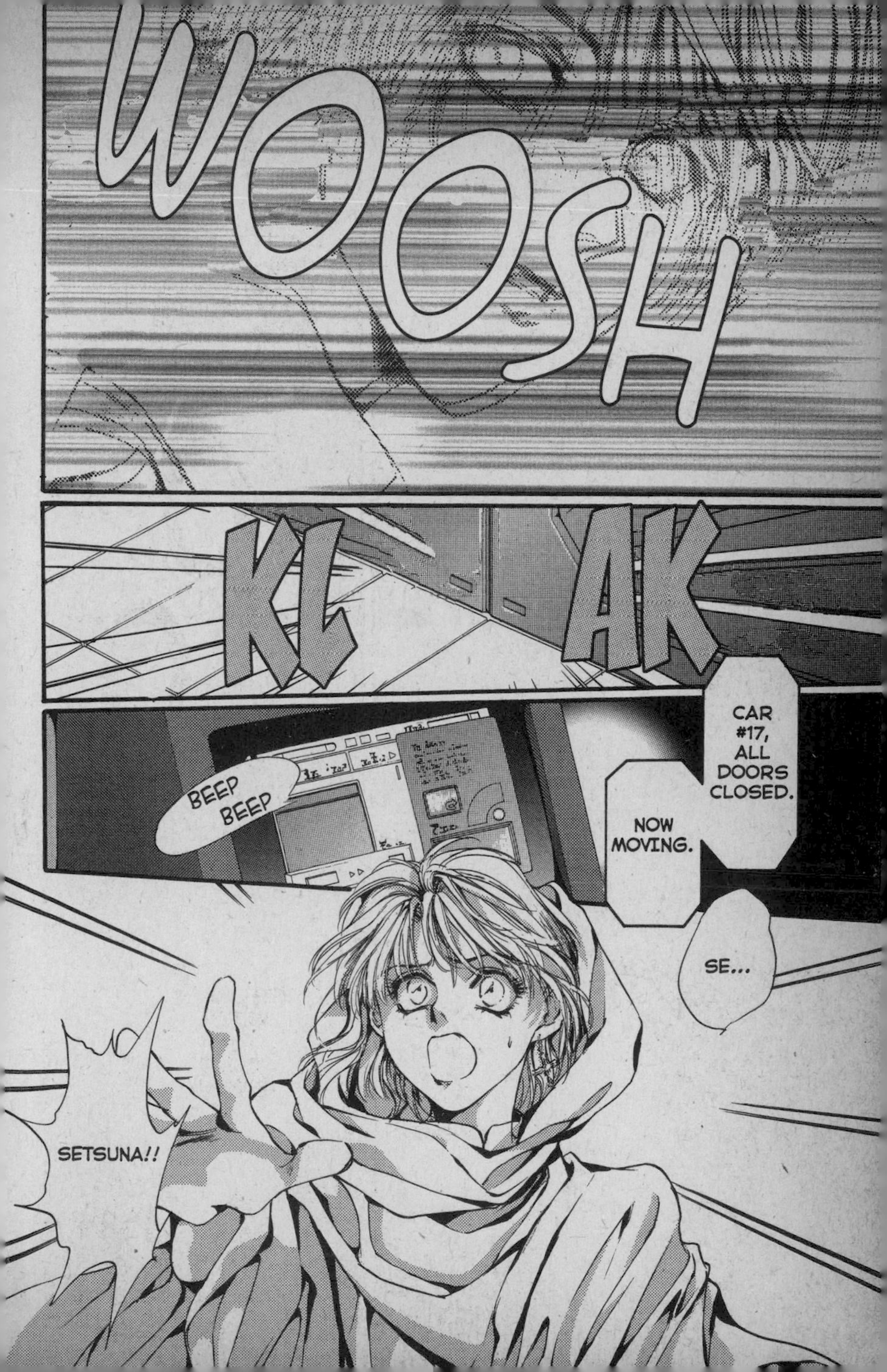
WOOSH
KLAK
CAR #17, ALL DOORS CLOSED.
NOW MOVING.
BEEP BEEP
SE...
SETSUNA!!

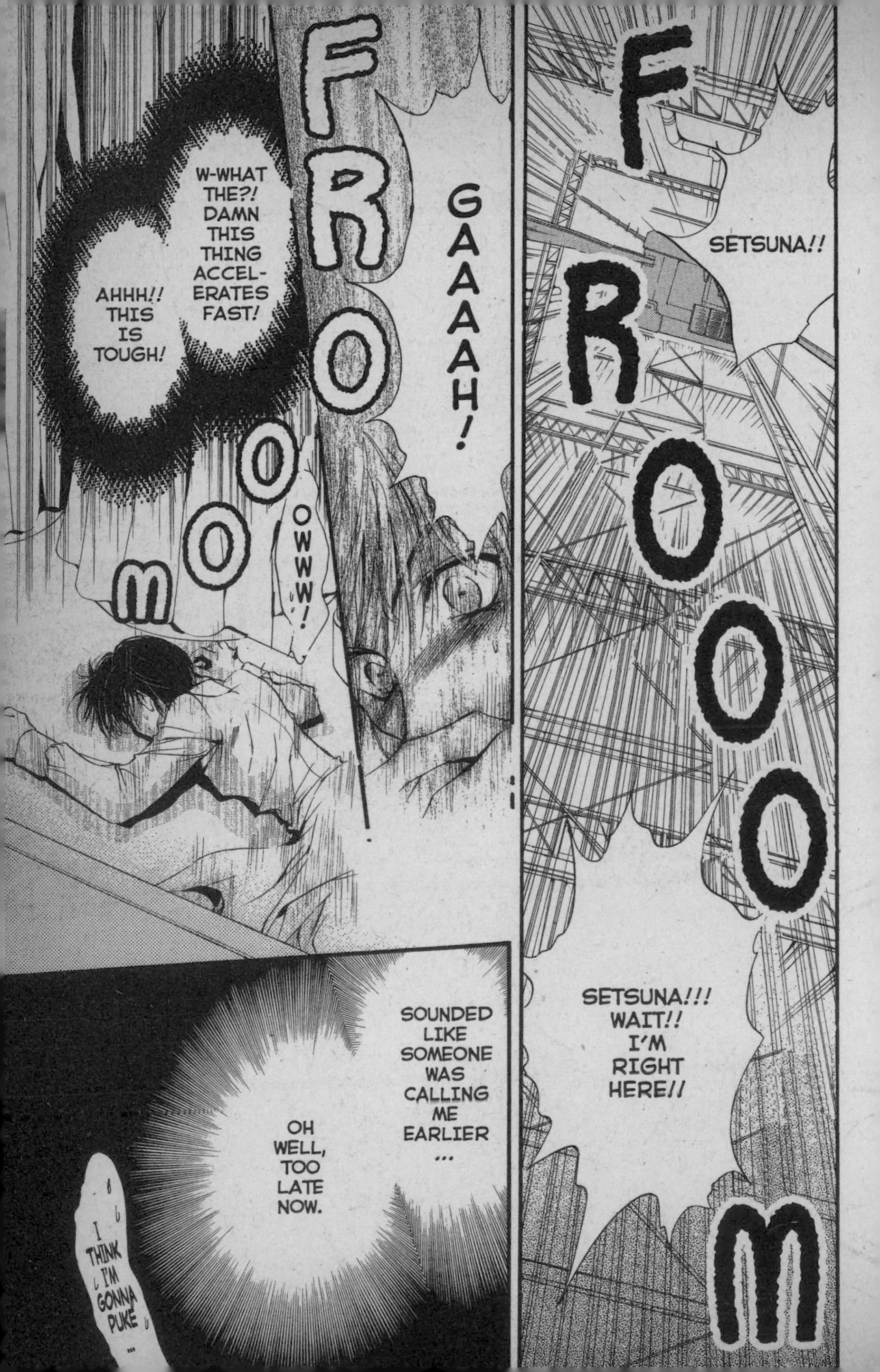
FROOOM
SETSUNA!!
SETSUNA!!! WAIT!! I'M RIGHT HERE!!
FROOOM
GAAAAH!
W-WHAT THE?! DAMN THIS THING ACCEL-ERATES FAST!
AHHH!! THIS IS TOUGH!
OWWW!
SOUNDED LIKE SOMEONE WAS CALLING ME EARLIER ...
OH WELL, TOO LATE NOW.
I THINK I'M GONNA PUKE ...

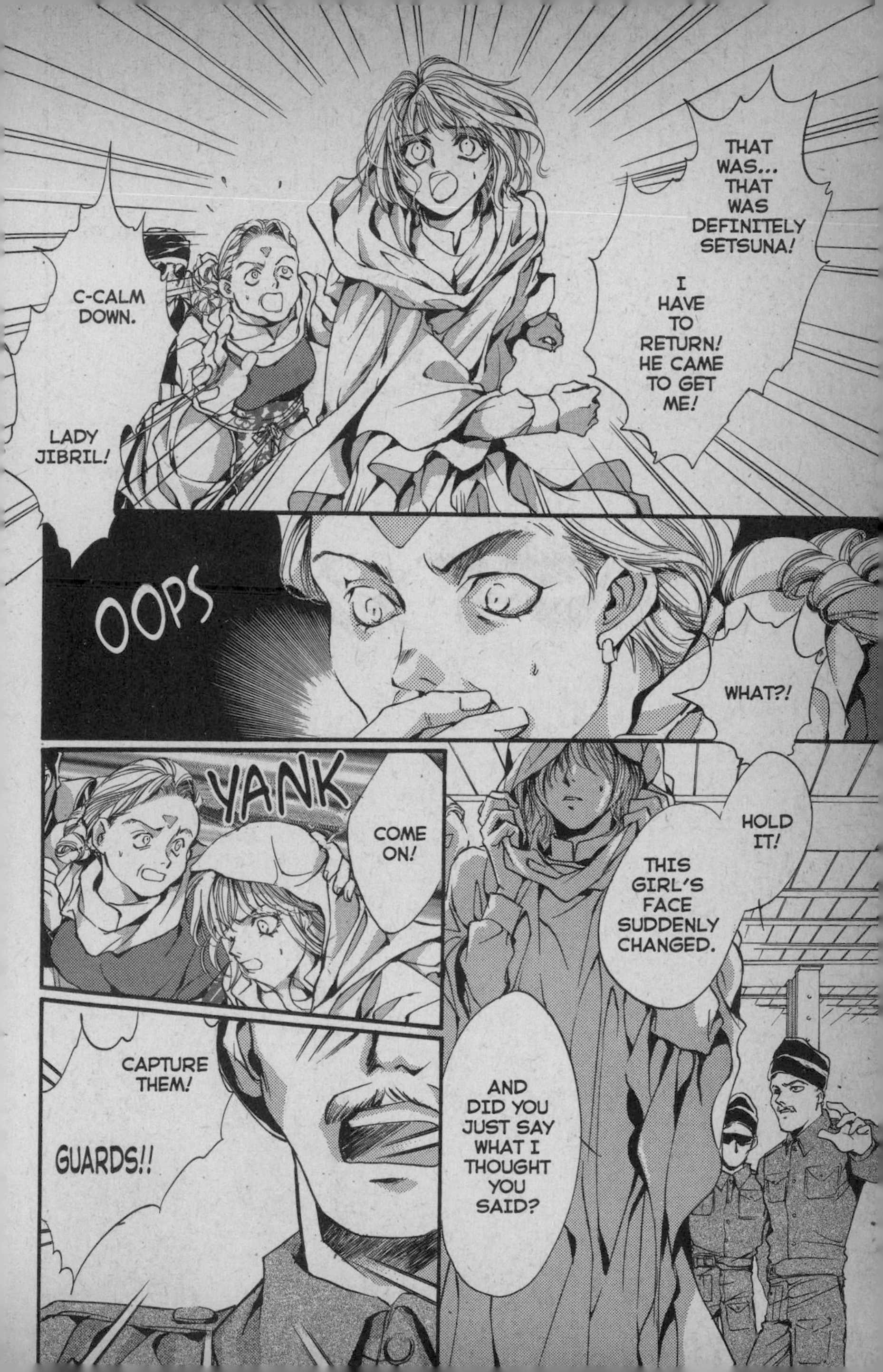
THAT WAS... THAT WAS DEFINITELY SETSUNA!
I HAVE TO RETURN! HE CAME TO GET ME!
C-CALM DOWN.
LADY JIBRIL!
WHAT?!
OOPS
HOLD IT!
THIS GIRL'S FACE SUDDENLY CHANGED.
AND DID YOU JUST SAY WHAT I THOUGHT YOU SAID?
YANK
COME ON!
CAPTURE THEM!
GUARDS!!

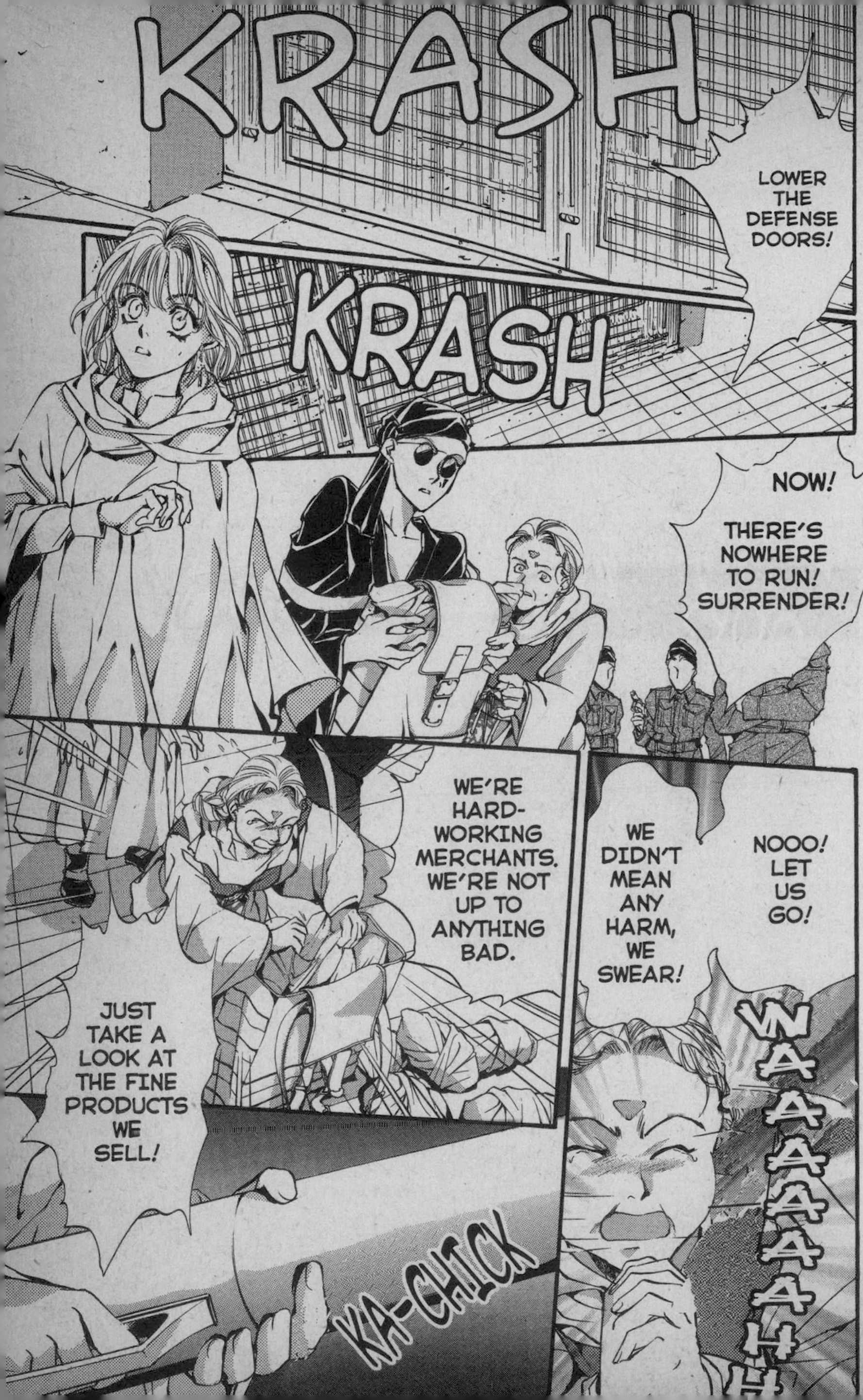
KRASH
LOWER THE DEFENSE DOORS!
KRASH
NOW!
THERE'S NOWHERE TO RUN! SURRENDER!
NOOO! LET US GO!
WE DIDN'T MEAN ANY HARM, WE SWEAR!
WAAAAAAHH
WE'RE HARD-WORKING MERCHANTS. WE'RE NOT UP TO ANYTHING BAD.
JUST TAKE A LOOK AT THE FINE PRODUCTS WE SELL!
KA-CHICK

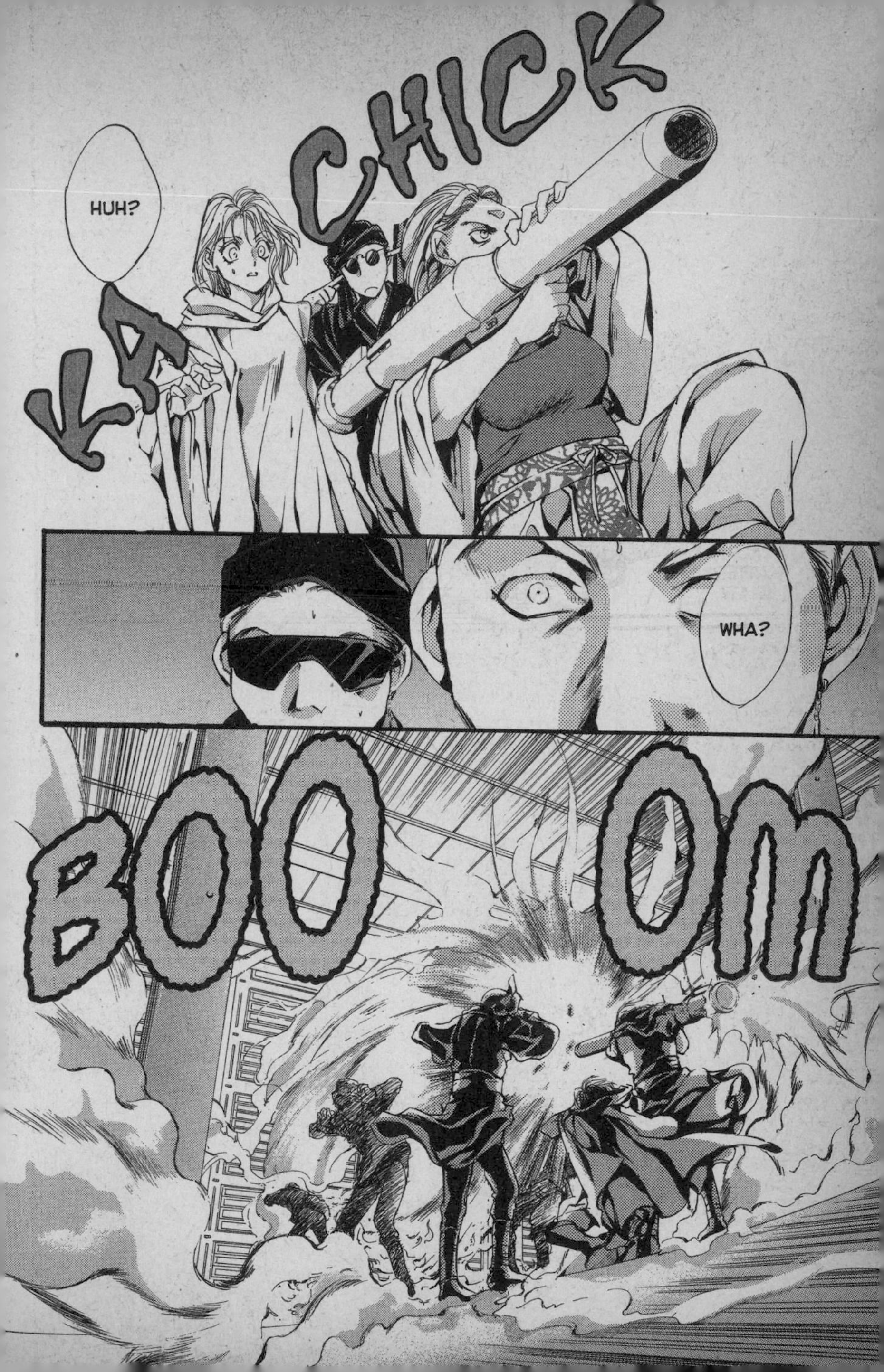
KA CHICK
HUH?
WHA?
BOOOM

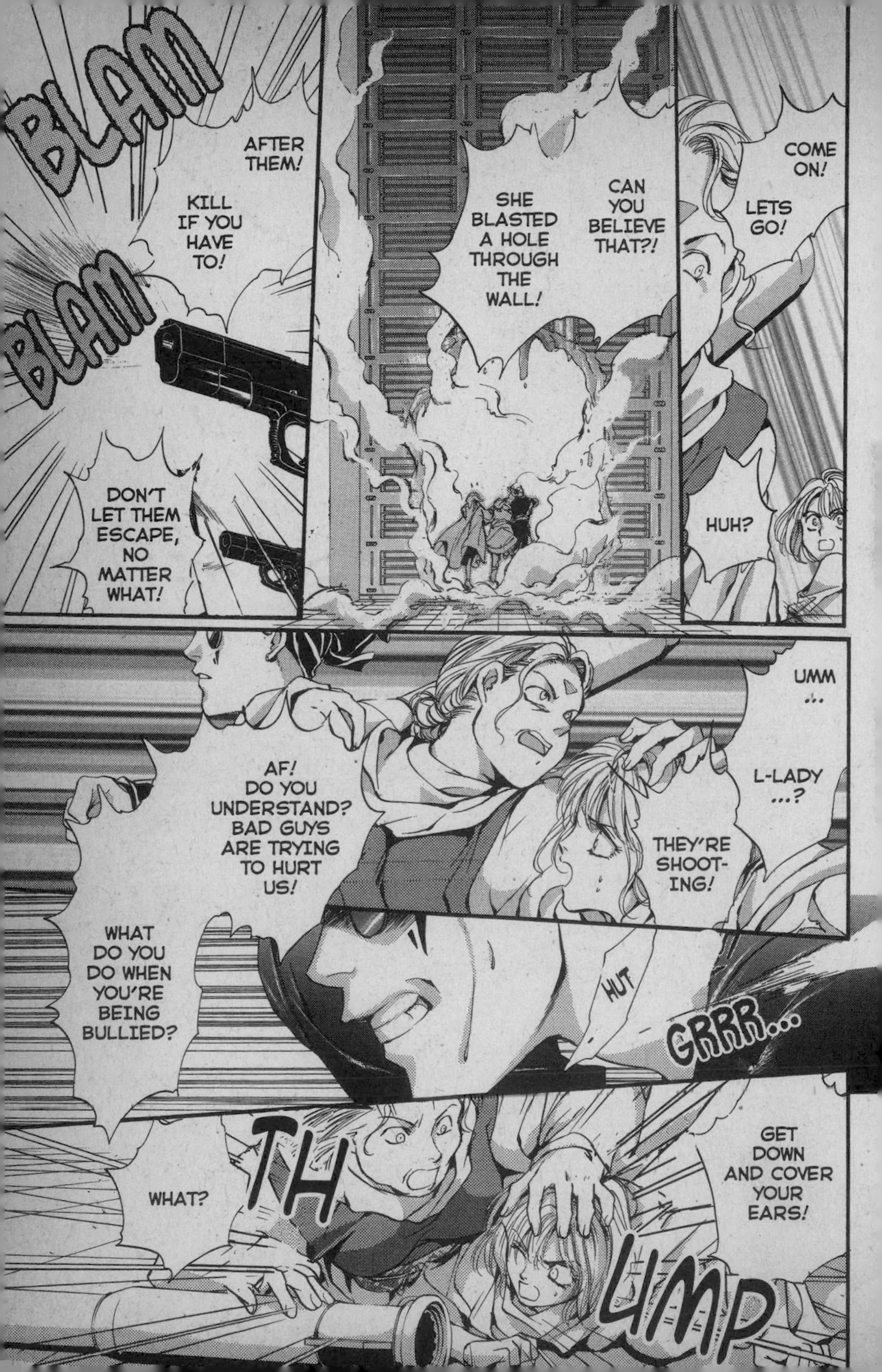
COME ON!
LETS GO!
HUH?
CAN YOU BELIEVE THAT?!
SHE BLASTED A HOLE THROUGH THE WALL!
AFTER THEM!
KILL IF YOU HAVE TO!
BLAM
BLAM
DON'T LET THEM ESCAPE, NO MATTER WHAT!
UMM ...
L-LADY ...?
THEY'RE SHOOTING!
AF! DO YOU UNDERSTAND? BAD GUYS ARE TRYING TO HURT US!
HUT
GRRR...
WHAT DO YOU DO WHEN YOU'RE BEING BULLIED?
GET DOWN AND COVER YOUR EARS!
WHAT?
TH
UMP

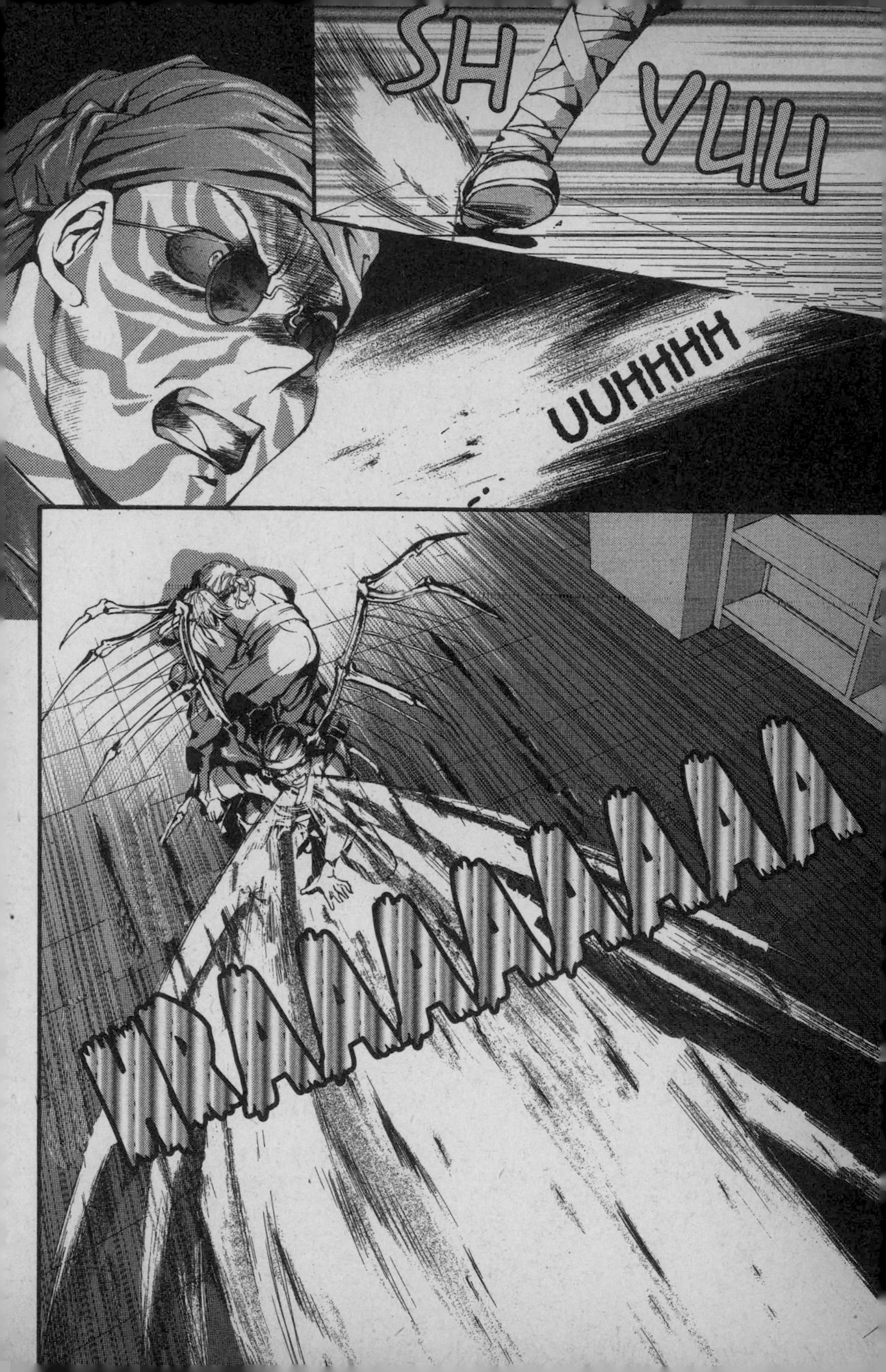
SHYUU
UUHHHH
WAAAAAAAAA

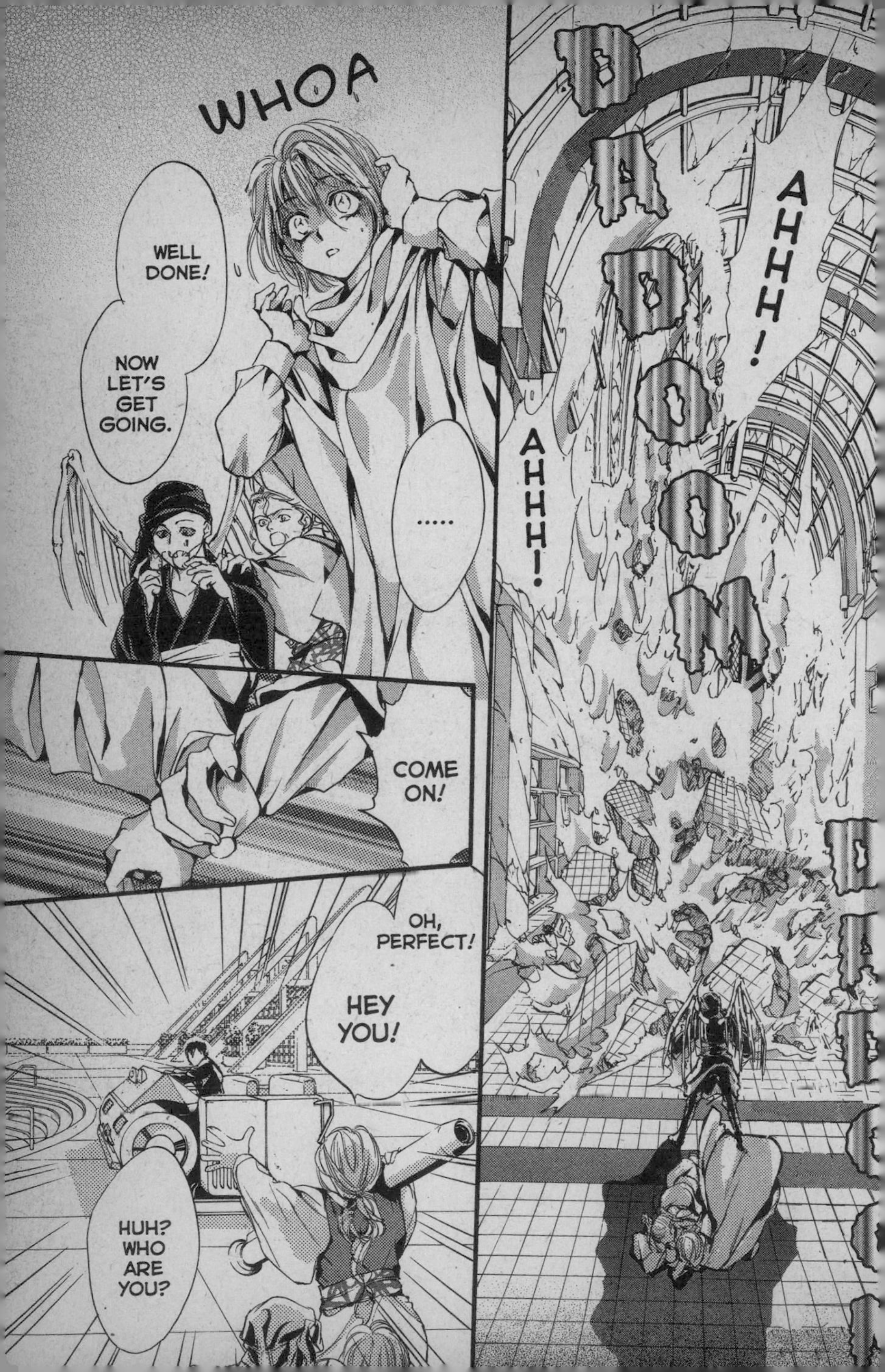
BOOOM
AHHH!
AHHH!
WHOA
WELL DONE!
NOW LET'S GET GOING.
.....
COME ON!
OH, PERFECT!
HEY YOU!
HUH? WHO ARE YOU?

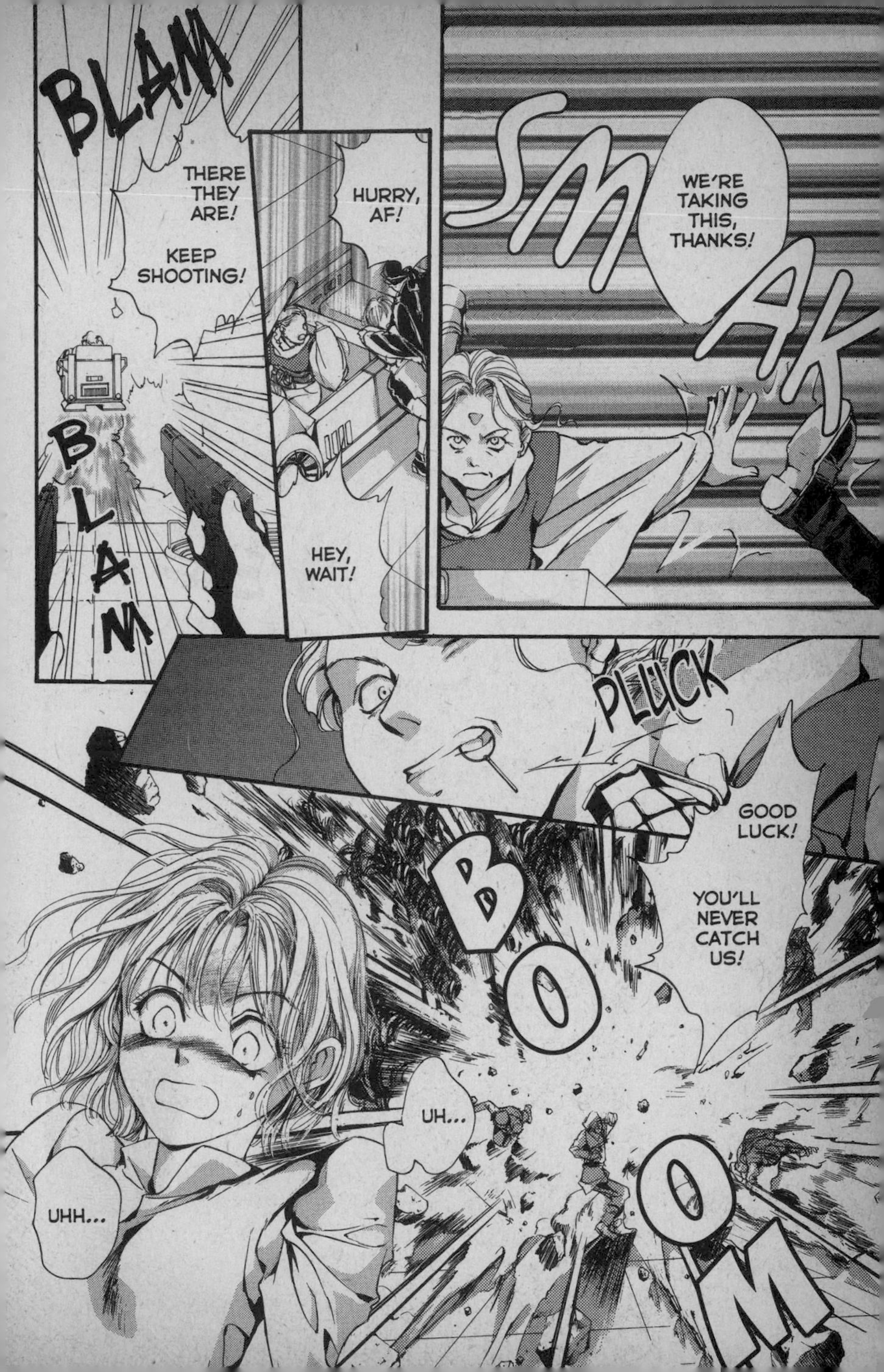
SMAK
WE'RE TAKING THIS, THANKS!
HURRY, AF!
HEY, WAIT!
BLAM
THERE THEY ARE!
KEEP SHOOTING!
BLAM
PLUCK
GOOD LUCK!
YOU'LL NEVER CATCH US!
BOOOM
UH...
UHH...

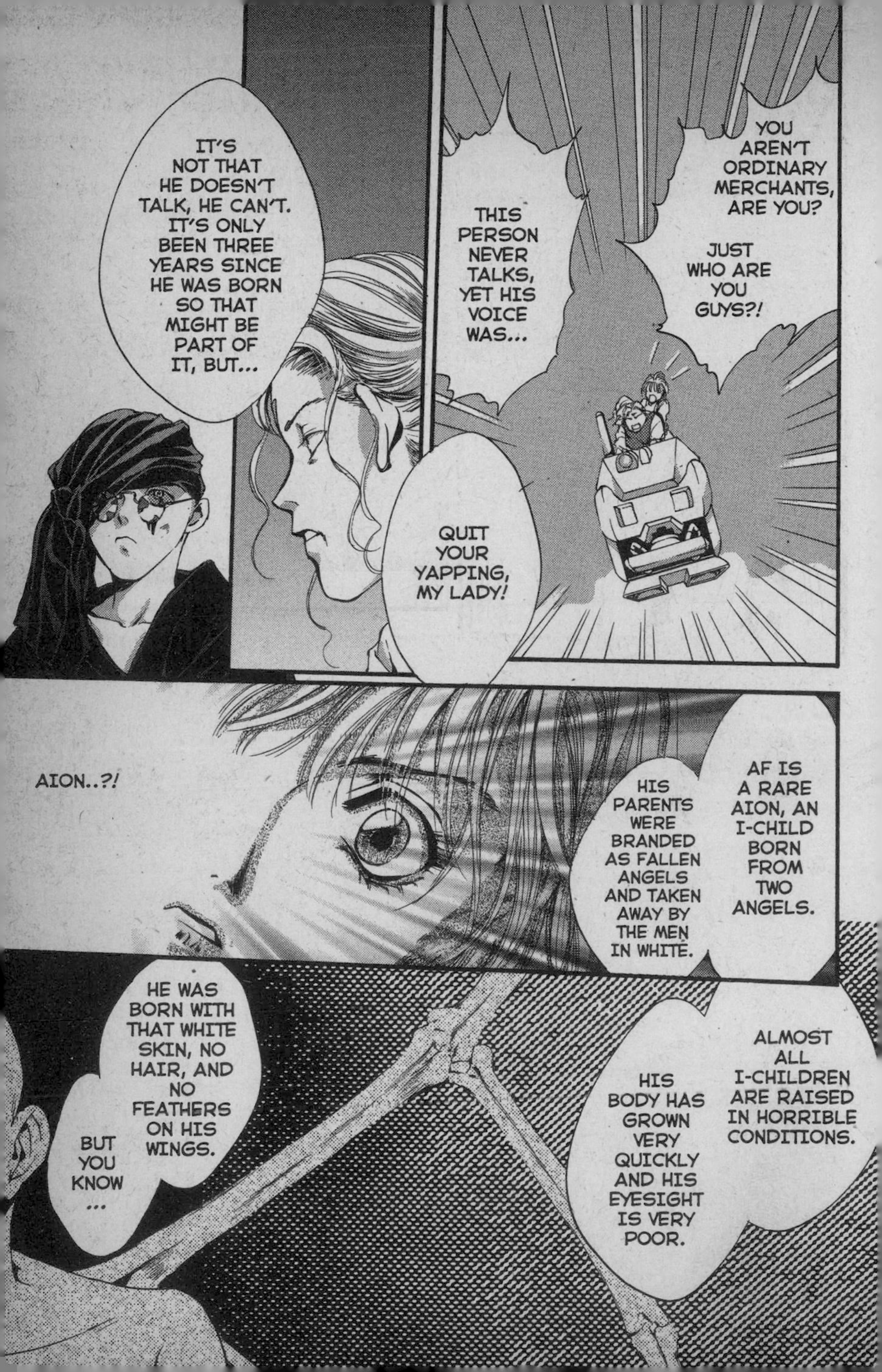
YOU AREN'T ORDINARY MERCHANTS, ARE YOU?
JUST WHO ARE YOU GUYS?!
THIS PERSON NEVER TALKS, YET HIS VOICE WAS...
QUIT YOUR YAPPING, MY LADY!
IT'S NOT THAT HE DOESN'T TALK, HE CAN'T. IT'S ONLY BEEN THREE YEARS SINCE HE WAS BORN SO THAT MIGHT BE PART OF IT, BUT...
AF IS A RARE AION, AN I-CHILD BORN FROM TWO ANGELS.
HIS PARENTS WERE BRANDED AS FALLEN ANGELS AND TAKEN AWAY BY THE MEN IN WHITE.
AION..?!
ALMOST ALL I-CHILDREN ARE RAISED IN HORRIBLE CONDITIONS.
HIS BODY HAS GROWN VERY QUICKLY AND HIS EYESIGHT IS VERY POOR.
HE WAS BORN WITH THAT WHITE SKIN, NO HAIR, AND NO FEATHERS ON HIS WINGS.
BUT YOU KNOW ...

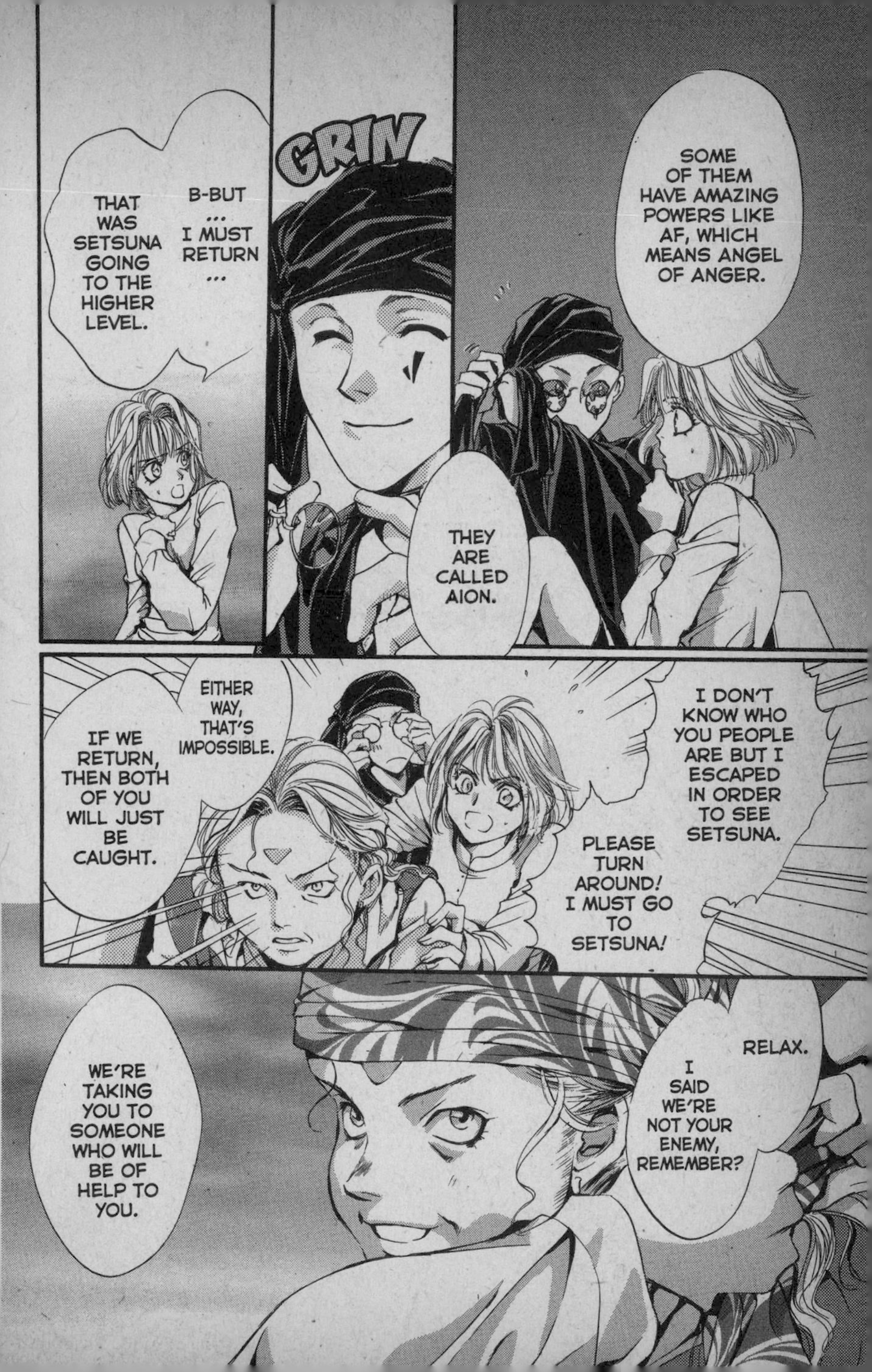
SOME OF THEM HAVE AMAZING POWERS LIKE AF, WHICH MEANS ANGEL OF ANGER.
THEY ARE CALLED AION.
GRIN
B-BUT ... I MUST RETURN ...
THAT WAS SETSUNA GOING TO THE HIGHER LEVEL.
I DON'T KNOW WHO YOU PEOPLE ARE BUT I ESCAPED IN ORDER TO SEE SETSUNA.
PLEASE TURN AROUND! I MUST GO TO SETSUNA!
EITHER WAY, THAT'S IMPOSSIBLE.
IF WE RETURN, THEN BOTH OF YOU WILL JUST BE CAUGHT.
RELAX.
I SAID WE'RE NOT YOUR ENEMY, REMEMBER?
WE'RE TAKING YOU TO SOMEONE WHO WILL BE OF HELP TO YOU.

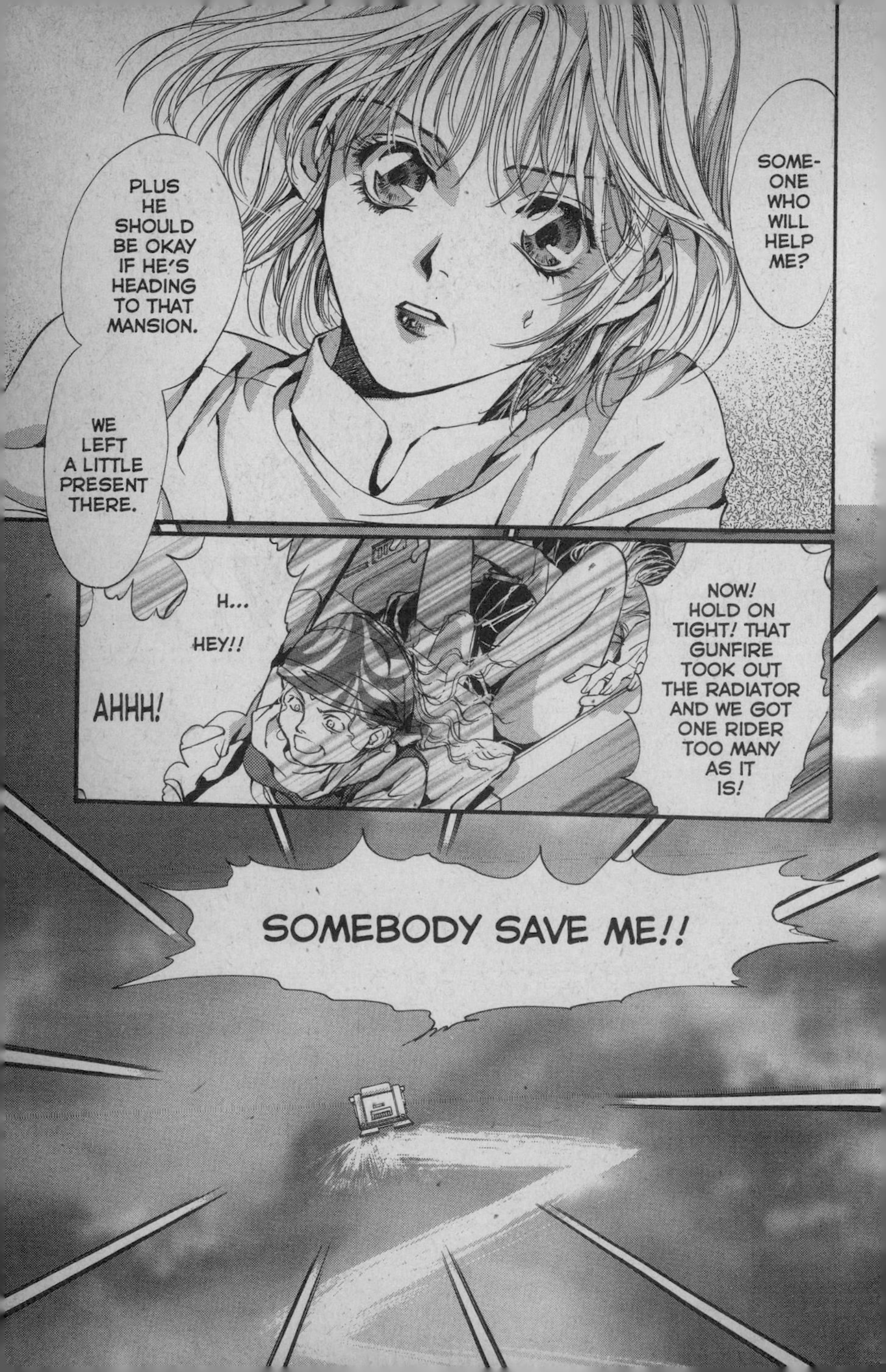
SOME-ONE WHO WILL HELP ME?
PLUS HE SHOULD BE OKAY IF HE'S HEADING TO THAT MANSION.
WE LEFT A LITTLE PRESENT THERE.
NOW! HOLD ON TIGHT! THAT GUNFIRE TOOK OUT THE RADIATOR AND WE GOT ONE RIDER TOO MANY AS IT IS!
H...
HEY!!
AHHH!
SOMEBODY SAVE ME!!

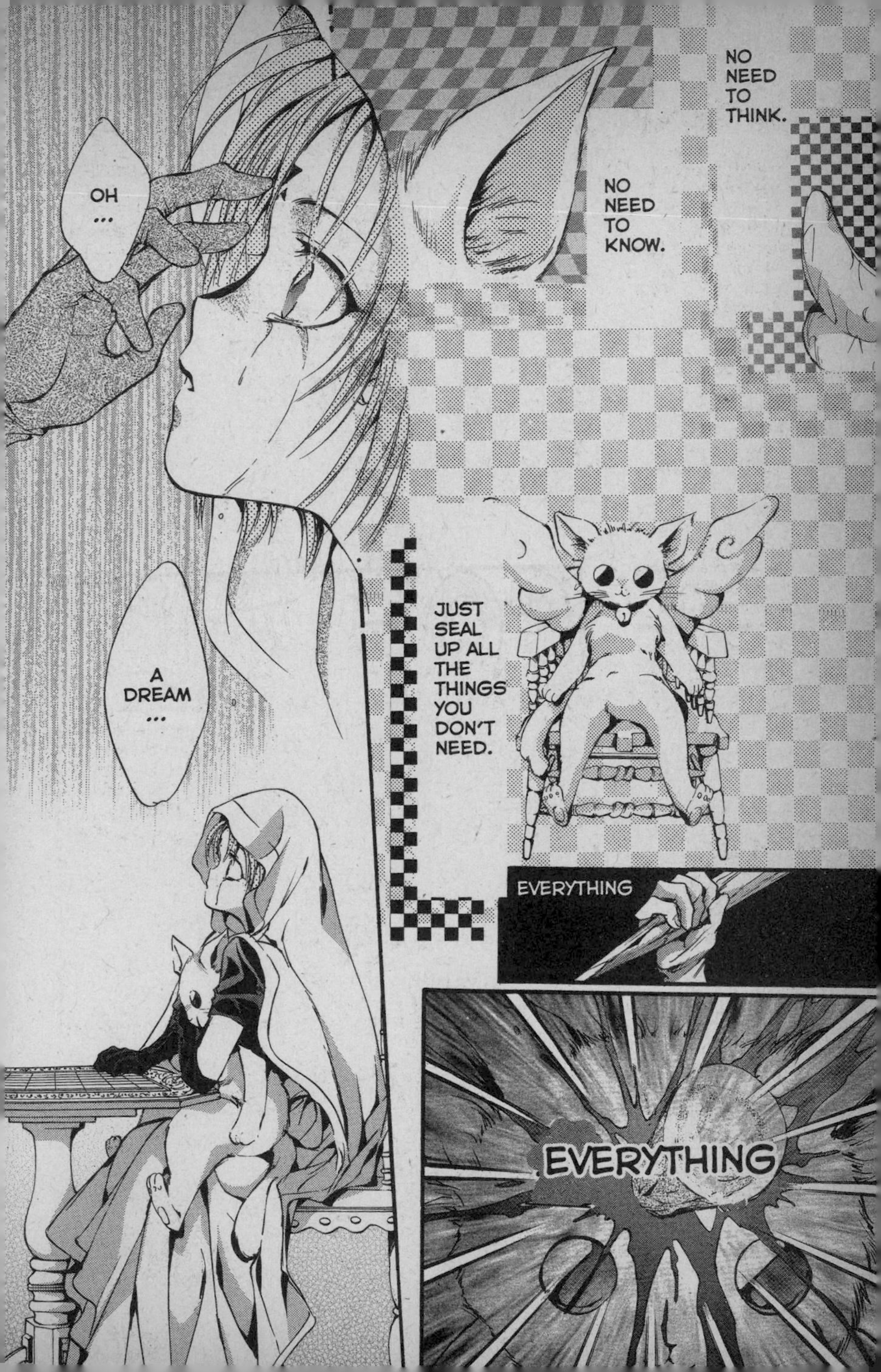
NO NEED TO THINK.
NO NEED TO KNOW.
JUST SEAL UP ALL THE THINGS YOU DON'T NEED.
EVERYTHING
EVERYTHING
OH ...
A DREAM ...

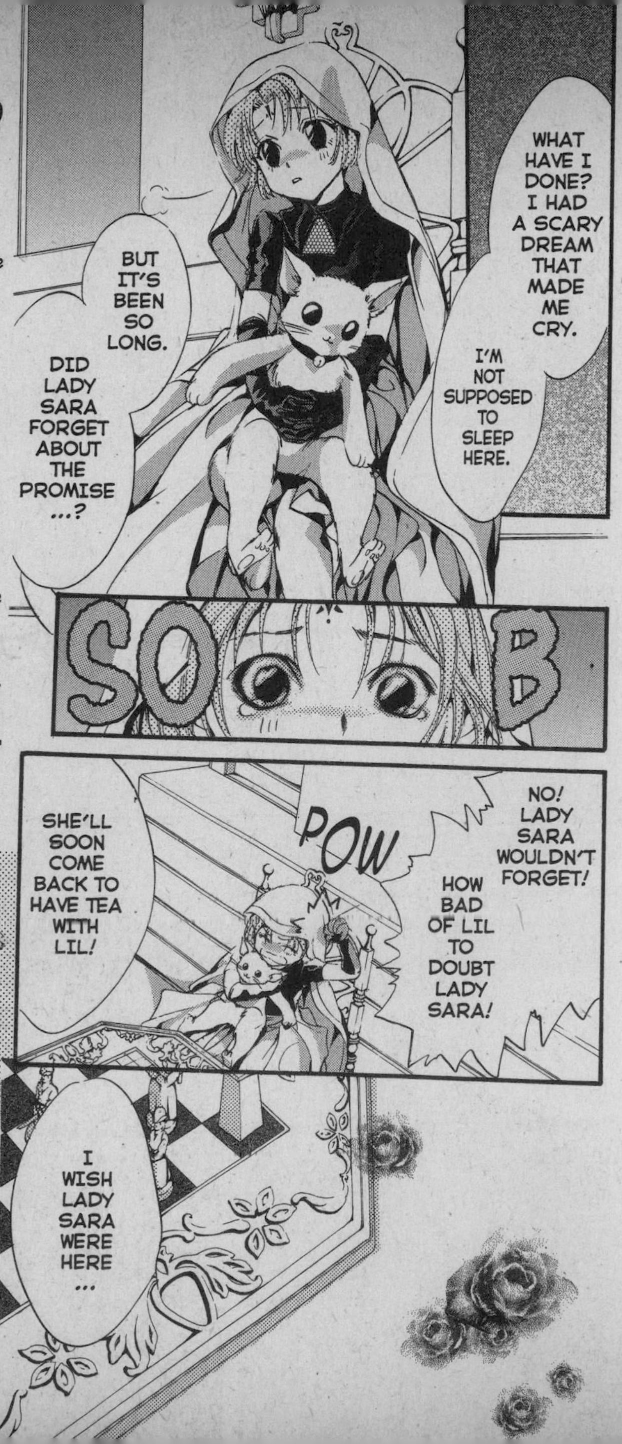
WHAT HAVE I DONE? I HAD A SCARY DREAM THAT MADE ME CRY.
I'M NOT SUPPOSED TO SLEEP HERE.
BUT IT'S BEEN SO LONG.
DID LADY SARA FORGET ABOUT THE PROMISE ...?
SOB
POW
NO! LADY SARA WOULDN'T FORGET!
HOW BAD OF LIL TO DOUBT LADY SARA!
SHE'LL SOON COME BACK TO HAVE TEA WITH LIL!
I WISH LADY SARA WERE HERE ...

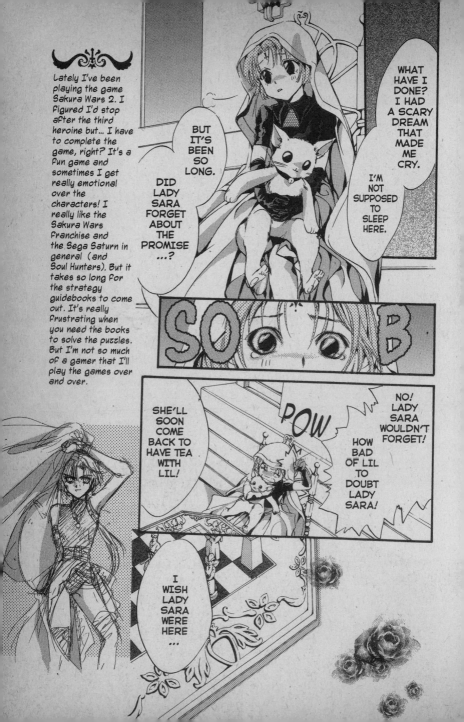

Lately I've been playing the game Sakura Wars 2. I figured I'd stop after the third heroine but... I have to complete the game, right? It's a fun game and sometimes I get really emotional over the characters! I really like the Sakura Wars franchise and the Sega Saturn in general (and Soul Hunters). But it takes so long for the strategy guidebooks to come out. It's really frustrating when you need the books to solve the puzzles. But I'm not so much of a gamer that I'll play the games over and over.

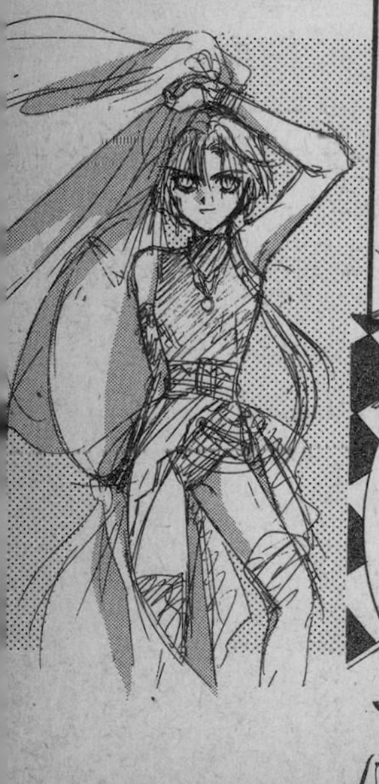

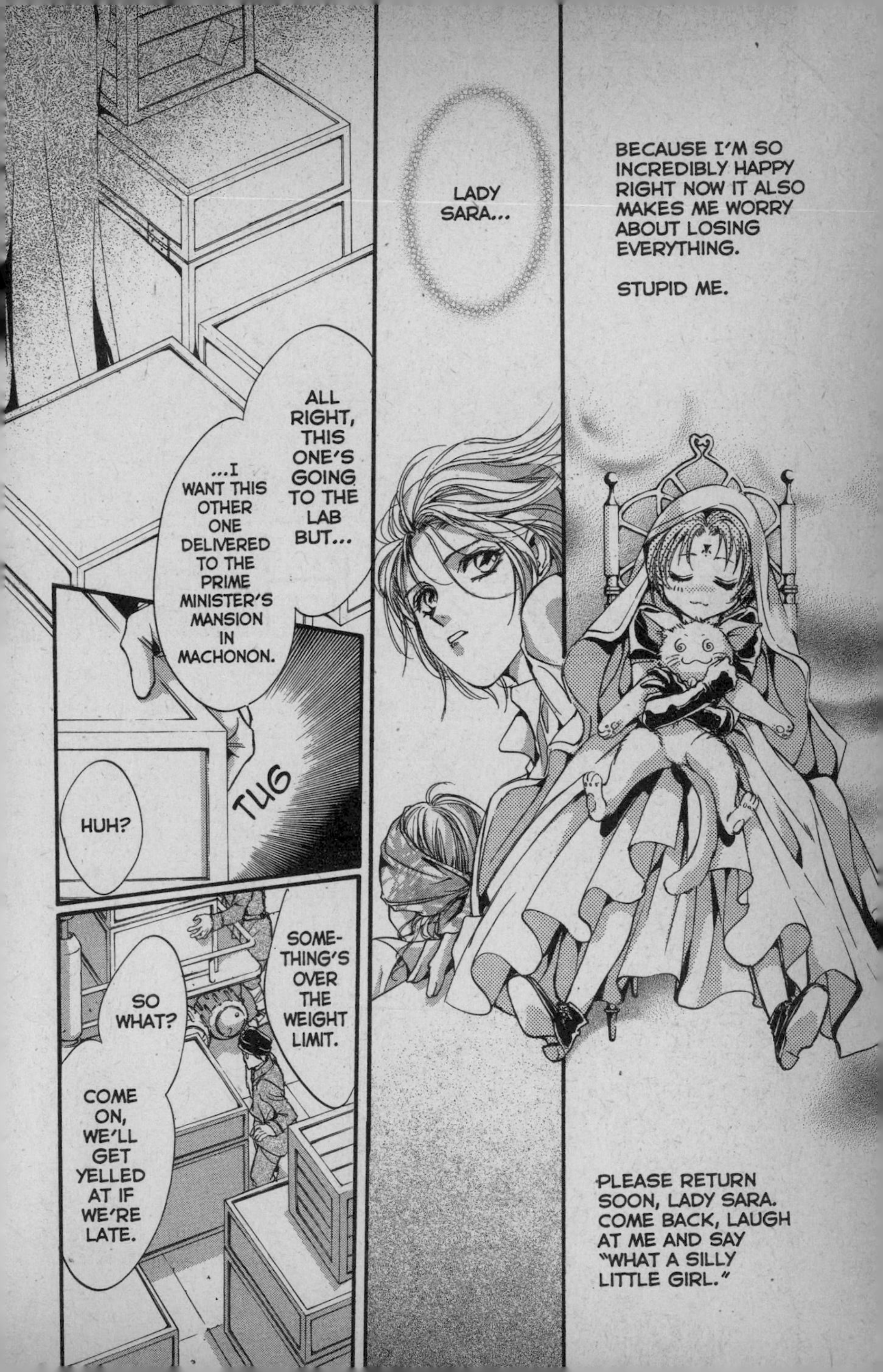
BECAUSE I'M SO INCREDIBLY HAPPY RIGHT NOW IT ALSO MAKES ME WORRY ABOUT LOSING EVERYTHING.
STUPID ME.
PLEASE RETURN SOON, LADY SARA. COME BACK, LAUGH AT ME AND SAY "WHAT A SILLY LITTLE GIRL."
LADY SARA...
ALL RIGHT, THIS ONE'S GOING TO THE LAB BUT...
...I WANT THIS OTHER ONE DELIVERED TO THE PRIME MINISTER'S MANSION IN MACHONON.
TUG
HUH?
SOME-THING'S OVER THE WEIGHT LIMIT.
SO WHAT?
COME ON, WE'LL GET YELLED AT IF WE'RE LATE.

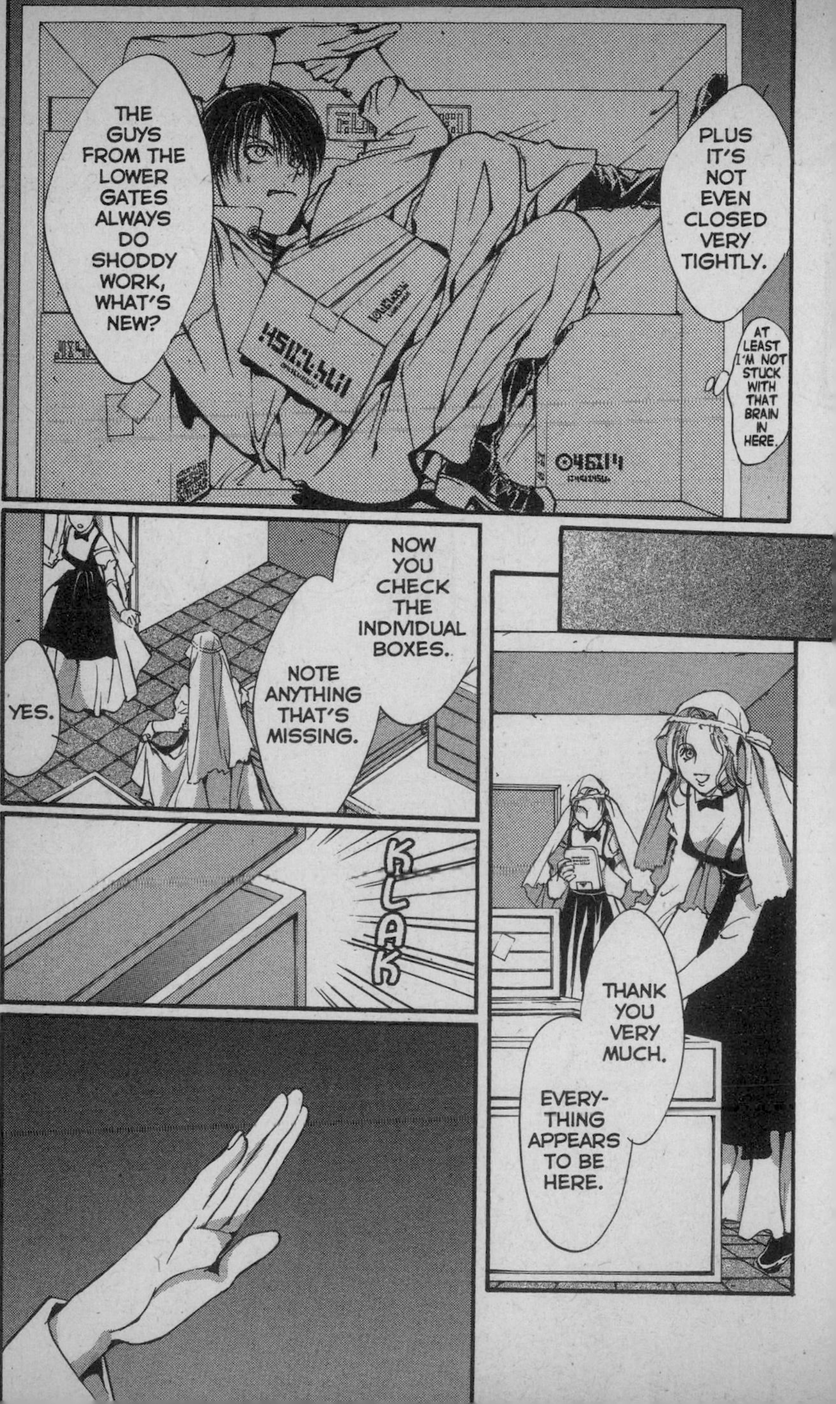
THE GUYS FROM THE LOWER GATES ALWAYS DO SHODDY WORK, WHAT'S NEW?
PLUS IT'S NOT EVEN CLOSED VERY TIGHTLY.
AT LEAST I'M NOT STUCK WITH THAT BRAIN IN HERE.
NOW YOU CHECK THE INDIVIDUAL BOXES.
NOTE ANYTHING THAT'S MISSING.
YES.
KLAK
THANK YOU VERY MUCH.
EVERY-THING APPEARS TO BE HERE.

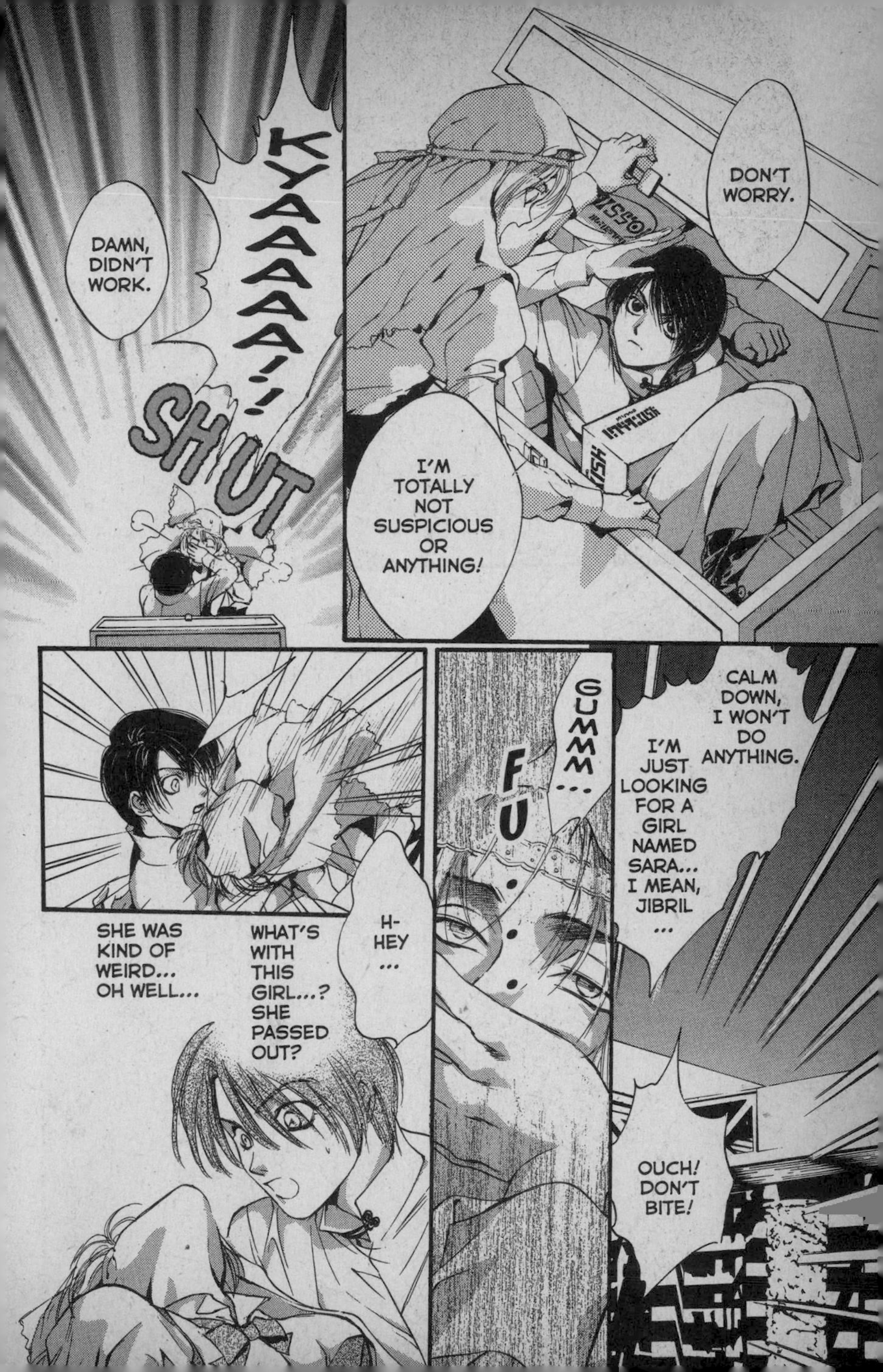
DON'T WORRY.
I'M TOTALLY NOT SUSPICIOUS OR ANYTHING!
KYAAAAAA!!!
DAMN, DIDN'T WORK.
SHUT
CALM DOWN, I WON'T DO ANYTHING.
I'M JUST LOOKING FOR A GIRL NAMED SARA... I MEAN, JIBRIL...
GUMMM...
FU...
OUCH! DON'T BITE!
H-HEY...
WHAT'S WITH THIS GIRL...? SHE PASSED OUT?
SHE WAS KIND OF WEIRD... OH WELL...

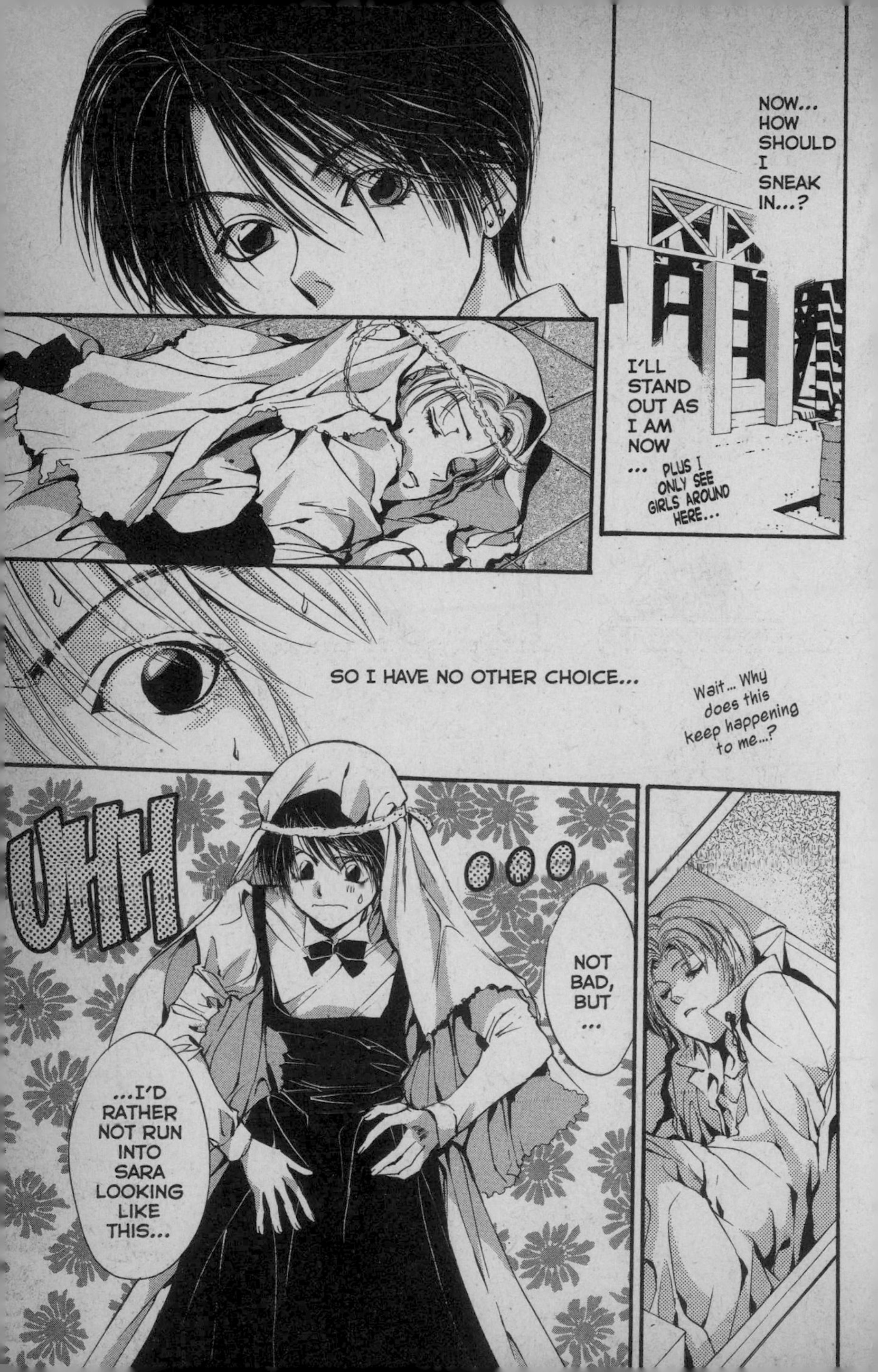
NOW... HOW SHOULD I SNEAK IN...?
I'LL STAND OUT AS I AM NOW ...
PLUS I ONLY SEE GIRLS AROUND HERE...
SO I HAVE NO OTHER CHOICE...
Wait... Why does this keep happening to me...?
UHH
...
NOT BAD, BUT ...
...I'D RATHER NOT RUN INTO SARA LOOKING LIKE THIS...

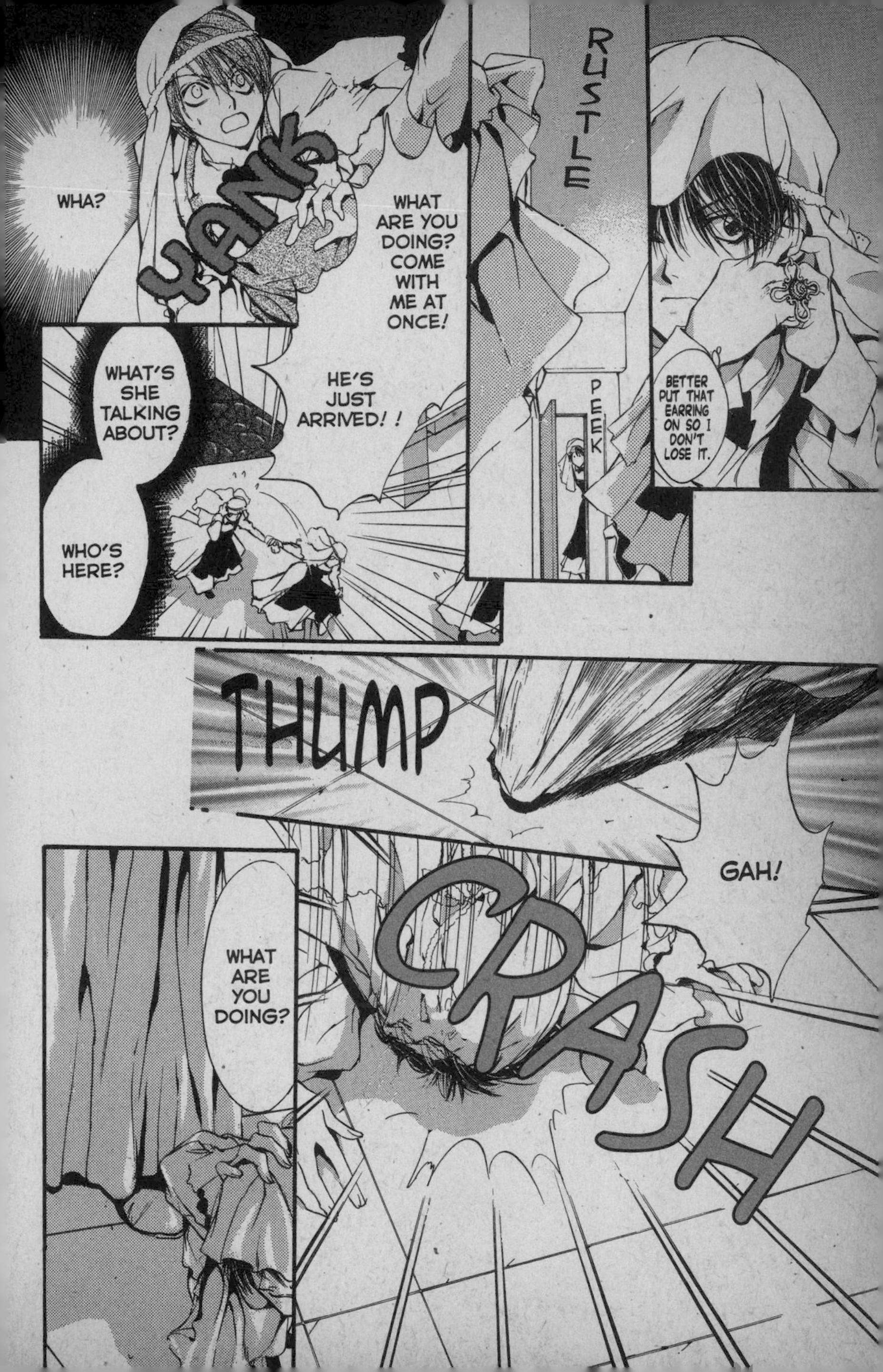

BETTER PUT THAT EARRING ON SO I DON'T LOSE IT.
RUSTLE
PEEK
WHAT ARE YOU DOING? COME WITH ME AT ONCE!
YANK
WHA?
HE'S JUST ARRIVED! !
WHAT'S SHE TALKING ABOUT?
WHO'S HERE?
THUMP
GAH!
CRASH
WHAT ARE YOU DOING?

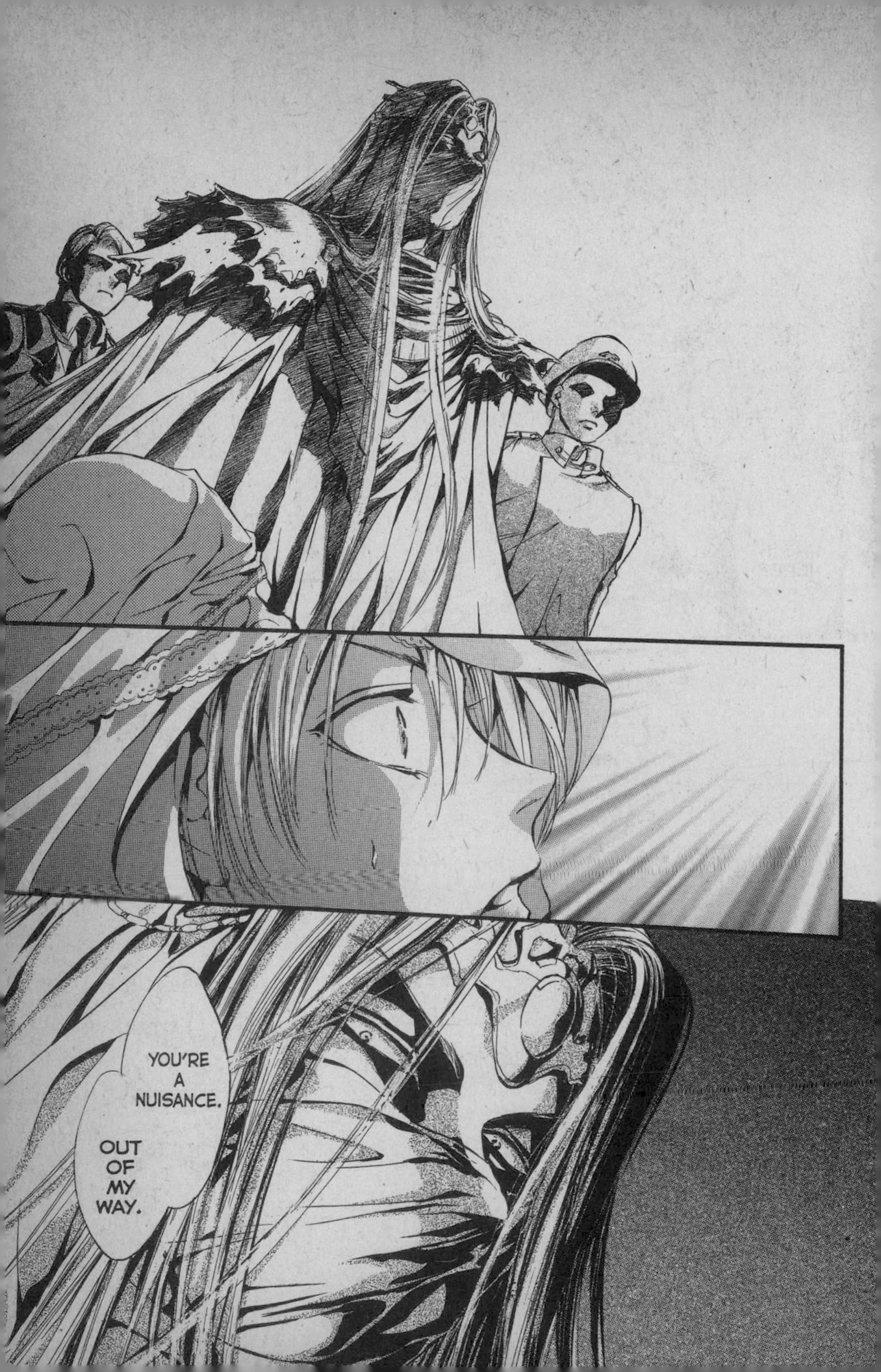
YOU'RE A NUISANCE.
OUT OF MY WAY.

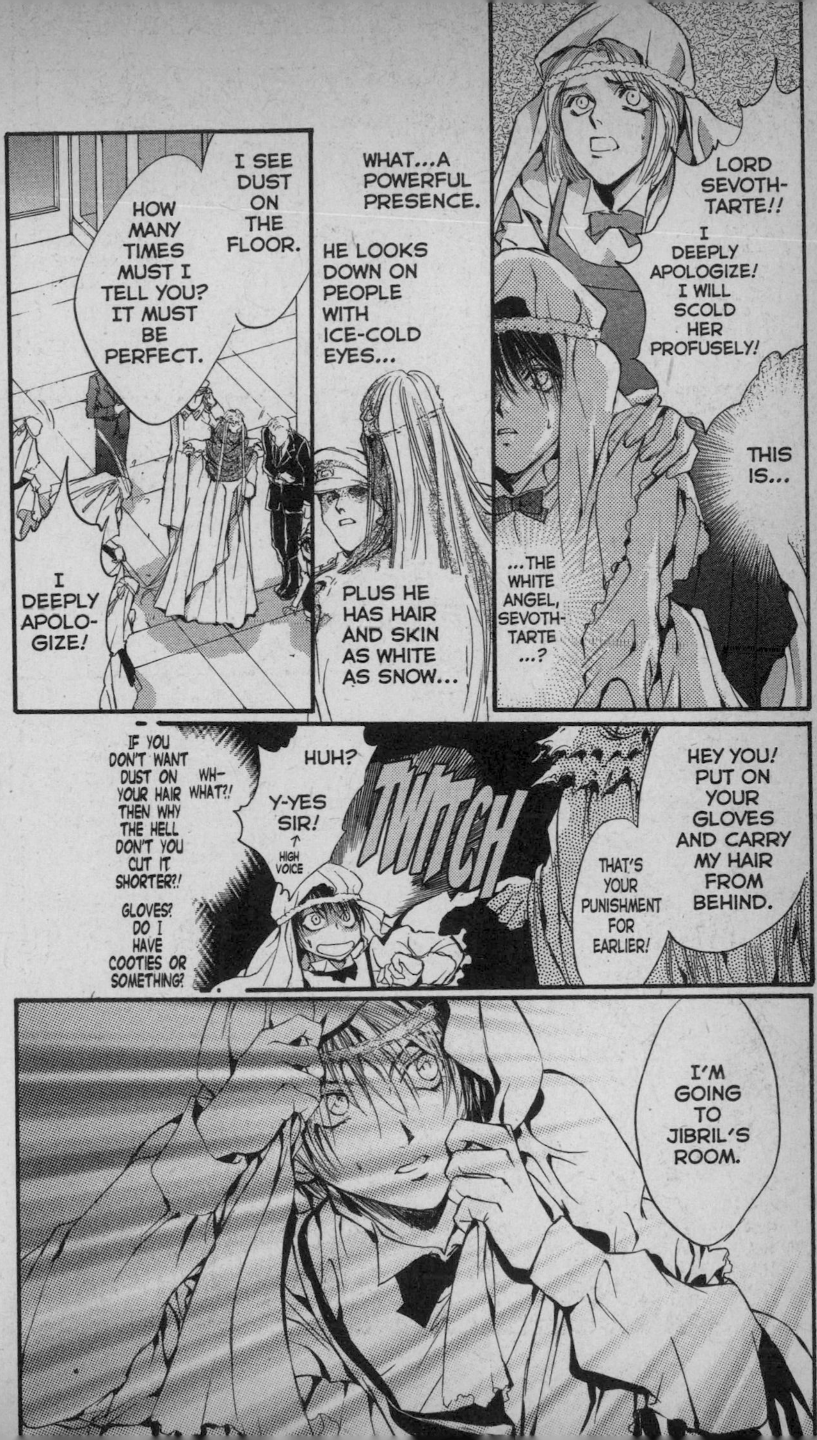
LORD SEVOTH-TARTE!!
I DEEPLY APOLOGIZE! I WILL SCOLD HER PROFUSELY!
THIS IS...
...THE WHITE ANGEL, SEVOTH-TARTE...?
WHAT...A POWERFUL PRESENCE.
HE LOOKS DOWN ON PEOPLE WITH ICE-COLD EYES...
PLUS HE HAS HAIR AND SKIN AS WHITE AS SNOW...
I SEE DUST ON THE FLOOR.
HOW MANY TIMES MUST I TELL YOU? IT MUST BE PERFECT.
I DEEPLY APOLO-GIZE!
HEY YOU! PUT ON YOUR GLOVES AND CARRY MY HAIR FROM BEHIND.
THAT'S YOUR PUNISHMENT FOR EARLIER!
TWITCH
HUH?
Y-YES SIR!
HIGH VOICE
WH-WHAT?!
IF YOU DON'T WANT DUST ON YOUR HAIR THEN WHY THE HELL DON'T YOU CUT IT SHORTER?!
GLOVES? DO I HAVE COOTIES OR SOMETHING?
I'M GOING TO JIBRIL'S ROOM.

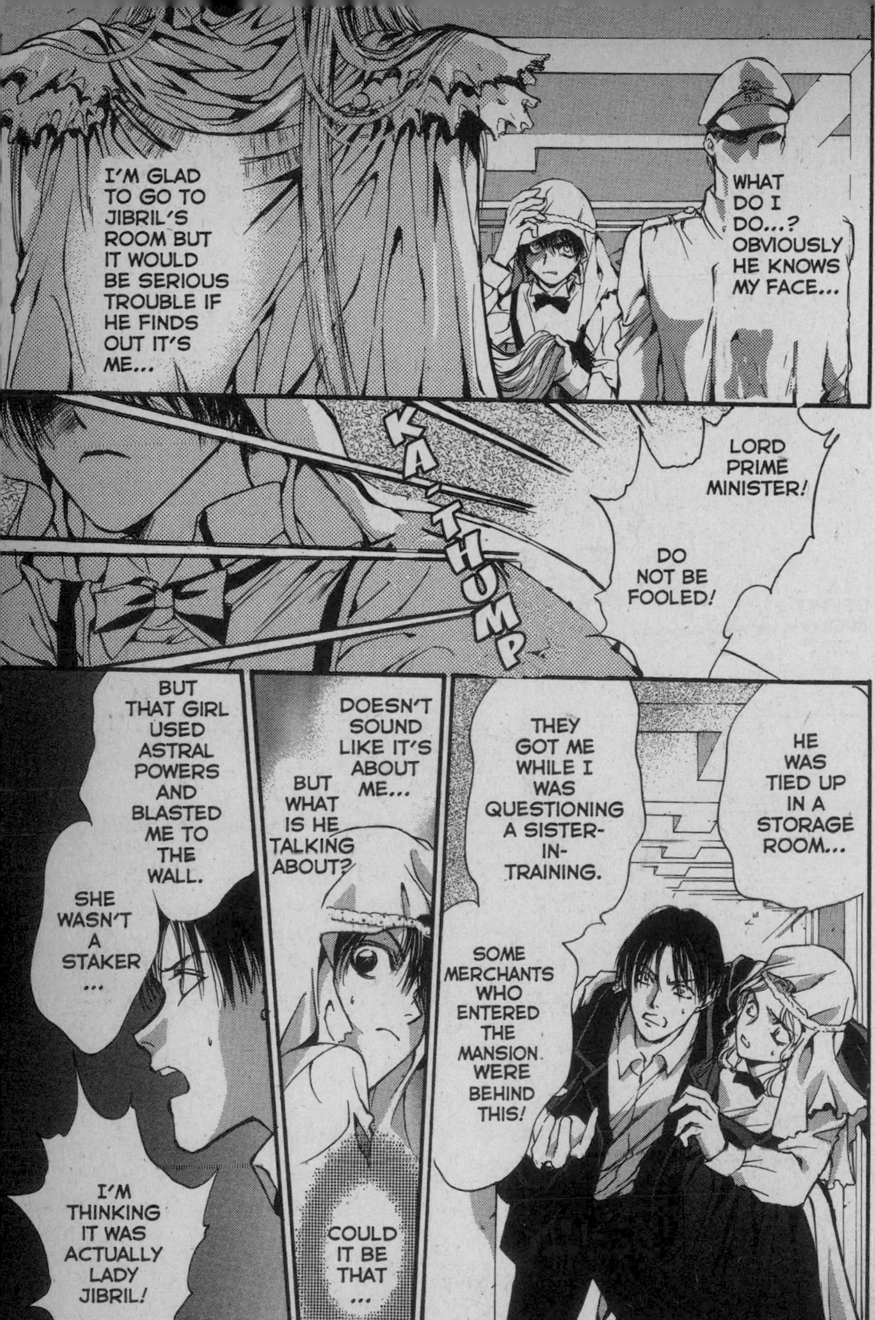
WHAT DO I DO...? OBVIOUSLY HE KNOWS MY FACE...
I'M GLAD TO GO TO JIBRIL'S ROOM BUT IT WOULD BE SERIOUS TROUBLE IF HE FINDS OUT IT'S ME...
LORD PRIME MINISTER!
DO NOT BE FOOLED!
KA-THUMP
HE WAS TIED UP IN A STORAGE ROOM...
THEY GOT ME WHILE I WAS QUESTIONING A SISTER-IN-TRAINING.
SOME MERCHANTS WHO ENTERED THE MANSION WERE BEHIND THIS!
DOESN'T SOUND LIKE IT'S ABOUT ME...
BUT WHAT IS HE TALKING ABOUT?
COULD IT BE THAT ...
BUT THAT GIRL USED ASTRAL POWERS AND BLASTED ME TO THE WALL.
SHE WASN'T A STAKER ...
I'M THINKING IT WAS ACTUALLY LADY JIBRIL!

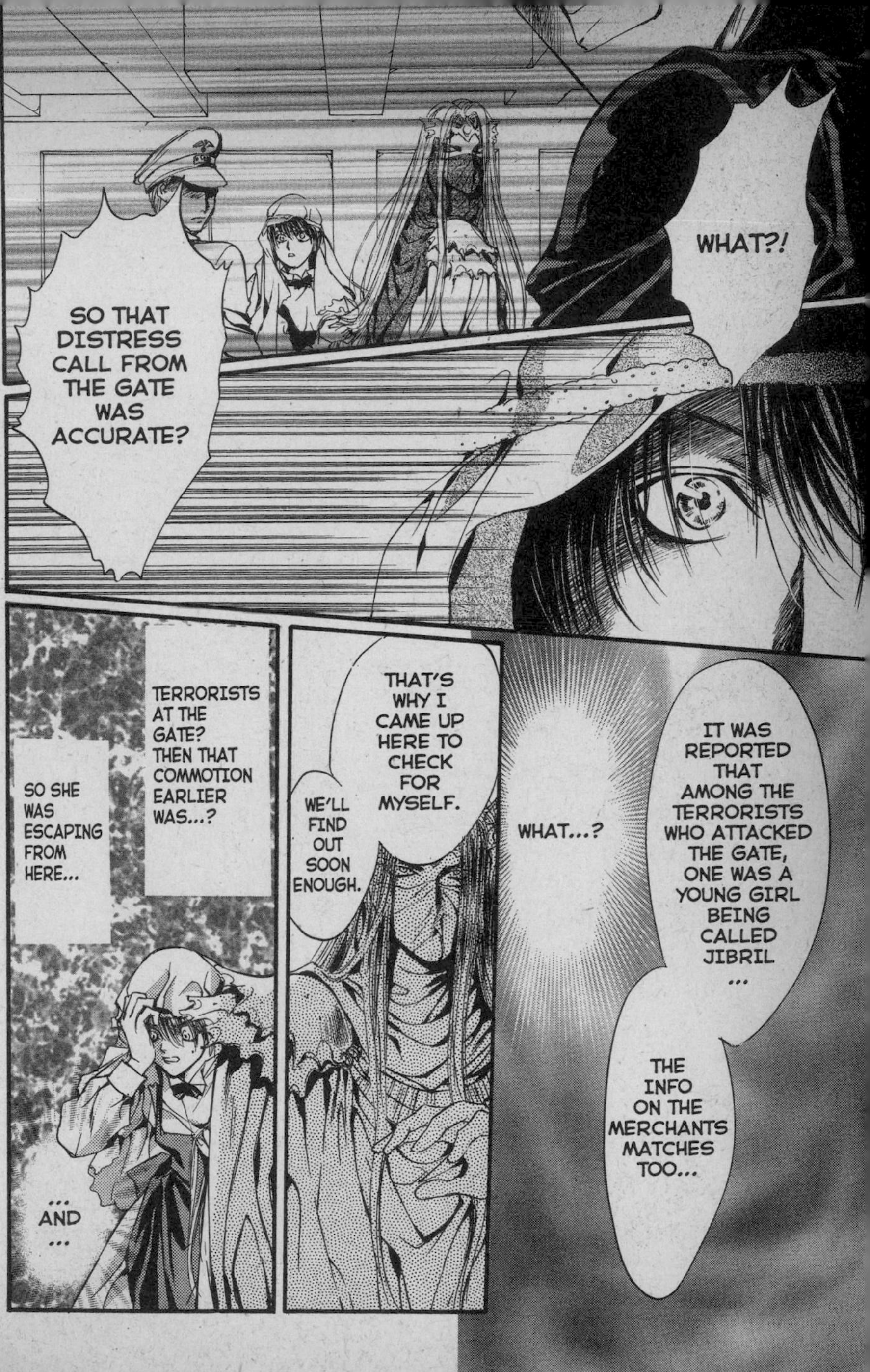
WHAT?!
SO THAT DISTRESS CALL FROM THE GATE WAS ACCURATE?
IT WAS REPORTED THAT AMONG THE TERRORISTS WHO ATTACKED THE GATE, ONE WAS A YOUNG GIRL BEING CALLED JIBRIL ...
WHAT...?
THE INFO ON THE MERCHANTS MATCHES TOO...
THAT'S WHY I CAME UP HERE TO CHECK FOR MYSELF.
WE'LL FIND OUT SOON ENOUGH.
TERRORISTS AT THE GATE? THEN THAT COMMOTION EARLIER WAS...?
SO SHE WAS ESCAPING FROM HERE...
... AND ...

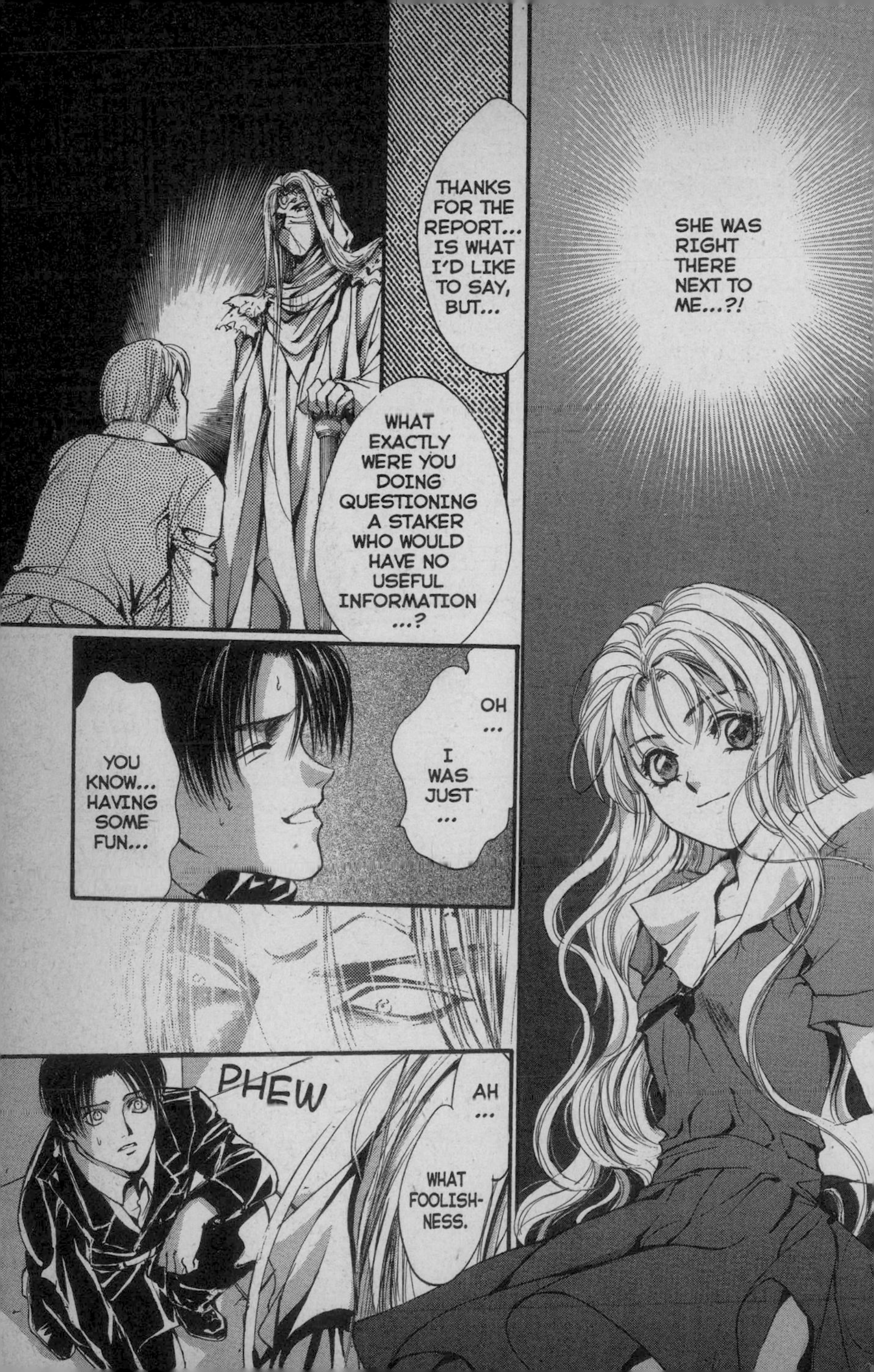
SHE WAS RIGHT THERE NEXT TO ME...?!
THANKS FOR THE REPORT... IS WHAT I'D LIKE TO SAY, BUT...
WHAT EXACTLY WERE YOU DOING QUESTIONING A STAKER WHO WOULD HAVE NO USEFUL INFORMATION ...?
OH ... I WAS JUST ...
YOU KNOW... HAVING SOME FUN...
AH ...
WHAT FOOLISH-NESS.
PHEW

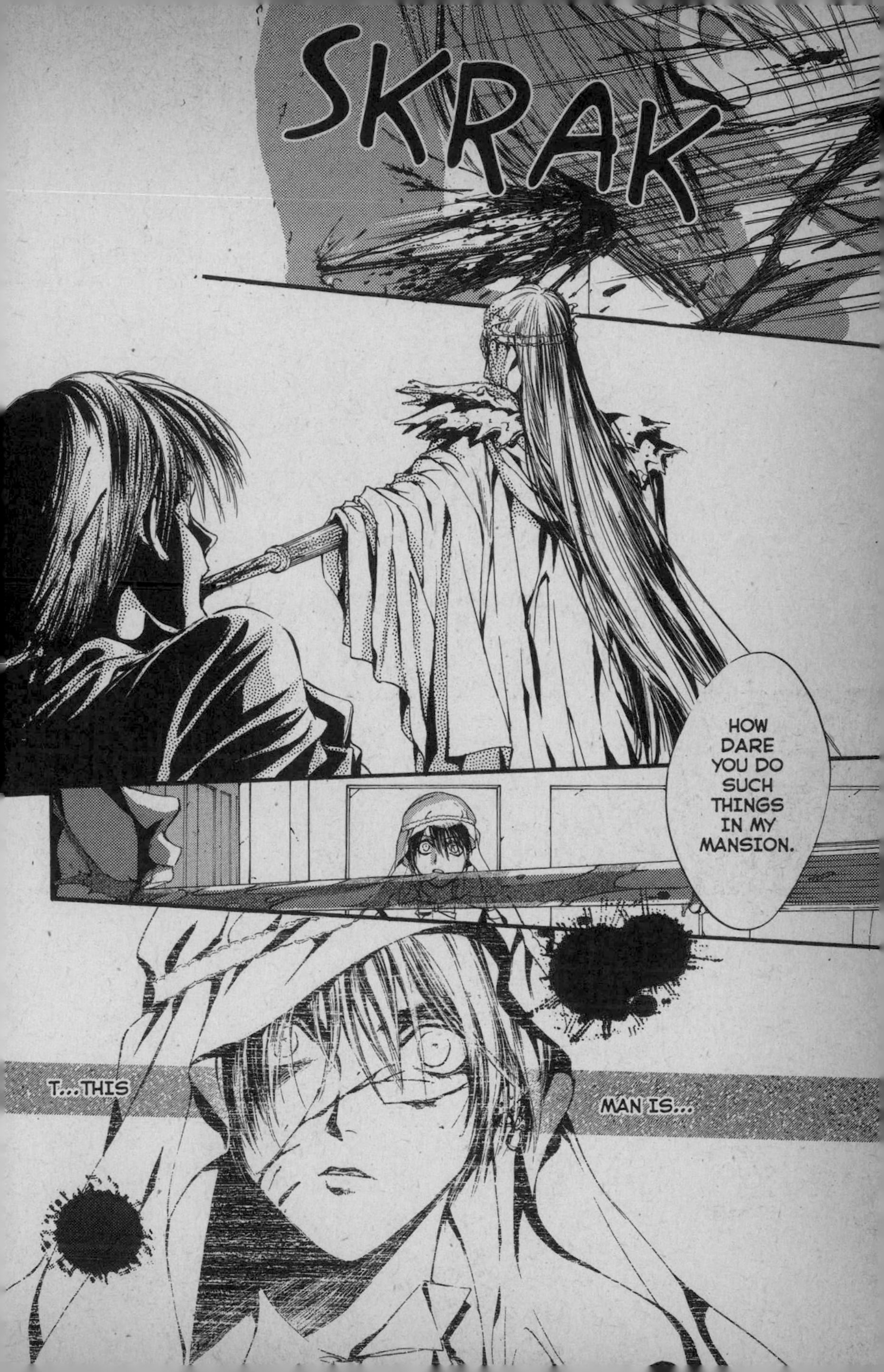
SKRAK
HOW DARE YOU DO SUCH THINGS IN MY MANSION.
T...THIS
MAN IS...

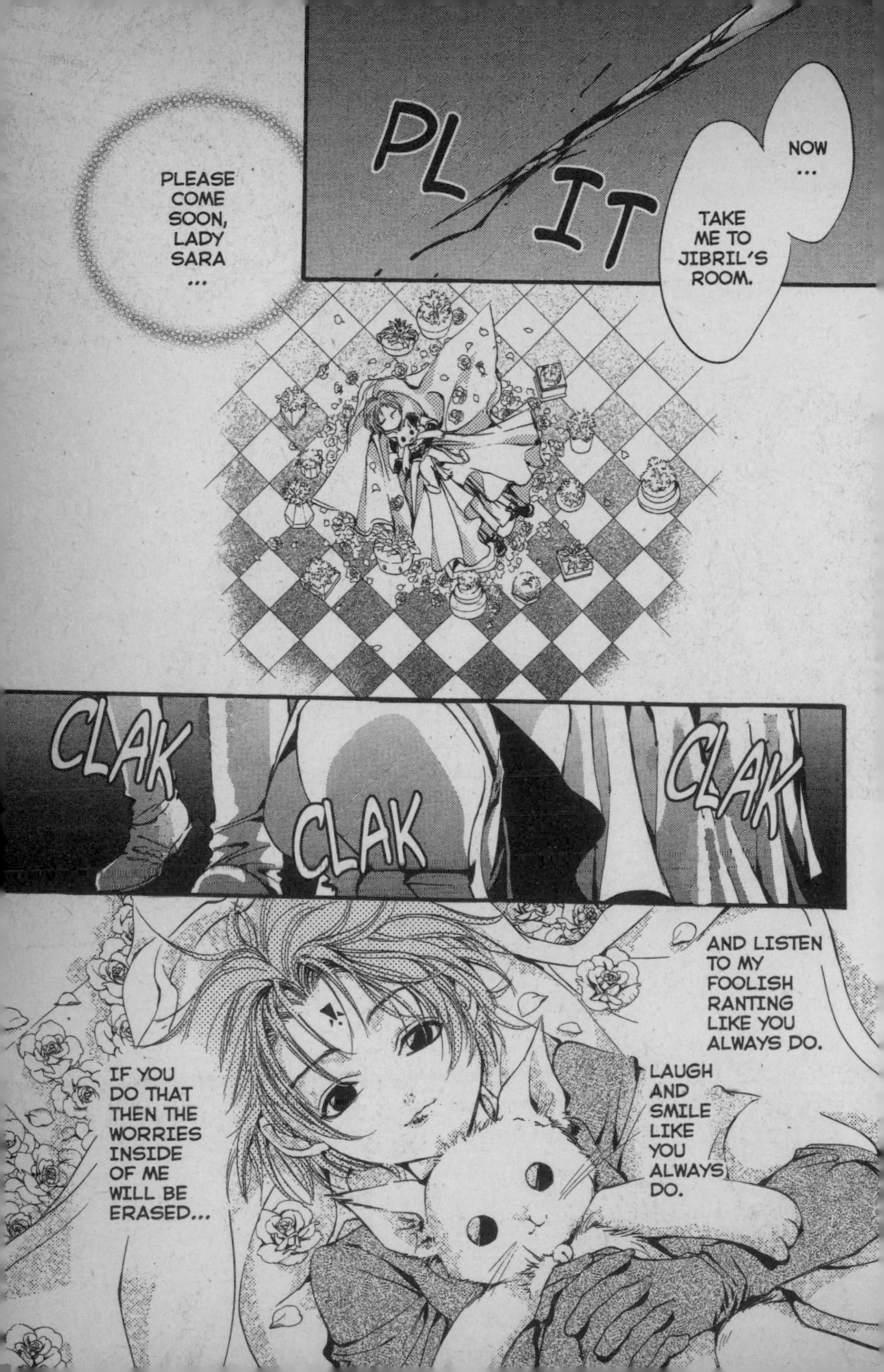
PLIT
NOW ...
TAKE ME TO JIBRIL'S ROOM.
PLEASE COME SOON, LADY SARA ...
CLAK
CLAK
CLAK
AND LISTEN TO MY FOOLISH RANTING LIKE YOU ALWAYS DO.
LAUGH AND SMILE LIKE YOU ALWAYS DO.
IF YOU DO THAT THEN THE WORRIES INSIDE OF ME WILL BE ERASED...

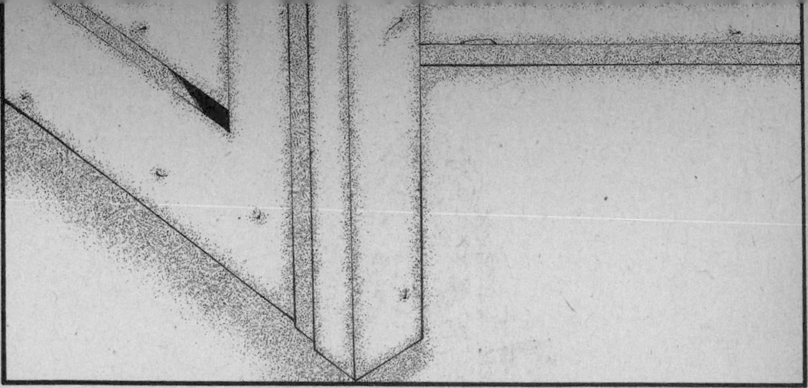

YES, EVEN FOR A GIRL LIKE ME...

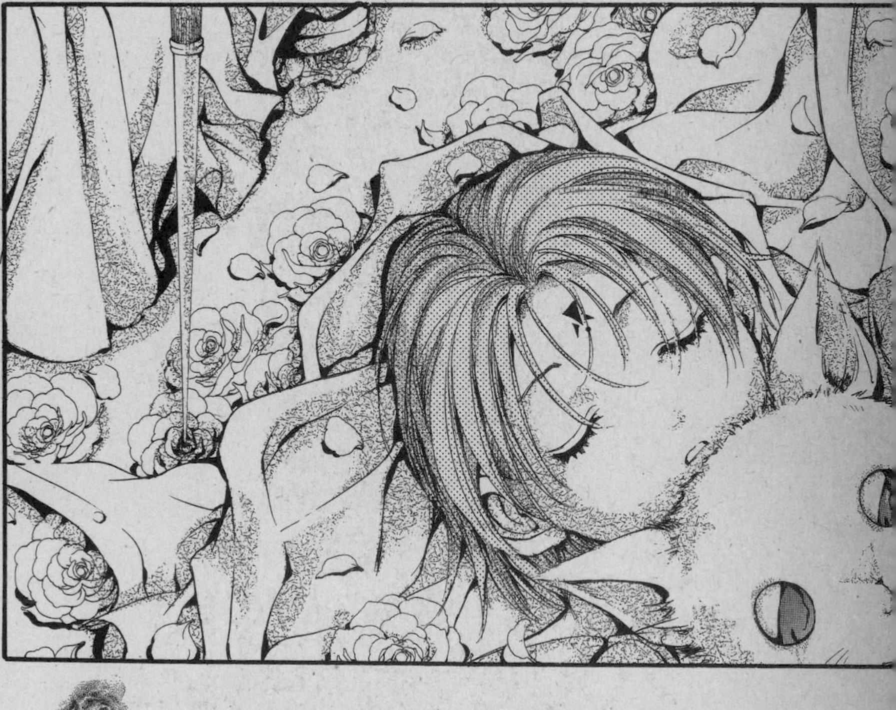

...THERE ARE NIGHTS SO PAINFUL THAT I WISH I WERE DEAD.

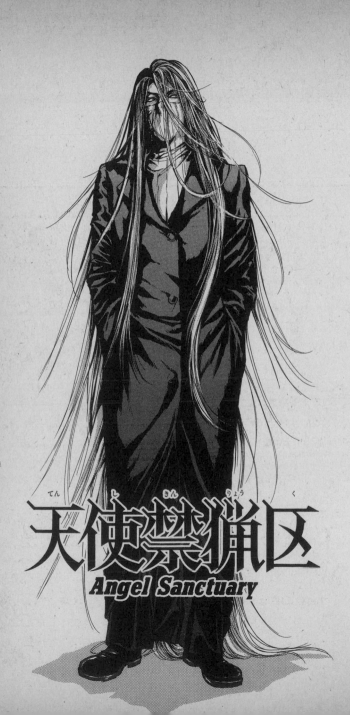

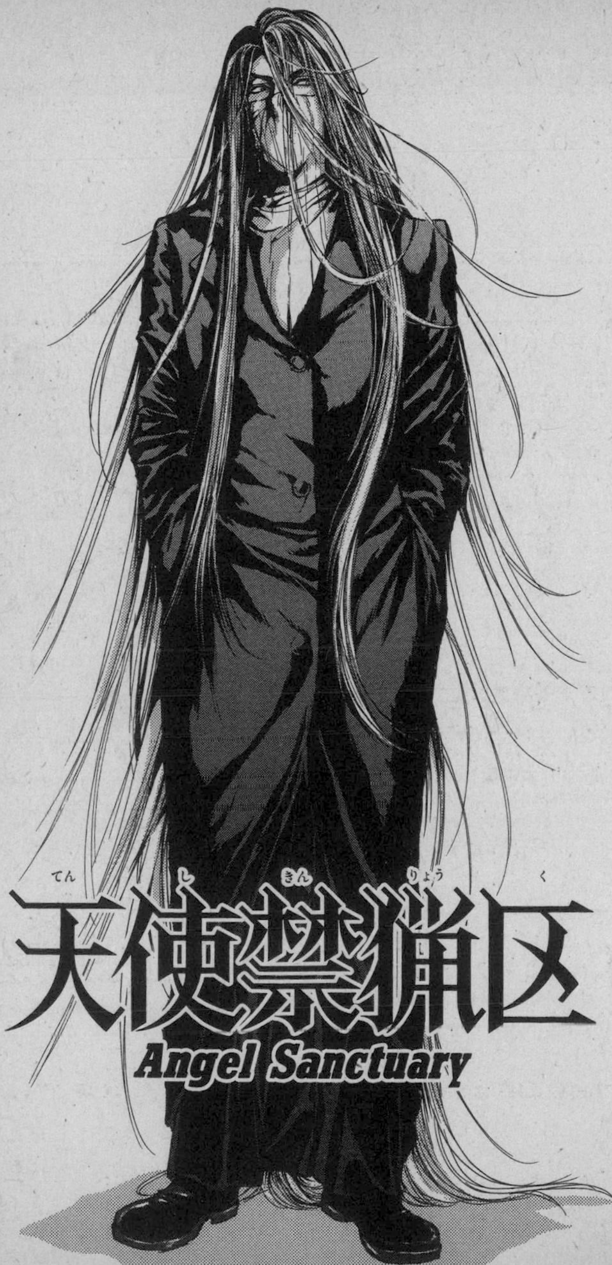
天使禁猟区
Angel Sanctuary

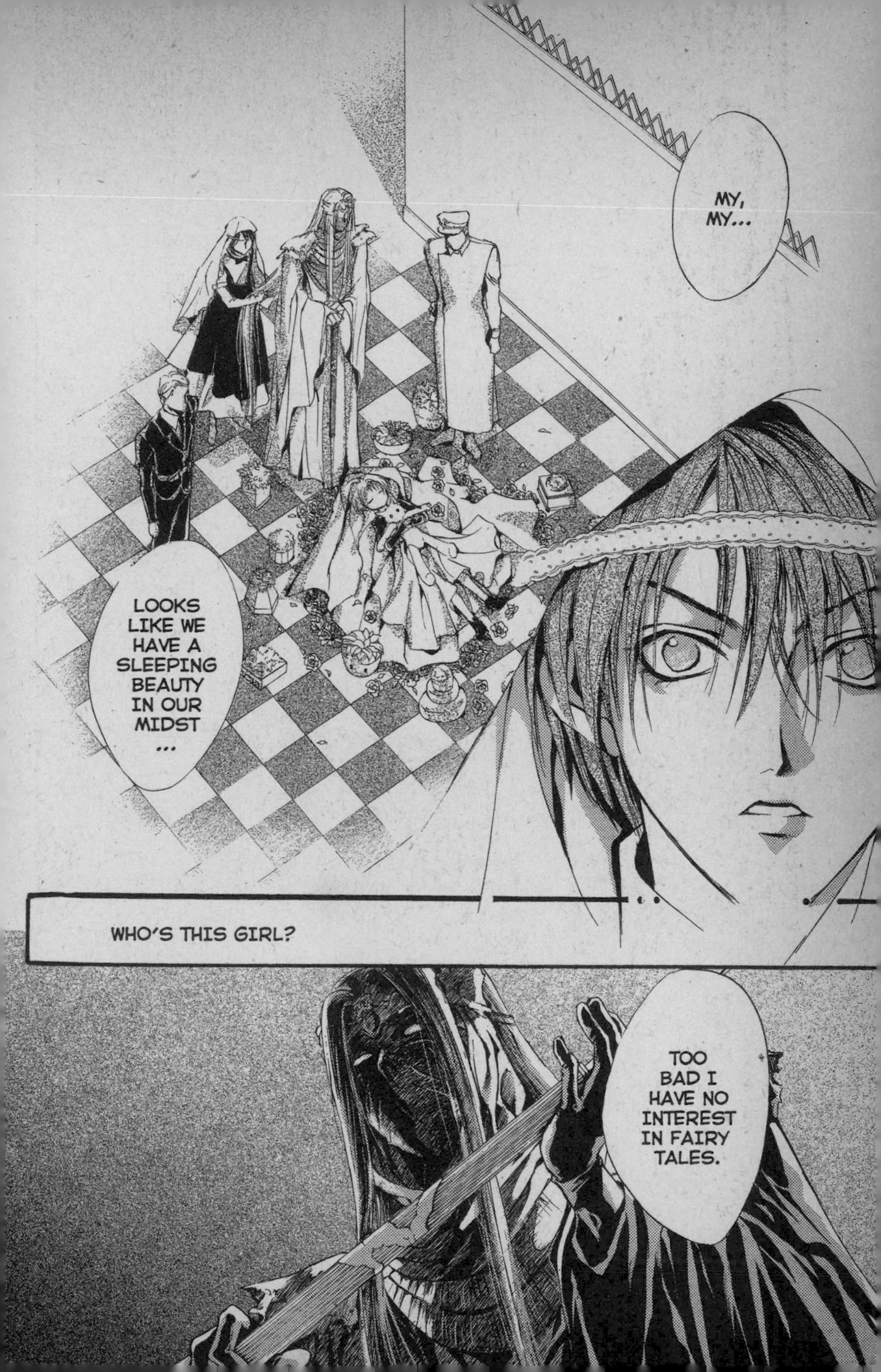
MY, MY...
LOOKS LIKE WE HAVE A SLEEPING BEAUTY IN OUR MIDST ...
WHO'S THIS GIRL?
TOO BAD I HAVE NO INTEREST IN FAIRY TALES.

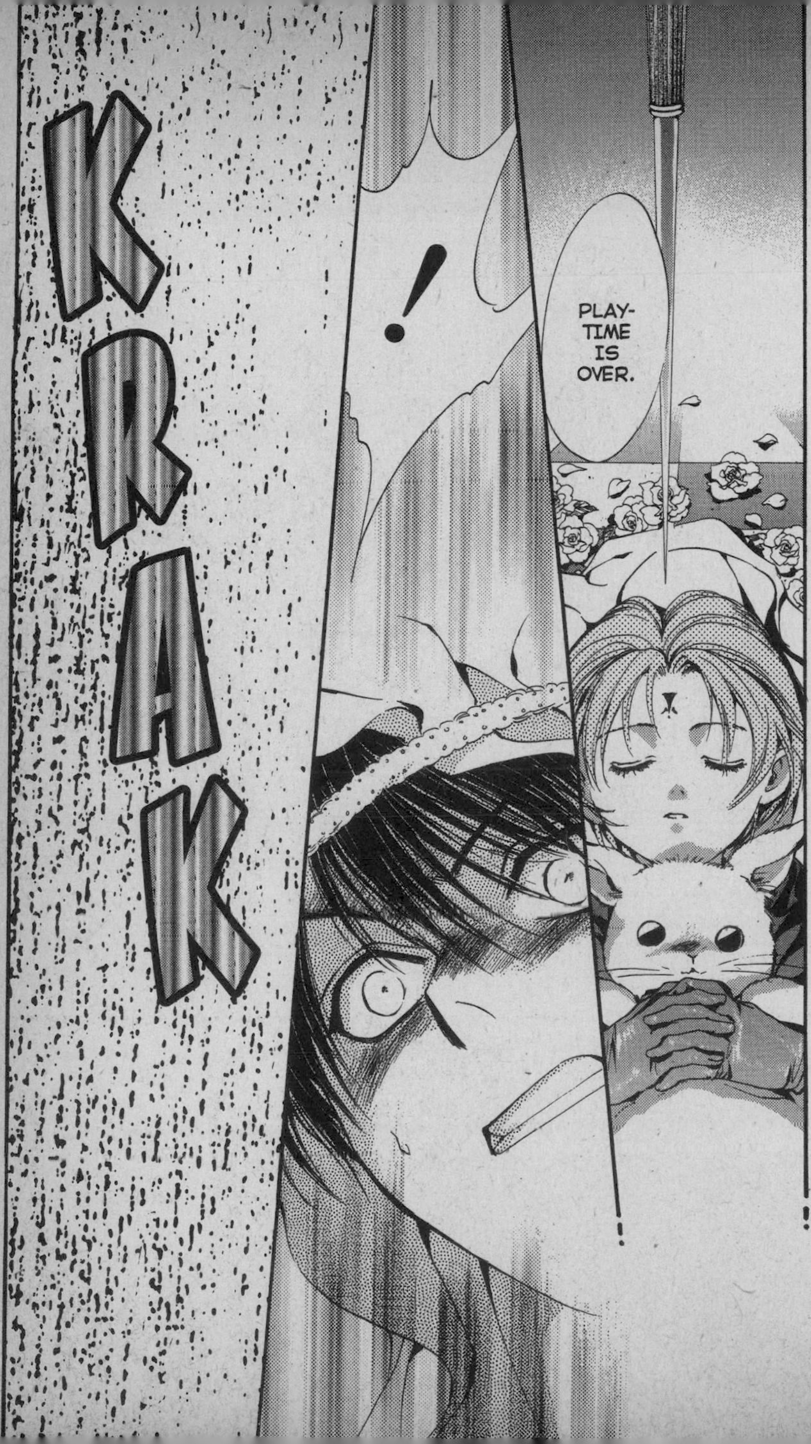
PLAY-
TIME
IS
OVER.
!
!
!
KRAK

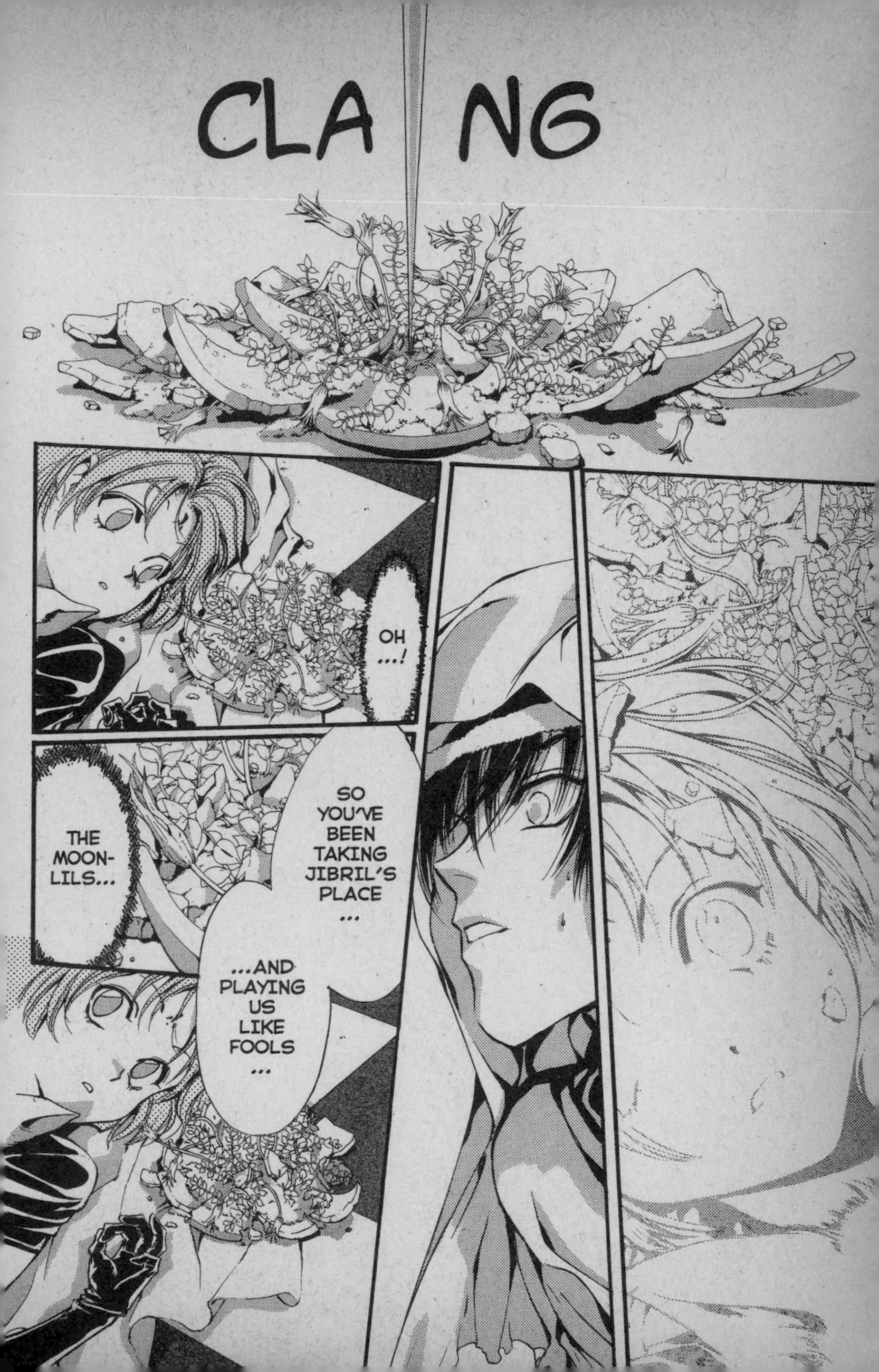
CLANG
OH ...!
THE MOON-LILS...
SO YOU'VE BEEN TAKING JIBRIL'S PLACE ...
...AND PLAYING US LIKE FOOLS ...

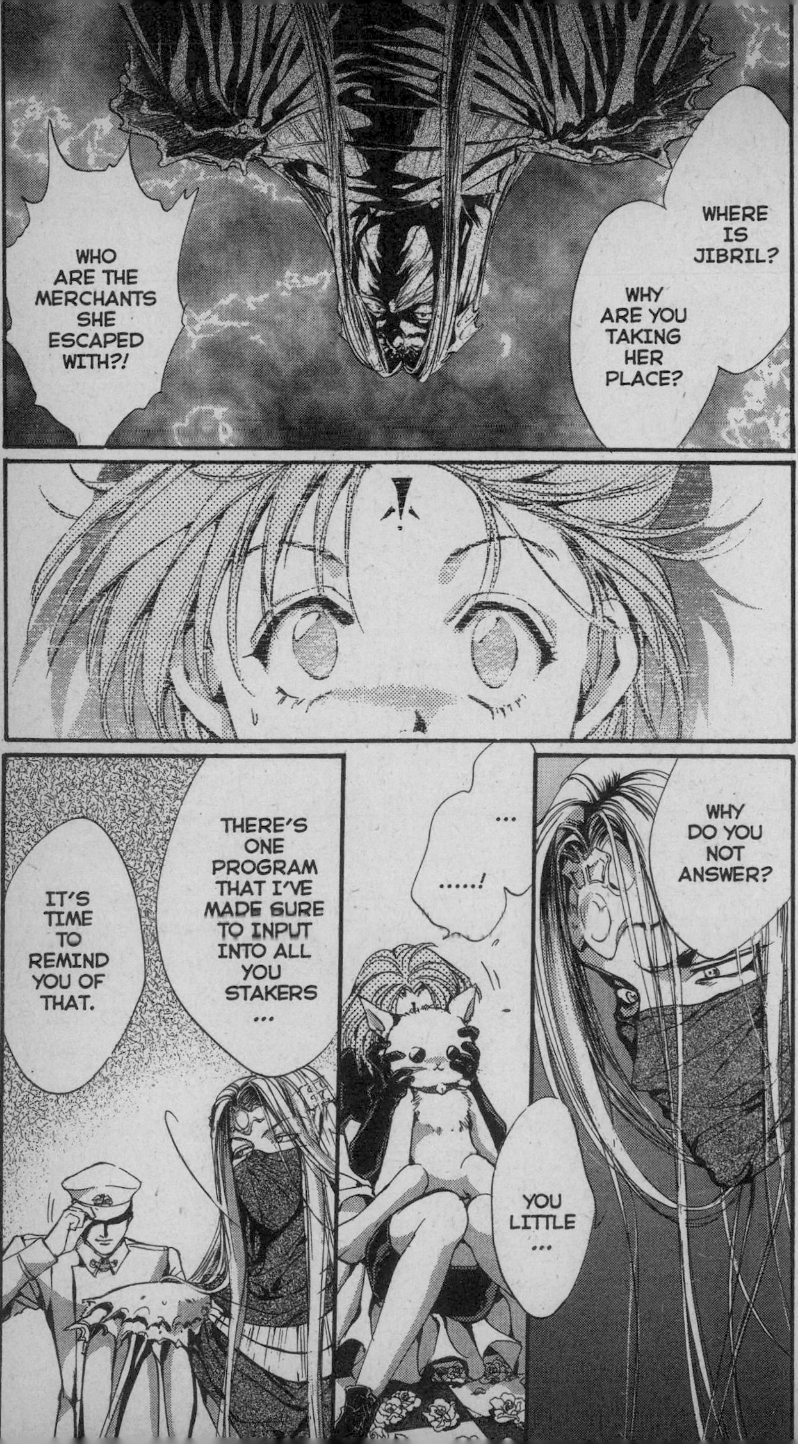
WHERE IS JIBRIL?
WHY ARE YOU TAKING HER PLACE?
WHO ARE THE MERCHANTS SHE ESCAPED WITH?!
WHY DO YOU NOT ANSWER?
YOU LITTLE ...
...
.....!
THERE'S ONE PROGRAM THAT I'VE MADE SURE TO INPUT INTO ALL YOU STAKERS ...
IT'S TIME TO REMIND YOU OF THAT.

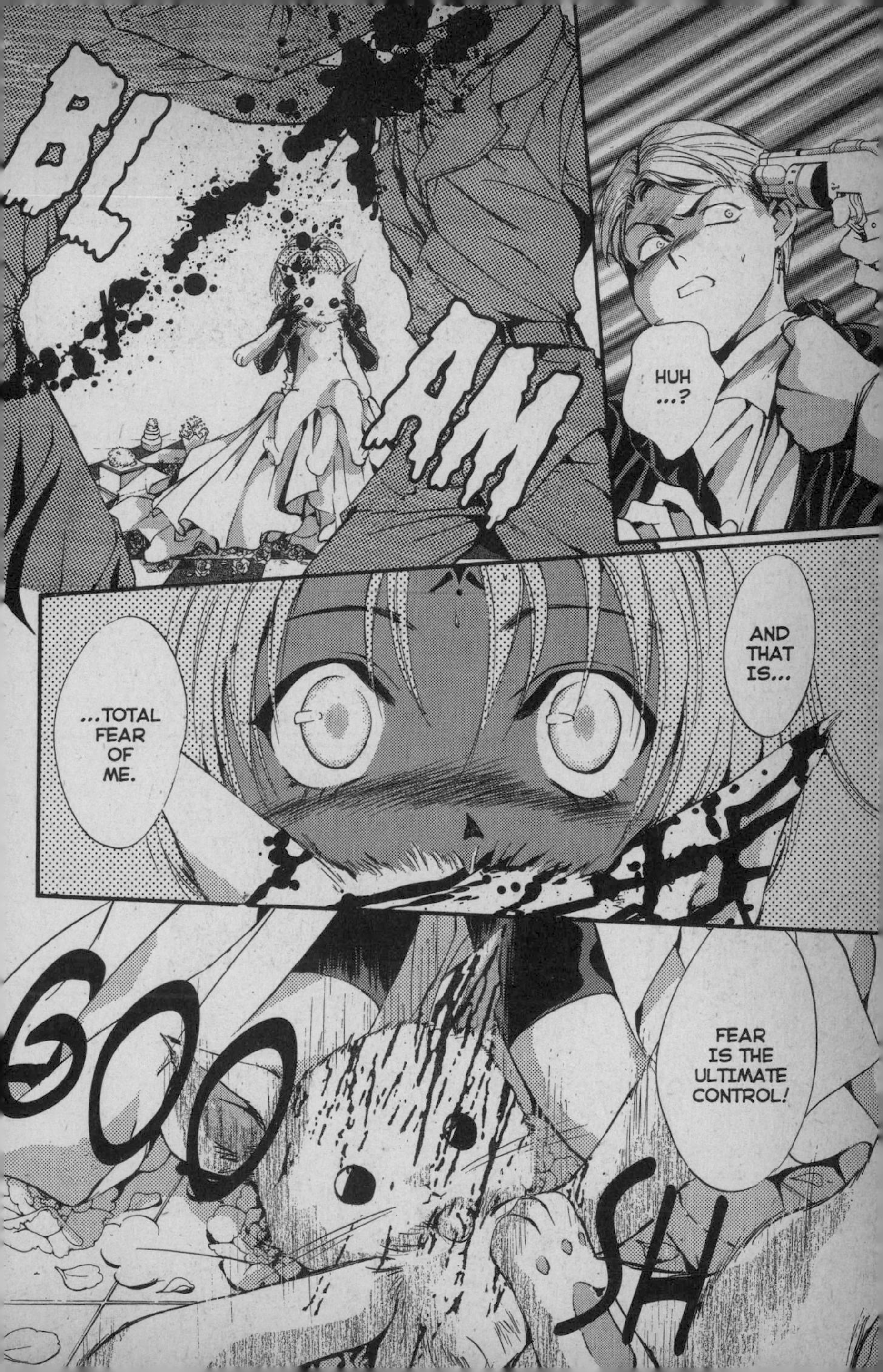
HUH ...?
BLAM
AND THAT IS...
...TOTAL FEAR OF ME.
FEAR IS THE ULTIMATE CONTROL!
GOOSH

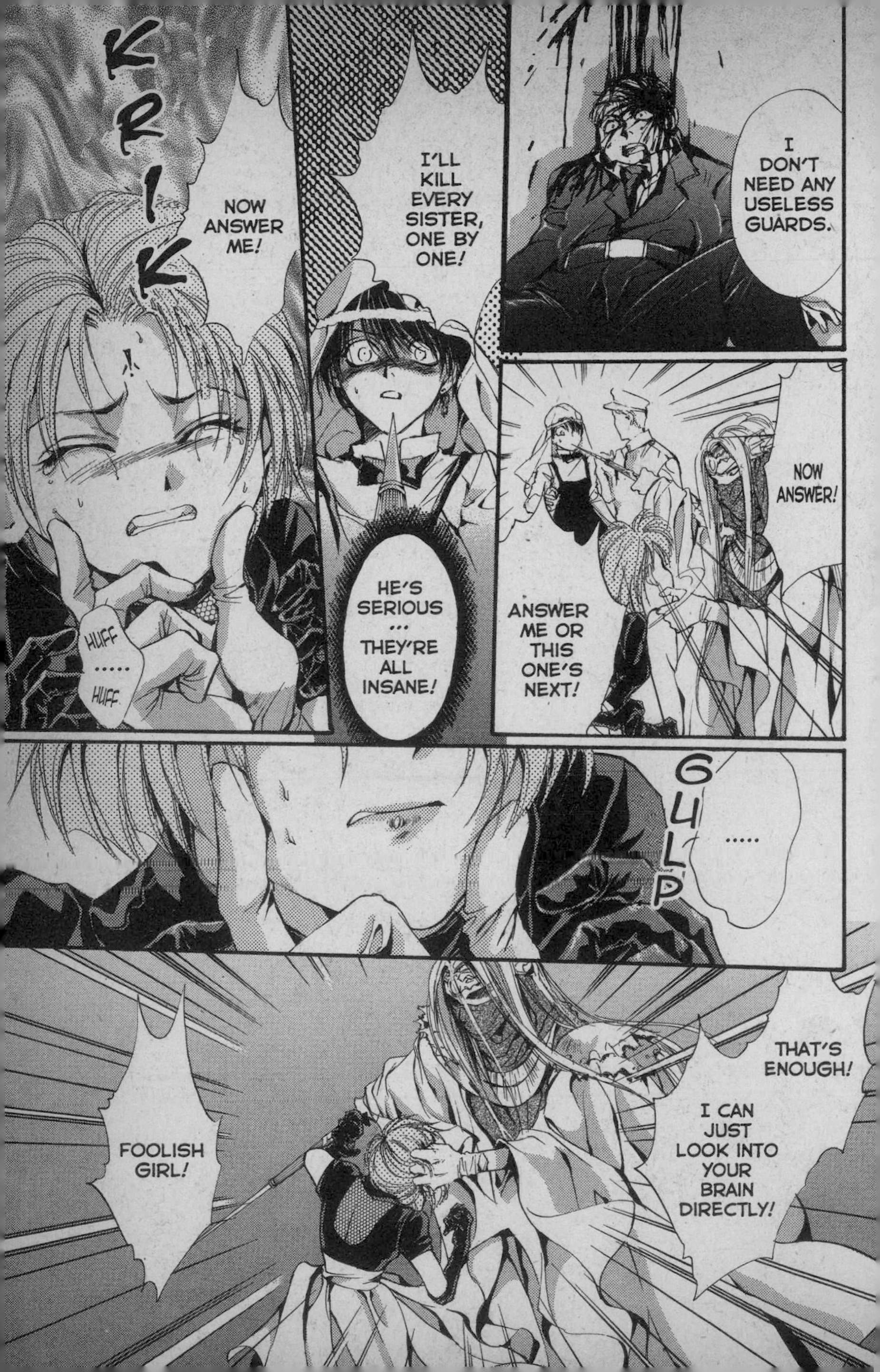
I DON'T NEED ANY USELESS GUARDS.
NOW ANSWER!
ANSWER ME OR THIS ONE'S NEXT!
I'LL KILL EVERY SISTER, ONE BY ONE!
HE'S SERIOUS... THEY'RE ALL INSANE!
KRIK
NOW ANSWER ME!
HUFF...... HUFF
GULP
.....
THAT'S ENOUGH!
I CAN JUST LOOK INTO YOUR BRAIN DIRECTLY!
FOOLISH GIRL!

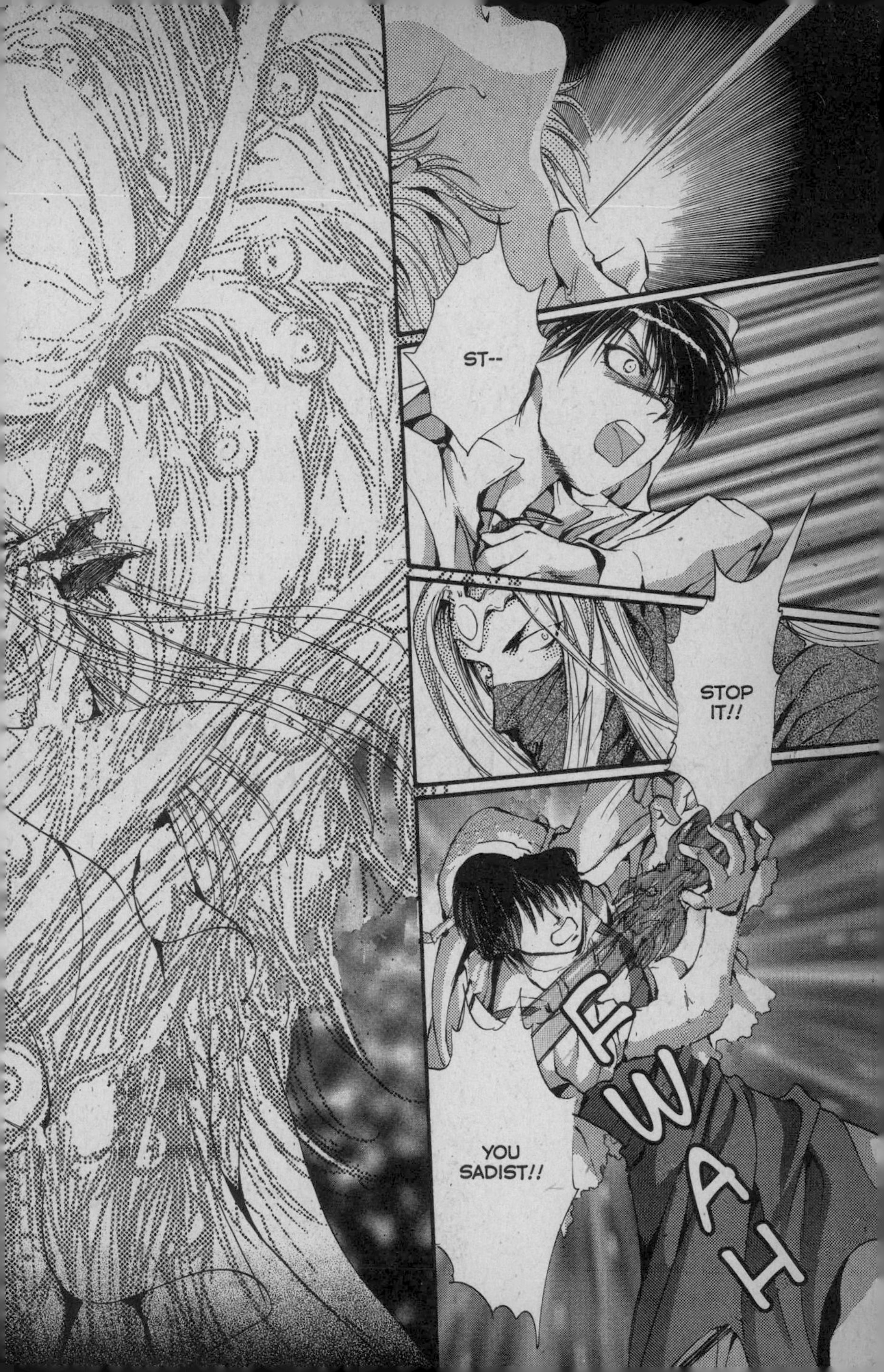
ST--
STOP IT!!
YOU SADIST!!
FWAH

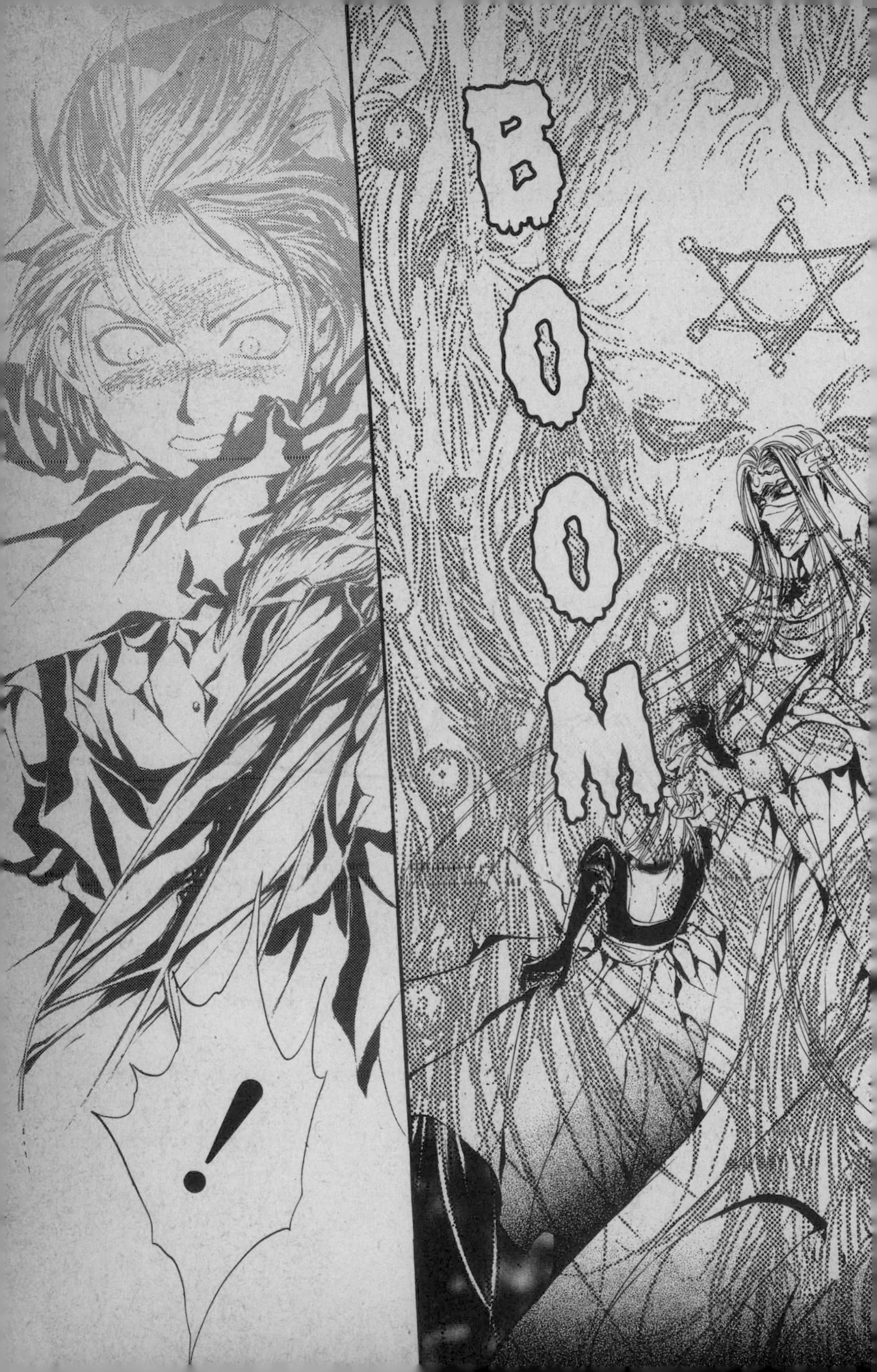
BOOM
!

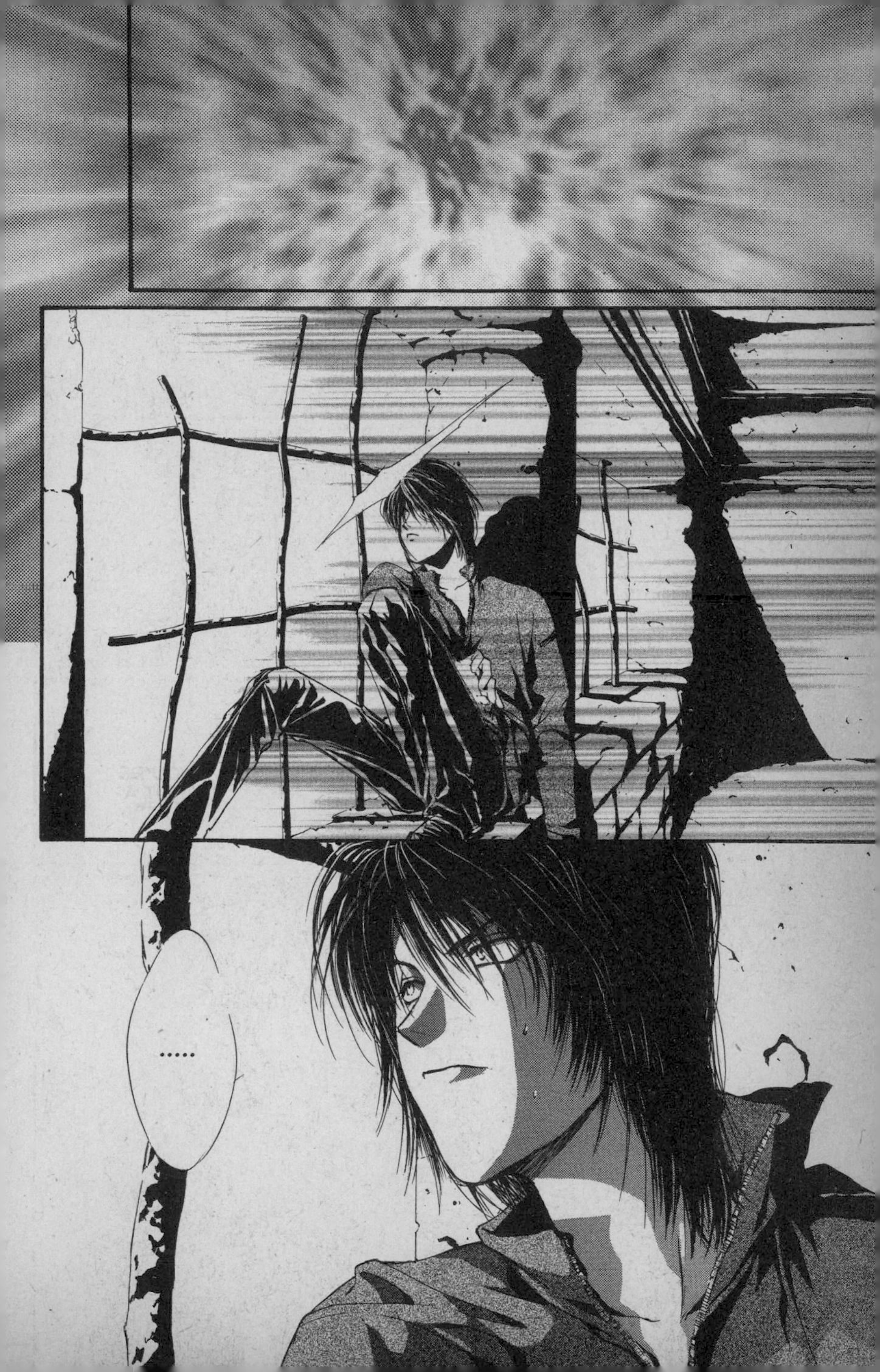
.....

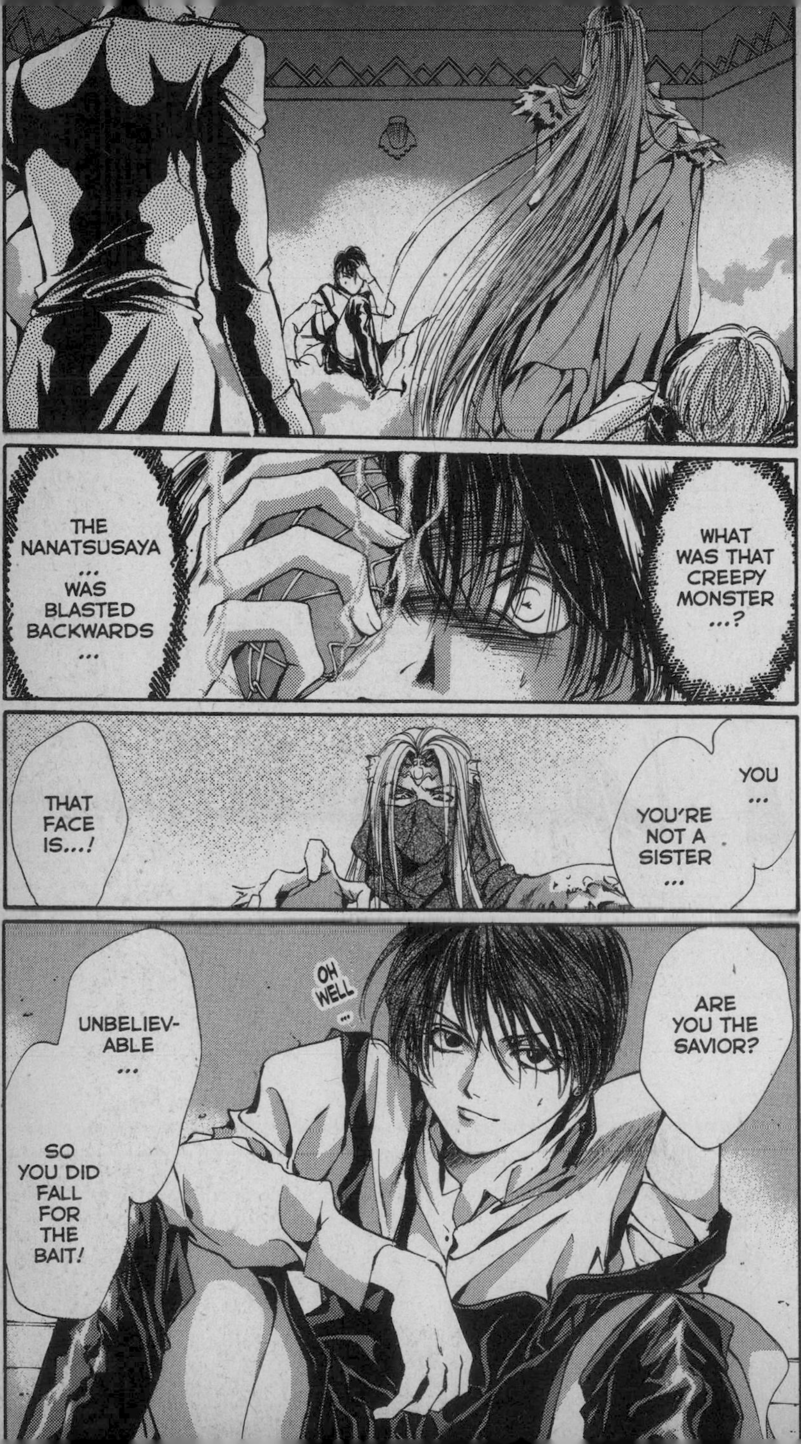
WHAT WAS THAT CREEPY MONSTER ...?
THE NANATSUSAYA ... WAS BLASTED BACKWARDS ...
YOU ... YOU'RE NOT A SISTER ...
THAT FACE IS...!
ARE YOU THE SAVIOR?
OH WELL ...
UNBELIEV-ABLE ...
SO YOU DID FALL FOR THE BAIT!

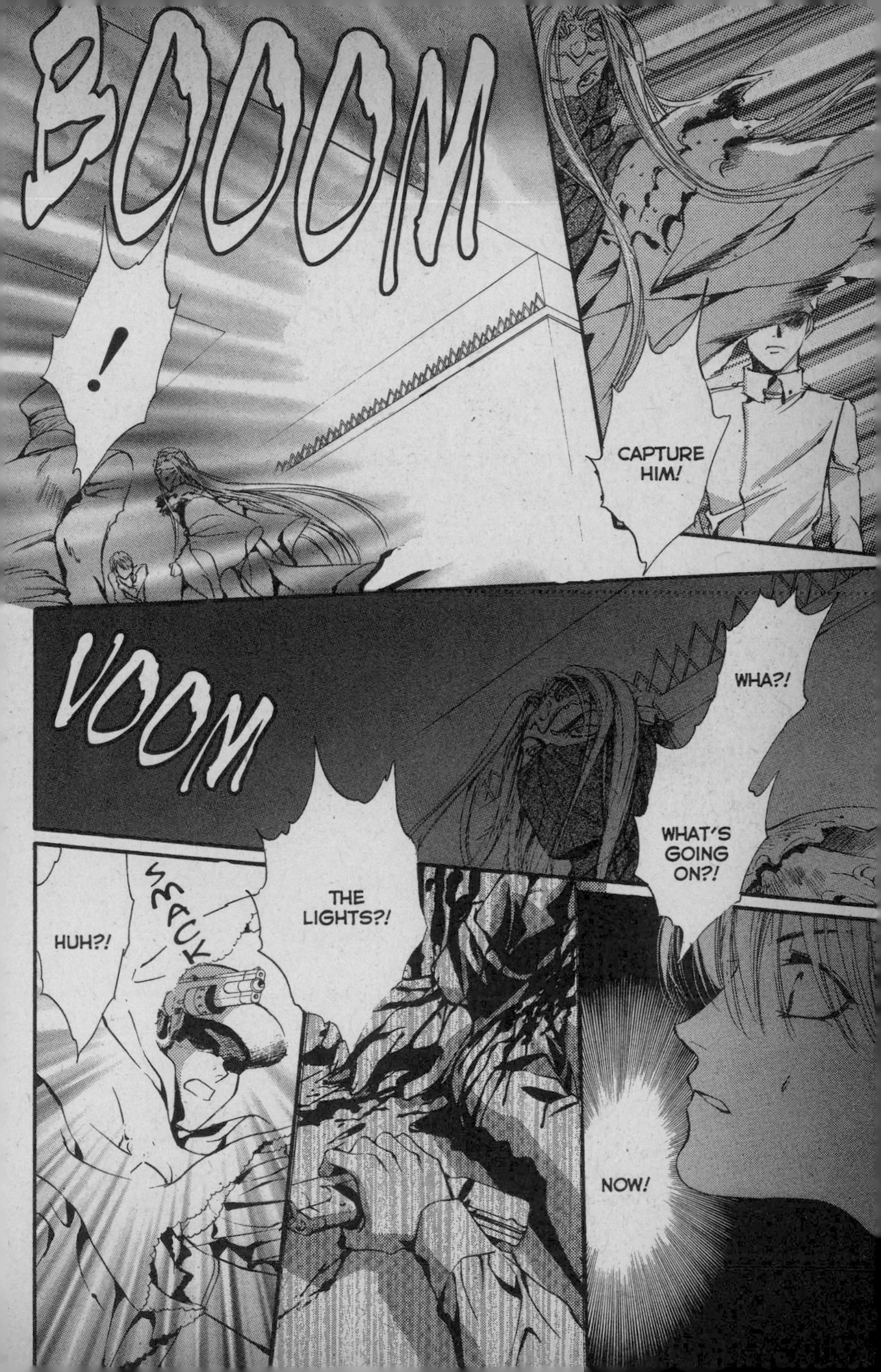
CAPTURE HIM!
BOOOM
!
WHA?!
WHAT'S GOING ON?!
VOOM
NOW!
THE LIGHTS?!
SMACK
HUH?!

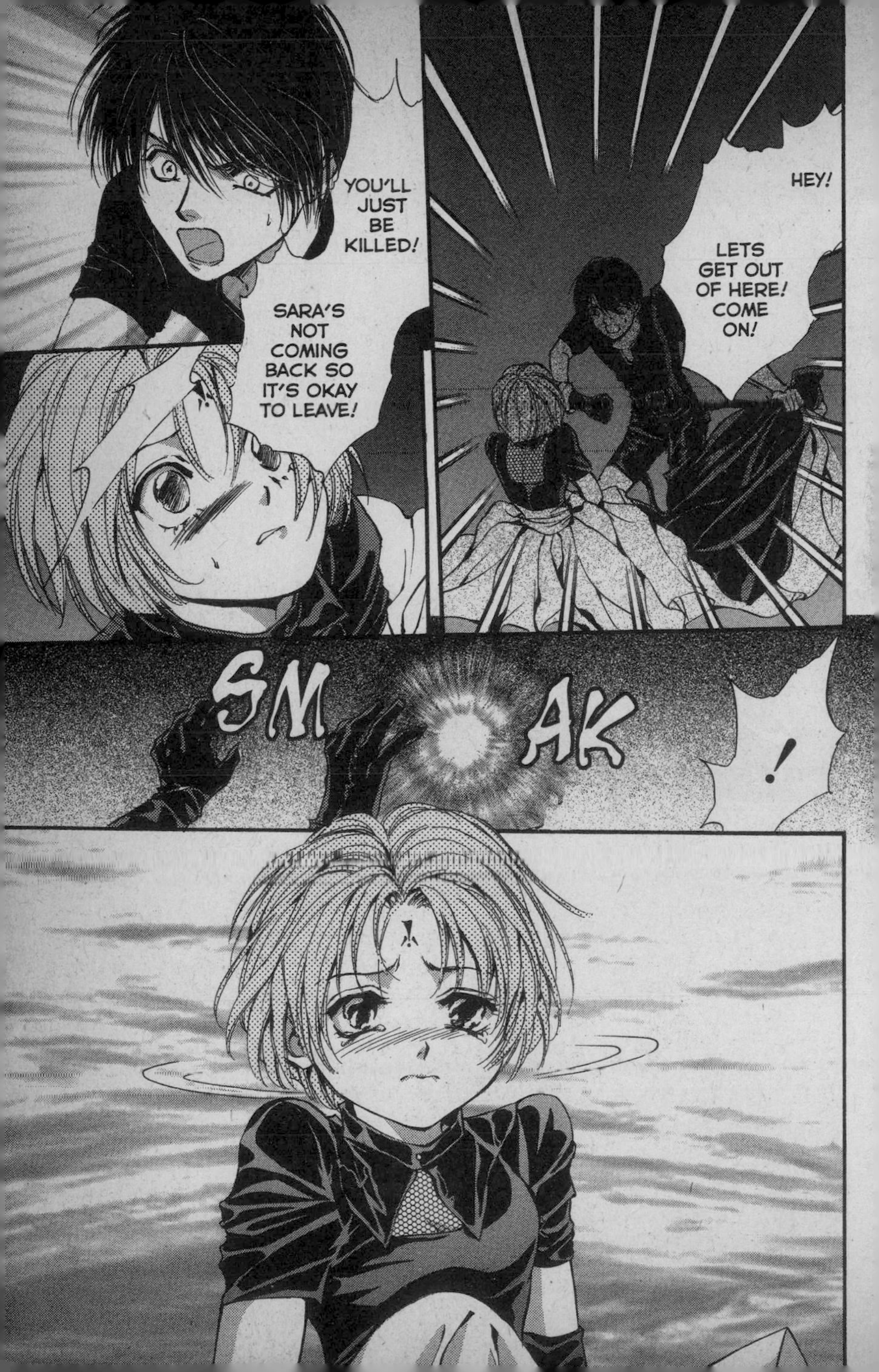
HEY!
LETS GET OUT OF HERE! COME ON!
YOU'LL JUST BE KILLED!
SARA'S NOT COMING BACK SO IT'S OKAY TO LEAVE!
SMAK
!

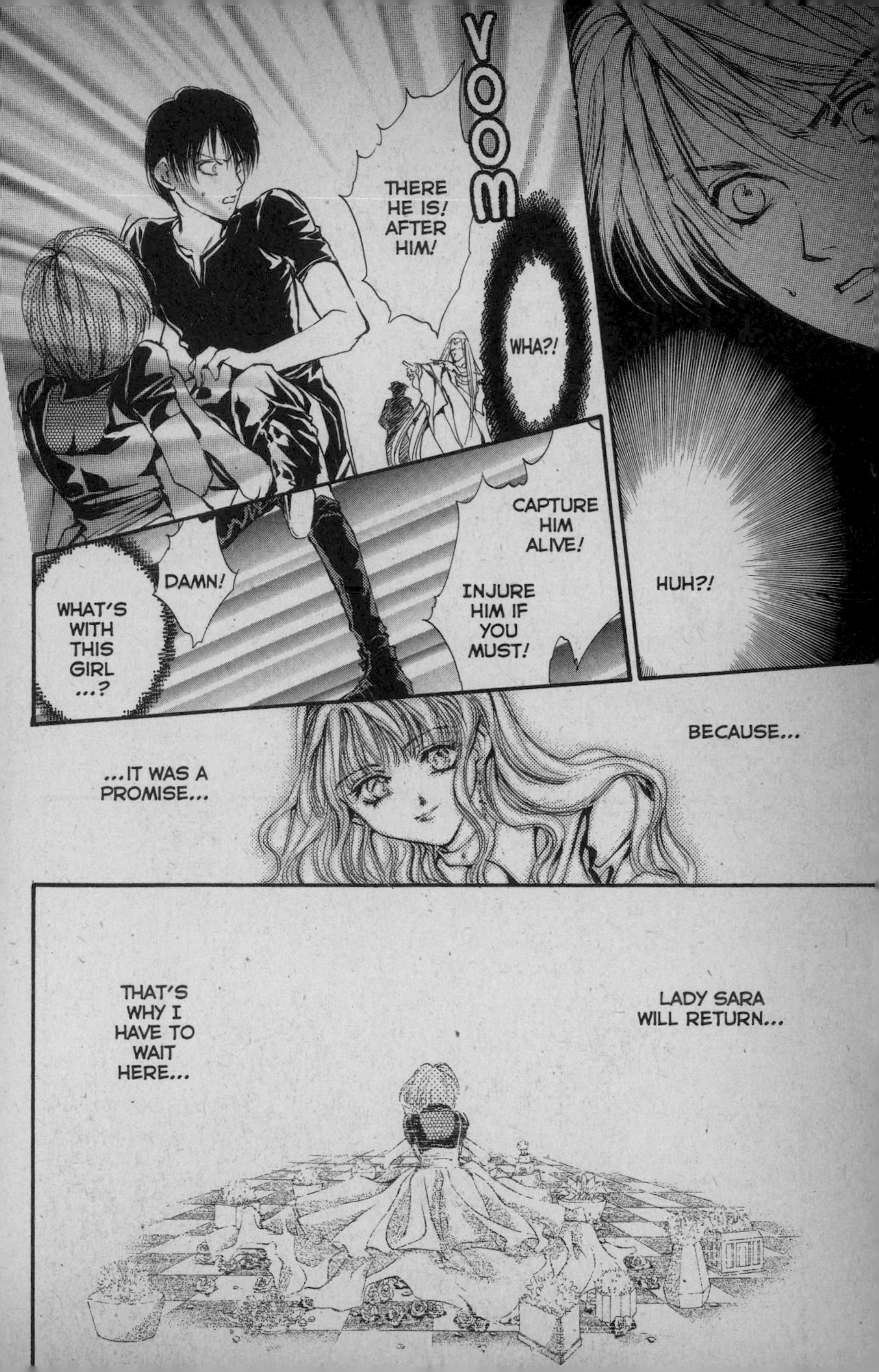
HUH?!
VOOM
WHA?!
THERE HE IS! AFTER HIM!
CAPTURE HIM ALIVE!
INJURE HIM IF YOU MUST!
DAMN!
WHAT'S WITH THIS GIRL ...?
BECAUSE...
...IT WAS A PROMISE...
LADY SARA WILL RETURN...
THAT'S WHY I HAVE TO WAIT HERE...

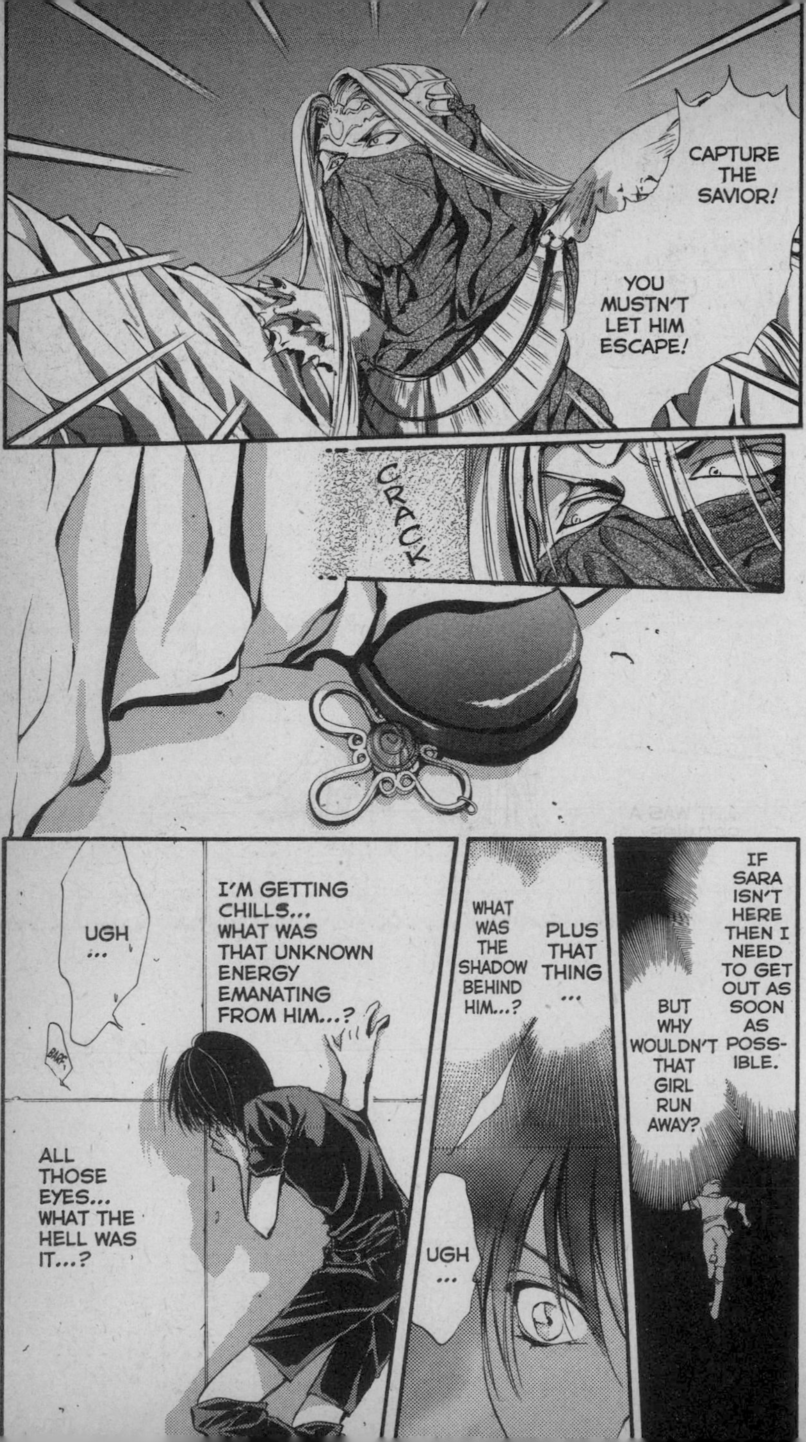
CAPTURE THE SAVIOR!
YOU MUSTN'T LET HIM ESCAPE!
CRACK
IF SARA ISN'T HERE THEN I NEED TO GET OUT AS SOON AS POSS-IBLE.
BUT WHY WOULDN'T THAT GIRL RUN AWAY?
PLUS THAT THING...
WHAT WAS THE SHADOW BEHIND HIM...?
UGH...
I'M GETTING CHILLS... WHAT WAS THAT UNKNOWN ENERGY EMANATING FROM HIM...?
UGH...
BARF
ALL THOSE EYES... WHAT THE HELL WAS IT...?

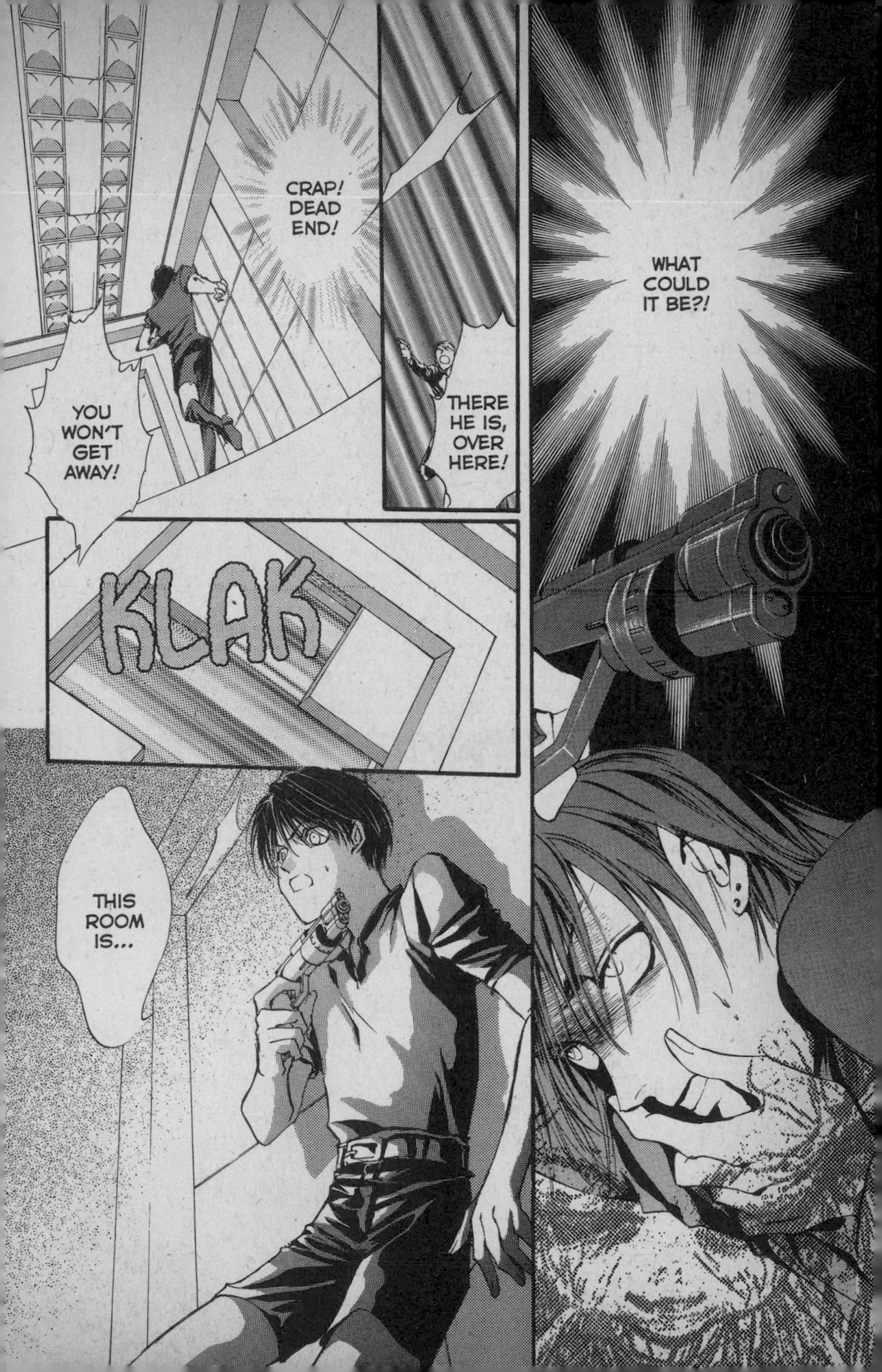
WHAT COULD IT BE?!
THERE HE IS, OVER HERE!
CRAP! DEAD END!
YOU WON'T GET AWAY!
KLAK
THIS ROOM IS...

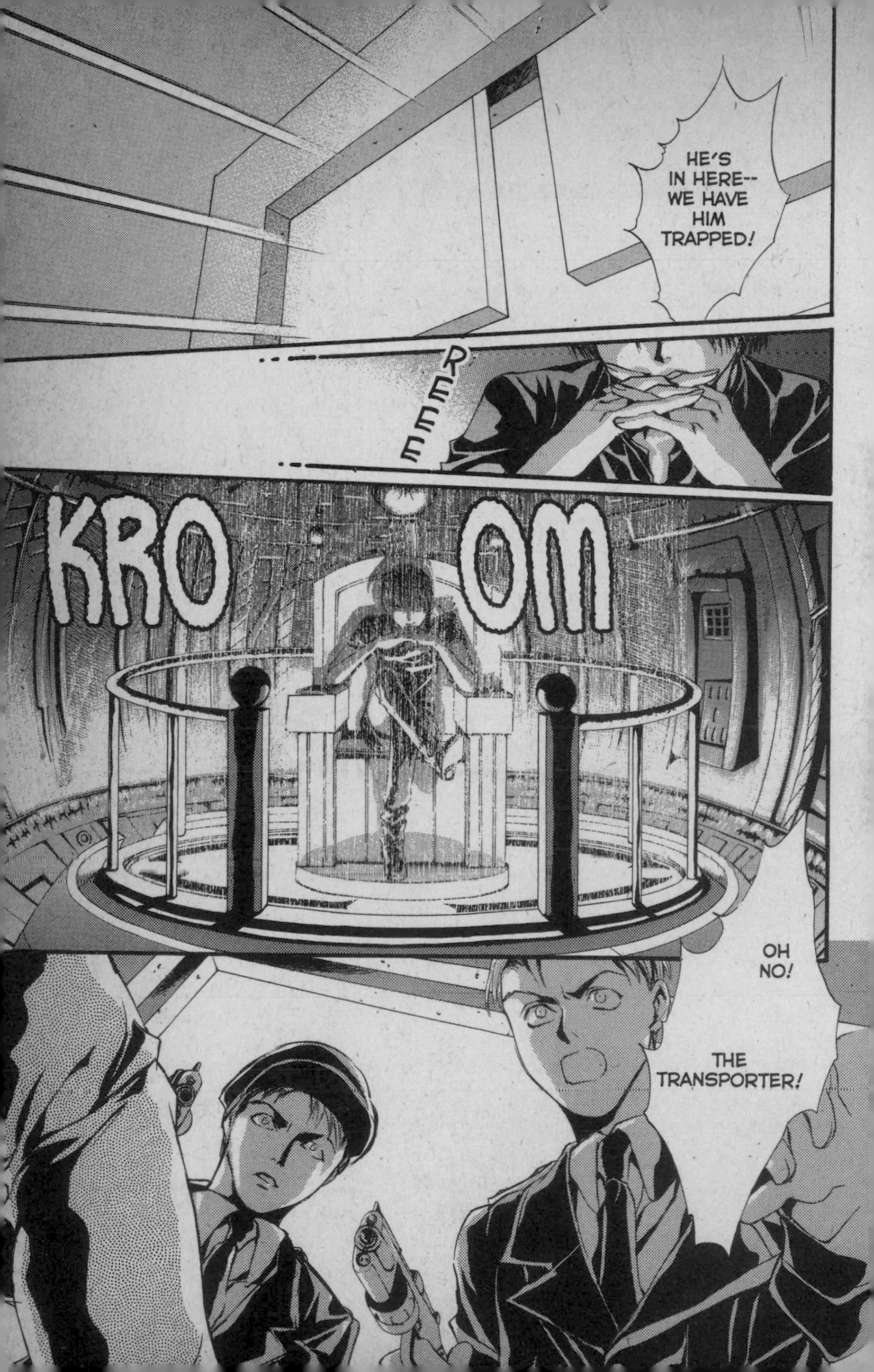
HE'S IN HERE-- WE HAVE HIM TRAPPED!
REEEE
KRO OM
OH NO!
THE TRANSPORTER!

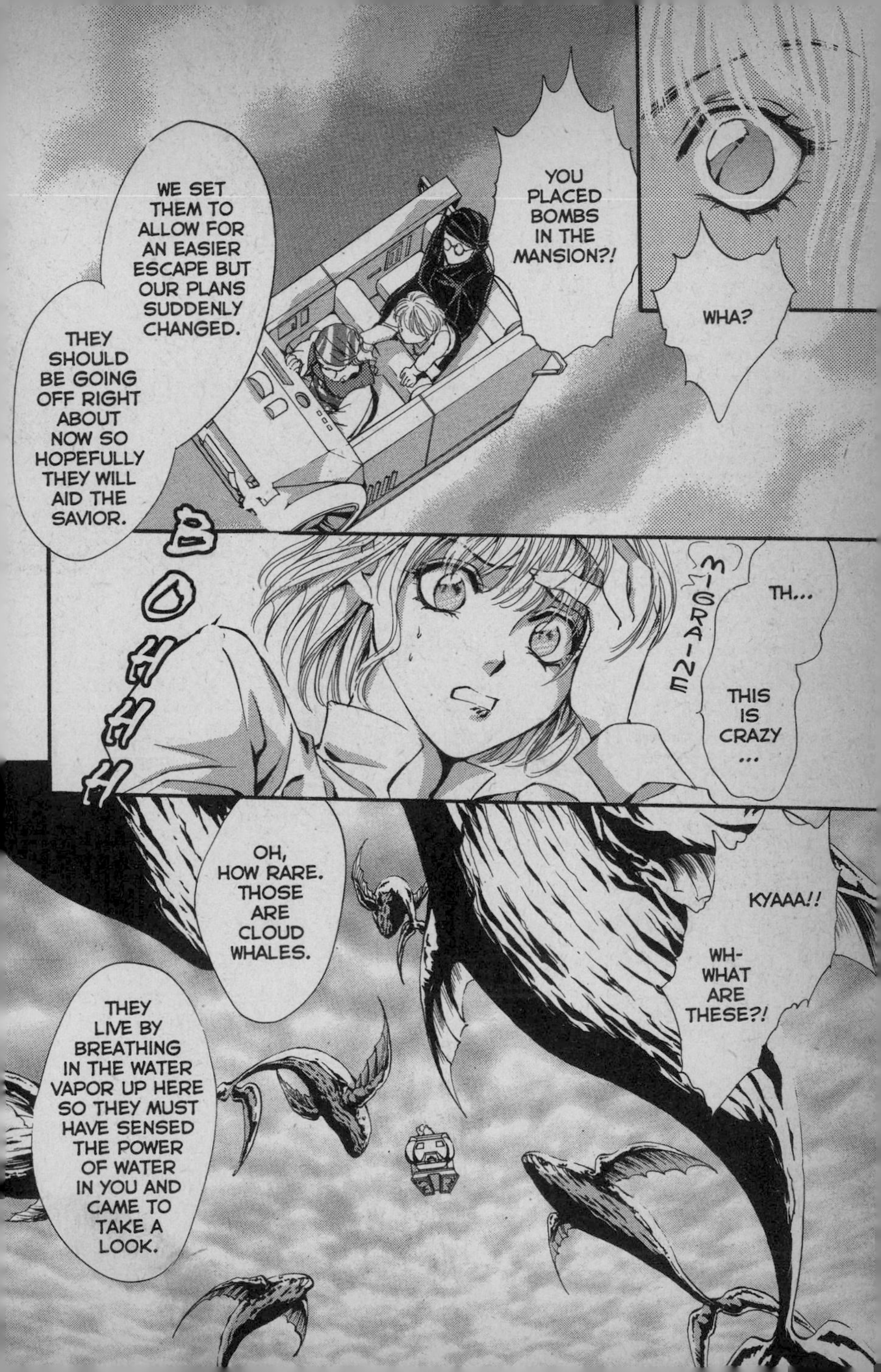
YOU PLACED BOMBS IN THE MANSION?!
WHA?
WE SET THEM TO ALLOW FOR AN EASIER ESCAPE BUT OUR PLANS SUDDENLY CHANGED.
THEY SHOULD BE GOING OFF RIGHT ABOUT NOW SO HOPEFULLY THEY WILL AID THE SAVIOR.
BOHHHH
TH...
THIS IS CRAZY ...
MIGRAINE
KYAAA!!
WH- WHAT ARE THESE?!
OH, HOW RARE. THOSE ARE CLOUD WHALES.
THEY LIVE BY BREATHING IN THE WATER VAPOR UP HERE SO THEY MUST HAVE SENSED THE POWER OF WATER IN YOU AND CAME TO TAKE A LOOK.

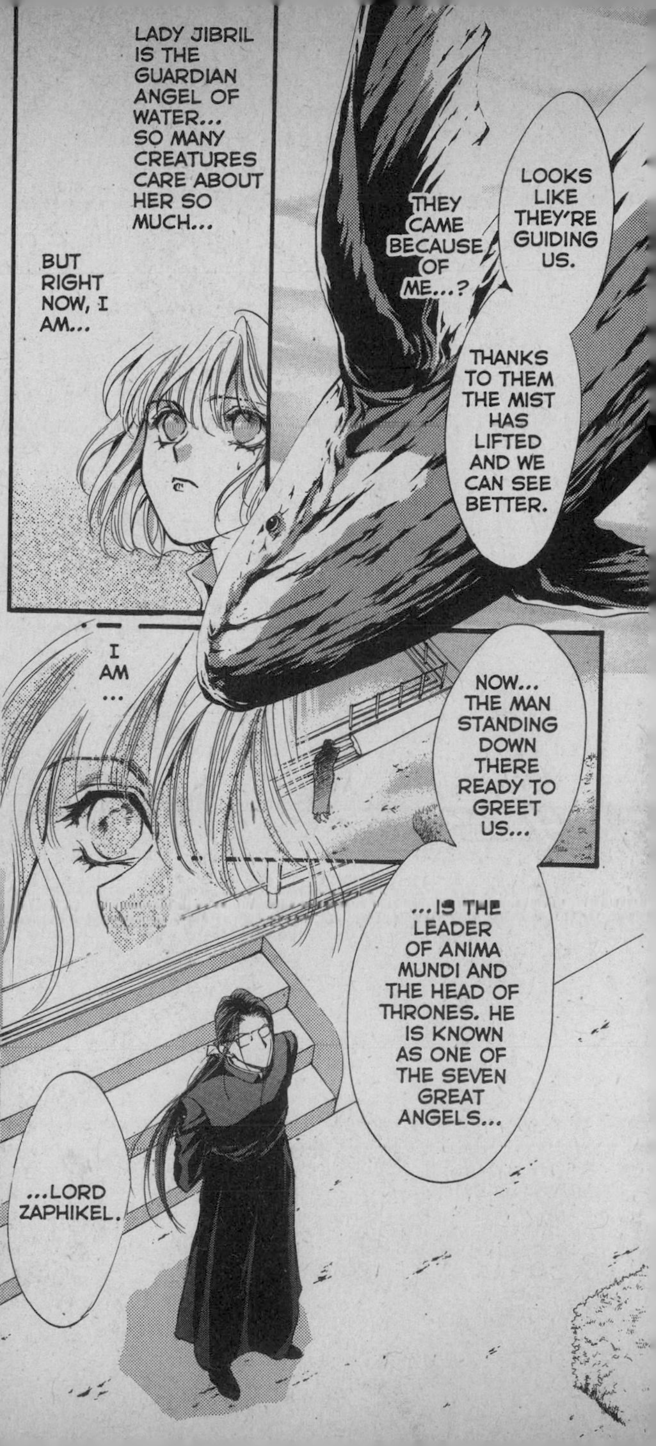
LOOKS LIKE THEY'RE GUIDING US.
THEY CAME BECAUSE OF ME...?
THANKS TO THEM THE MIST HAS LIFTED AND WE CAN SEE BETTER.
LADY JIBRIL IS THE GUARDIAN ANGEL OF WATER... SO MANY CREATURES CARE ABOUT HER SO MUCH...
BUT RIGHT NOW, I AM...
I AM ...
NOW... THE MAN STANDING DOWN THERE READY TO GREET US...
...IS THE LEADER OF ANIMA MUNDI AND THE HEAD OF THRONES. HE IS KNOWN AS ONE OF THE SEVEN GREAT ANGELS...
...LORD ZAPHIKEL.

I really liked the picture of Sevy at the beginning of this chapter but everyone hates him... Well, that's how I'm writing him so it's going exactly as planned... He really is hated! I guess some people do like him but it's a very small minority. Well, duh. Even if he was really good-looking, you can't tell because of the mask. Oh, the art from below is Kira who hasn't been appearing much at all lately. (Neither has Kato...) I'm not doing it on purpose--he should be appearing a lot in the next book. I forgot to add this to the popularity poll in the last book but first place Setsuna and second place Kira were really close in the voting. Kato was far behind in third. Kira really is popular. Can't go wrong with those good looks, I guess...

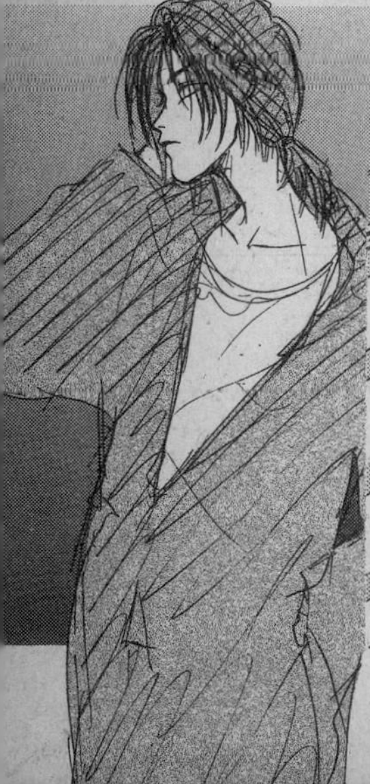

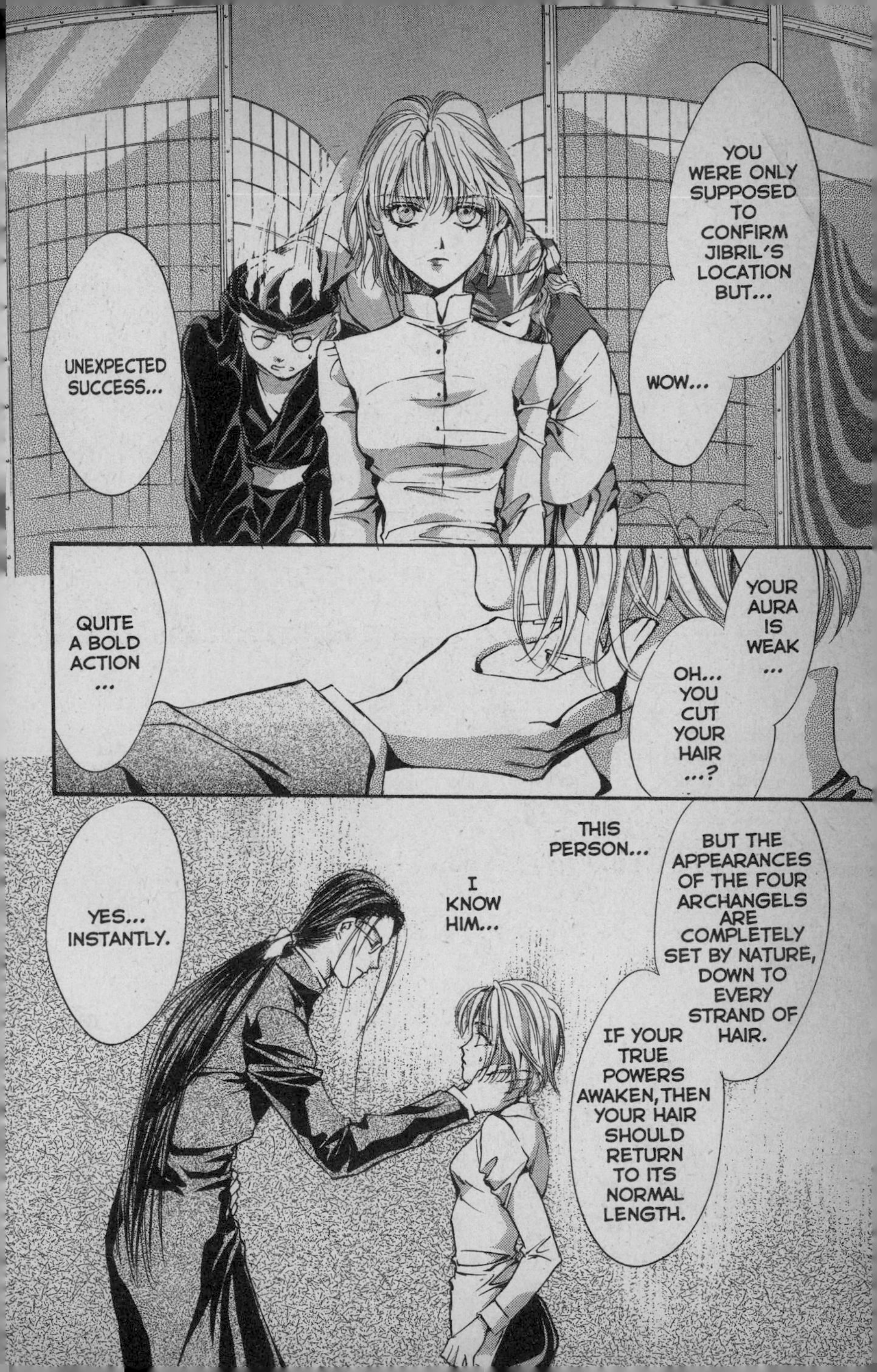
YOU WERE ONLY SUPPOSED TO CONFIRM JIBRIL'S LOCATION BUT...
WOW...
UNEXPECTED SUCCESS...
YOUR AURA IS WEAK...
OH... YOU CUT YOUR HAIR...?
QUITE A BOLD ACTION...
BUT THE APPEARANCES OF THE FOUR ARCHANGELS ARE COMPLETELY SET BY NATURE, DOWN TO EVERY STRAND OF HAIR.
IF YOUR TRUE POWERS AWAKEN, THEN YOUR HAIR SHOULD RETURN TO ITS NORMAL LENGTH.
THIS PERSON...
I KNOW HIM...
YES... INSTANTLY.

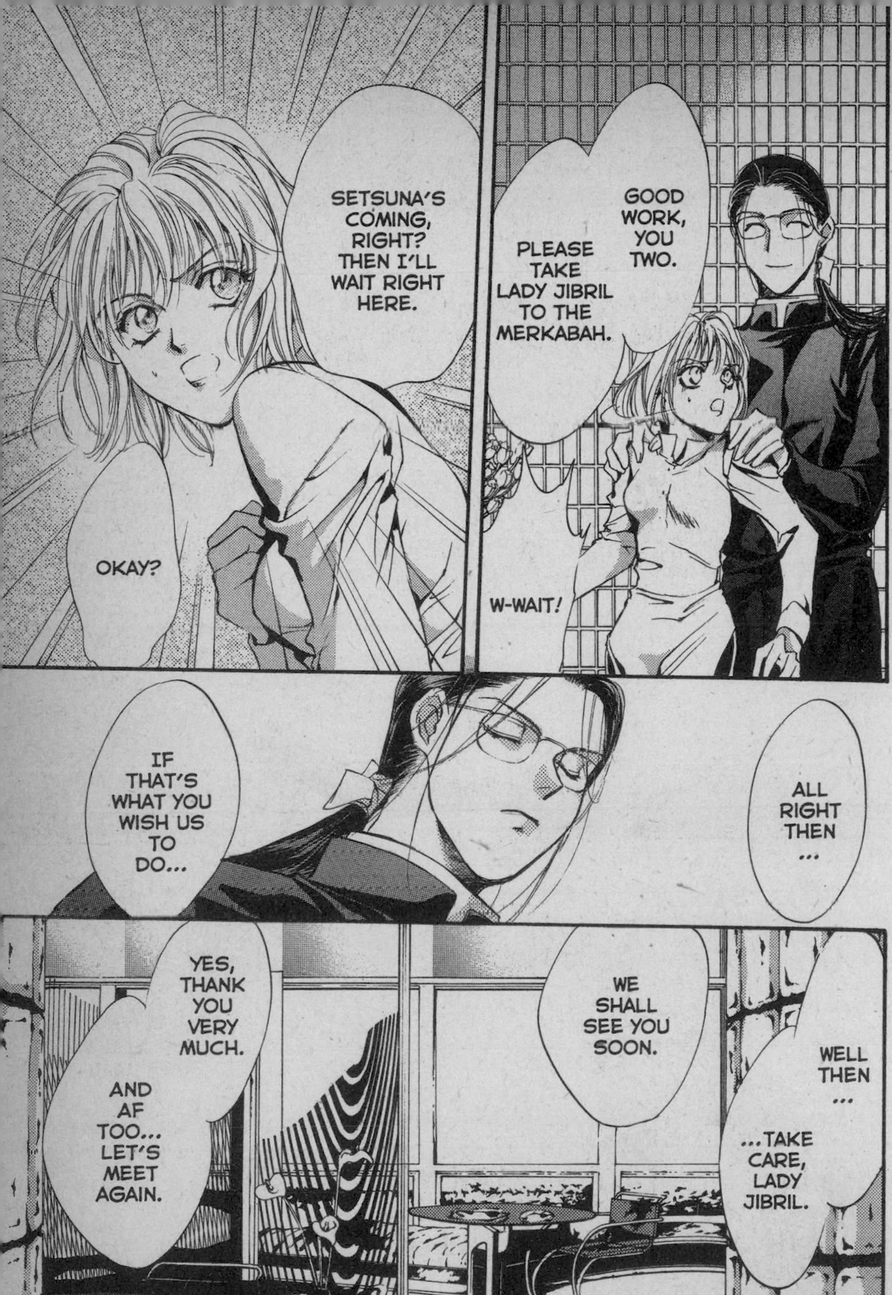
GOOD WORK, YOU TWO.
PLEASE TAKE LADY JIBRIL TO THE MERKABAH.
W-WAIT!
SETSUNA'S COMING, RIGHT? THEN I'LL WAIT RIGHT HERE.
OKAY?
ALL RIGHT THEN ...
IF THAT'S WHAT YOU WISH US TO DO...
WELL THEN ...
...TAKE CARE, LADY JIBRIL.
WE SHALL SEE YOU SOON.
YES, THANK YOU VERY MUCH.
AND AF TOO... LET'S MEET AGAIN.

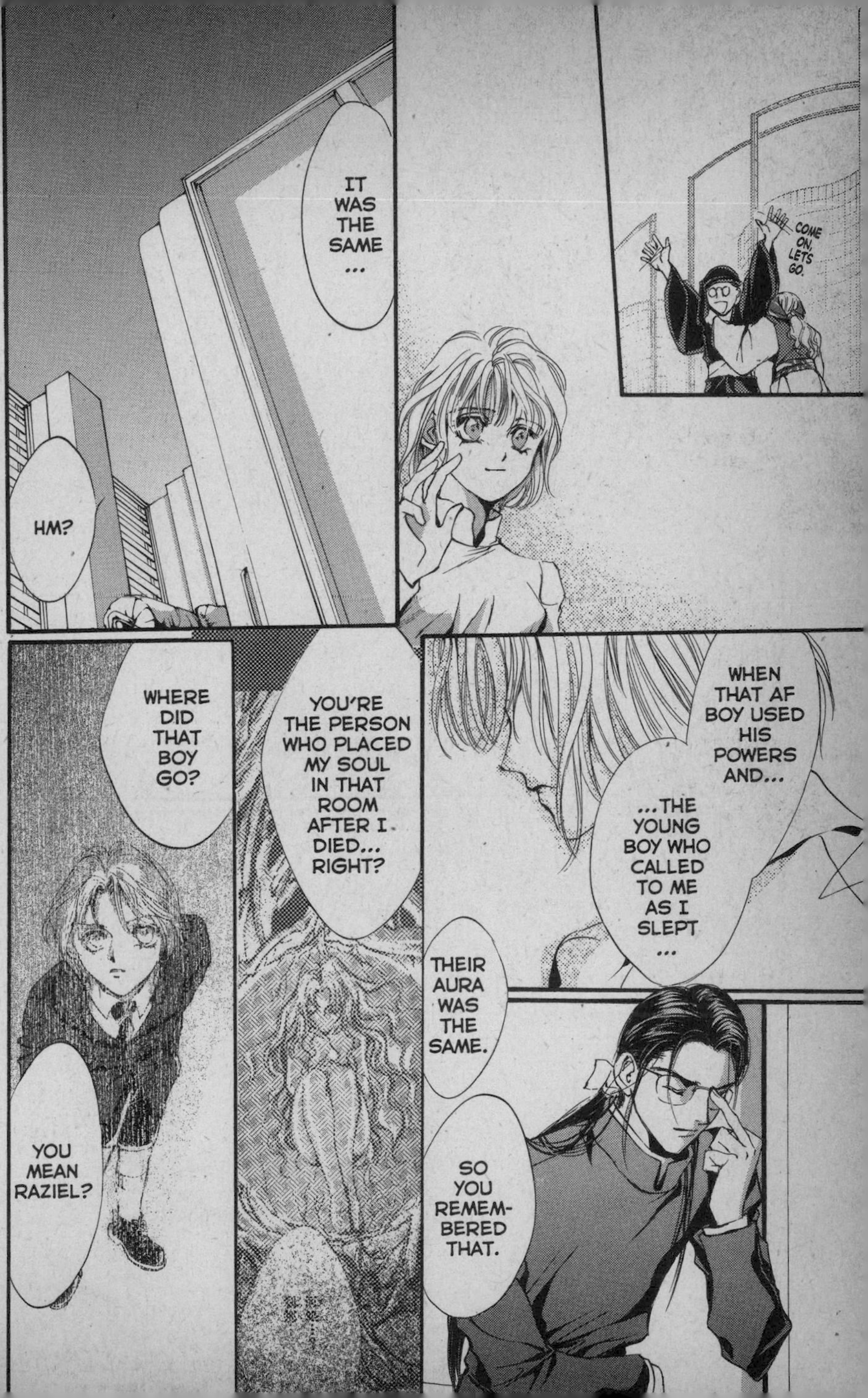
COME ON, LETS GO.
IT WAS THE SAME...
HM?
WHEN THAT AF BOY USED HIS POWERS AND...
...THE YOUNG BOY WHO CALLED TO ME AS I SLEPT...
THEIR AURA WAS THE SAME.
SO YOU REMEM-BERED THAT.
YOU'RE THE PERSON WHO PLACED MY SOUL IN THAT ROOM AFTER I DIED... RIGHT?
WHERE DID THAT BOY GO?
YOU MEAN RAZIEL?

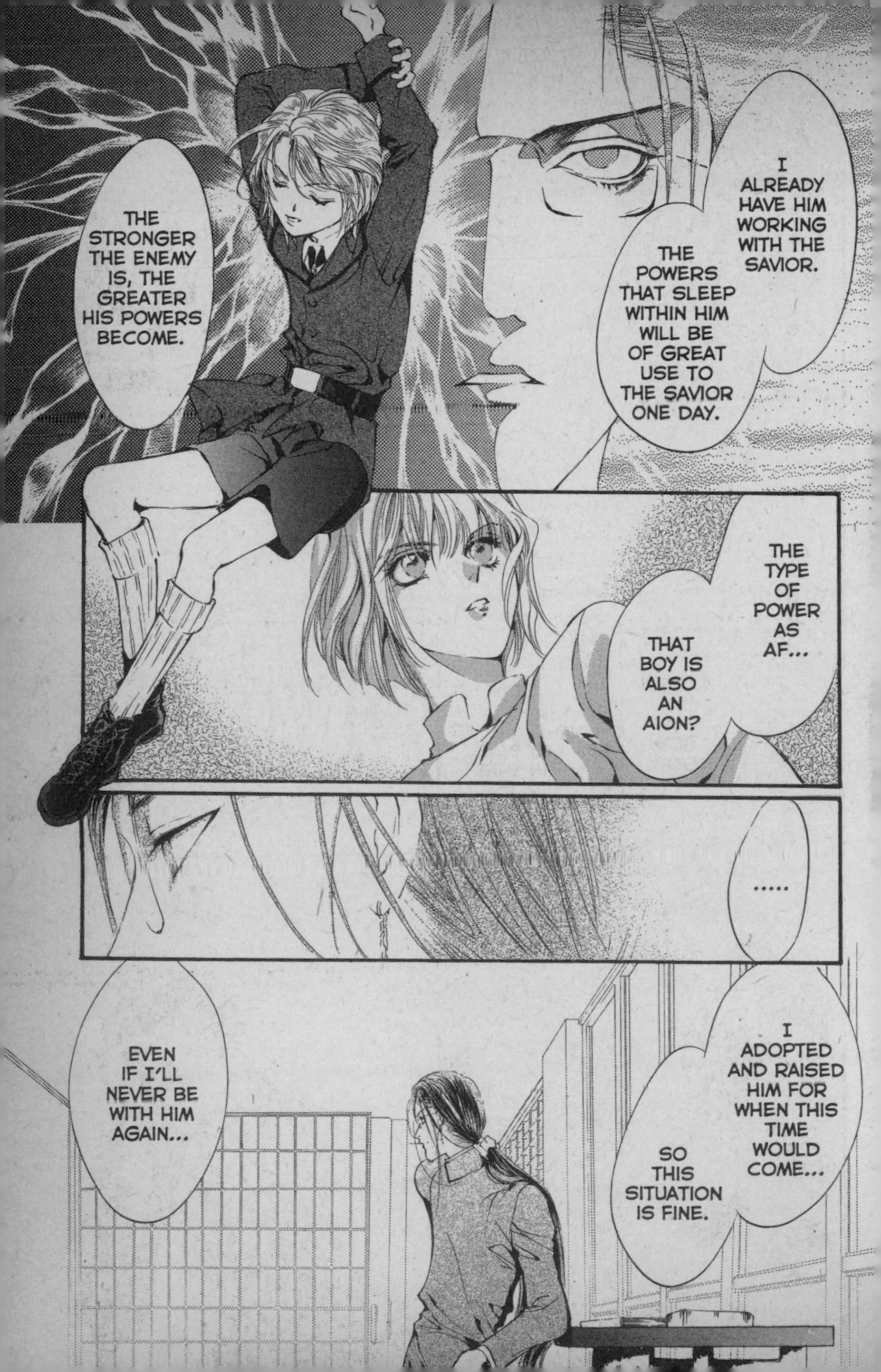
I ALREADY HAVE HIM WORKING WITH THE SAVIOR.
THE POWERS THAT SLEEP WITHIN HIM WILL BE OF GREAT USE TO THE SAVIOR ONE DAY.
THE STRONGER THE ENEMY IS, THE GREATER HIS POWERS BECOME.
THE TYPE OF POWER AS AF...
THAT BOY IS ALSO AN AION?
.....
I ADOPTED AND RAISED HIM FOR WHEN THIS TIME WOULD COME...
SO THIS SITUATION IS FINE.
EVEN IF I'LL NEVER BE WITH HIM AGAIN...

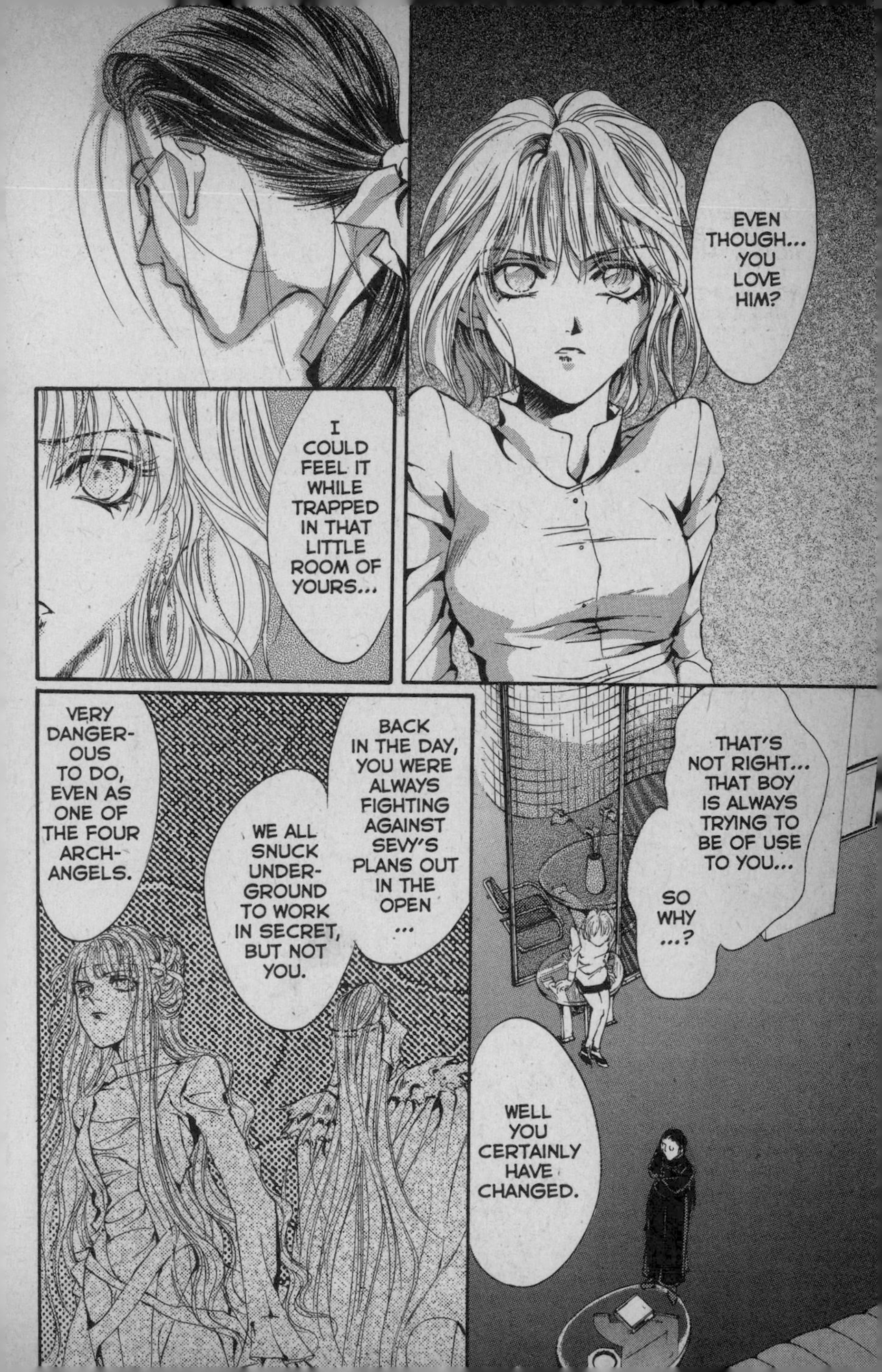
EVEN THOUGH... YOU LOVE HIM?
I COULD FEEL IT WHILE TRAPPED IN THAT LITTLE ROOM OF YOURS...
THAT'S NOT RIGHT... THAT BOY IS ALWAYS TRYING TO BE OF USE TO YOU...
SO WHY ...?
WELL YOU CERTAINLY HAVE CHANGED.
BACK IN THE DAY, YOU WERE ALWAYS FIGHTING AGAINST SEVY'S PLANS OUT IN THE OPEN ...
WE ALL SNUCK UNDER-GROUND TO WORK IN SECRET, BUT NOT YOU.
VERY DANGER-OUS TO DO, EVEN AS ONE OF THE FOUR ARCH-ANGELS.

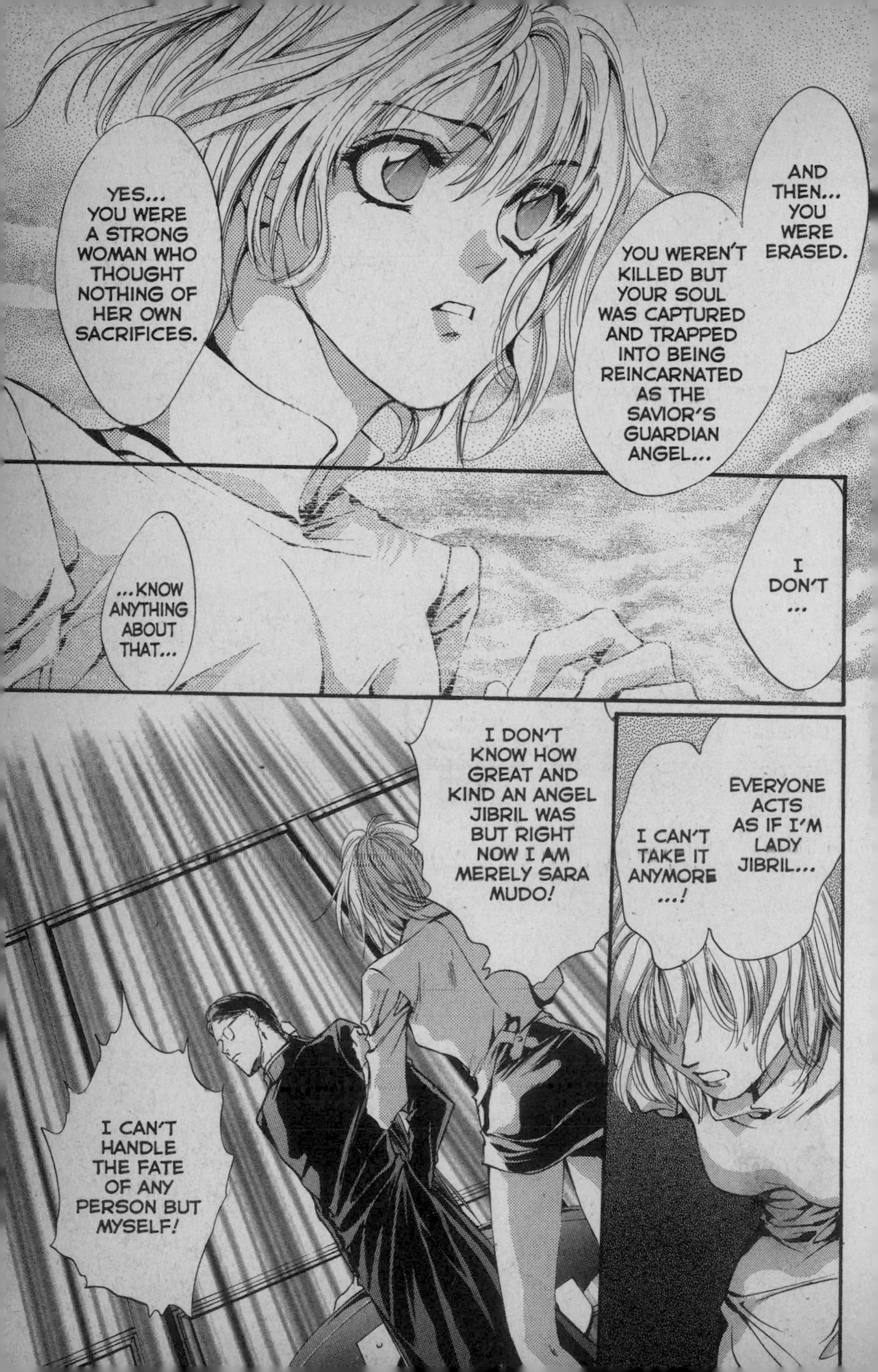
AND THEN... YOU WERE ERASED.
YOU WEREN'T KILLED BUT YOUR SOUL WAS CAPTURED AND TRAPPED INTO BEING REINCARNATED AS THE SAVIOR'S GUARDIAN ANGEL...
YES... YOU WERE A STRONG WOMAN WHO THOUGHT NOTHING OF HER OWN SACRIFICES.
I DON'T ...
...KNOW ANYTHING ABOUT THAT...
EVERYONE ACTS AS IF I'M LADY JIBRIL...
I CAN'T TAKE IT ANYMORE ...!
I DON'T KNOW HOW GREAT AND KIND AN ANGEL JIBRIL WAS BUT RIGHT NOW I AM MERELY SARA MUDO!
I CAN'T HANDLE THE FATE OF ANY PERSON BUT MYSELF!

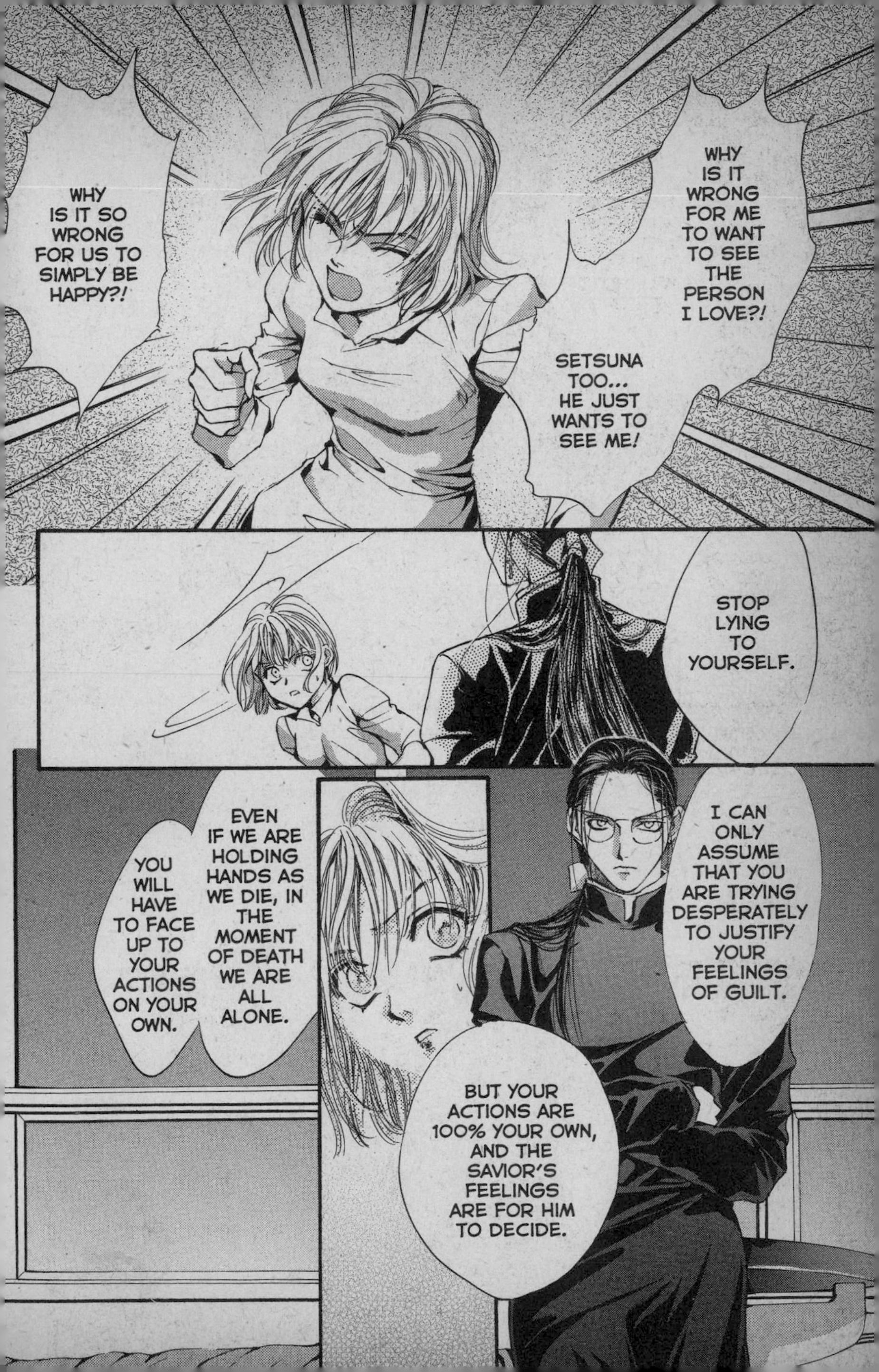
WHY IS IT WRONG FOR ME TO WANT TO SEE THE PERSON I LOVE?!
WHY IS IT SO WRONG FOR US TO SIMPLY BE HAPPY?!
SETSUNA TOO... HE JUST WANTS TO SEE ME!
STOP LYING TO YOURSELF.
I CAN ONLY ASSUME THAT YOU ARE TRYING DESPERATELY TO JUSTIFY YOUR FEELINGS OF GUILT.
BUT YOUR ACTIONS ARE 100% YOUR OWN, AND THE SAVIOR'S FEELINGS ARE FOR HIM TO DECIDE.
EVEN IF WE ARE HOLDING HANDS AS WE DIE, IN THE MOMENT OF DEATH WE ARE ALL ALONE.
YOU WILL HAVE TO FACE UP TO YOUR ACTIONS ON YOUR OWN.

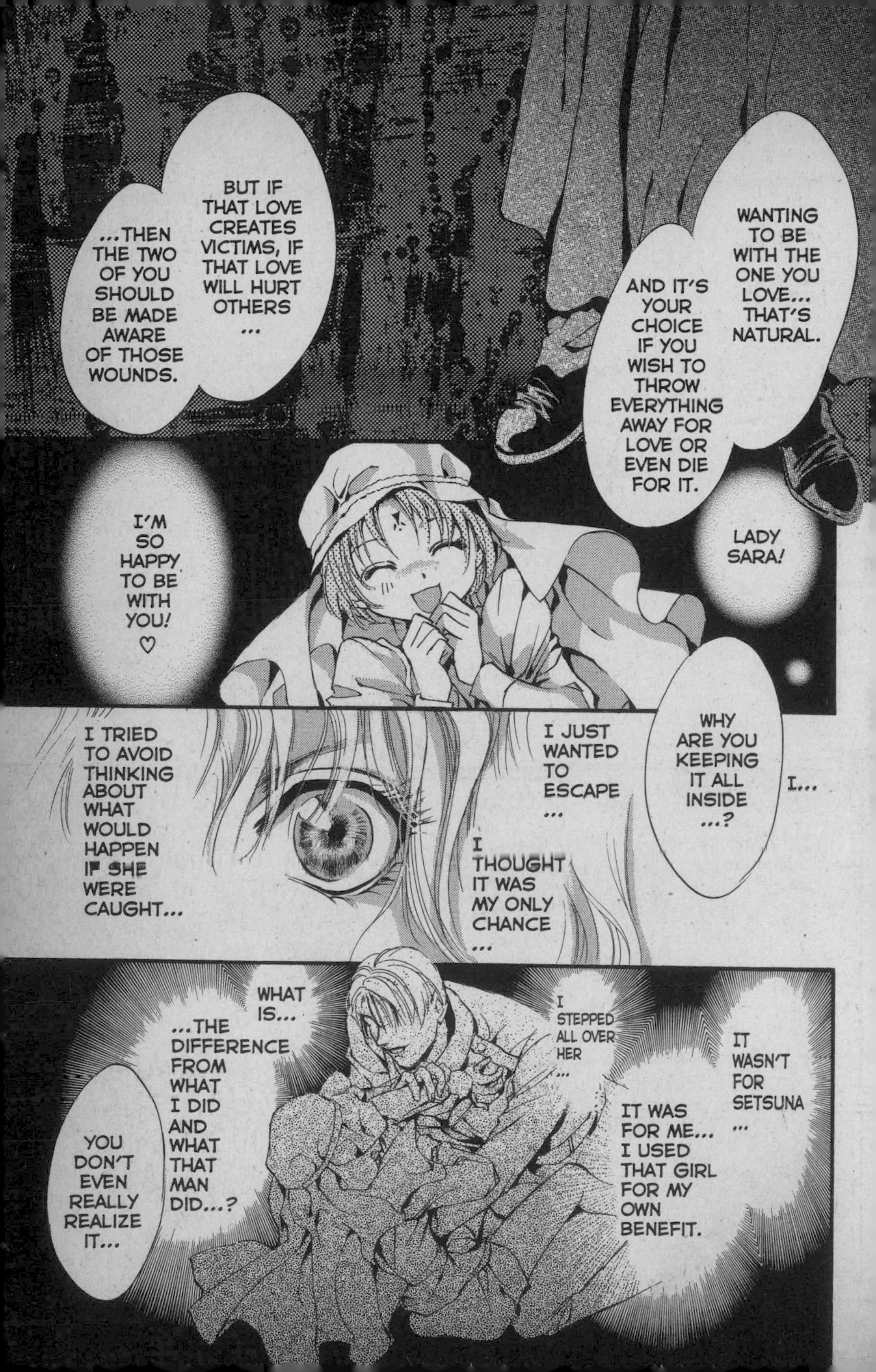
WANTING TO BE WITH THE ONE YOU LOVE... THAT'S NATURAL.
AND IT'S YOUR CHOICE IF YOU WISH TO THROW EVERYTHING AWAY FOR LOVE OR EVEN DIE FOR IT.
BUT IF THAT LOVE CREATES VICTIMS, IF THAT LOVE WILL HURT OTHERS ...
...THEN THE TWO OF YOU SHOULD BE MADE AWARE OF THOSE WOUNDS.
LADY SARA!
I'M SO HAPPY TO BE WITH YOU! ♡
I...
WHY ARE YOU KEEPING IT ALL INSIDE ...?
I JUST WANTED TO ESCAPE ...
I THOUGHT IT WAS MY ONLY CHANCE ...
I TRIED TO AVOID THINKING ABOUT WHAT WOULD HAPPEN IF SHE WERE CAUGHT...
IT WASN'T FOR SETSUNA ...
IT WAS FOR ME... I USED THAT GIRL FOR MY OWN BENEFIT.
I STEPPED ALL OVER HER ...
WHAT IS...
...THE DIFFERENCE FROM WHAT I DID AND WHAT THAT MAN DID...?
YOU DON'T EVEN REALLY REALIZE IT...

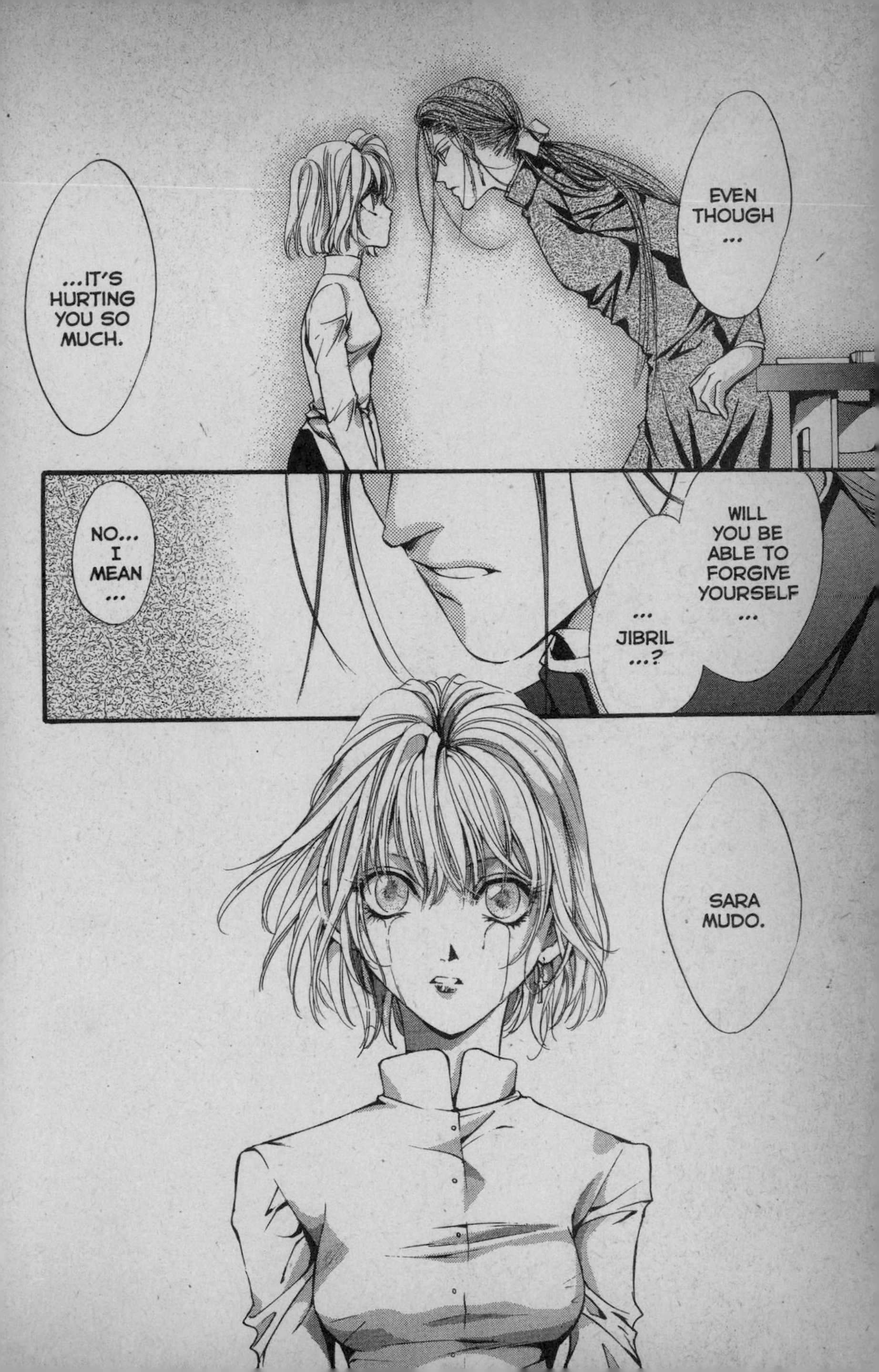
EVEN THOUGH ...
...IT'S HURTING YOU SO MUCH.
WILL YOU BE ABLE TO FORGIVE YOURSELF ... ... JIBRIL ...?
NO... I MEAN ...
SARA MUDO.

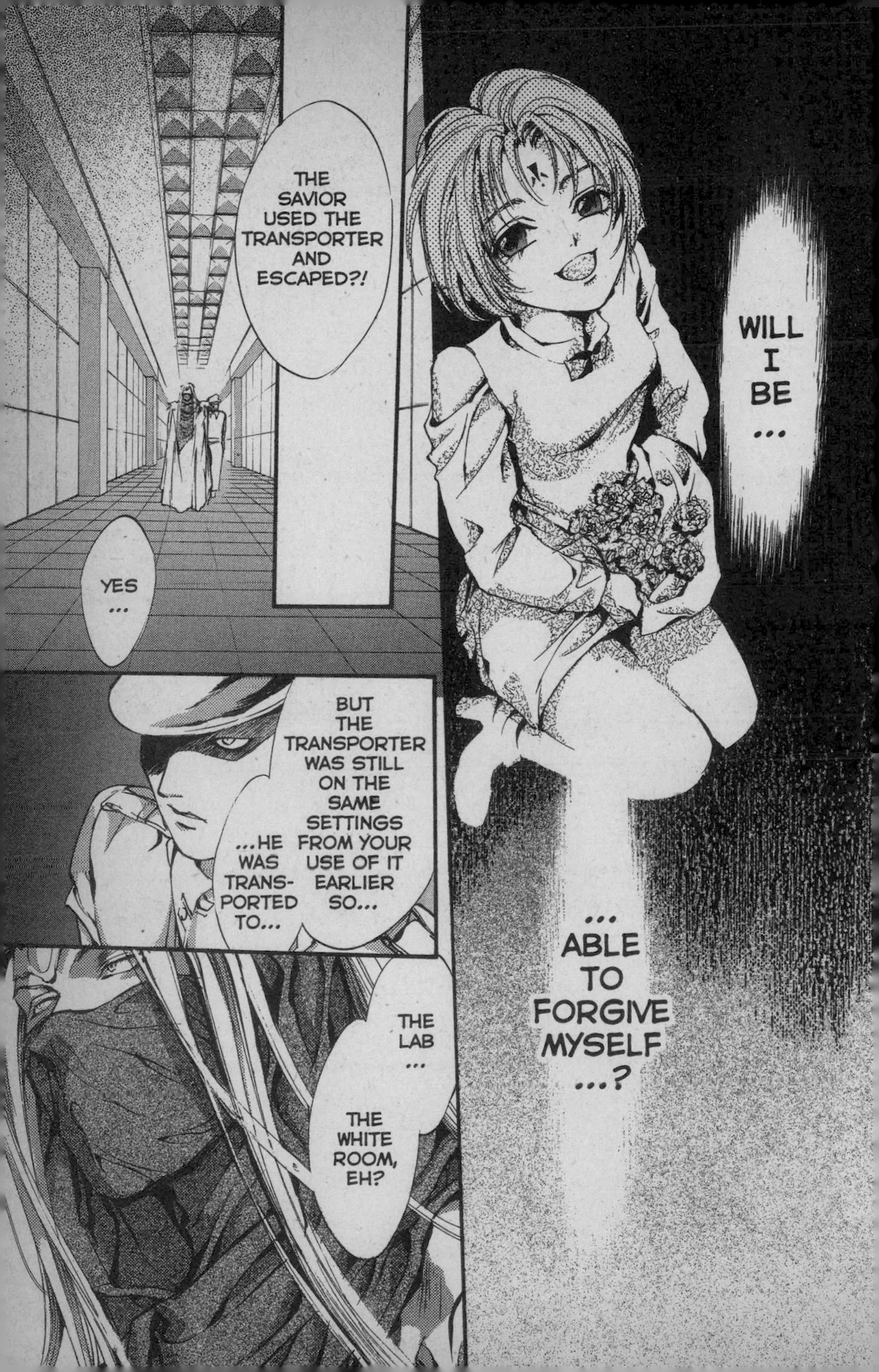
WILL I BE ...
... ABLE TO FORGIVE MYSELF ...?
THE SAVIOR USED THE TRANSPORTER AND ESCAPED?!
YES ...
BUT THE TRANSPORTER WAS STILL ON THE SAME SETTINGS FROM YOUR USE OF IT EARLIER SO...
...HE WAS TRANS-PORTED TO...
THE LAB ...
THE WHITE ROOM, EH?

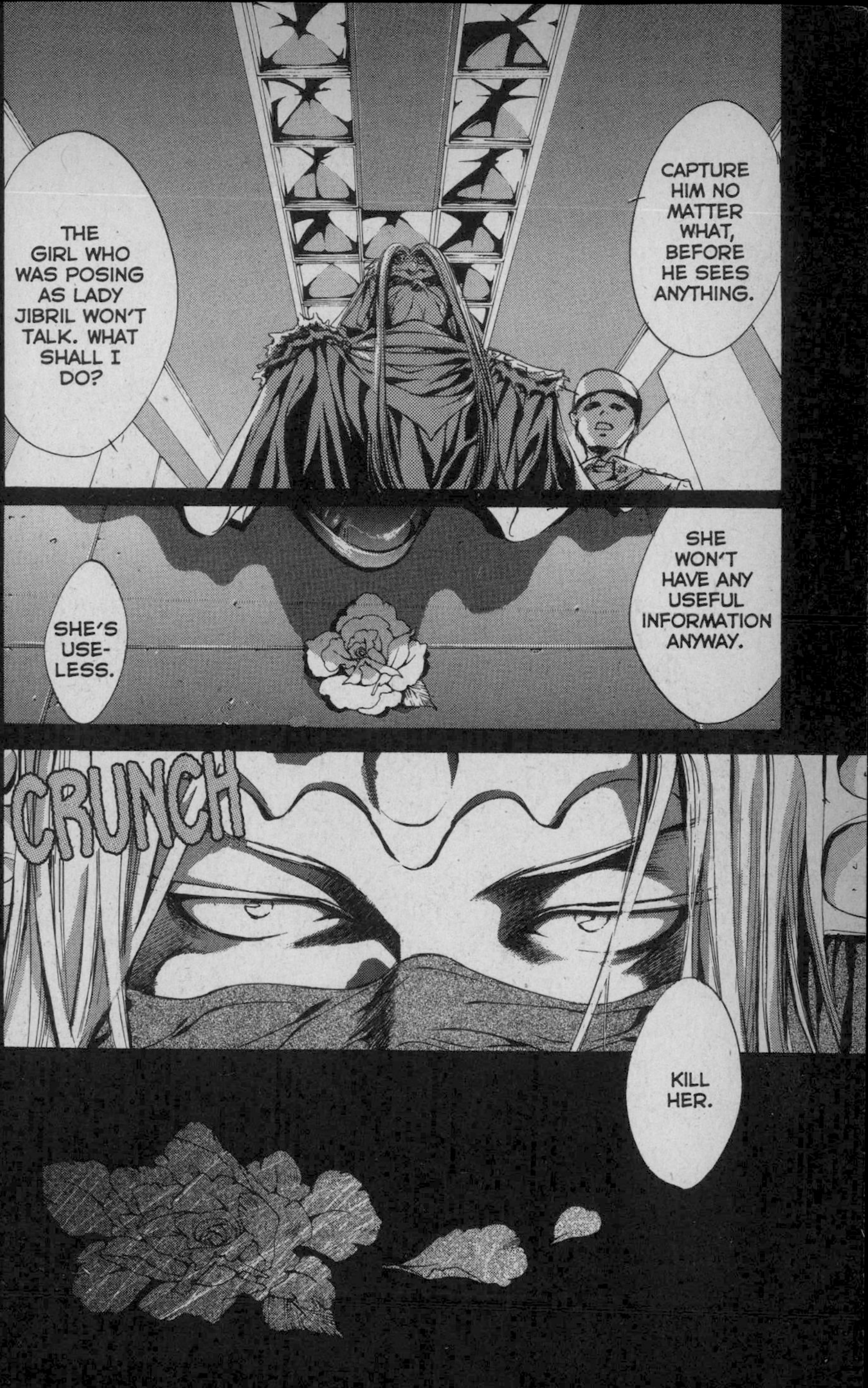
CAPTURE HIM NO MATTER WHAT, BEFORE HE SEES ANYTHING.
THE GIRL WHO WAS POSING AS LADY JIBRIL WON'T TALK. WHAT SHALL I DO?
SHE WON'T HAVE ANY USEFUL INFORMATION ANYWAY.
SHE'S USE-LESS.
CRUNCH
KILL HER.

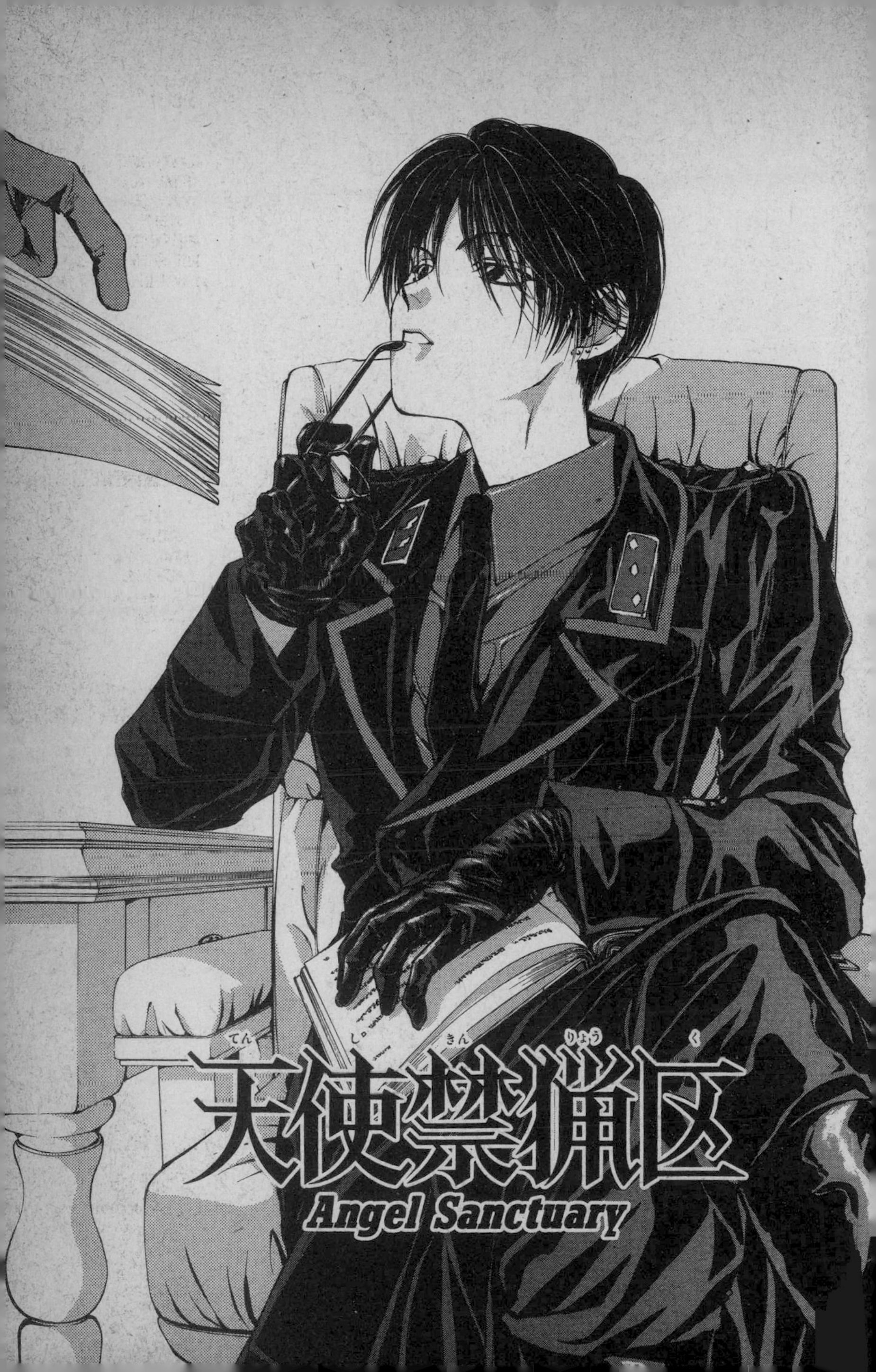
天使禁猟区
てんしきんりょうく
Angel Sanctuary

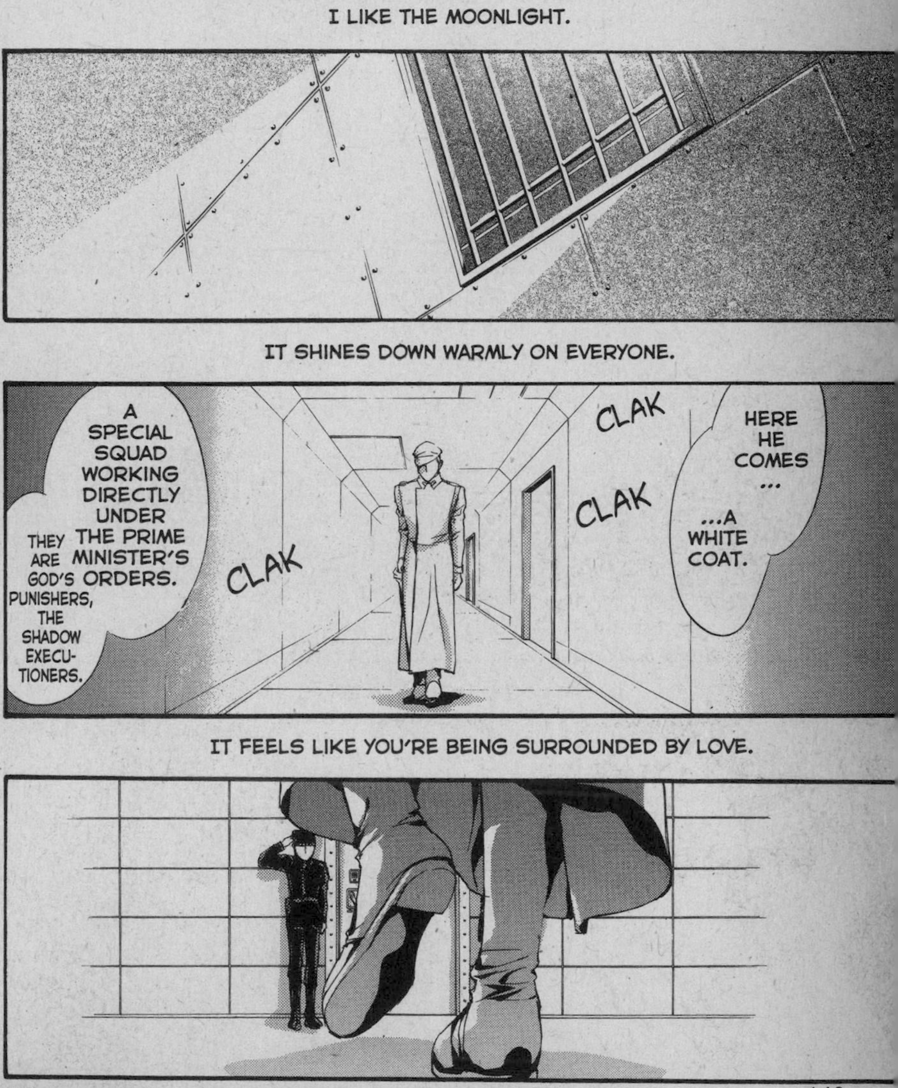
I LIKE THE MOONLIGHT.
IT SHINES DOWN WARMLY ON EVERYONE.
HERE HE COMES... ...A WHITE COAT.
CLAK
CLAK
CLAK
A SPECIAL SQUAD WORKING DIRECTLY UNDER THE PRIME MINISTER'S ORDERS.
THEY ARE GOD'S PUNISHERS, THE SHADOW EXECUTIONERS.
IT FEELS LIKE YOU'RE BEING SURROUNDED BY LOVE.

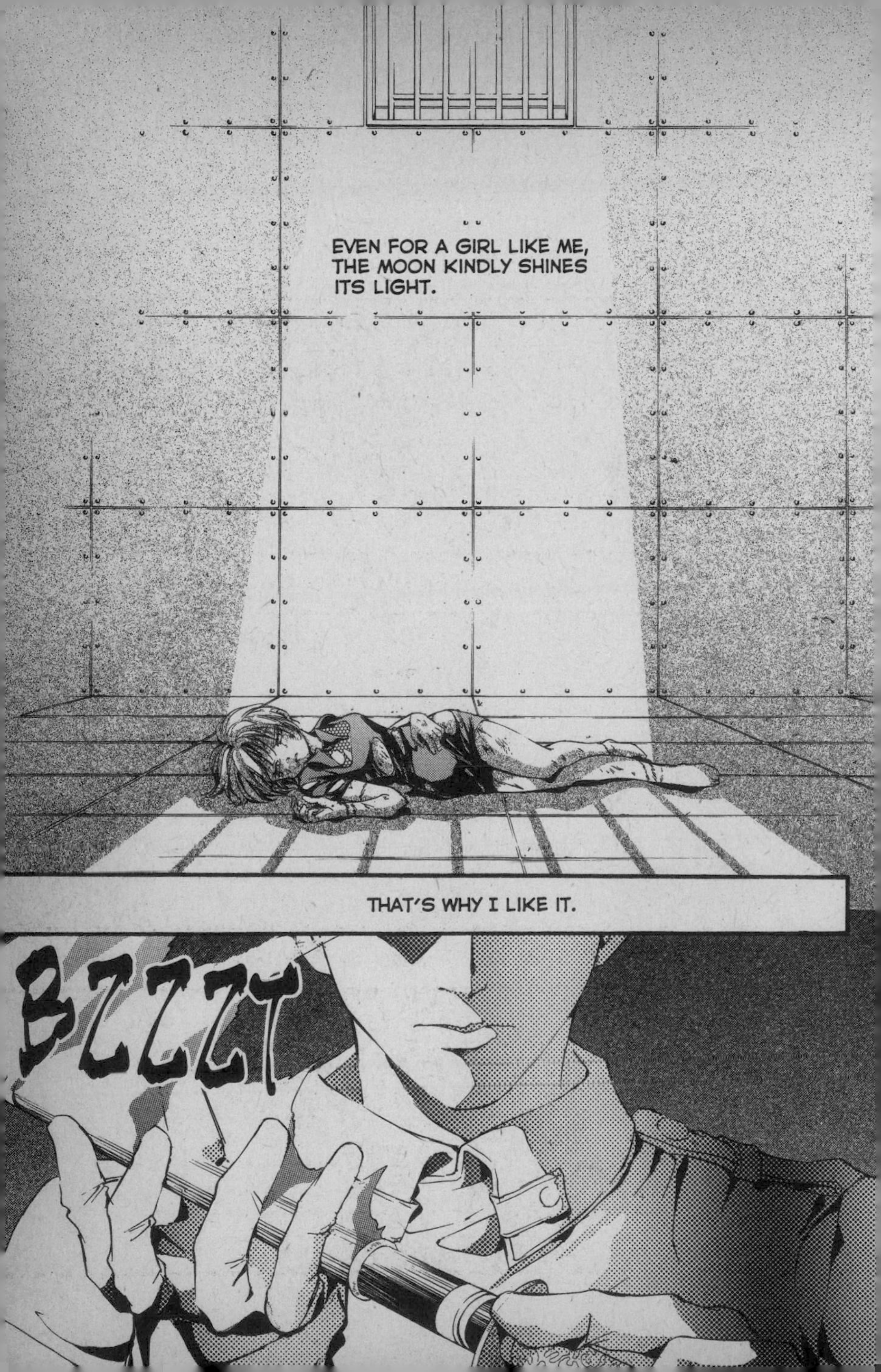
EVEN FOR A GIRL LIKE ME, THE MOON KINDLY SHINES ITS LIGHT.
THAT'S WHY I LIKE IT.
BZZZT

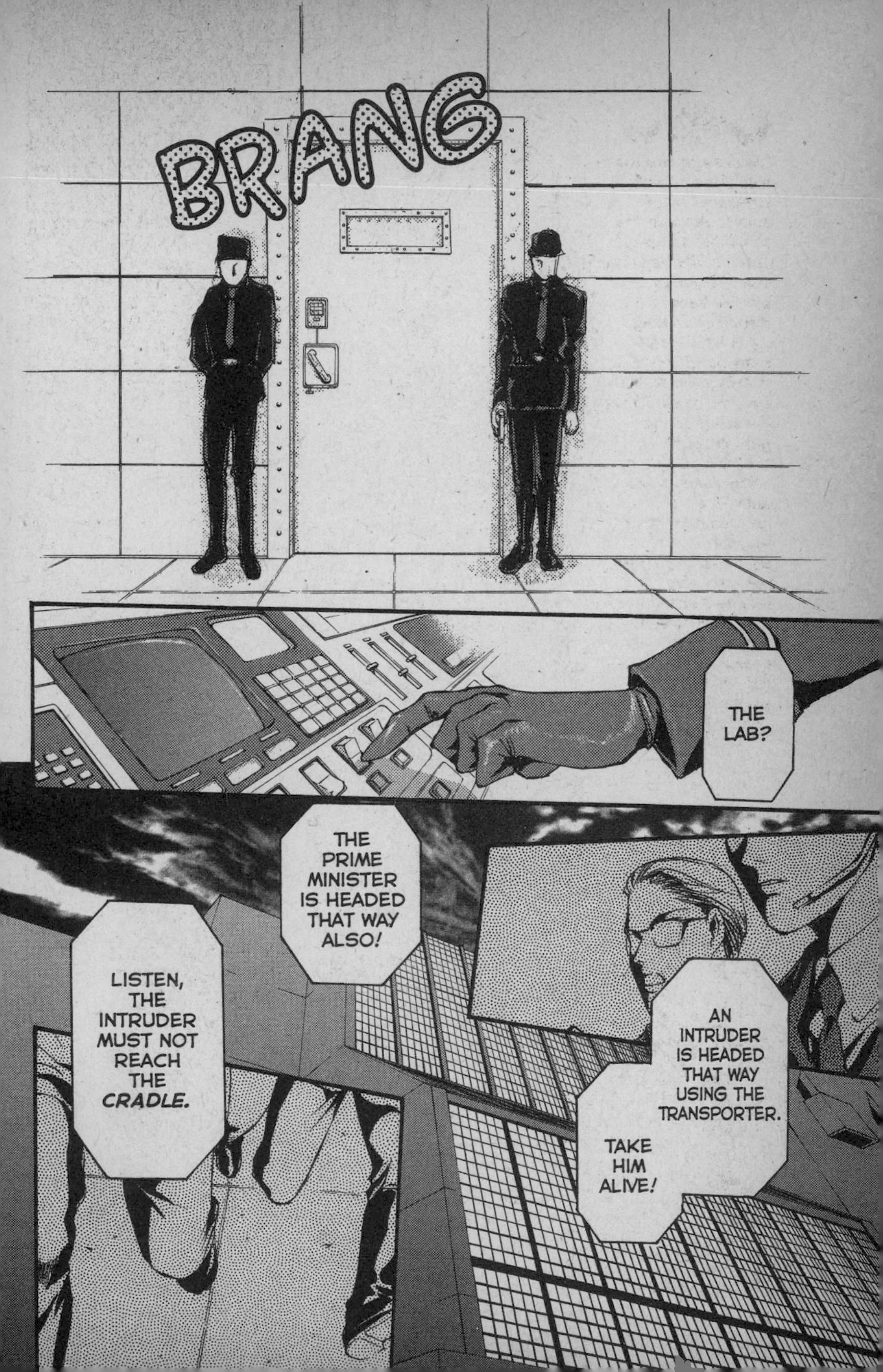
BRANG
THE LAB?
AN INTRUDER IS HEADED THAT WAY USING THE TRANSPORTER.
TAKE HIM ALIVE!
THE PRIME MINISTER IS HEADED THAT WAY ALSO!
LISTEN, THE INTRUDER MUST NOT REACH THE *CRADLE.*

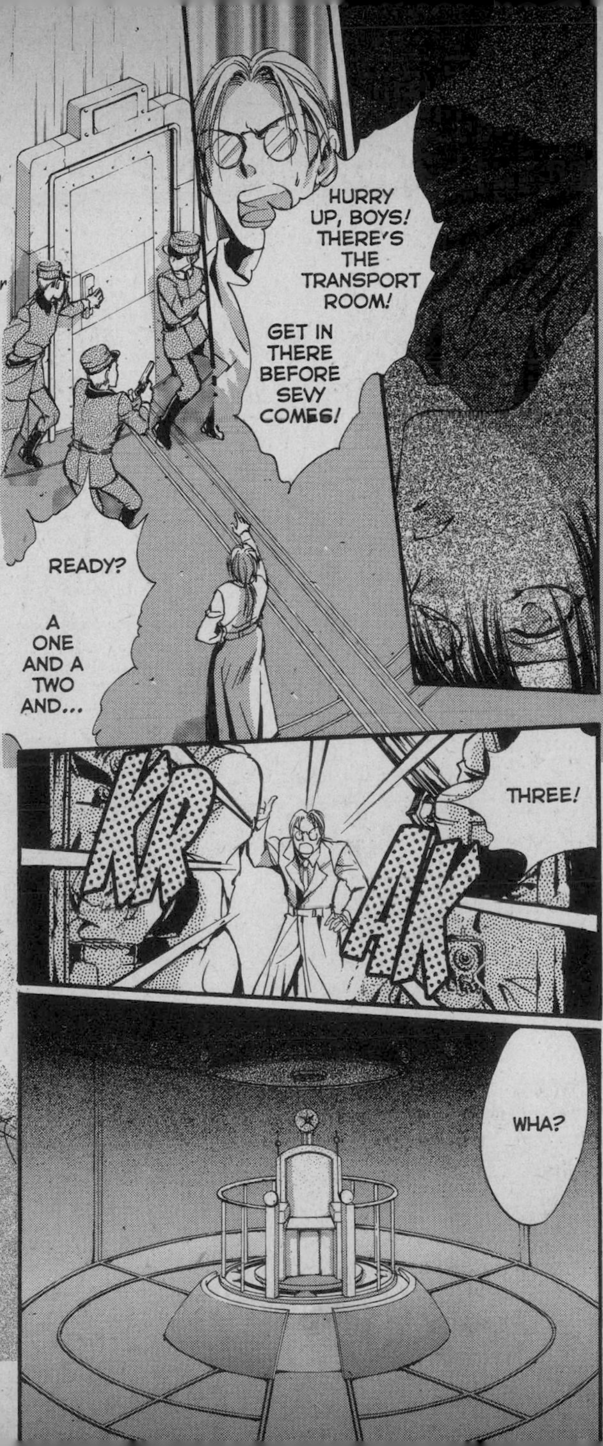
HURRY UP, BOYS! THERE'S THE TRANSPORT ROOM!
GET IN THERE BEFORE SEVY COMES!
READY?
A ONE AND A TWO AND...
THREE!
KRAK
WHA?

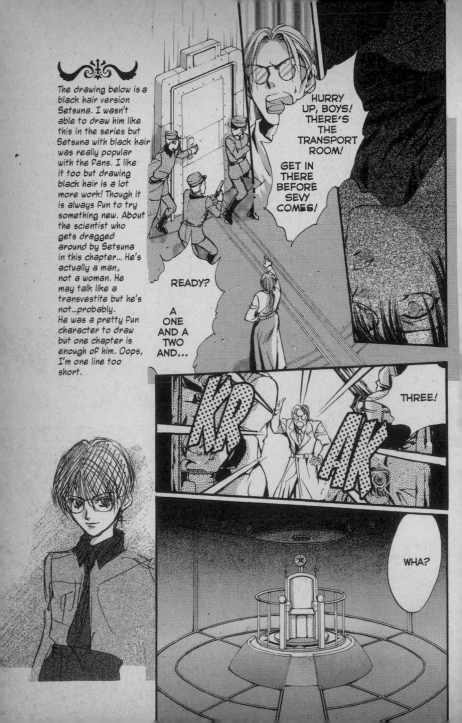

The drawing below is a black hair version Setsuna. I wasn't able to draw him like this in the series but Setsuna with black hair was really popular with the fans. I like it too but drawing black hair is a lot more work! Though it is always fun to try something new. About the scientist who gets dragged around by Setsuna in this chapter... He's actually a man, not a woman. He may talk like a transvestite but he's not...probably. He was a pretty fun character to draw but one chapter is enough of him. Oops, I'm one line too short.

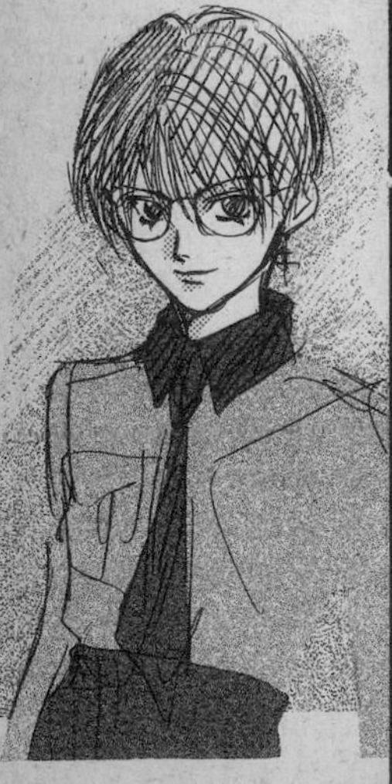

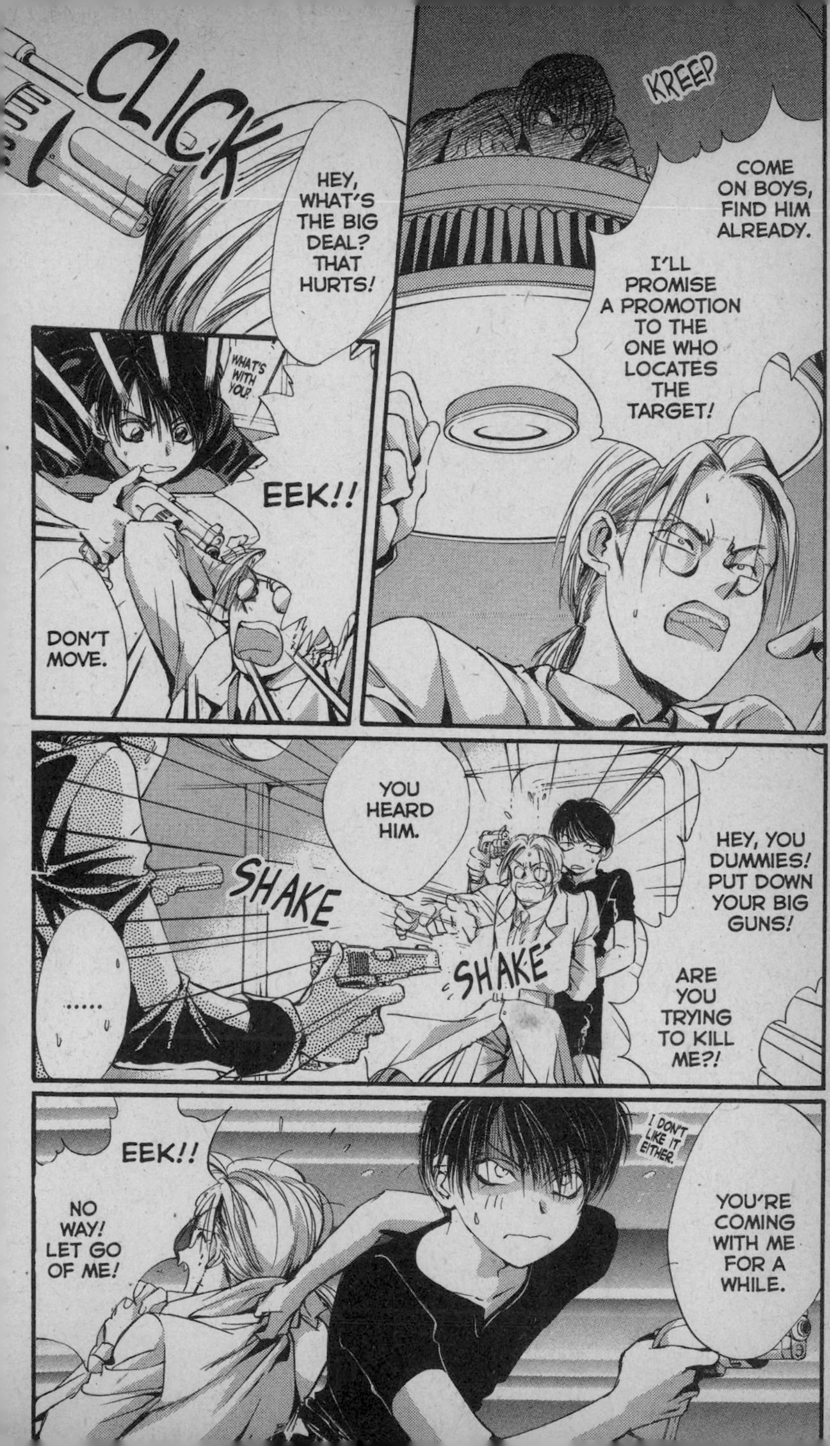
KREEP
COME ON BOYS, FIND HIM ALREADY.
I'LL PROMISE A PROMOTION TO THE ONE WHO LOCATES THE TARGET!
CLICK
HEY, WHAT'S THE BIG DEAL? THAT HURTS!
WHAT'S WITH YOU?
EEK!!
DON'T MOVE.
HEY, YOU DUMMIES! PUT DOWN YOUR BIG GUNS!
ARE YOU TRYING TO KILL ME?!
SHAKE
YOU HEARD HIM.
SHAKE
.....
YOU'RE COMING WITH ME FOR A WHILE.
I DON'T LIKE IT EITHER.
EEK!!
NO WAY! LET GO OF ME!

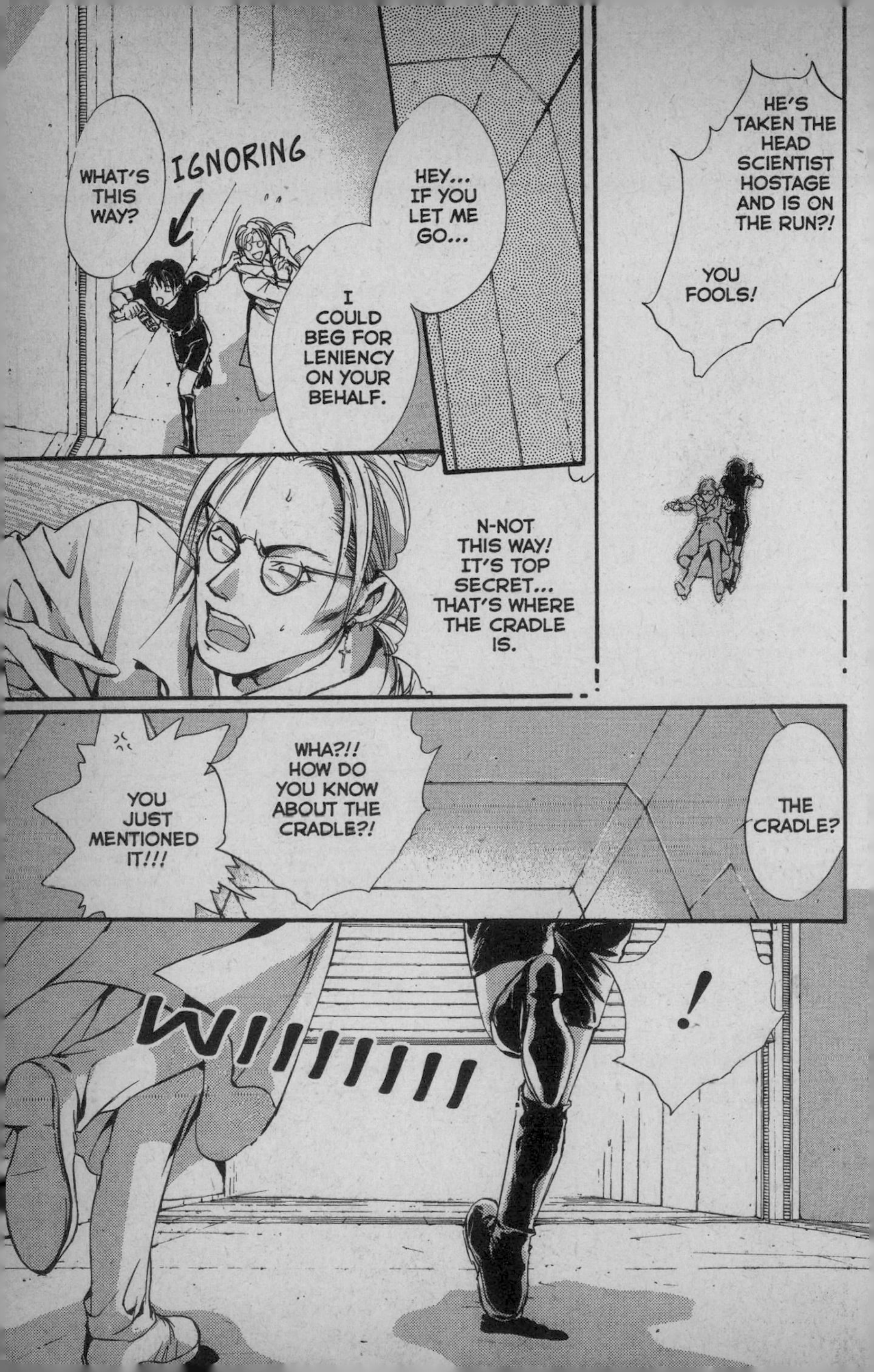
HE'S TAKEN THE HEAD SCIENTIST HOSTAGE AND IS ON THE RUN?!
YOU FOOLS!
HEY... IF YOU LET ME GO...
I COULD BEG FOR LENIENCY ON YOUR BEHALF.
IGNORING
WHAT'S THIS WAY?
N-NOT THIS WAY! IT'S TOP SECRET... THAT'S WHERE THE CRADLE IS.
THE CRADLE?
WHA?!! HOW DO YOU KNOW ABOUT THE CRADLE?!
YOU JUST MENTIONED IT!!!
!
WIIIIIIII

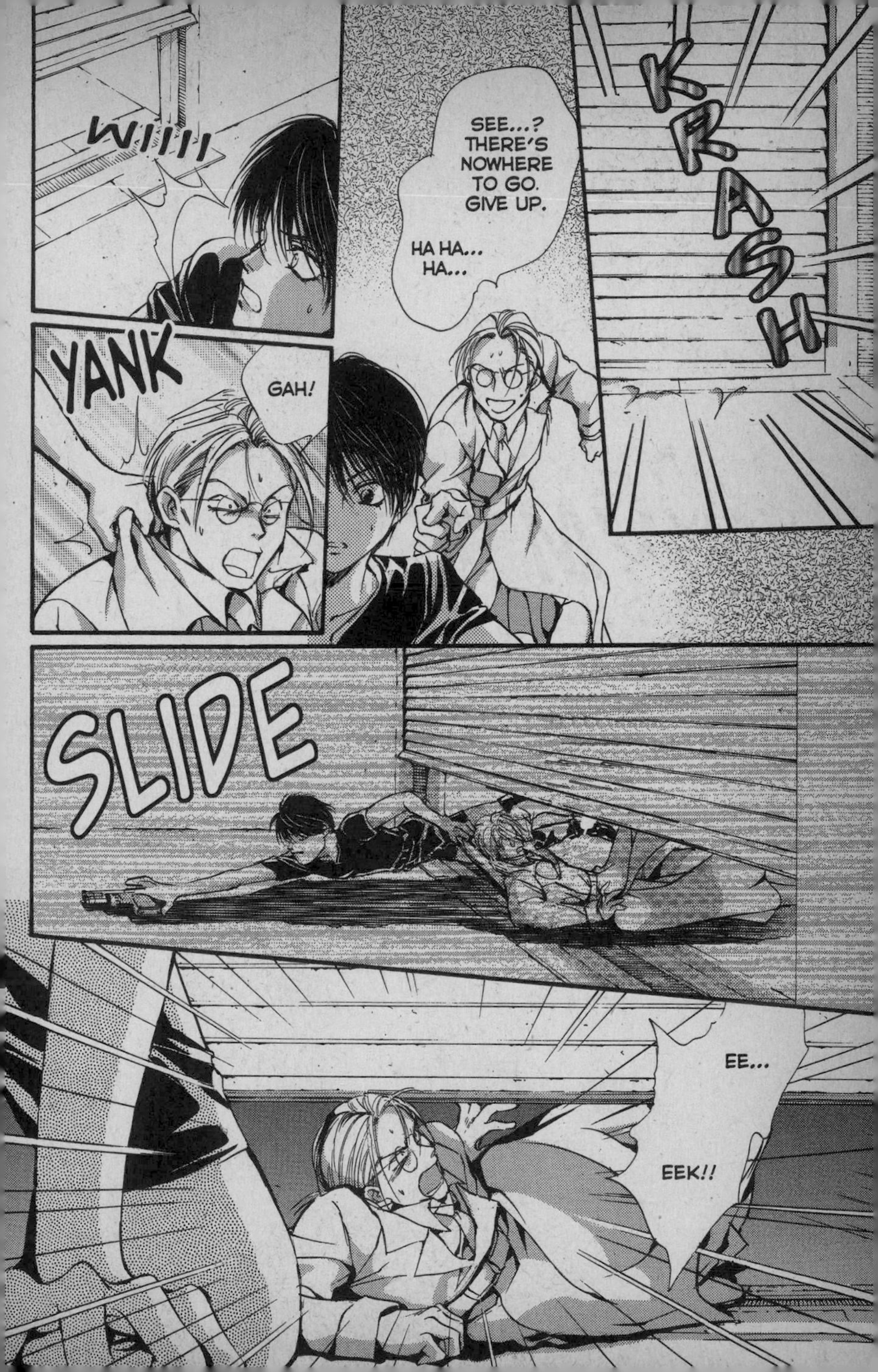
KRASH
SEE...? THERE'S NOWHERE TO GO. GIVE UP.
HA HA... HA...
WIIII
GAH!
YANK
SLIDE
EE...
EEK!!

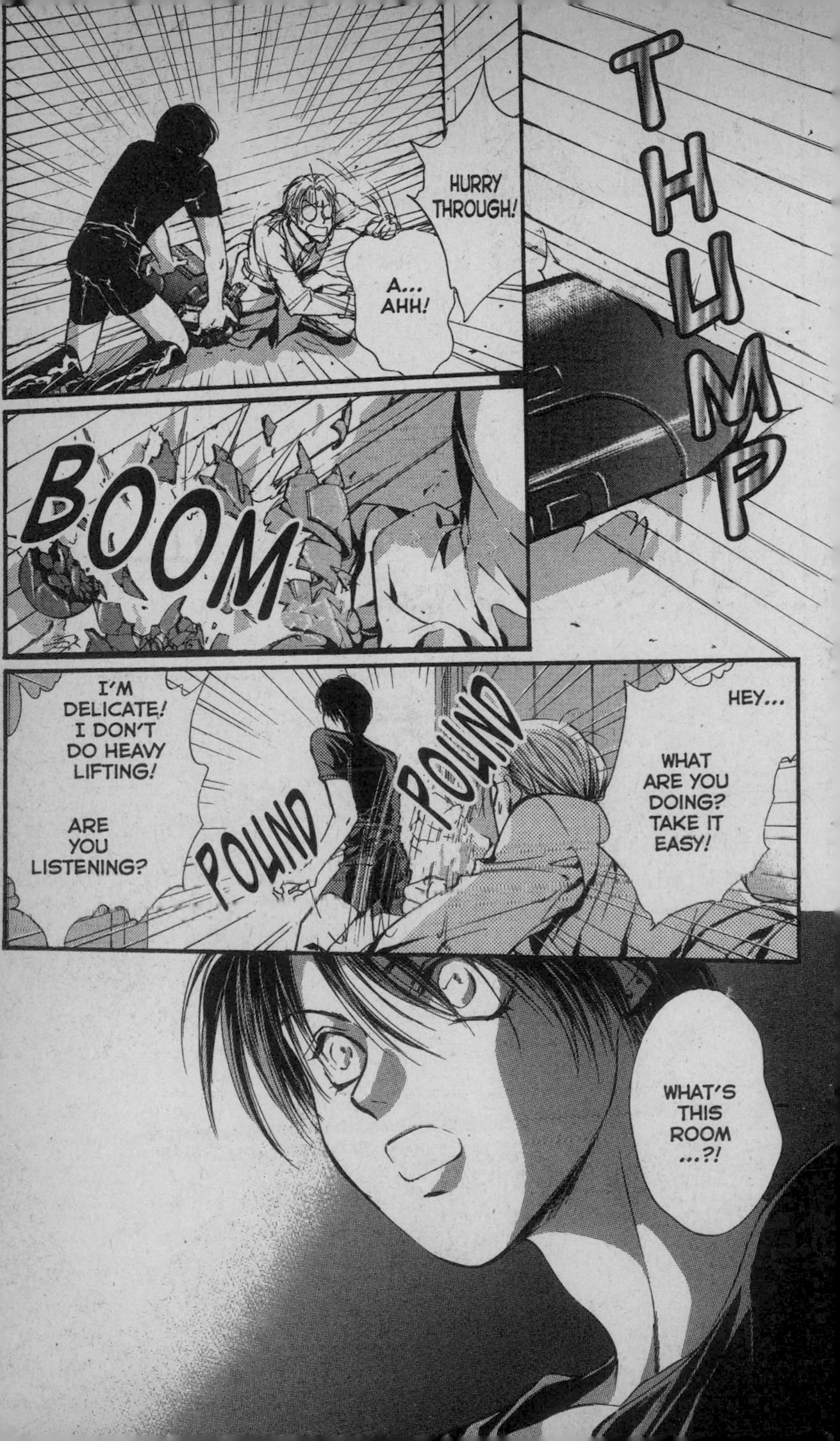
THUMP
HURRY THROUGH!
A... AHH!
BOOM
HEY...
WHAT ARE YOU DOING? TAKE IT EASY!
POUND
POUND
I'M DELICATE! I DON'T DO HEAVY LIFTING!
ARE YOU LISTENING?
WHAT'S THIS ROOM ...?!

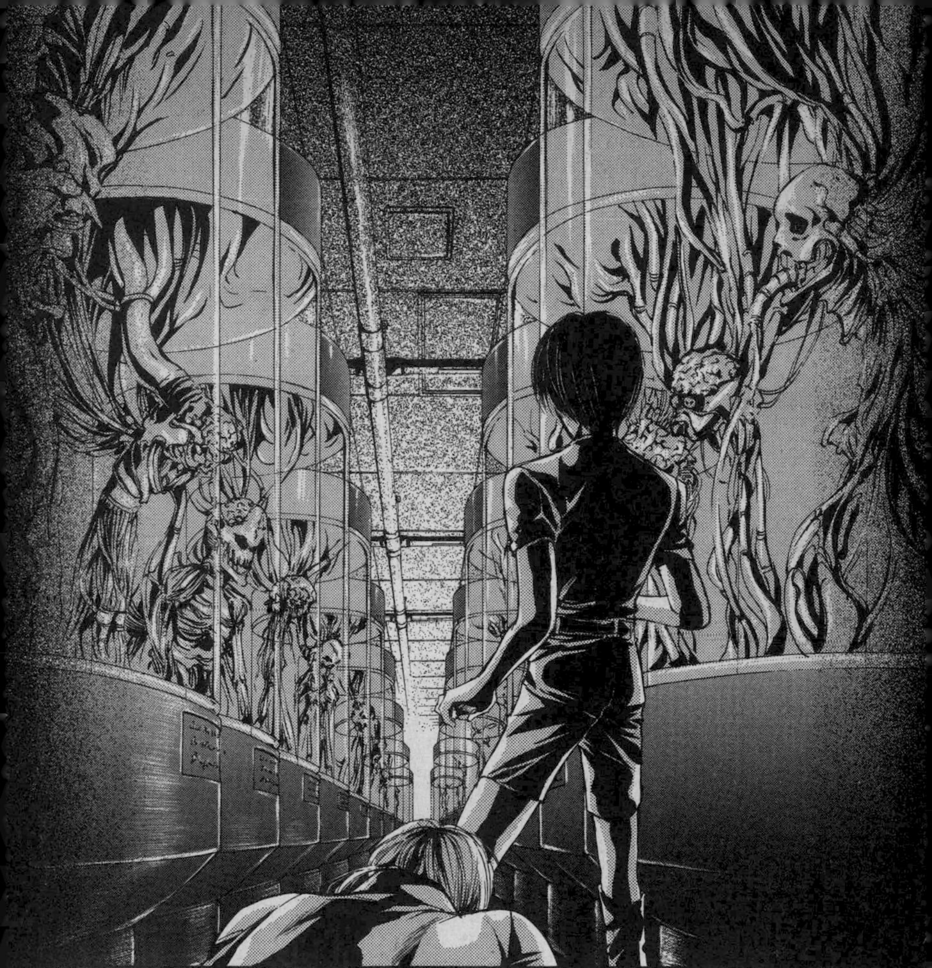

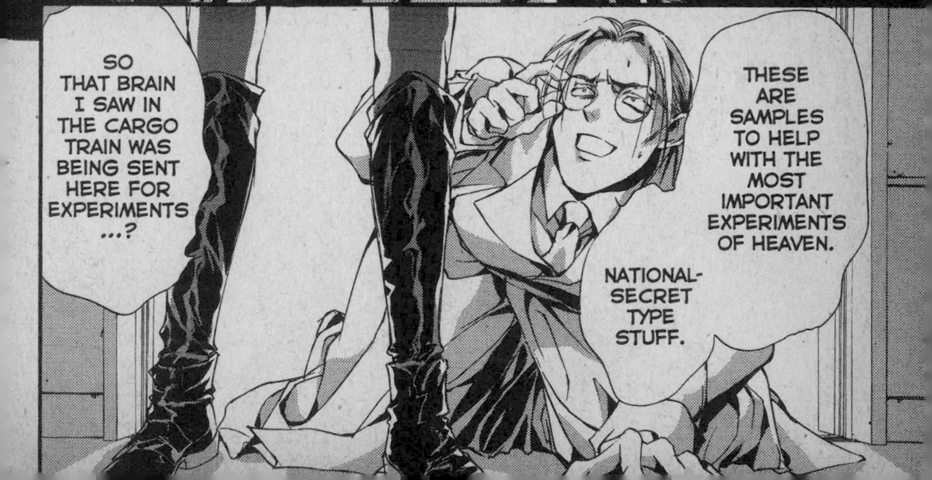
THESE ARE SAMPLES TO HELP WITH THE MOST IMPORTANT EXPERIMENTS OF HEAVEN.
NATIONAL-SECRET TYPE STUFF.
SO THAT BRAIN I SAW IN THE CARGO TRAIN WAS BEING SENT HERE FOR EXPERIMENTS ...?

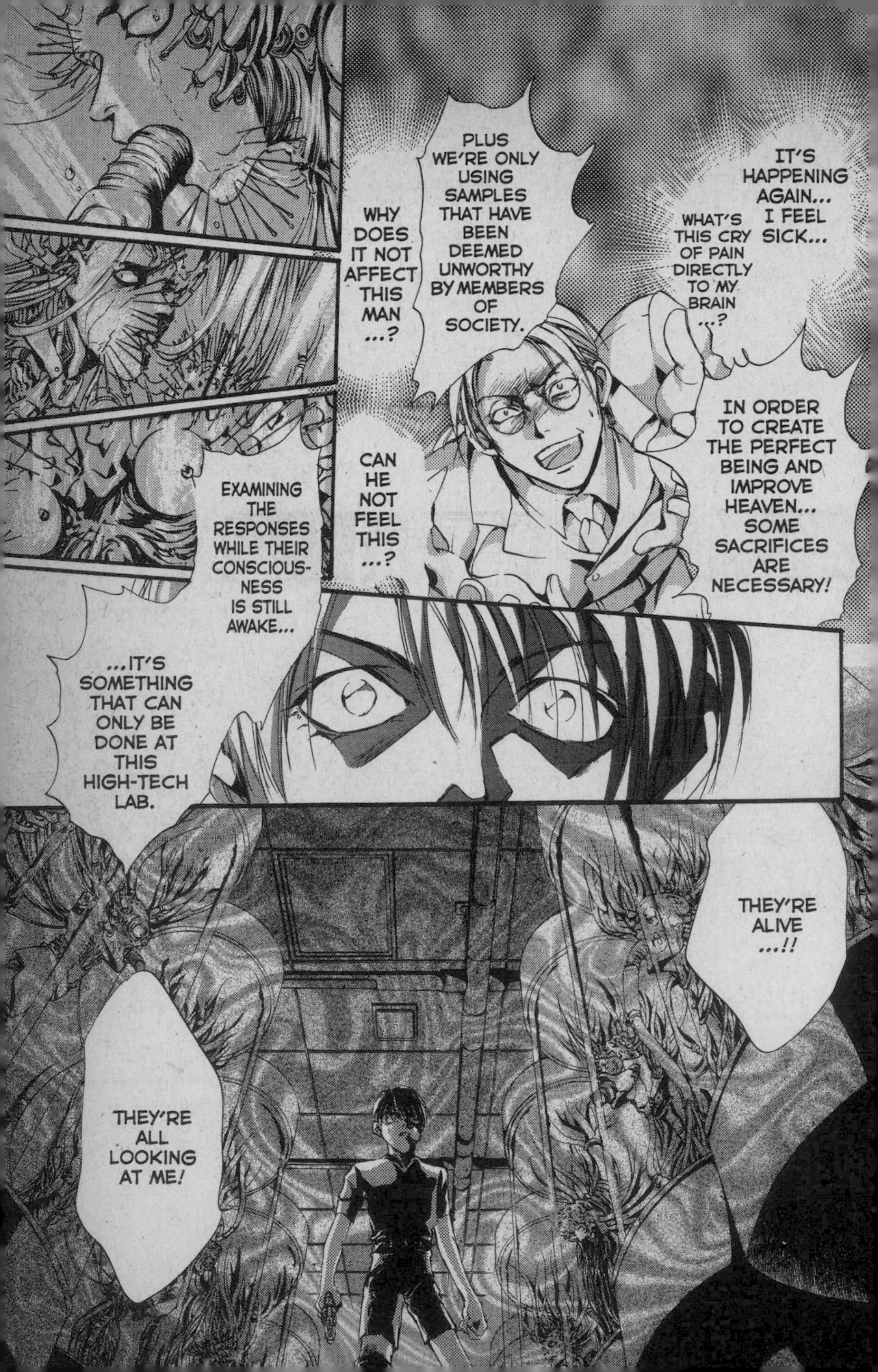
IT'S HAPPENING AGAIN... I FEEL SICK...
WHAT'S THIS CRY OF PAIN DIRECTLY TO MY BRAIN ...?
PLUS WE'RE ONLY USING SAMPLES THAT HAVE BEEN DEEMED UNWORTHY BY MEMBERS OF SOCIETY.
WHY DOES IT NOT AFFECT THIS MAN ...?
IN ORDER TO CREATE THE PERFECT BEING AND IMPROVE HEAVEN... SOME SACRIFICES ARE NECESSARY!
CAN HE NOT FEEL THIS ...?
EXAMINING THE RESPONSES WHILE THEIR CONSCIOUS-NESS IS STILL AWAKE...
...IT'S SOMETHING THAT CAN ONLY BE DONE AT THIS HIGH-TECH LAB.
THEY'RE ALIVE ...!!
THEY'RE ALL LOOKING AT ME!

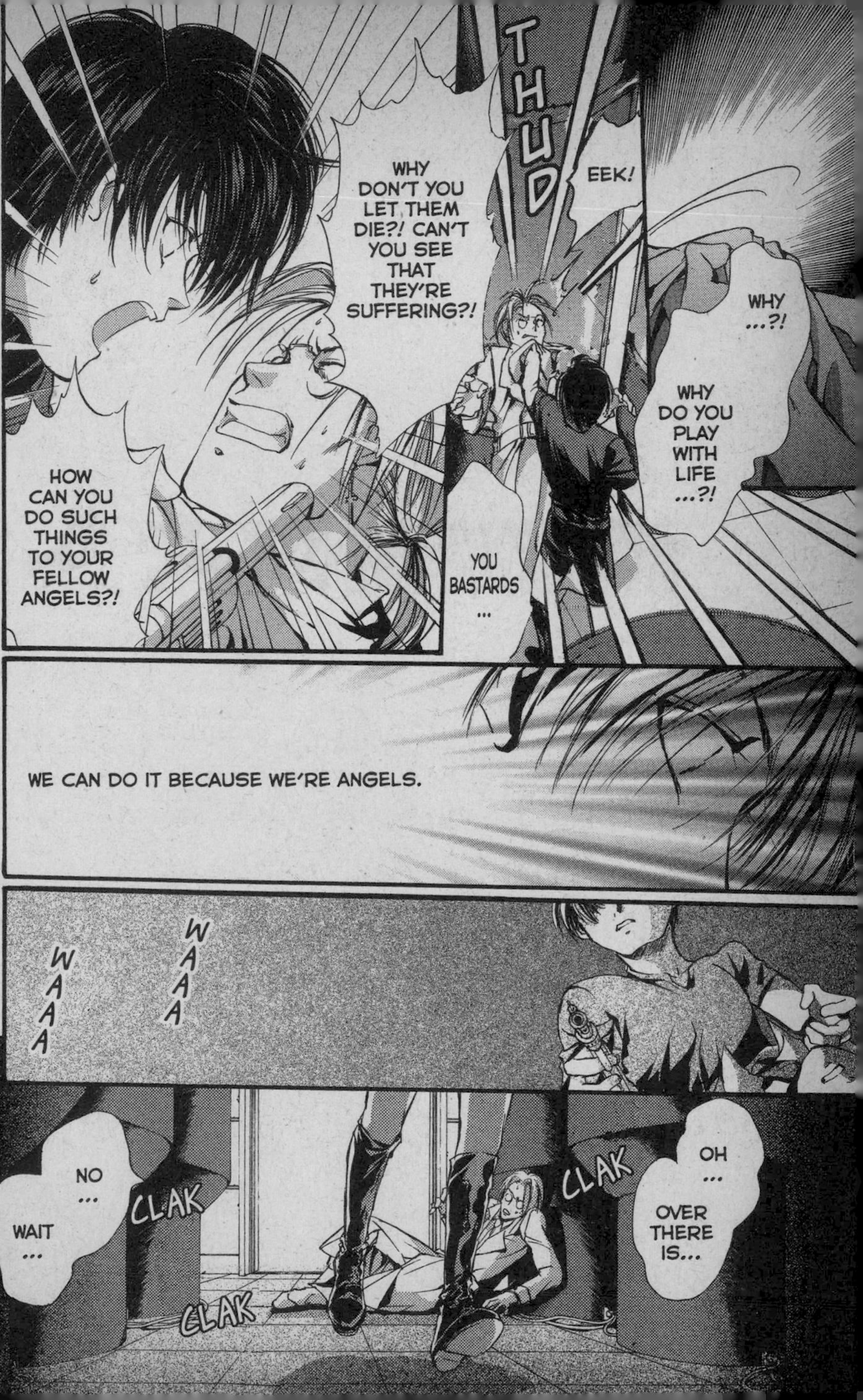
THUD
EEK!
WHY ...?!
WHY DO YOU PLAY WITH LIFE ...?!
YOU BASTARDS ...
WHY DON'T YOU LET THEM DIE?! CAN'T YOU SEE THAT THEY'RE SUFFERING?!
HOW CAN YOU DO SUCH THINGS TO YOUR FELLOW ANGELS?!
WE CAN DO IT BECAUSE WE'RE ANGELS.
WAAAA
WAAAA
OH ... OVER THERE IS...
CLAK
CLAK
NO ... WAIT ...
CLAK

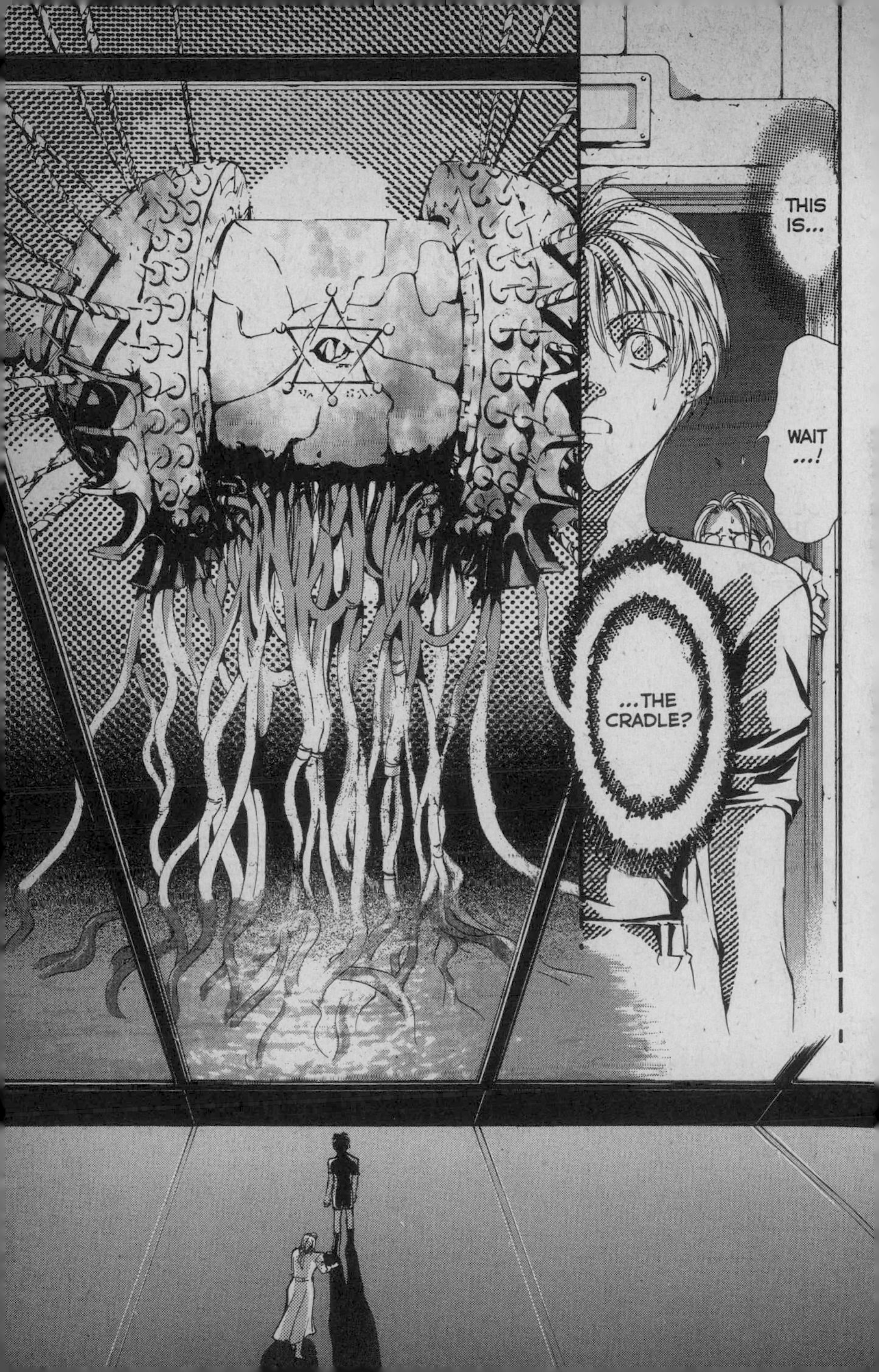
THIS IS...
WAIT ...!
...THE CRADLE?

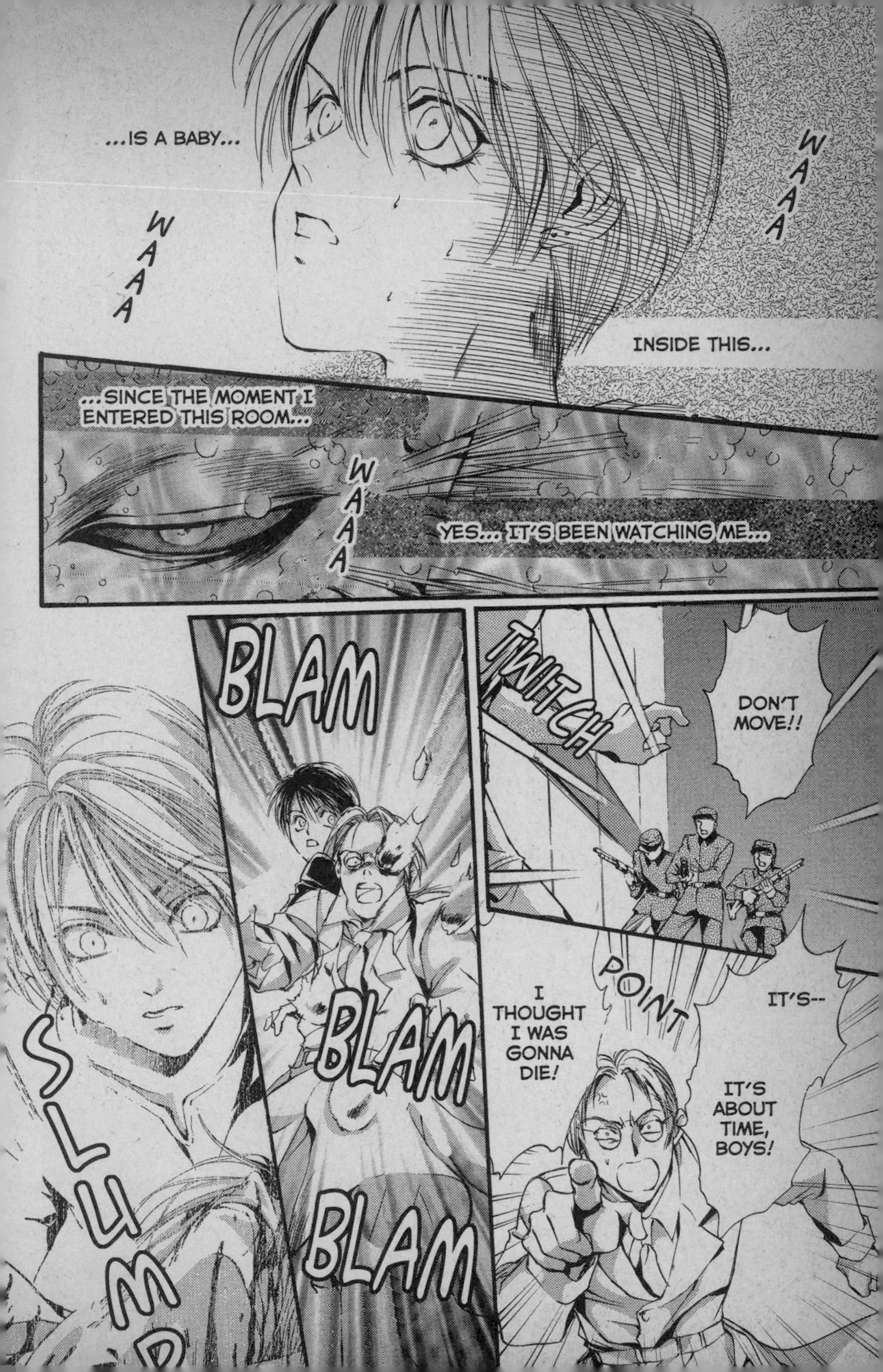
WAAAA
INSIDE THIS...
...IS A BABY...
WAAA
YES... IT'S BEEN WATCHING ME...
WAAAA
...SINCE THE MOMENT I ENTERED THIS ROOM...
TWITCH
DON'T MOVE!!
IT'S--
IT'S ABOUT TIME, BOYS!
POINT
I THOUGHT I WAS GONNA DIE!
BLAM
BLAM
BLAM
SLUM

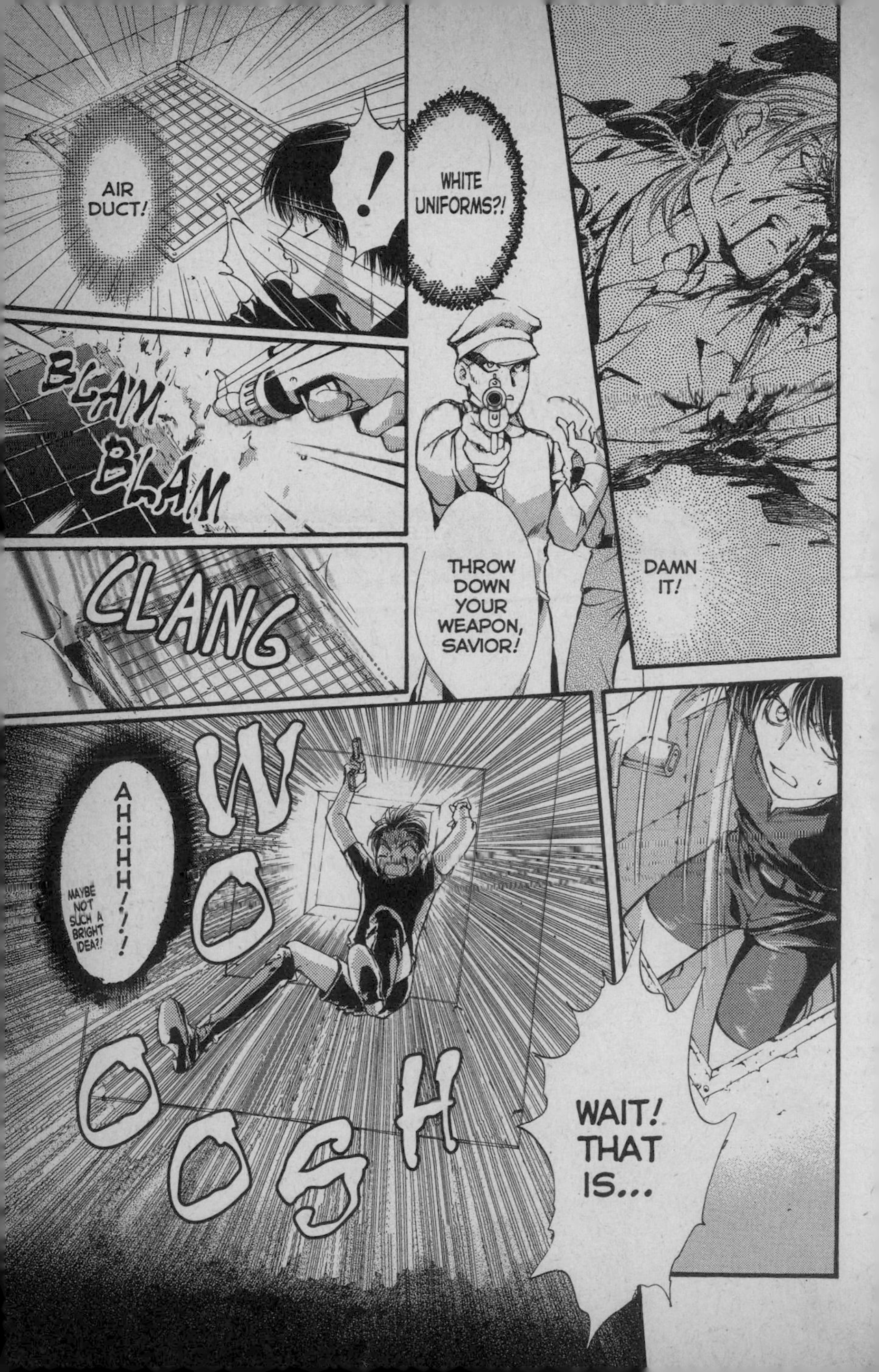
DAMN IT!
WHITE UNIFORMS?!
THROW DOWN YOUR WEAPON, SAVIOR!
!
AIR DUCT!
BLAM BLAM
CLANG
WAIT! THAT IS...
WHOOSH
AHHHH!!!
MAYBE NOT SUCH A BRIGHT IDEA?!

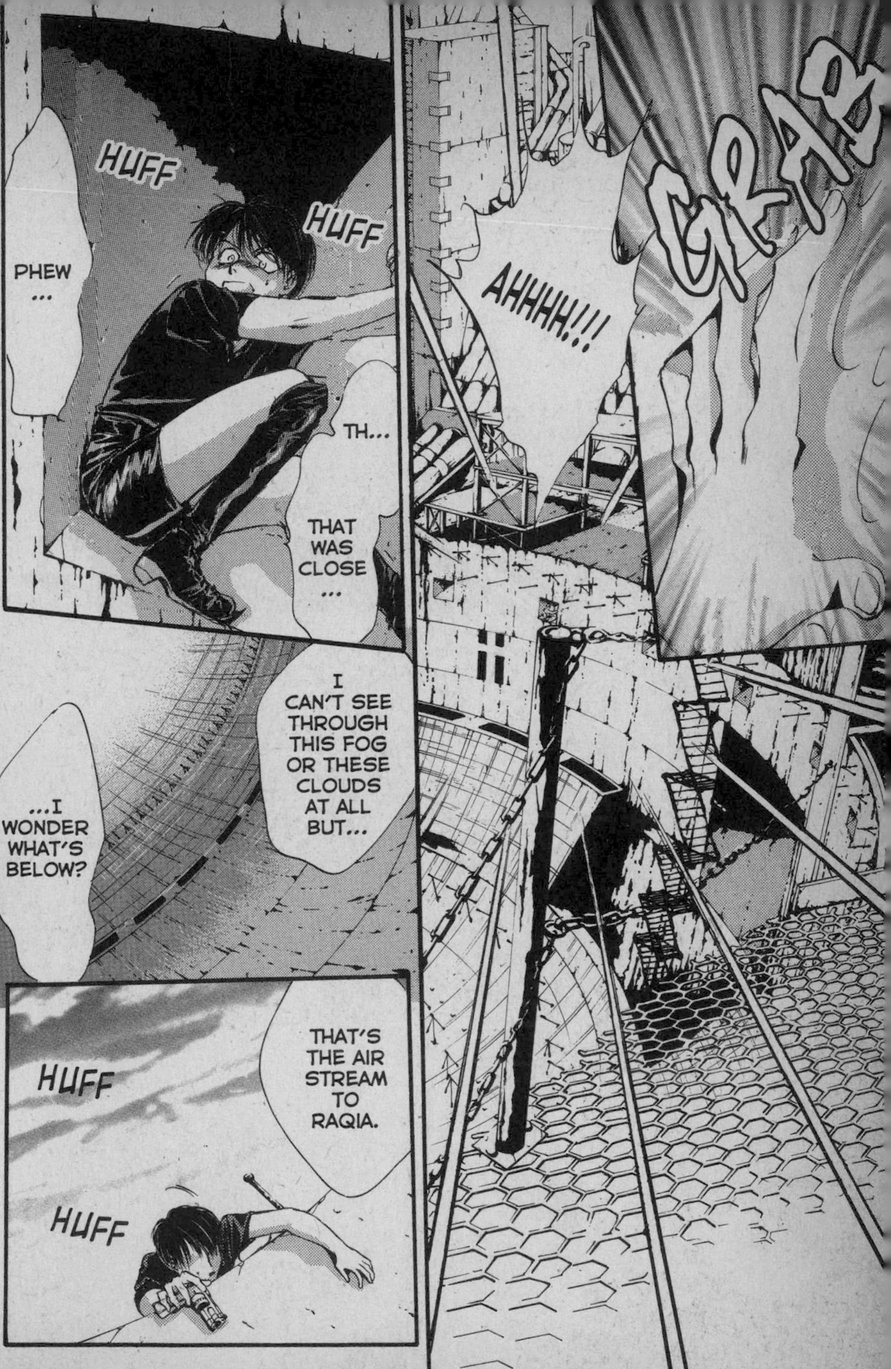
GRAB
AHHHH!!!
HUFF
HUFF
PHEW...
TH...
THAT WAS CLOSE...
I CAN'T SEE THROUGH THIS FOG OR THESE CLOUDS AT ALL BUT...
...I WONDER WHAT'S BELOW?
THAT'S THE AIR STREAM TO RAQIA.
HUFF
HUFF

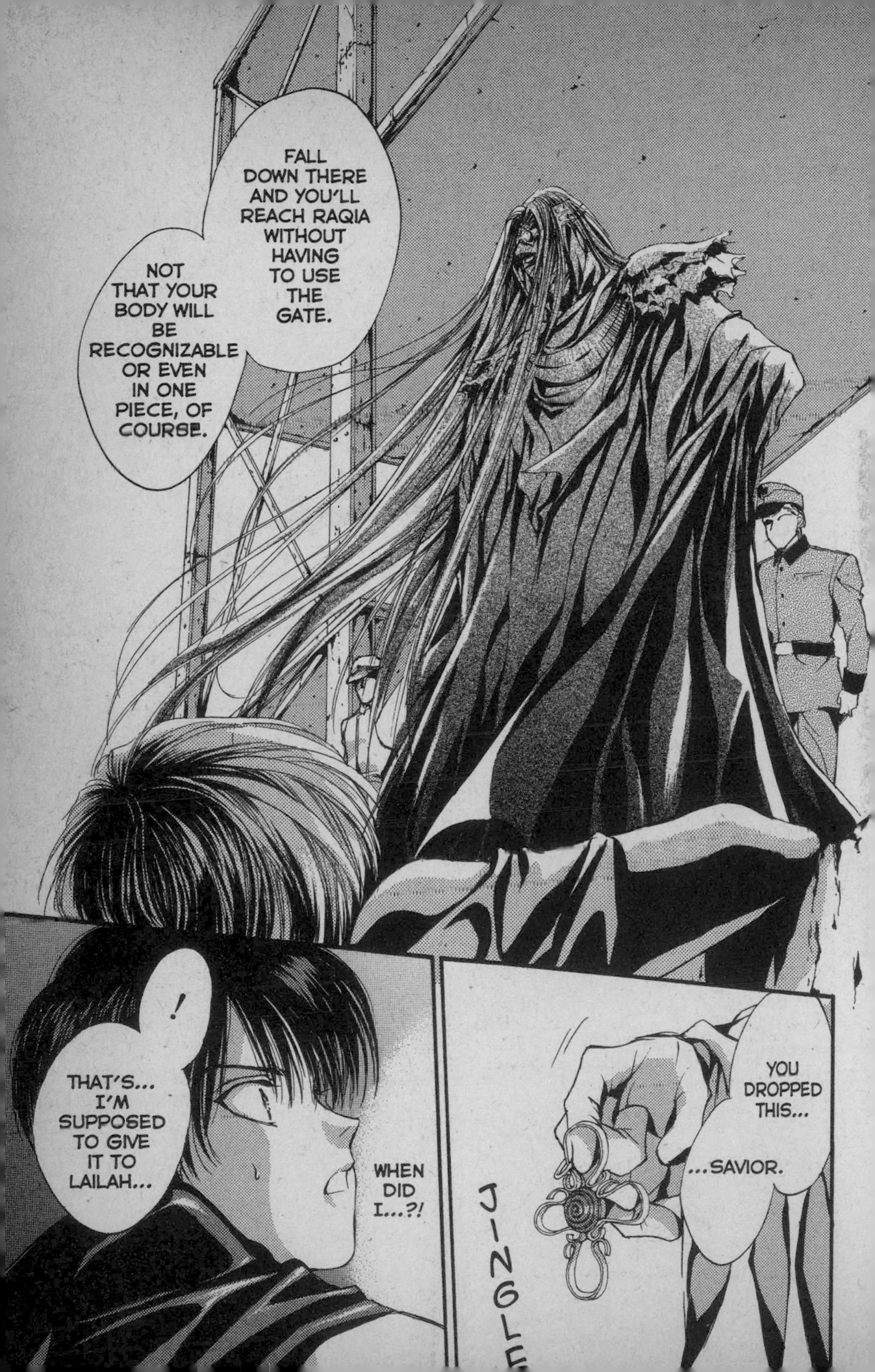
FALL DOWN THERE AND YOU'LL REACH RAQIA WITHOUT HAVING TO USE THE GATE.
NOT THAT YOUR BODY WILL BE RECOGNIZABLE OR EVEN IN ONE PIECE, OF COURSE.
YOU DROPPED THIS...
...SAVIOR.
JINGLE
!
WHEN DID I...?!
THAT'S... I'M SUPPOSED TO GIVE IT TO LAILAH...

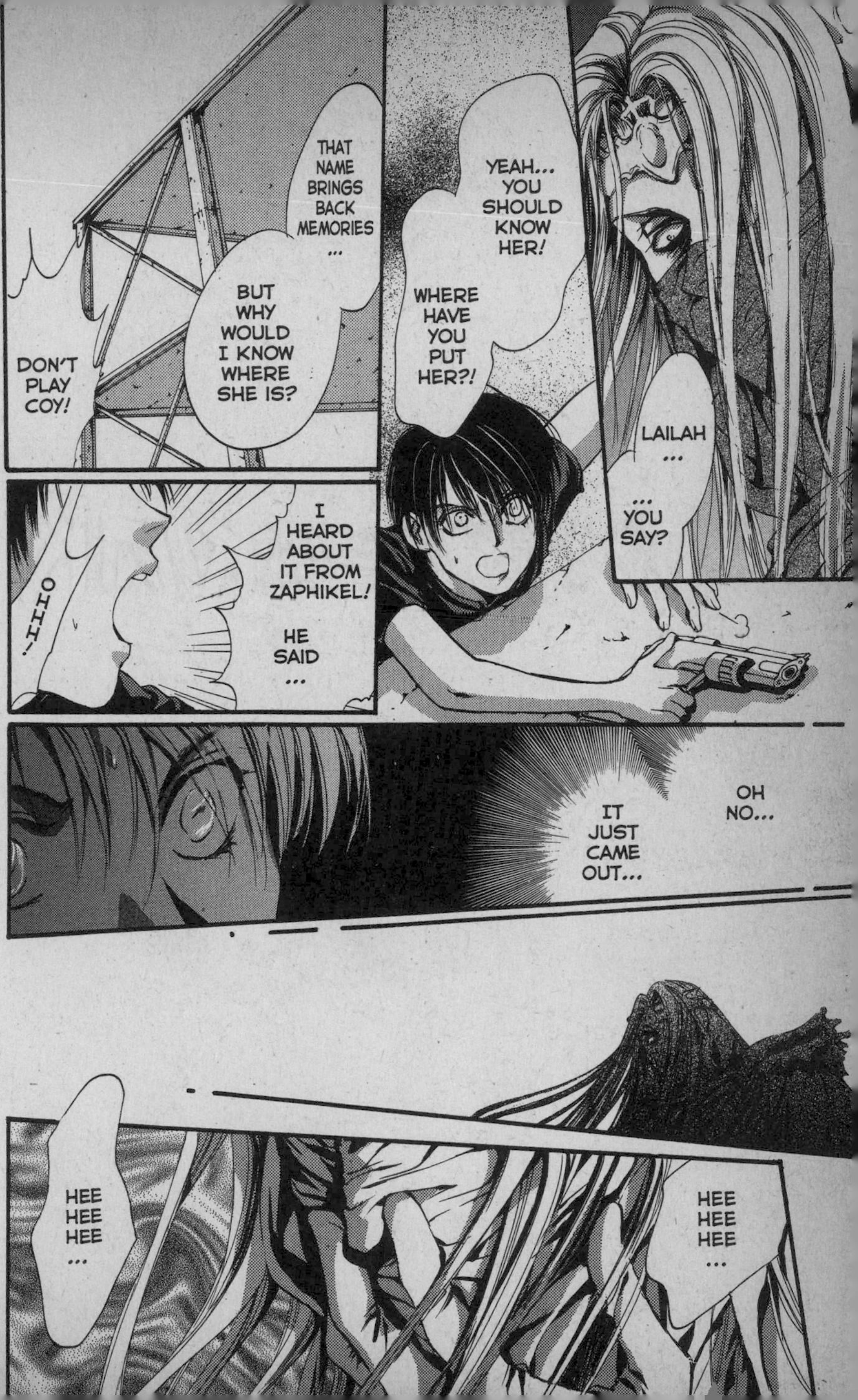
LAILAH... ...YOU SAY?
YEAH... YOU SHOULD KNOW HER!
WHERE HAVE YOU PUT HER?!
THAT NAME BRINGS BACK MEMORIES...
BUT WHY WOULD I KNOW WHERE SHE IS?
DON'T PLAY COY!
I HEARD ABOUT IT FROM ZAPHIKEL!
HE SAID...
OHHH!
OH NO...
IT JUST CAME OUT...
HEE HEE HEE...
HEE HEE HEE...

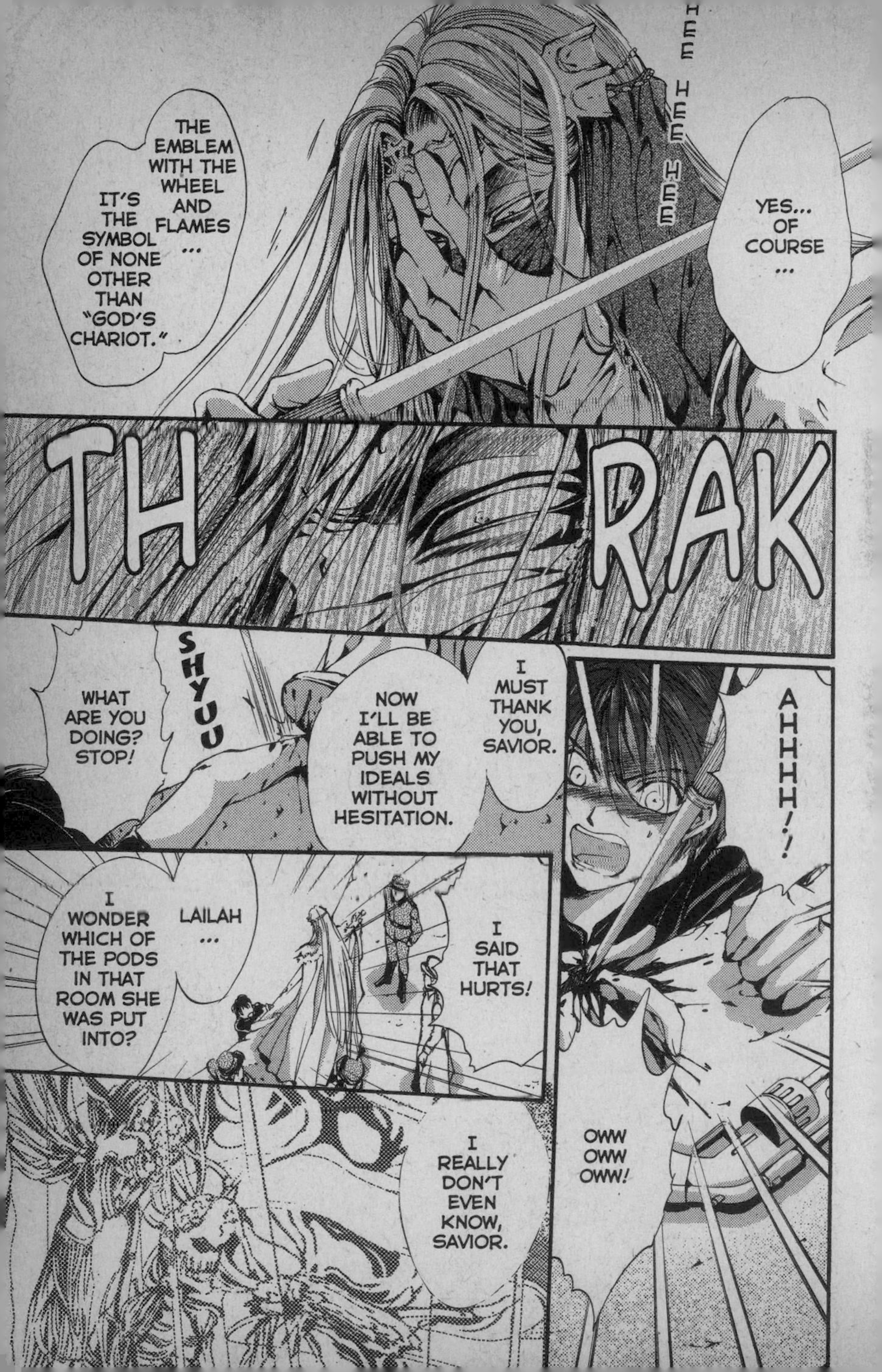
HEE HEE HEE
YES... OF COURSE...
THE EMBLEM WITH THE WHEEL AND FLAMES...
IT'S THE SYMBOL OF NONE OTHER THAN "GOD'S CHARIOT."
THRAK
AHHHH!!
OWW OWW OWW!
I MUST THANK YOU, SAVIOR.
NOW I'LL BE ABLE TO PUSH MY IDEALS WITHOUT HESITATION.
SHYUU
WHAT ARE YOU DOING? STOP!
I SAID THAT HURTS!
LAILAH...
I WONDER WHICH OF THE PODS IN THAT ROOM SHE WAS PUT INTO?
I REALLY DON'T EVEN KNOW, SAVIOR.

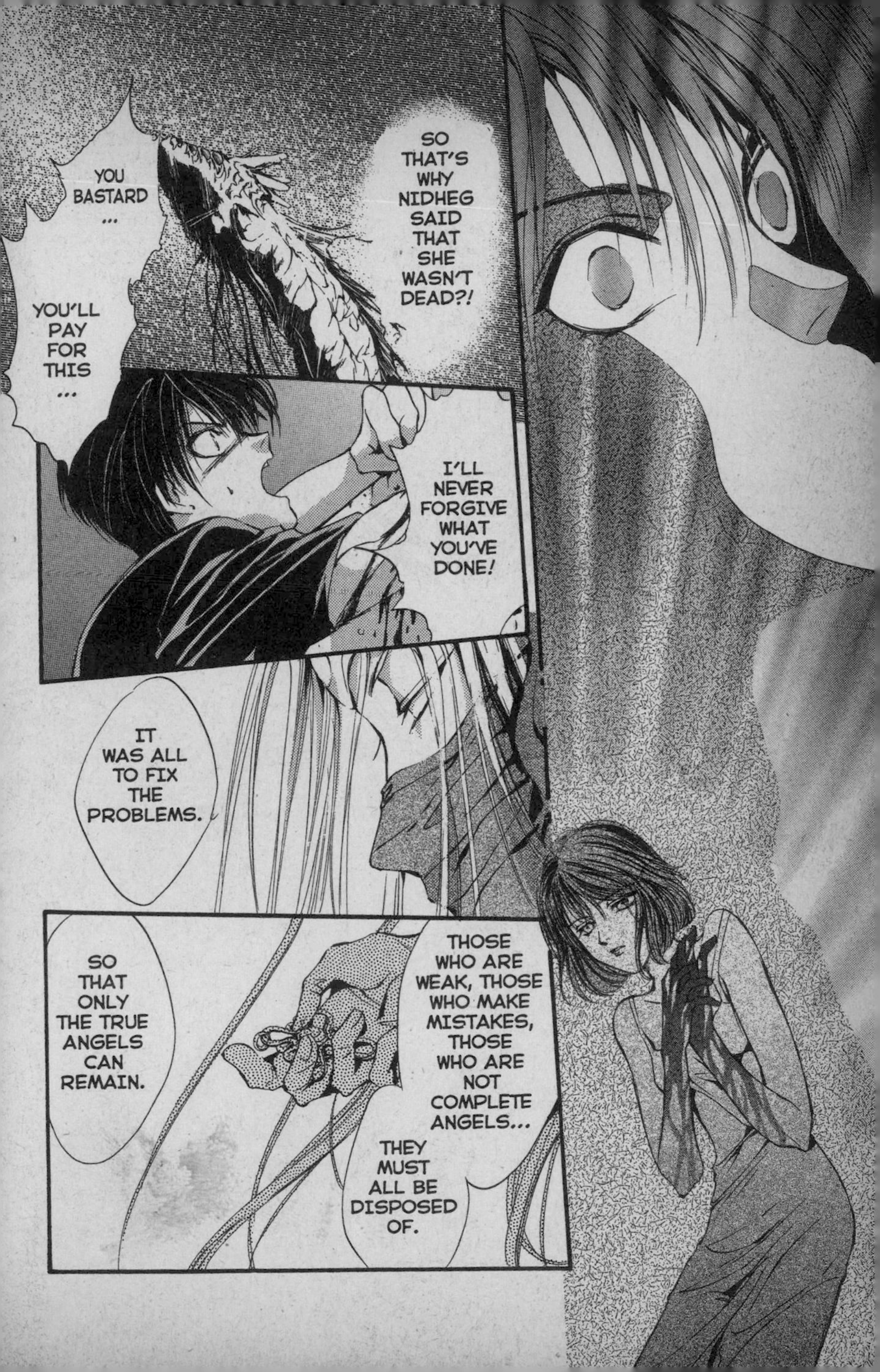
SO THAT'S WHY NIDHEG SAID THAT SHE WASN'T DEAD?!
YOU BASTARD ...
YOU'LL PAY FOR THIS ...
I'LL NEVER FORGIVE WHAT YOU'VE DONE!
IT WAS ALL TO FIX THE PROBLEMS.
THOSE WHO ARE WEAK, THOSE WHO MAKE MISTAKES, THOSE WHO ARE NOT COMPLETE ANGELS...
THEY MUST ALL BE DISPOSED OF.
SO THAT ONLY THE TRUE ANGELS CAN REMAIN.

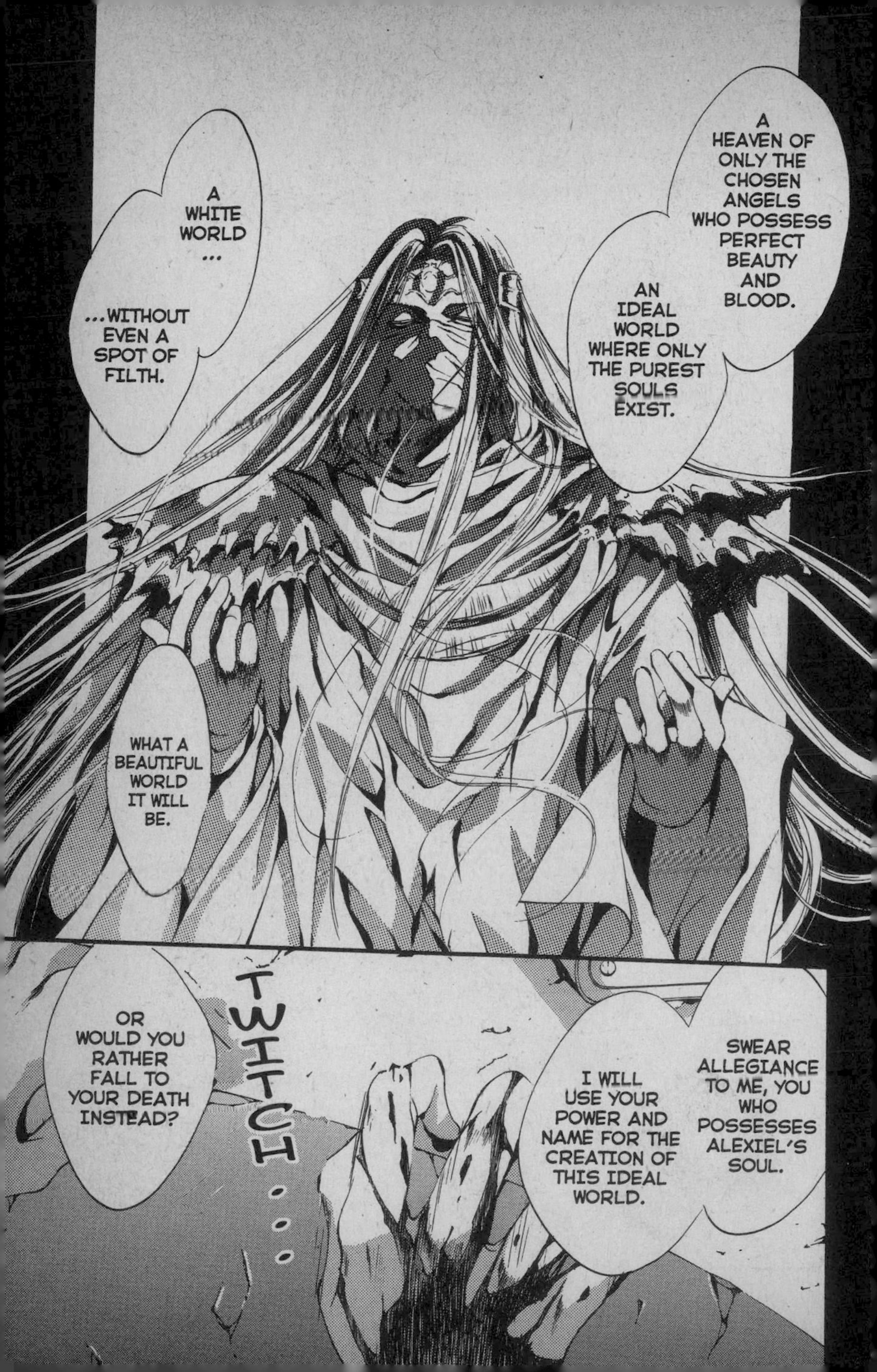
A HEAVEN OF ONLY THE CHOSEN ANGELS WHO POSSESS PERFECT BEAUTY AND BLOOD.
AN IDEAL WORLD WHERE ONLY THE PUREST SOULS EXIST.
A WHITE WORLD ...
...WITHOUT EVEN A SPOT OF FILTH.
WHAT A BEAUTIFUL WORLD IT WILL BE.
SWEAR ALLEGIANCE TO ME, YOU WHO POSSESSES ALEXIEL'S SOUL.
I WILL USE YOUR POWER AND NAME FOR THE CREATION OF THIS IDEAL WORLD.
TWITCH...
OR WOULD YOU RATHER FALL TO YOUR DEATH INSTEAD?

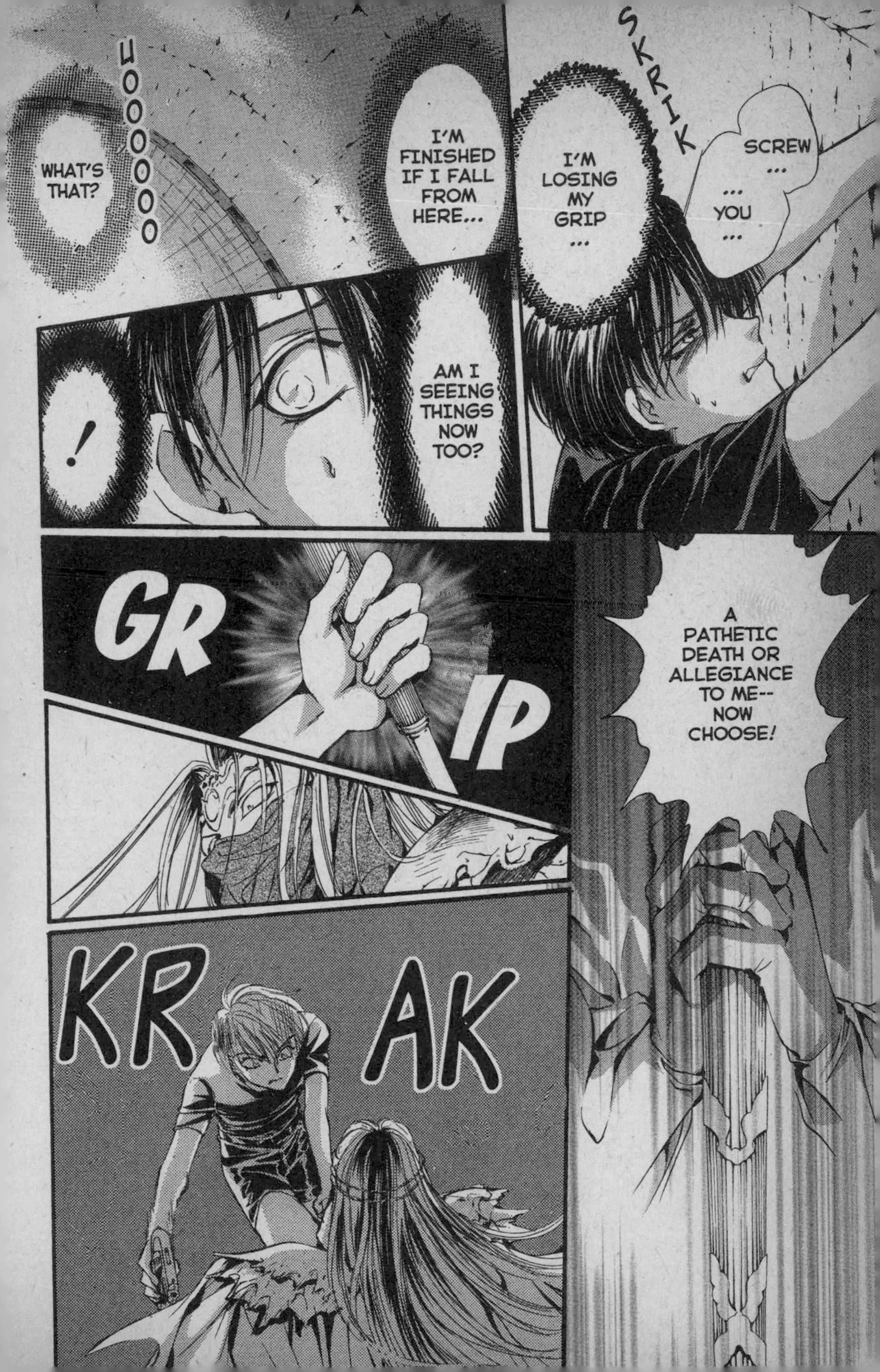
SCREW ... ... YOU ...
SKRIK
I'M LOSING MY GRIP ...
I'M FINISHED IF I FALL FROM HERE...
WOOOOOO
WHAT'S THAT?
AM I SEEING THINGS NOW TOO?
!
A PATHETIC DEATH OR ALLEGIANCE TO ME-- NOW CHOOSE!
GRIP
KRAK

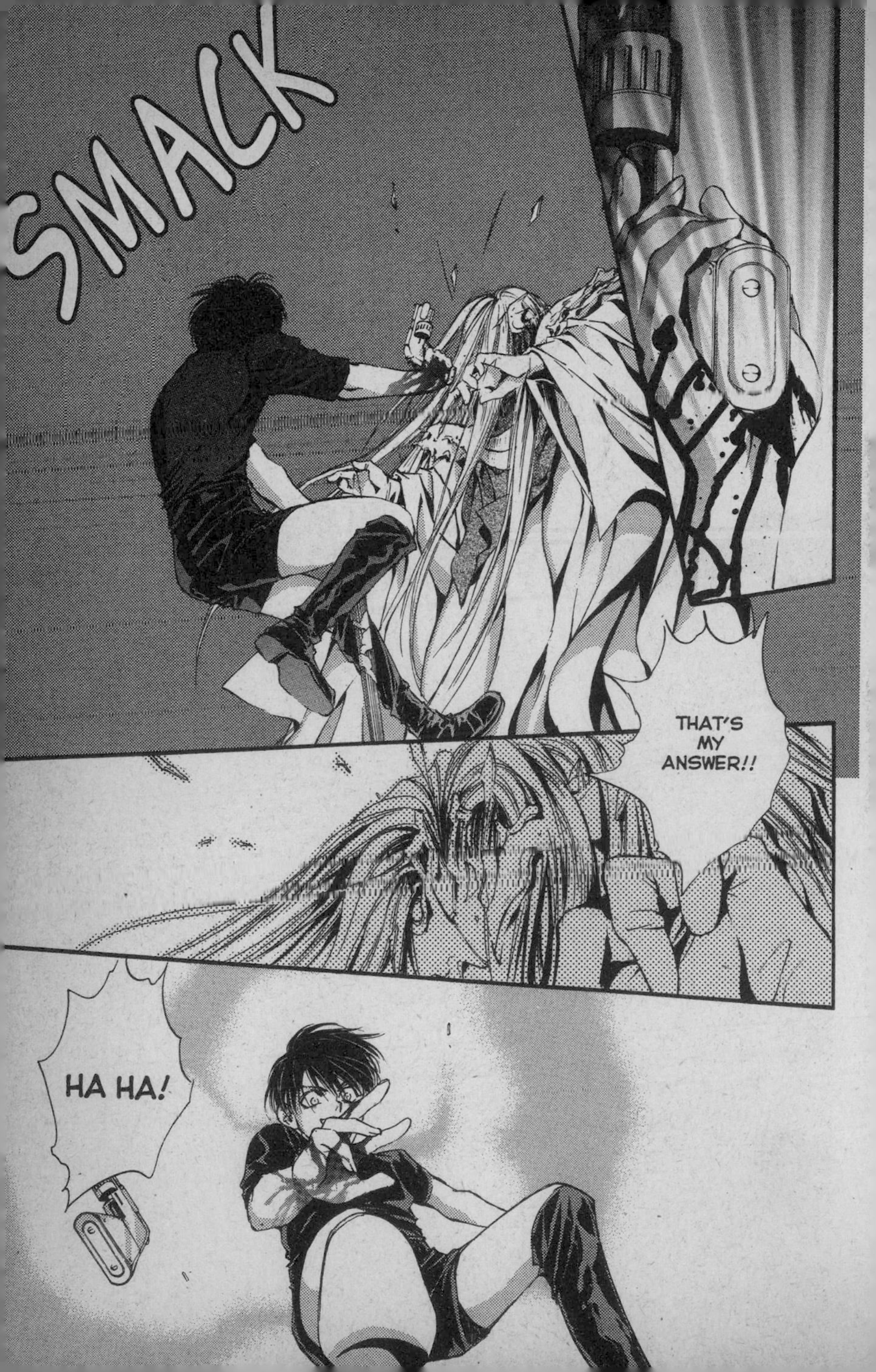
SMACK
THAT'S MY ANSWER!!
HA HA!

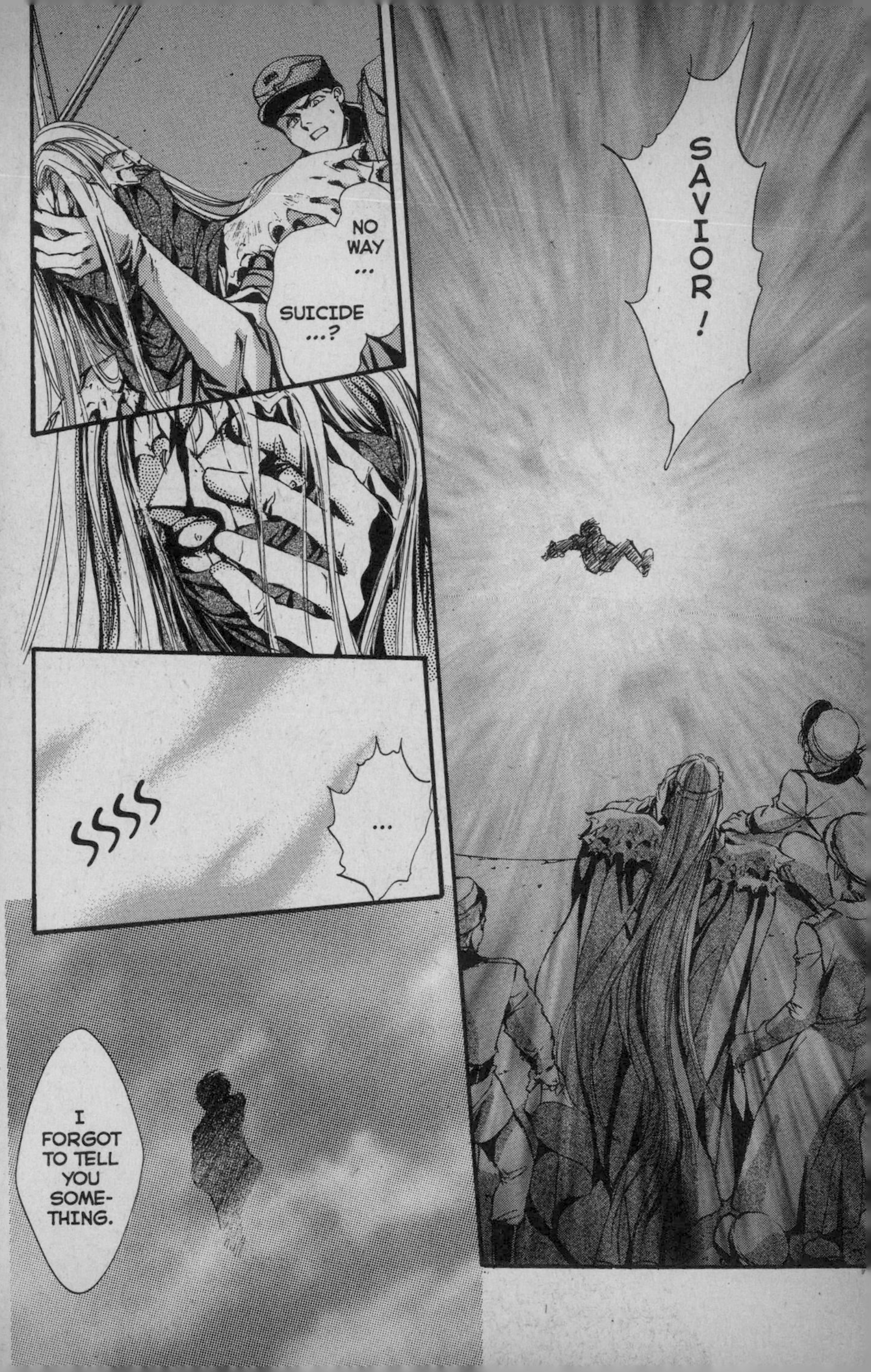
SAVIOR!
NO WAY... SUICIDE...?
...
I FORGOT TO TELL YOU SOME-THING.

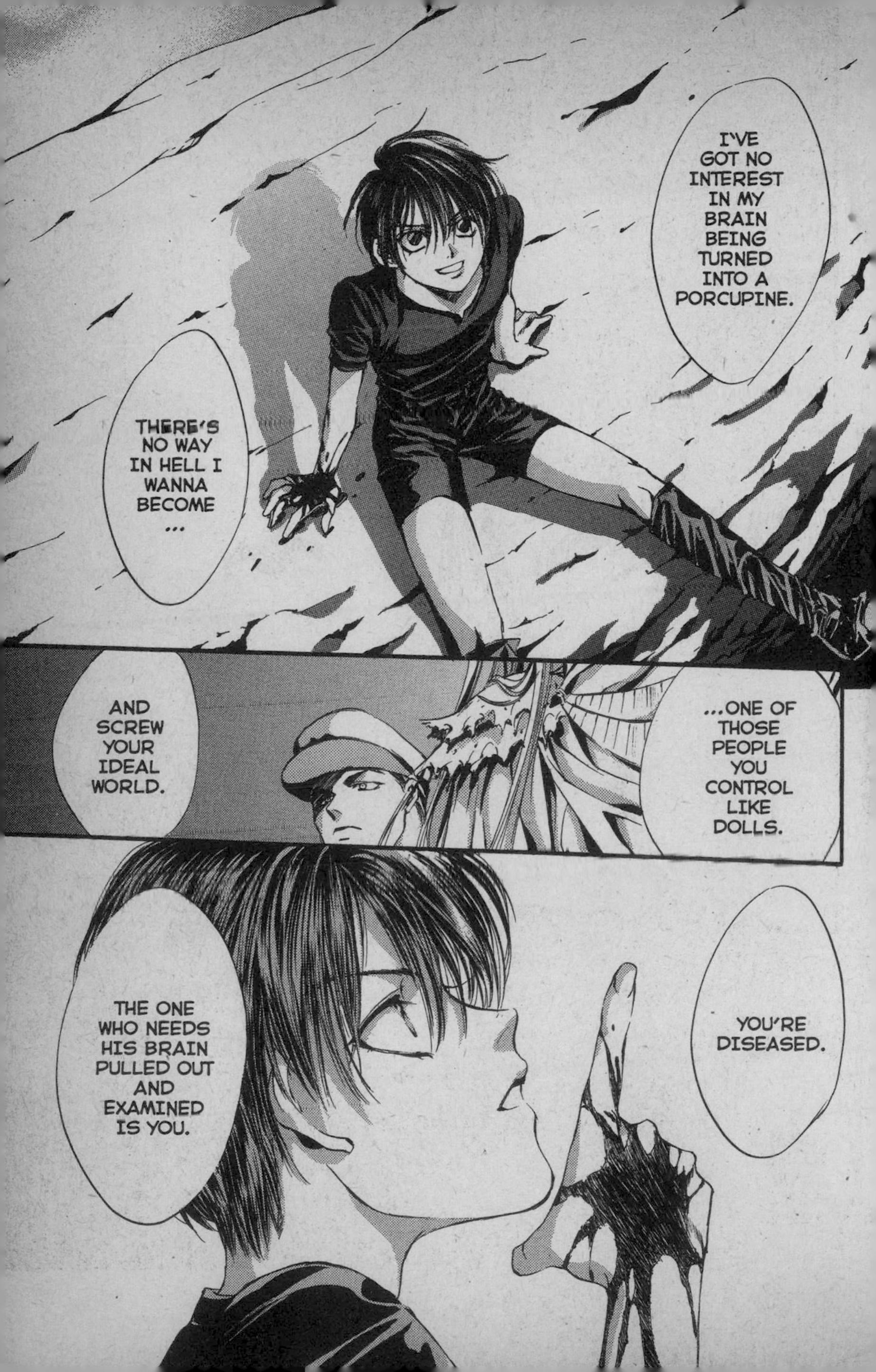
I'VE GOT NO INTEREST IN MY BRAIN BEING TURNED INTO A PORCUPINE.
THERE'S NO WAY IN HELL I WANNA BECOME ...
...ONE OF THOSE PEOPLE YOU CONTROL LIKE DOLLS.
AND SCREW YOUR IDEAL WORLD.
YOU'RE DISEASED.
THE ONE WHO NEEDS HIS BRAIN PULLED OUT AND EXAMINED IS YOU.

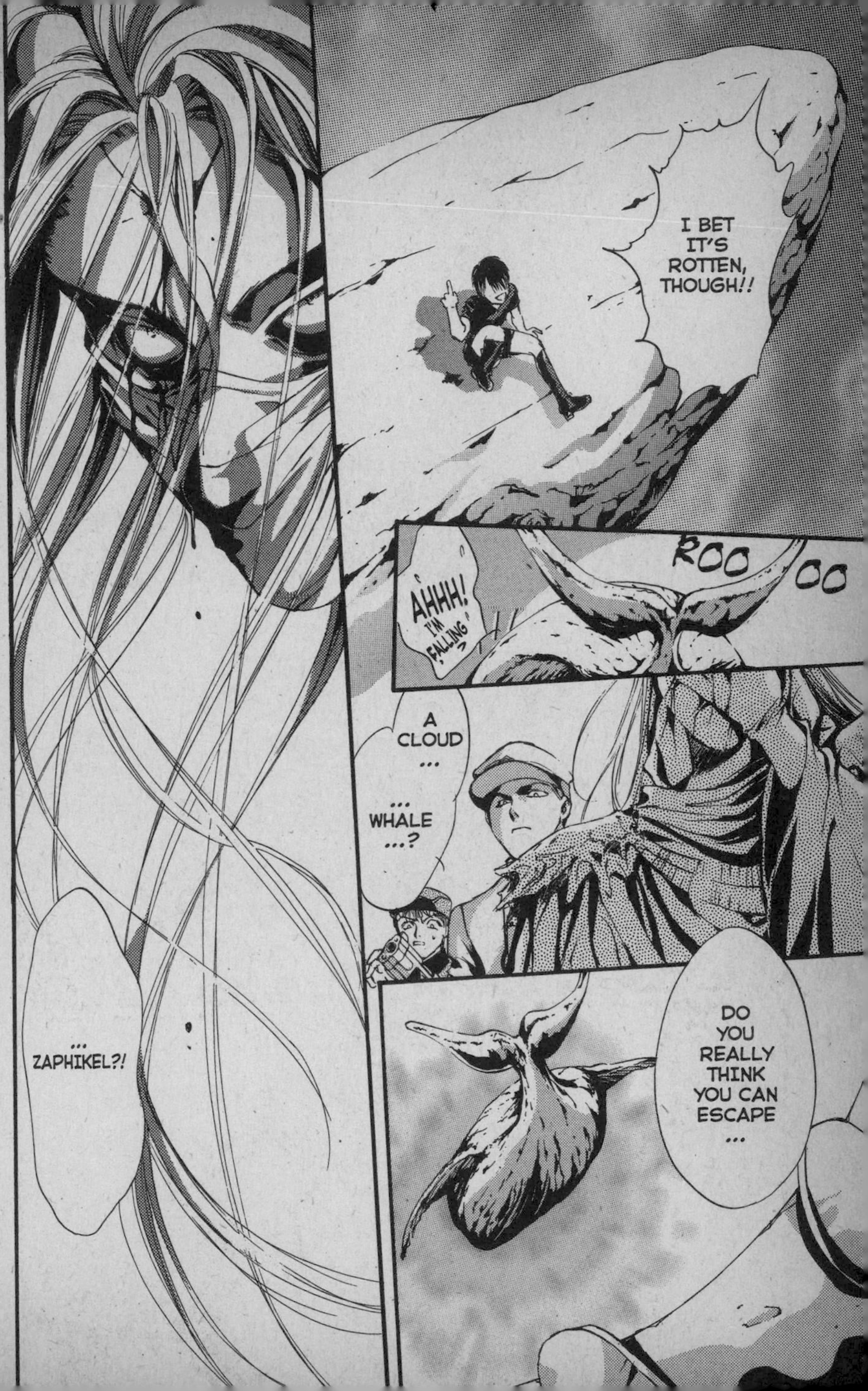
I BET IT'S ROTTEN, THOUGH!!
ROO OO
AHHH! I'M FALLING?
A CLOUD ...
... WHALE ...?
DO YOU REALLY THINK YOU CAN ESCAPE ...
... ZAPHIKEL?!

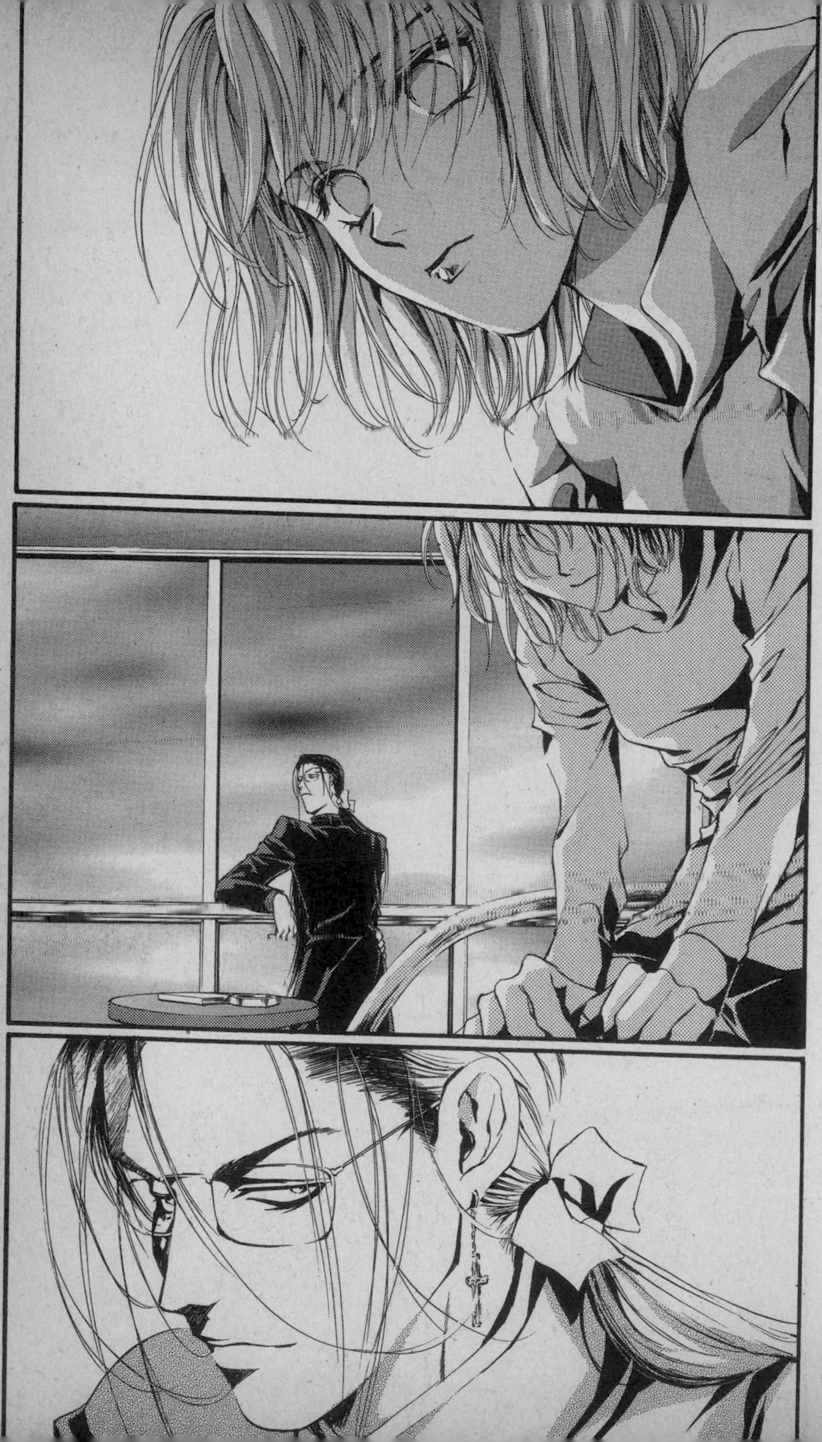

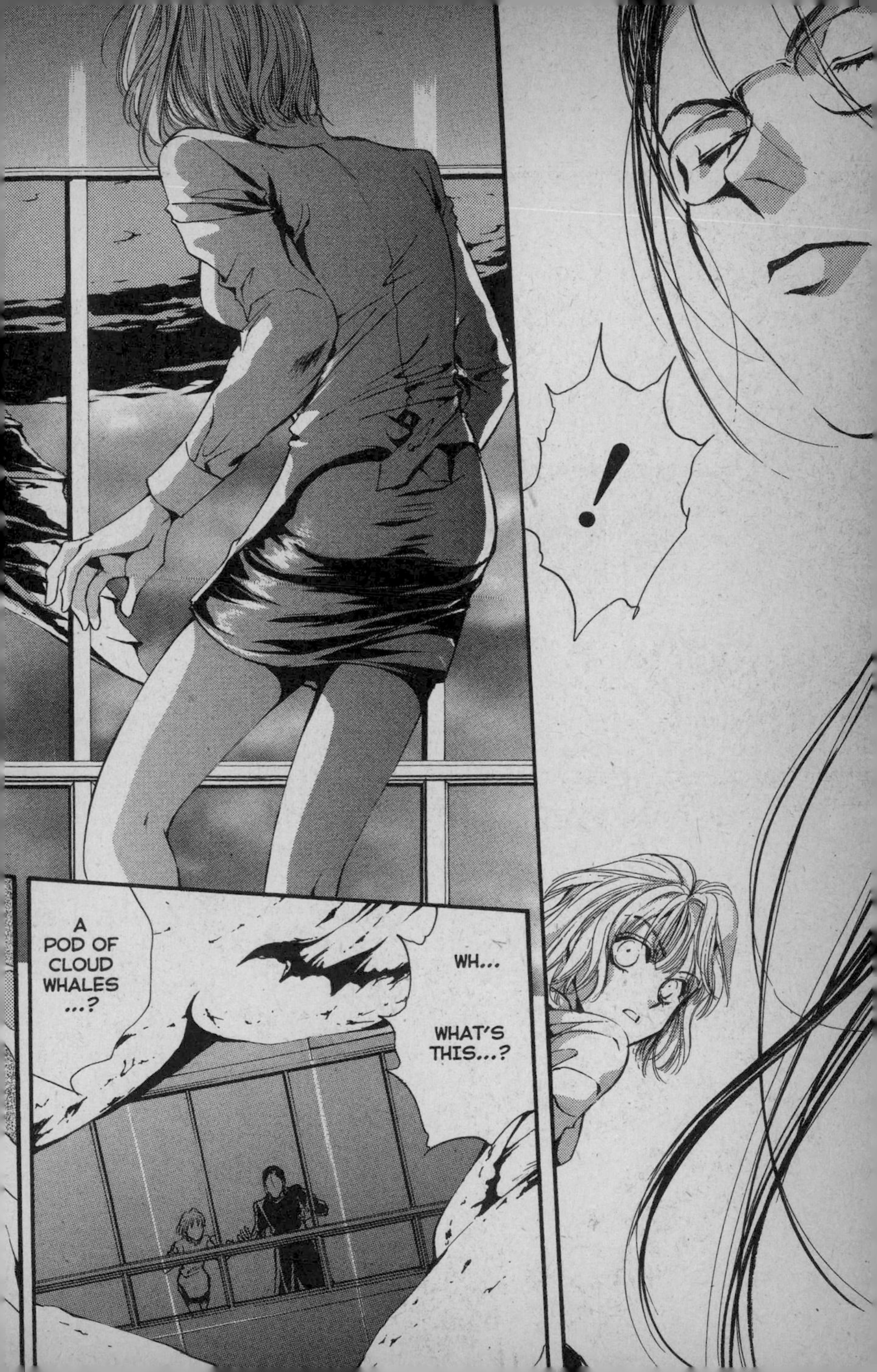
!
WH...
WHAT'S THIS...?
A POD OF CLOUD WHALES ...?

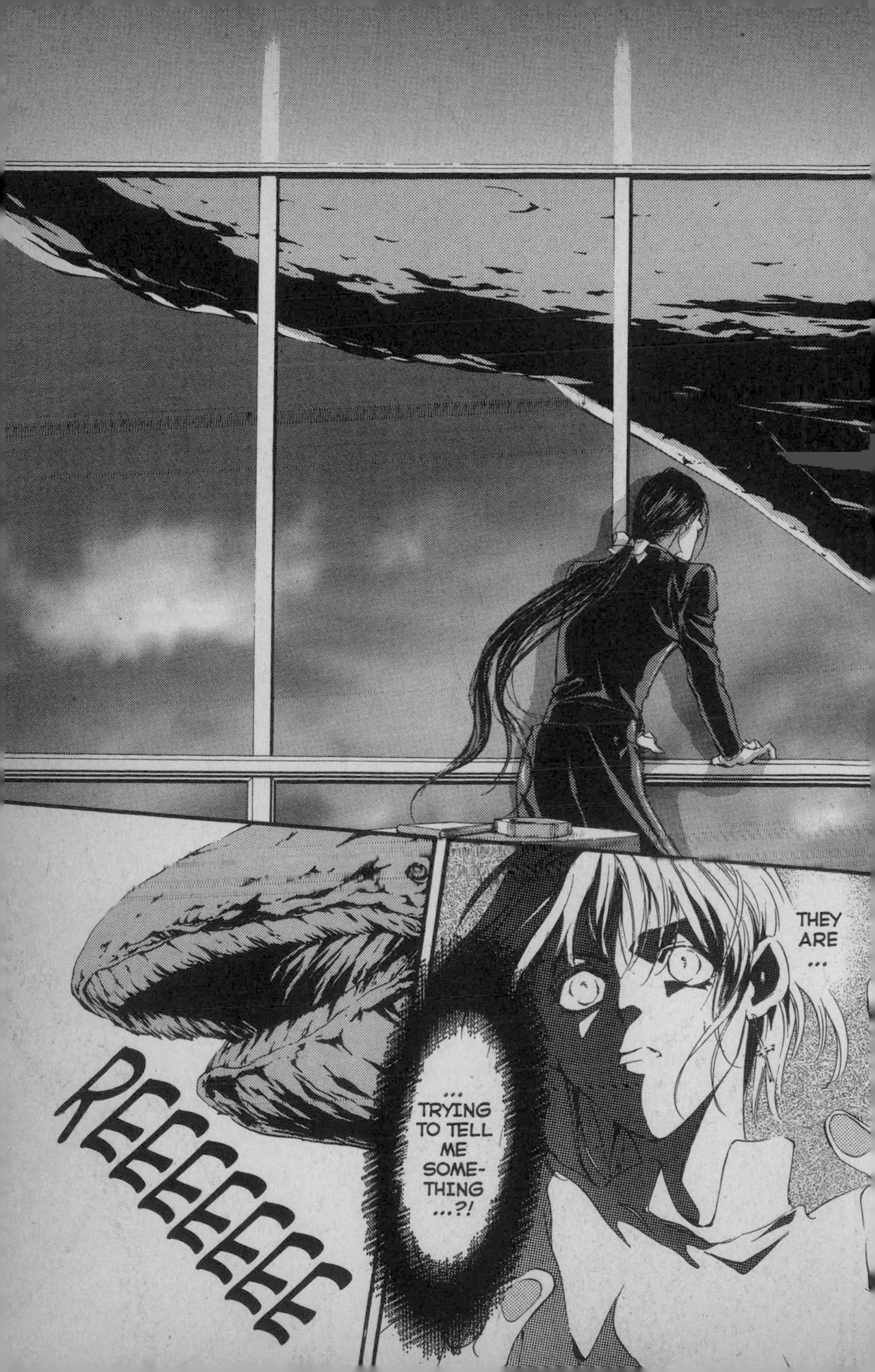
THEY ARE ...
... TRYING TO TELL ME SOMETHING ...?!
REEEEEEE

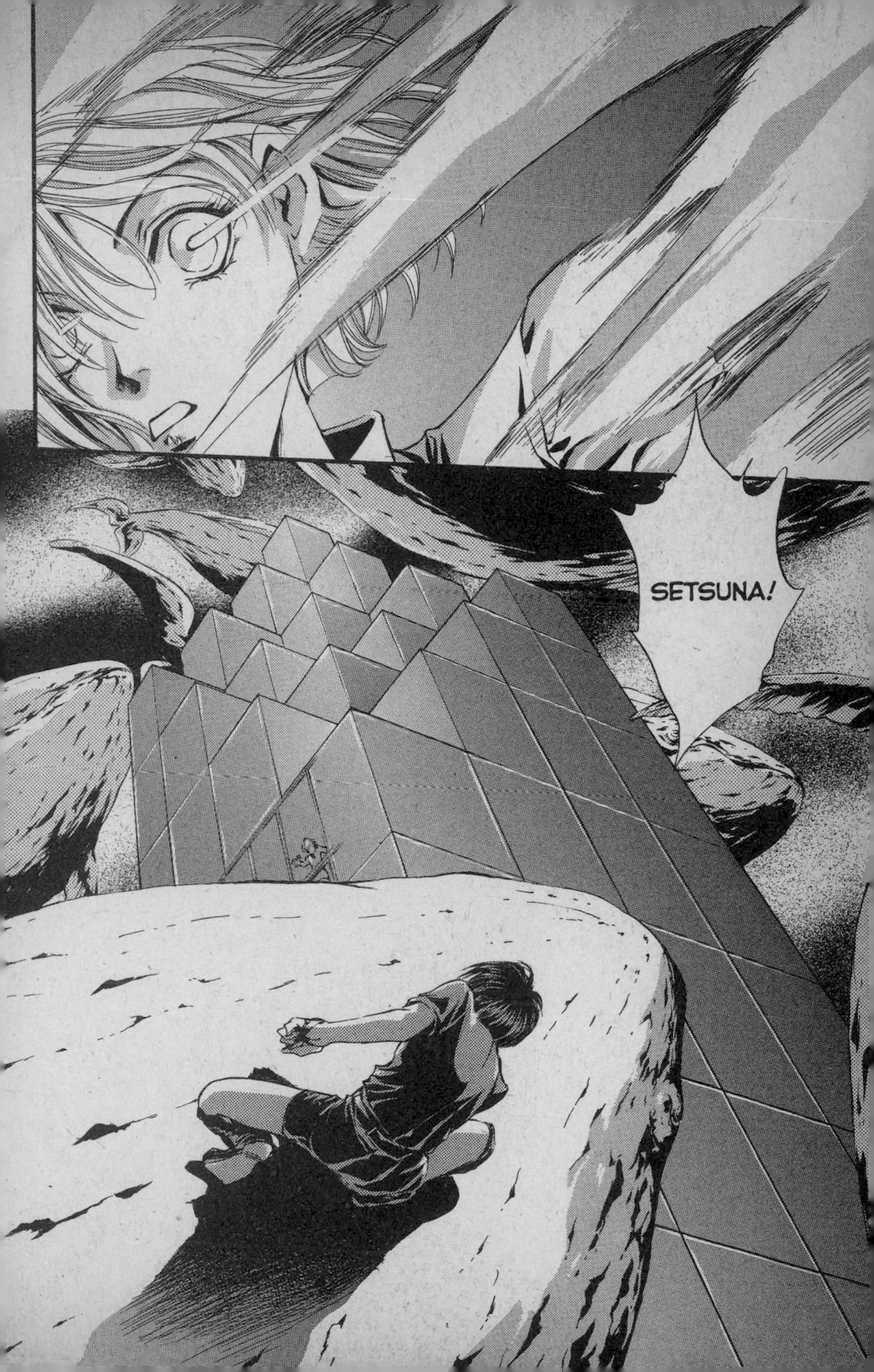
SETSUNA!

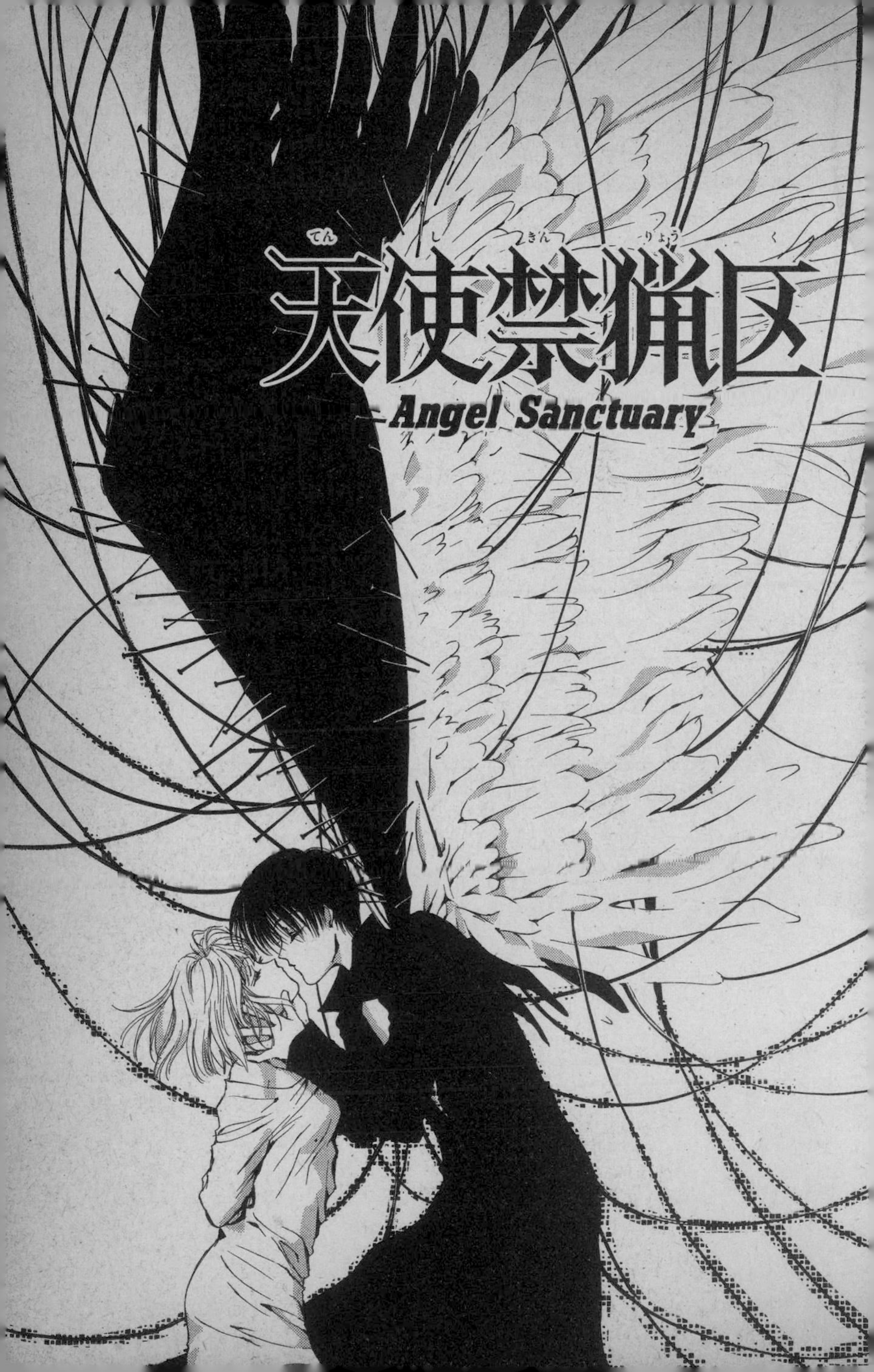
天使禁猟区
Angel Sanctuary

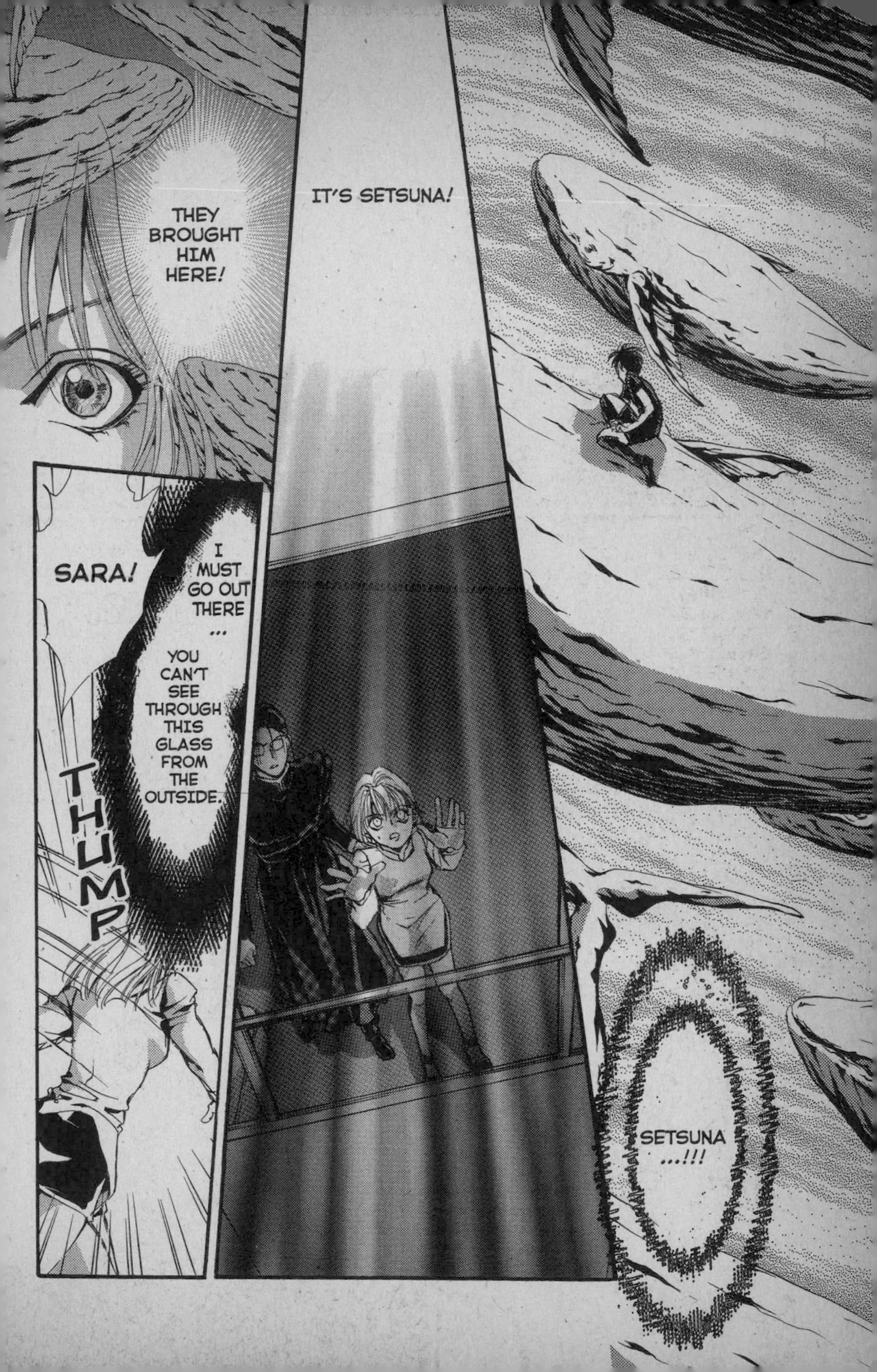
SETSUNA ...!!!
IT'S SETSUNA!
THEY BROUGHT HIM HERE!
I MUST GO OUT THERE ...
SARA!
YOU CAN'T SEE THROUGH THIS GLASS FROM THE OUTSIDE.
THUMP

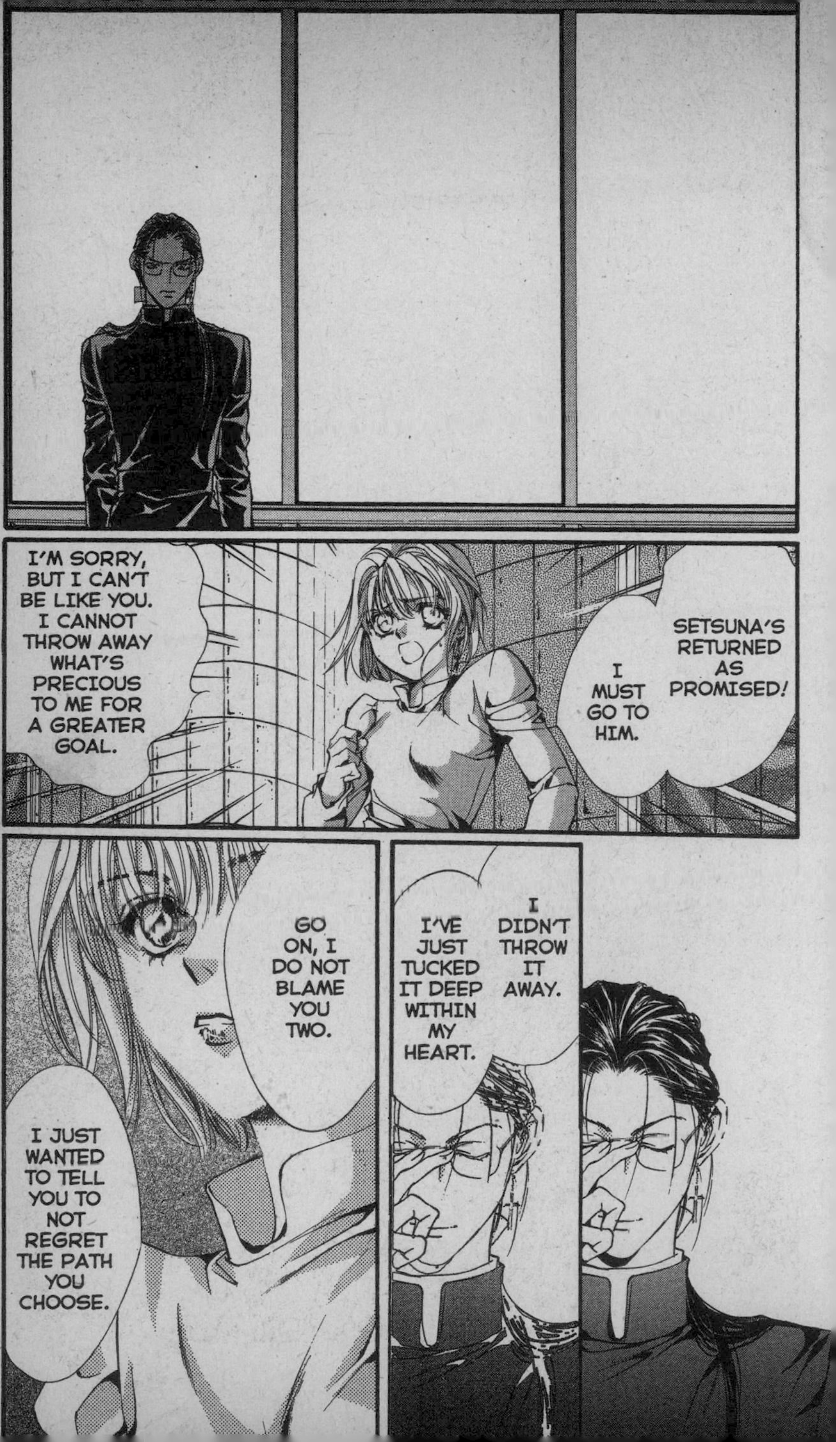
SETSUNA'S RETURNED AS PROMISED!
I MUST GO TO HIM.
I'M SORRY, BUT I CAN'T BE LIKE YOU. I CANNOT THROW AWAY WHAT'S PRECIOUS TO ME FOR A GREATER GOAL.
I DIDN'T THROW IT AWAY.
I'VE JUST TUCKED IT DEEP WITHIN MY HEART.
GO ON, I DO NOT BLAME YOU TWO.
I JUST WANTED TO TELL YOU TO NOT REGRET THE PATH YOU CHOOSE.

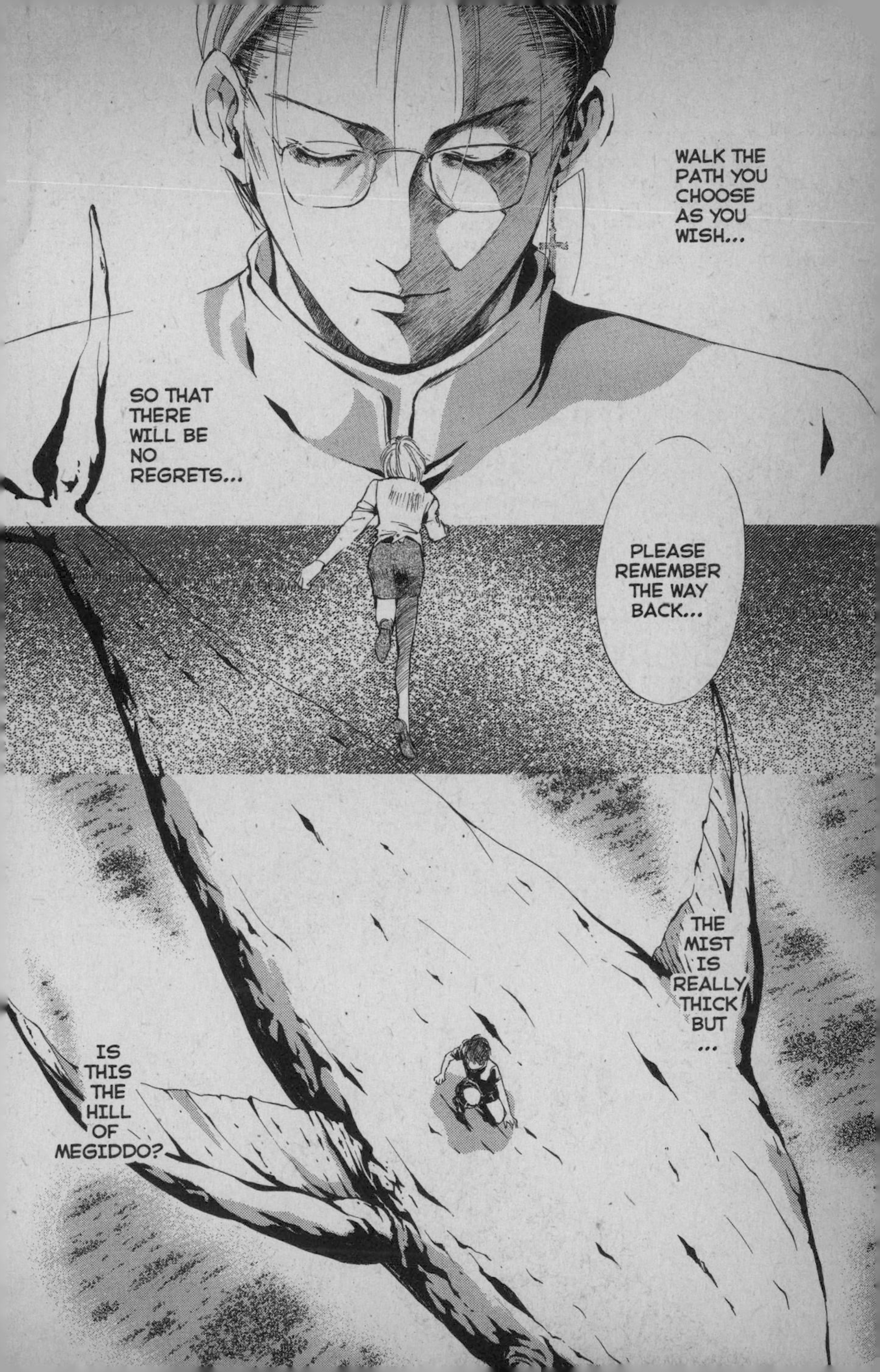
WALK THE PATH YOU CHOOSE AS YOU WISH...
SO THAT THERE WILL BE NO REGRETS...
PLEASE REMEMBER THE WAY BACK...
THE MIST IS REALLY THICK BUT ...
IS THIS THE HILL OF MEGIDDO?

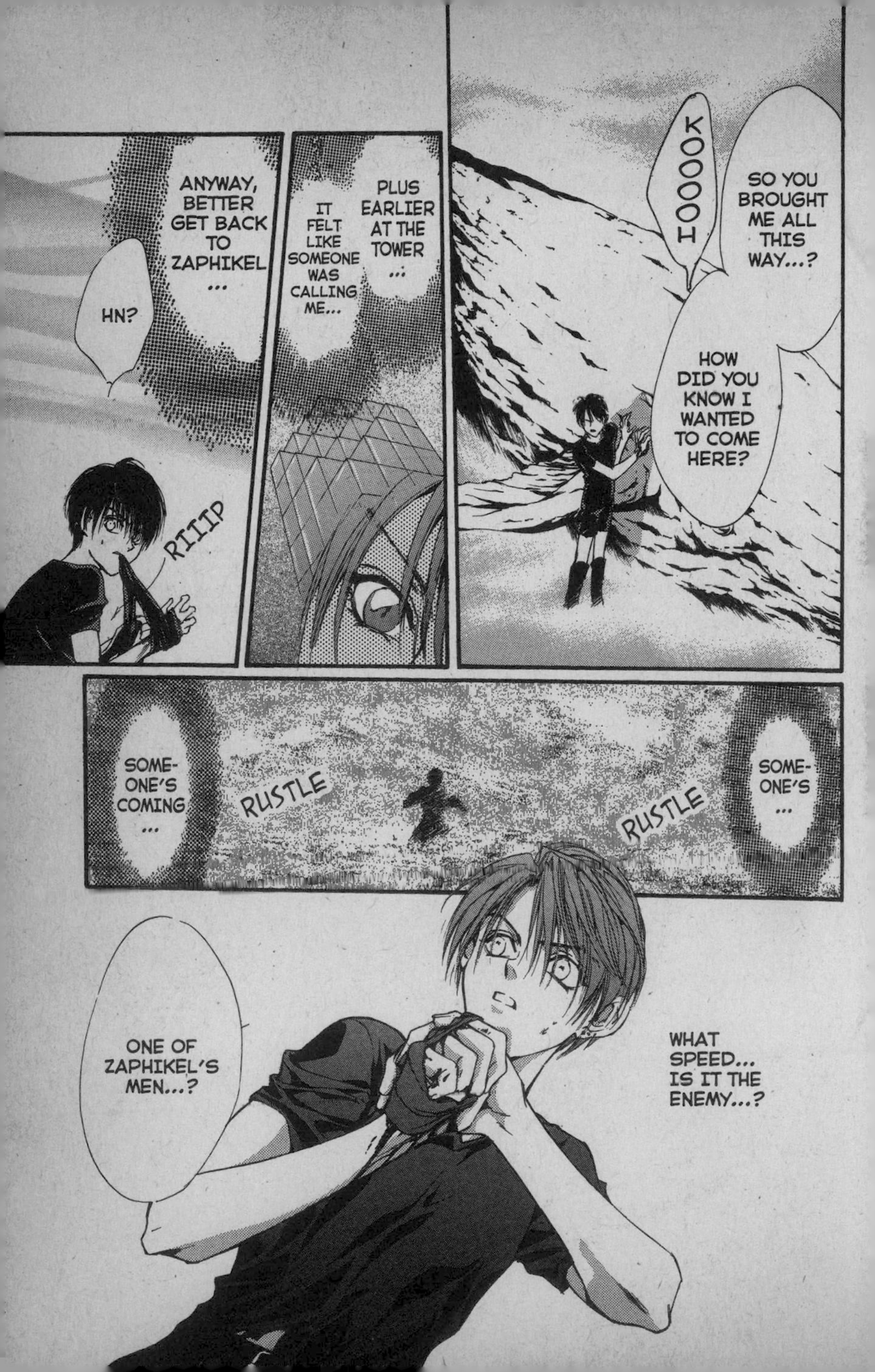
SO YOU BROUGHT ME ALL THIS WAY...?
KOOOOH
HOW DID YOU KNOW I WANTED TO COME HERE?
PLUS EARLIER AT THE TOWER ...
IT FELT LIKE SOMEONE WAS CALLING ME...
ANYWAY, BETTER GET BACK TO ZAPHIKEL ...
HN?
RIIIP
SOME-ONE'S ...
RUSTLE
RUSTLE
SOME-ONE'S COMING ...
WHAT SPEED... IS IT THE ENEMY...?
ONE OF ZAPHIKEL'S MEN...?

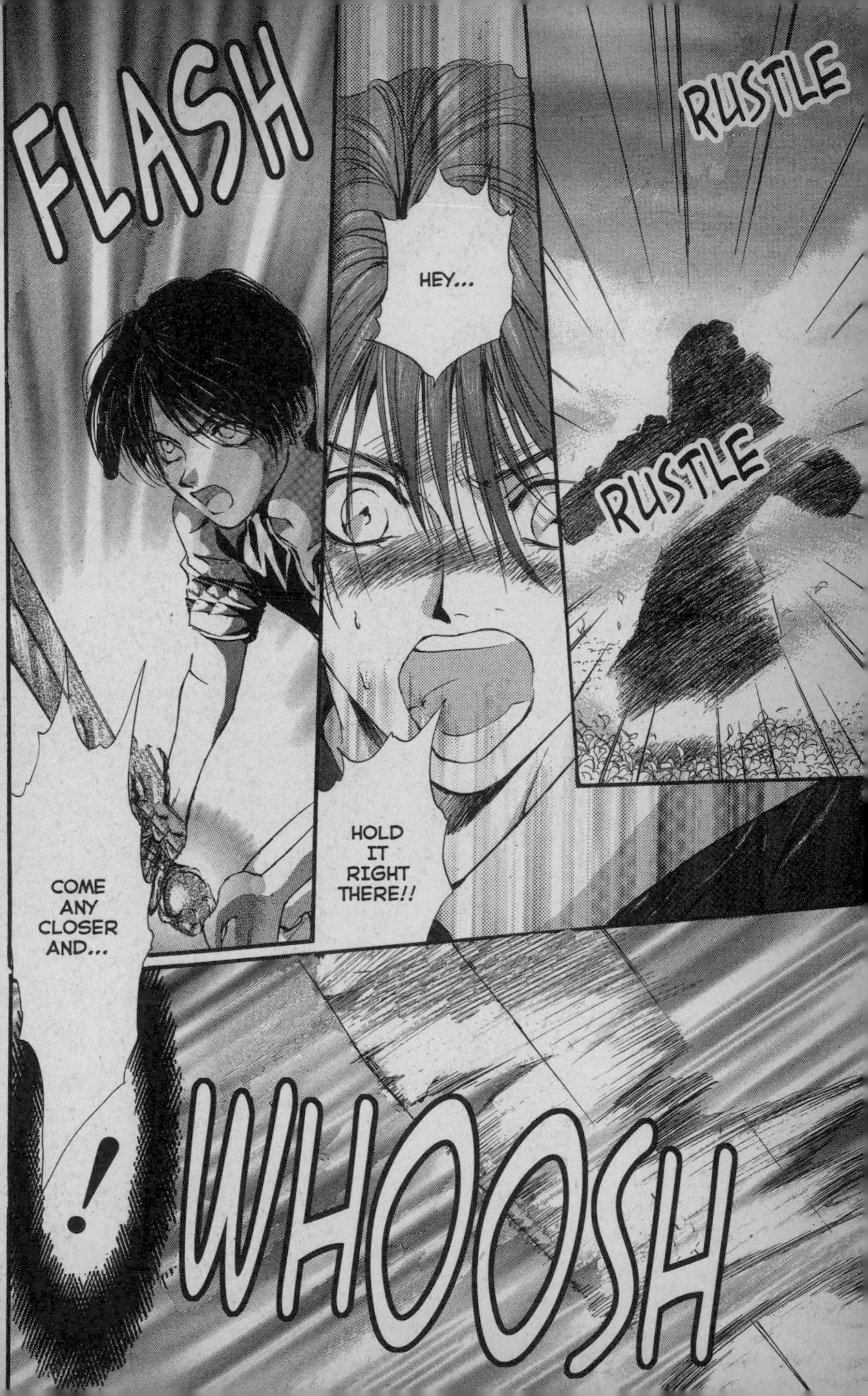
RUSTLE
RUSTLE
HEY...
HOLD IT RIGHT THERE!!
FLASH
COME ANY CLOSER AND...
!
WHOOSH

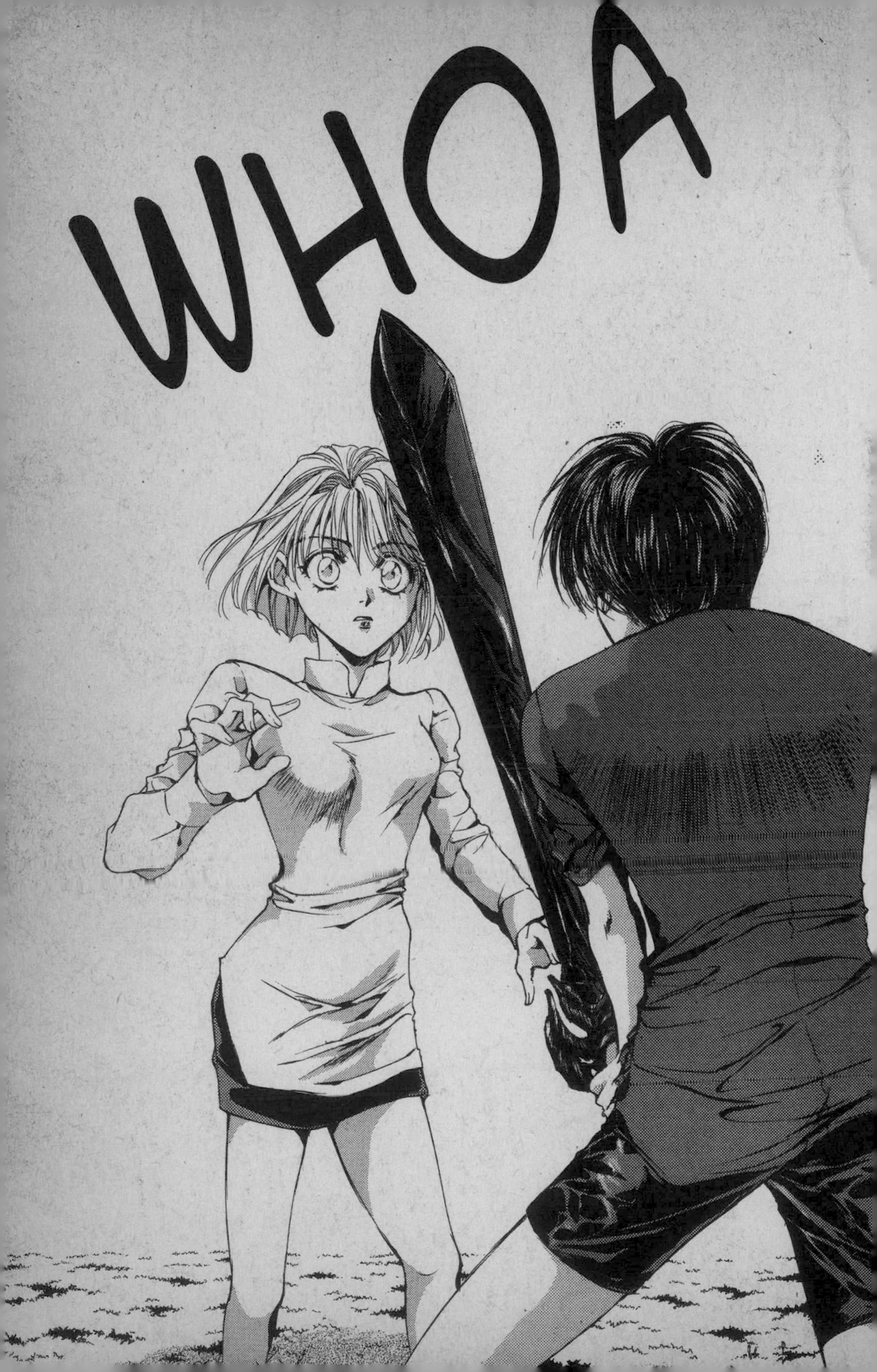
WHOA

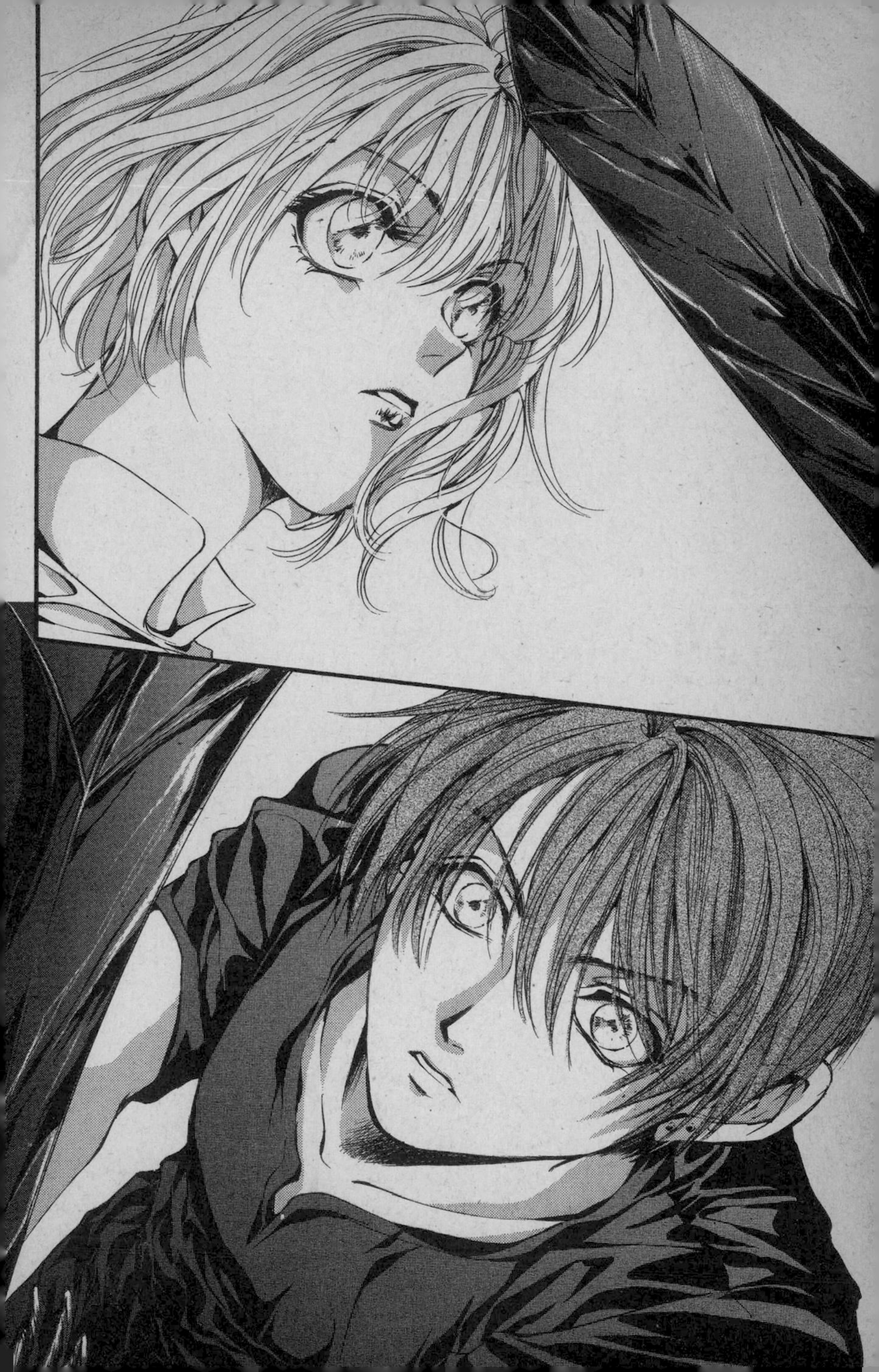

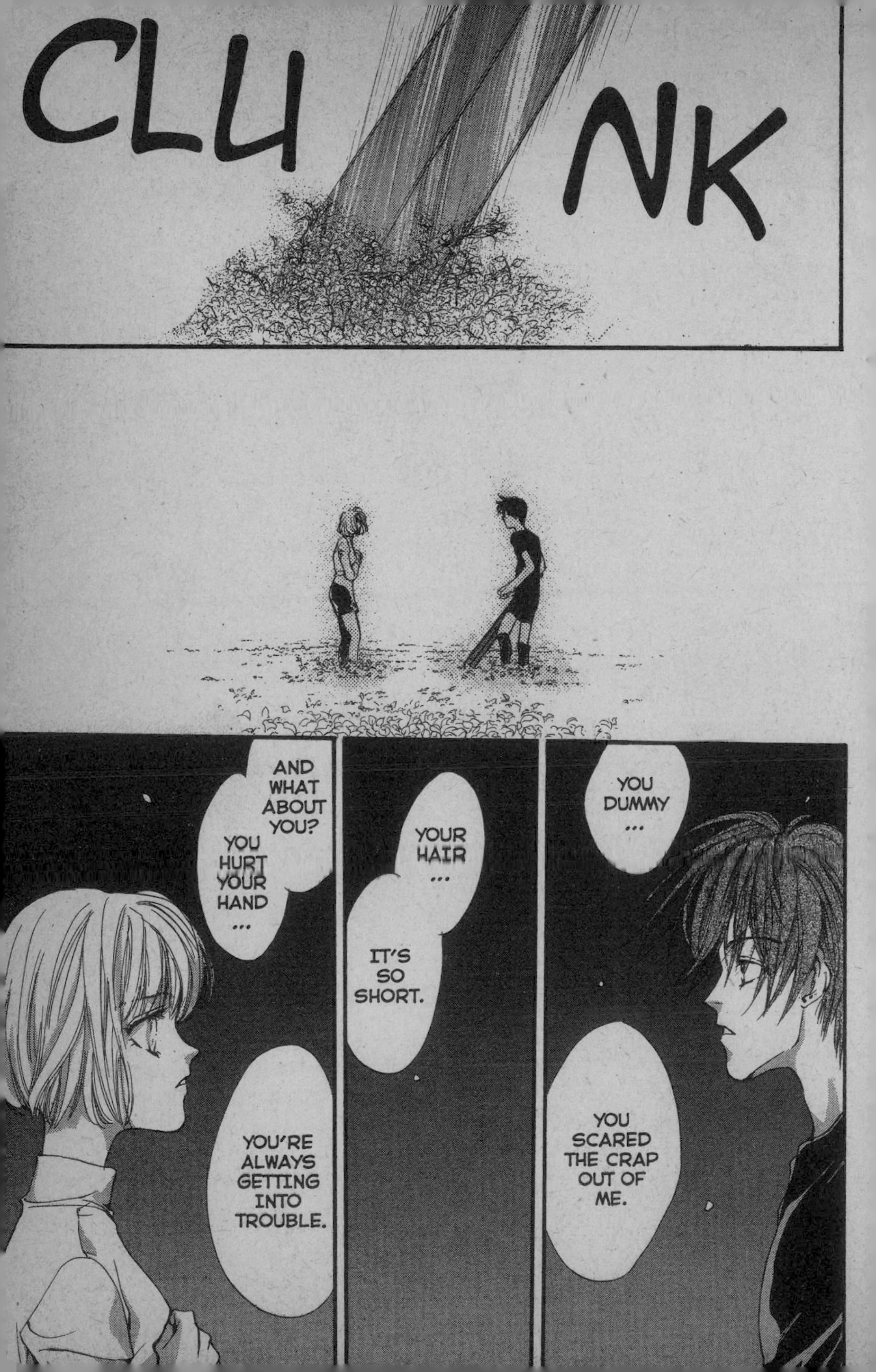
CLUNK
YOU DUMMY ...
YOU SCARED THE CRAP OUT OF ME.
YOUR HAIR ...
IT'S SO SHORT.
AND WHAT ABOUT YOU?
YOU HURT YOUR HAND ...
YOU'RE ALWAYS GETTING INTO TROUBLE.

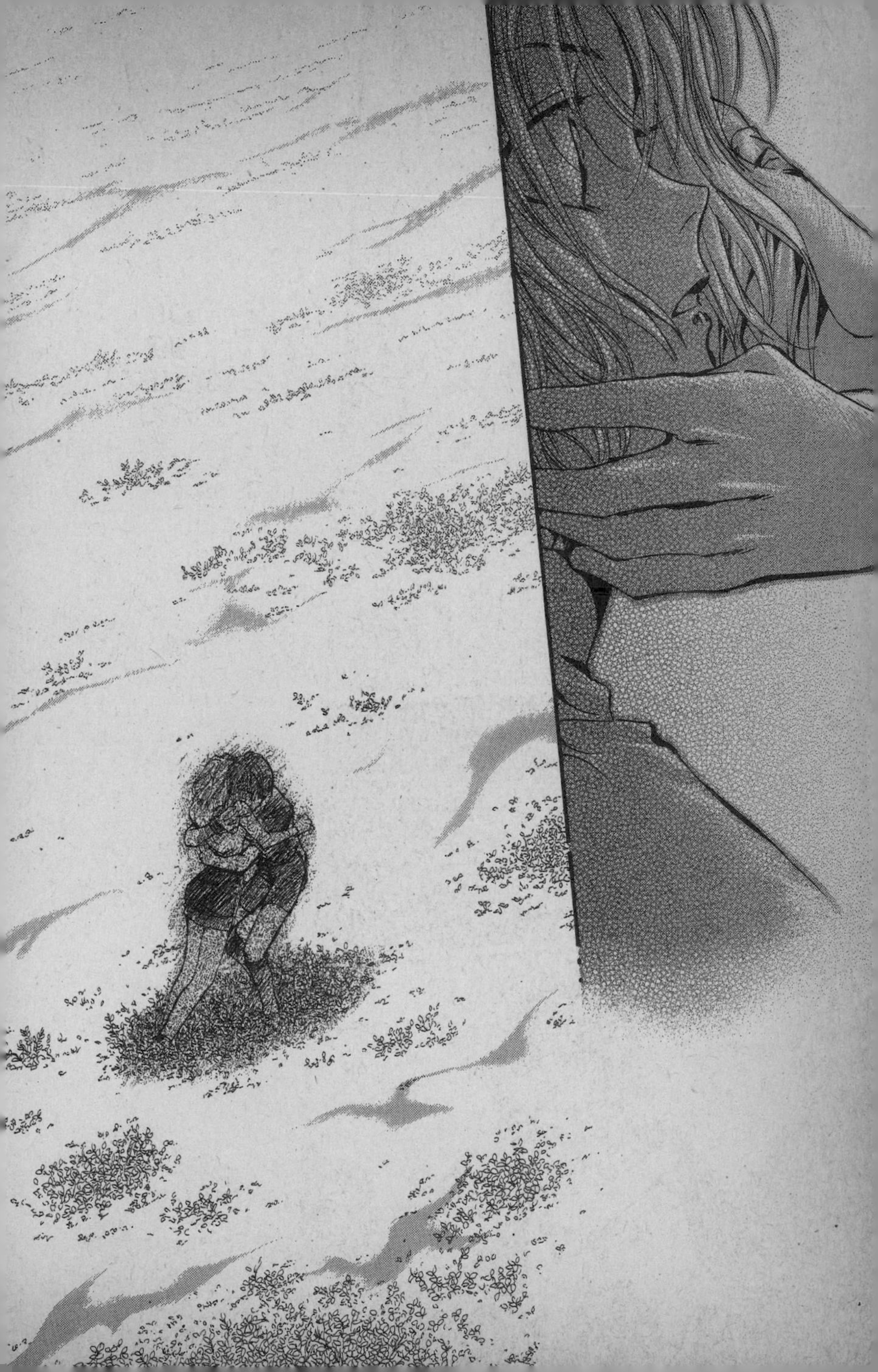

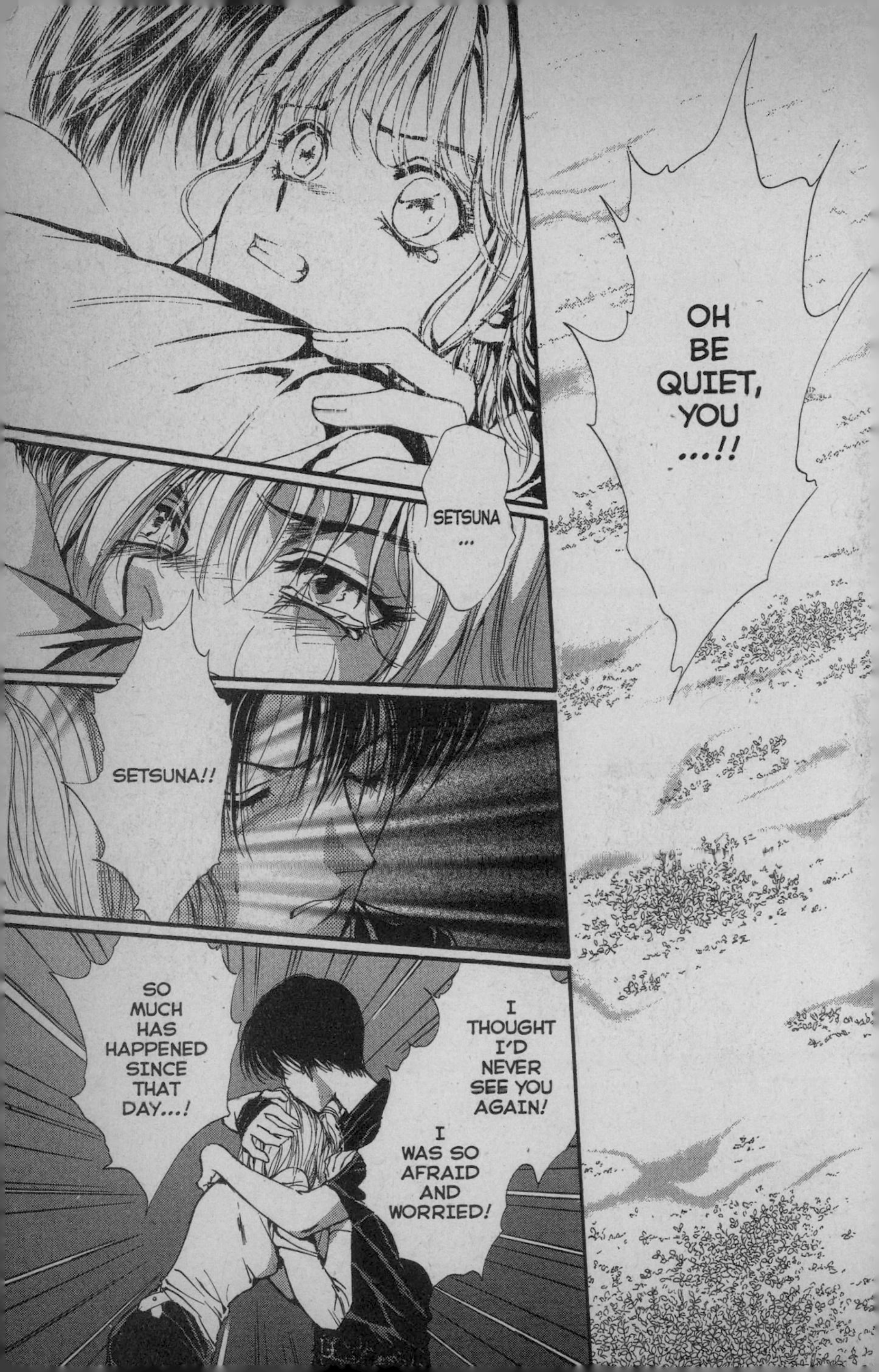
OH BE QUIET, YOU ...!!
SETSUNA ...
SETSUNA!!
I THOUGHT I'D NEVER SEE YOU AGAIN!
I WAS SO AFRAID AND WORRIED!
SO MUCH HAS HAPPENED SINCE THAT DAY...!

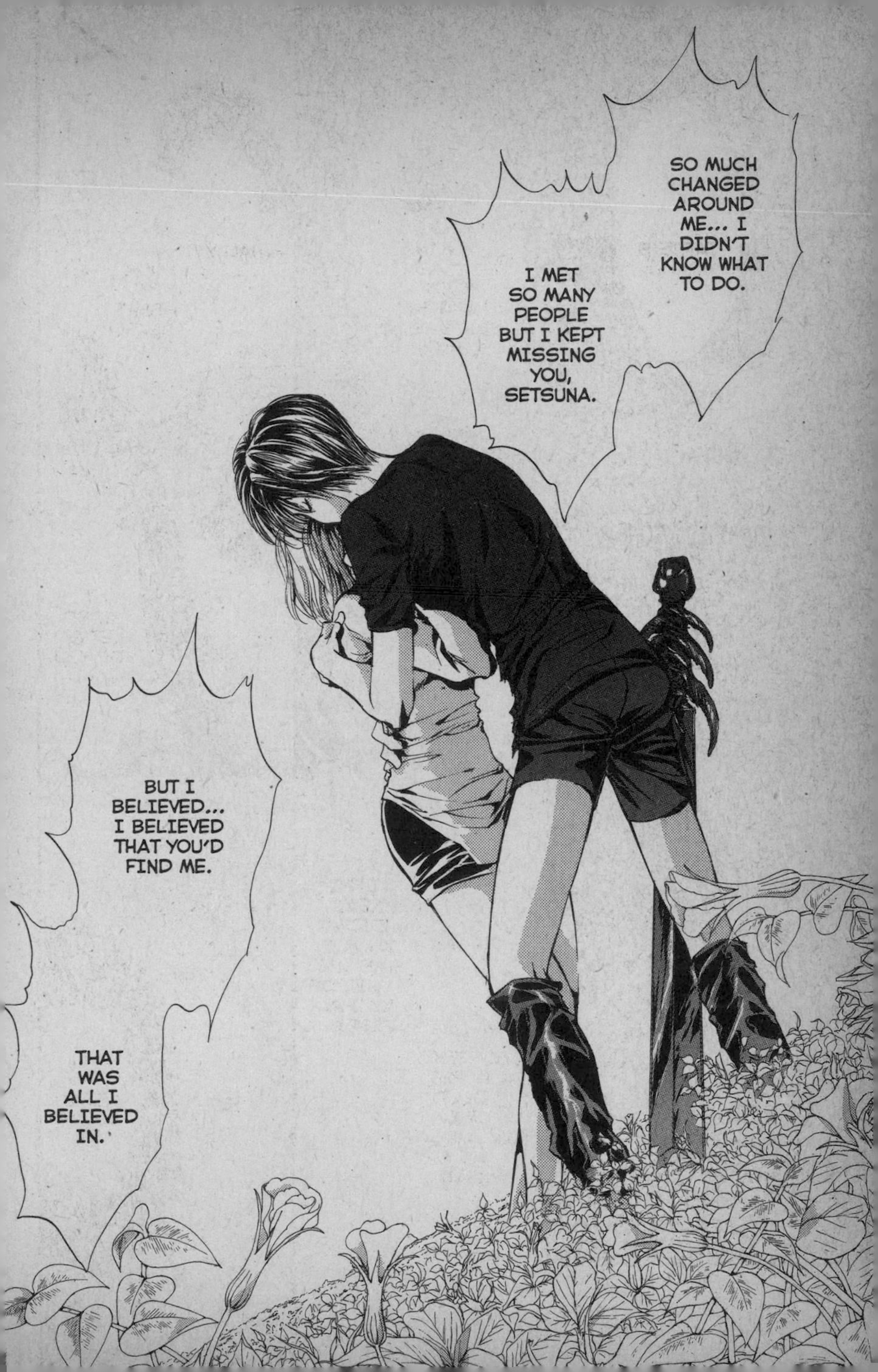
SO MUCH CHANGED AROUND ME... I DIDN'T KNOW WHAT TO DO.
I MET SO MANY PEOPLE BUT I KEPT MISSING YOU, SETSUNA.
BUT I BELIEVED... I BELIEVED THAT YOU'D FIND ME.
THAT WAS ALL I BELIEVED IN.

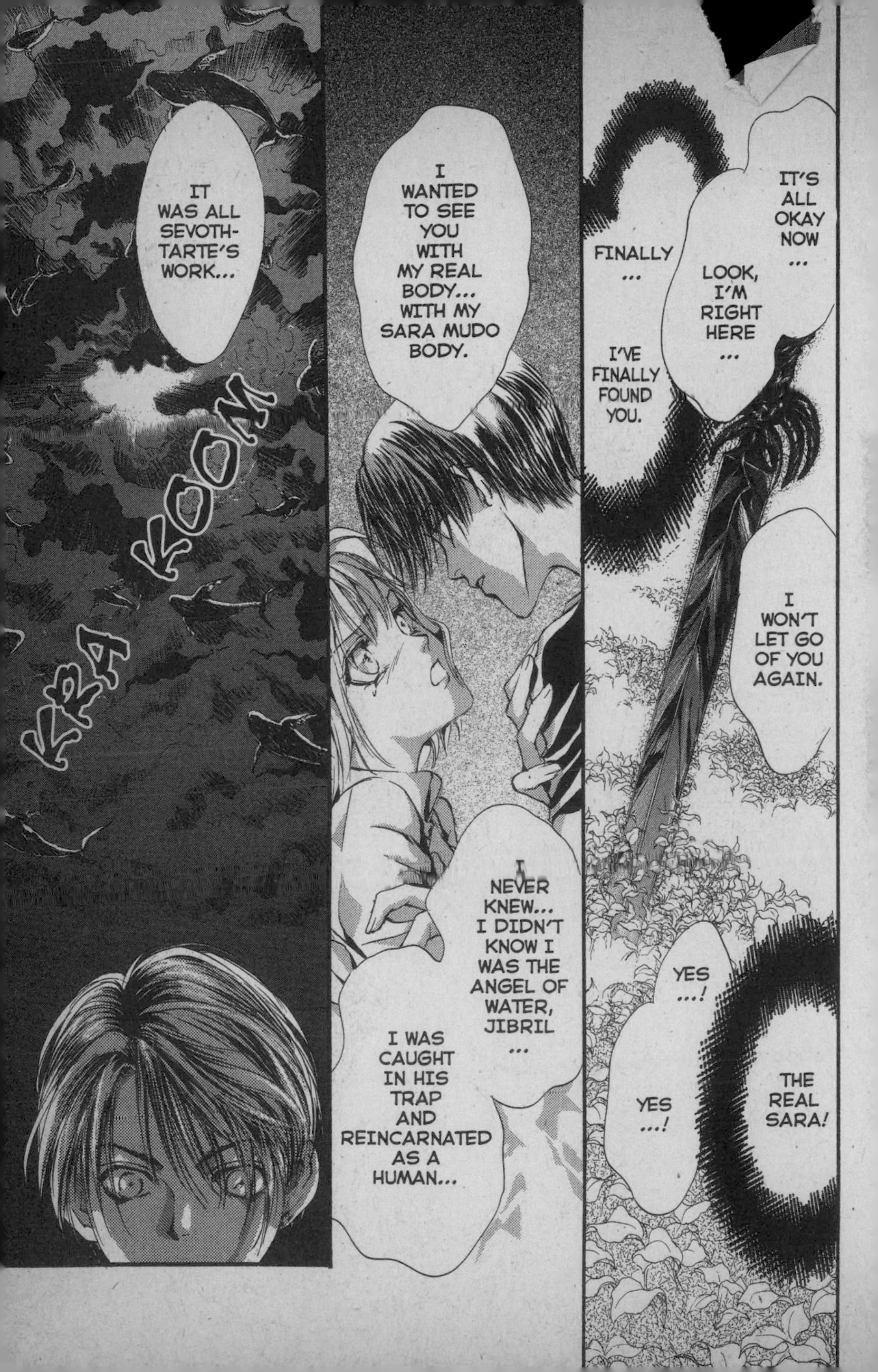
IT'S ALL OKAY NOW ...
LOOK, I'M RIGHT HERE ...
FINALLY ...
I'VE FINALLY FOUND YOU.
I WON'T LET GO OF YOU AGAIN.
THE REAL SARA!
YES ...!
YES ...!
I WANTED TO SEE YOU WITH MY REAL BODY... WITH MY SARA MUDO BODY.
I NEVER KNEW... I DIDN'T KNOW I WAS THE ANGEL OF WATER, JIBRIL ...
I WAS CAUGHT IN HIS TRAP AND REINCARNATED AS A HUMAN...
IT WAS ALL SEVOTH-TARTE'S WORK...
KRA KOOM

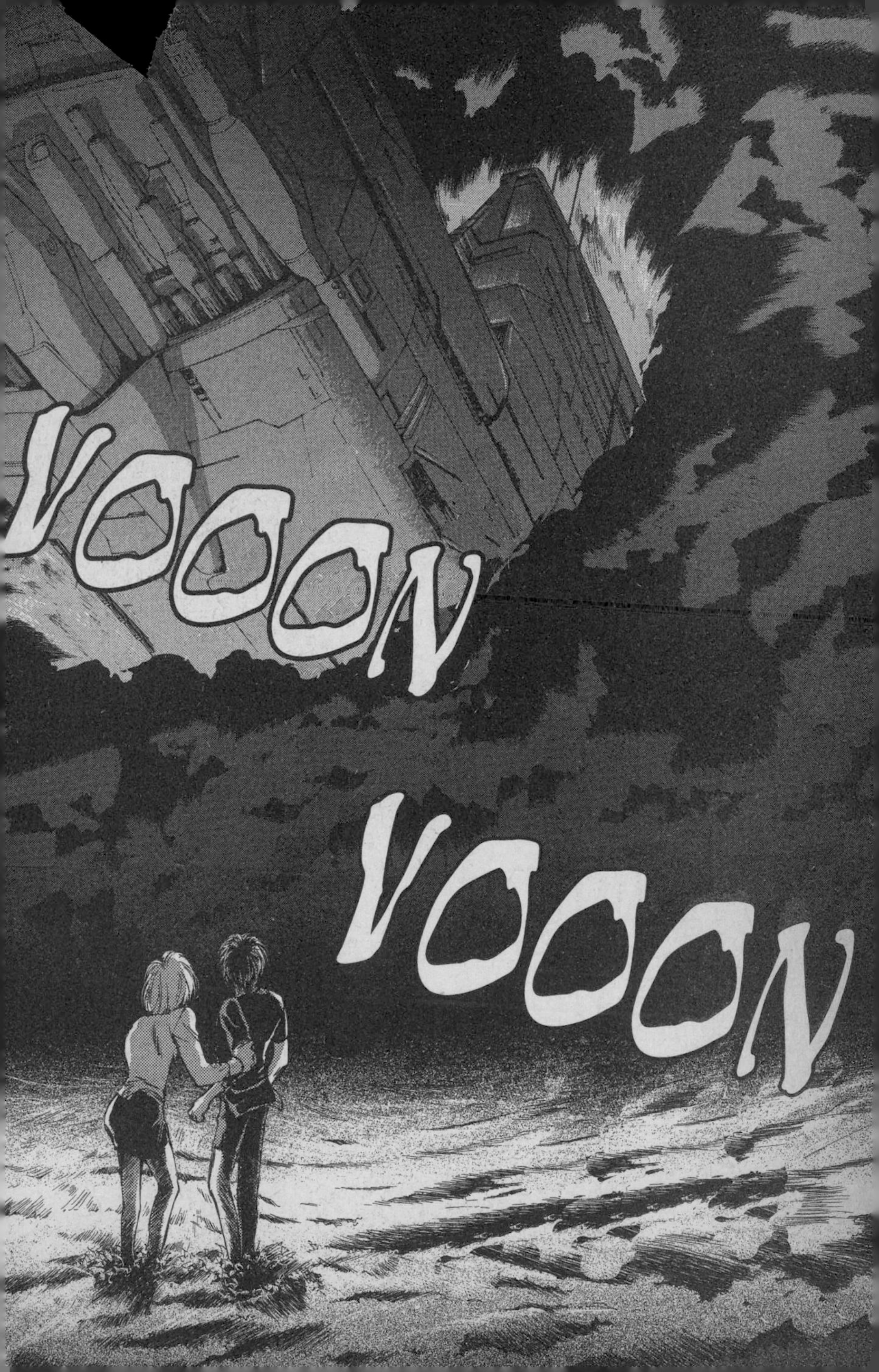
VOOON
VOOON

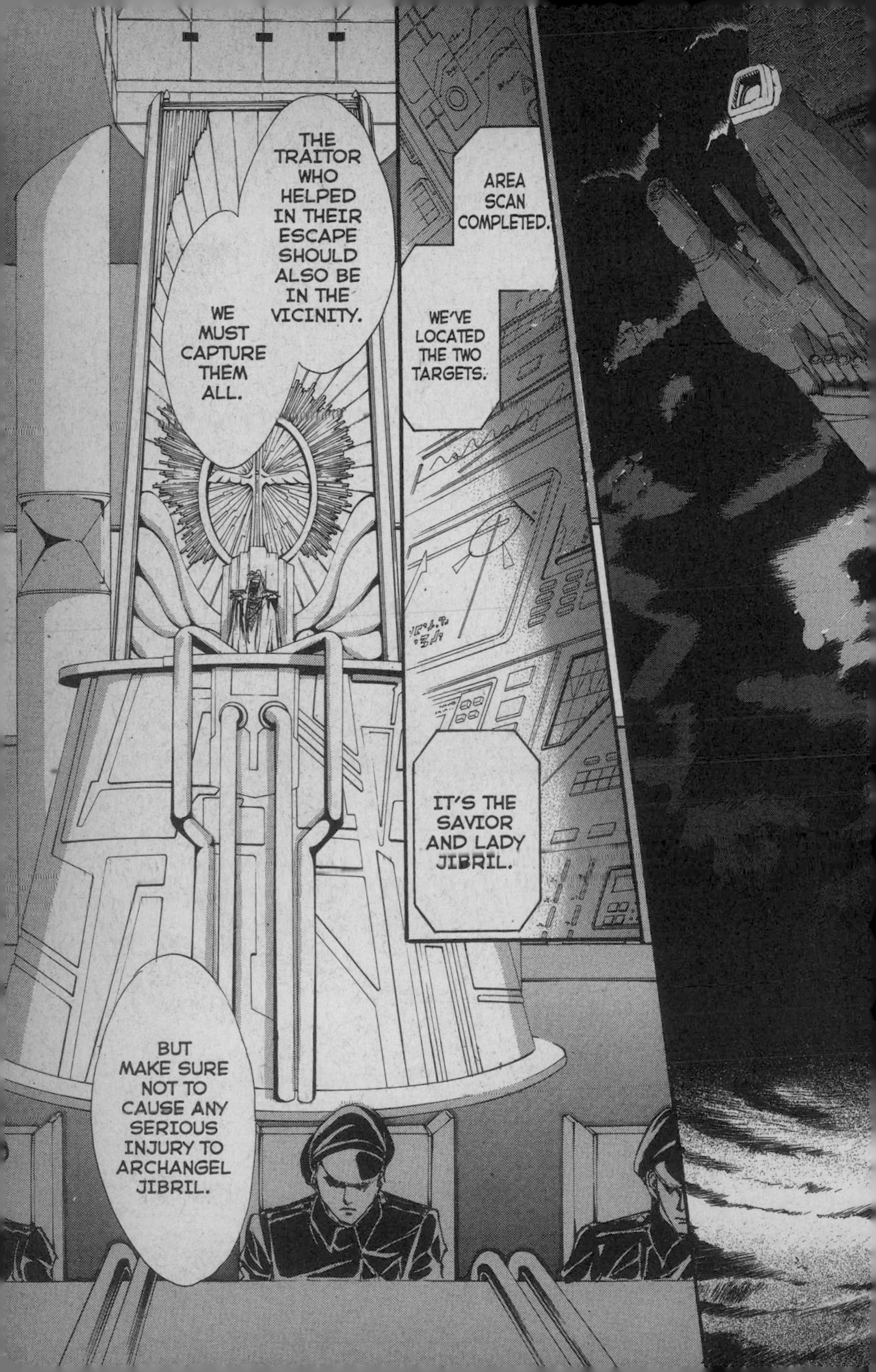
AREA SCAN COMPLETED.
WE'VE LOCATED THE TWO TARGETS.
IT'S THE SAVIOR AND LADY JIBRIL.
THE TRAITOR WHO HELPED IN THEIR ESCAPE SHOULD ALSO BE IN THE VICINITY.
WE MUST CAPTURE THEM ALL.
BUT MAKE SURE NOT TO CAUSE ANY SERIOUS INJURY TO ARCHANGEL JIBRIL.

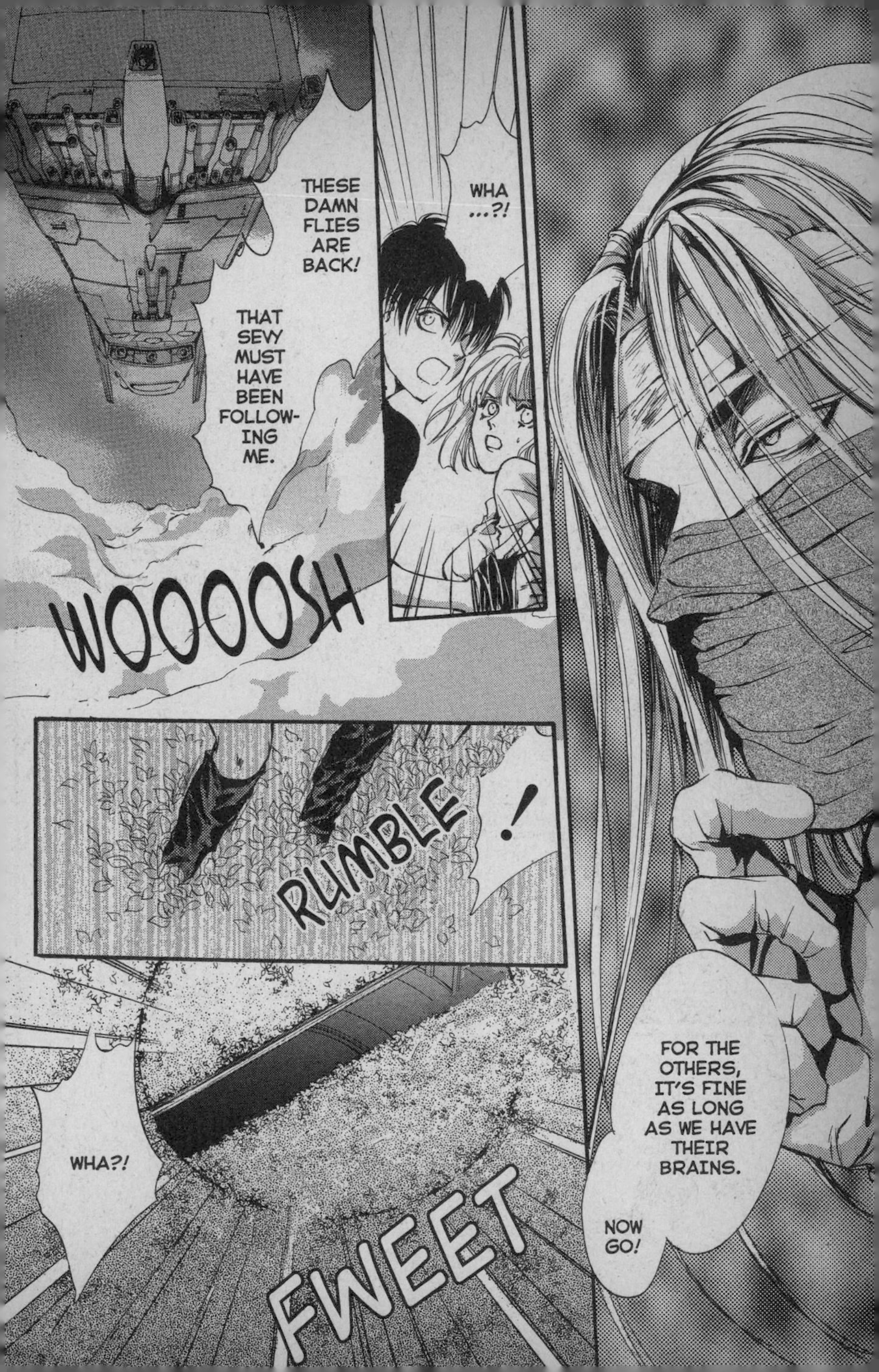

FOR THE OTHERS, IT'S FINE AS LONG AS WE HAVE THEIR BRAINS.
NOW GO!
WHA ...?!
THESE DAMN FLIES ARE BACK!
THAT SEVY MUST HAVE BEEN FOLLOW-ING ME.
WOOOOSH
!
RUMBLE
WHA?!
FWEET

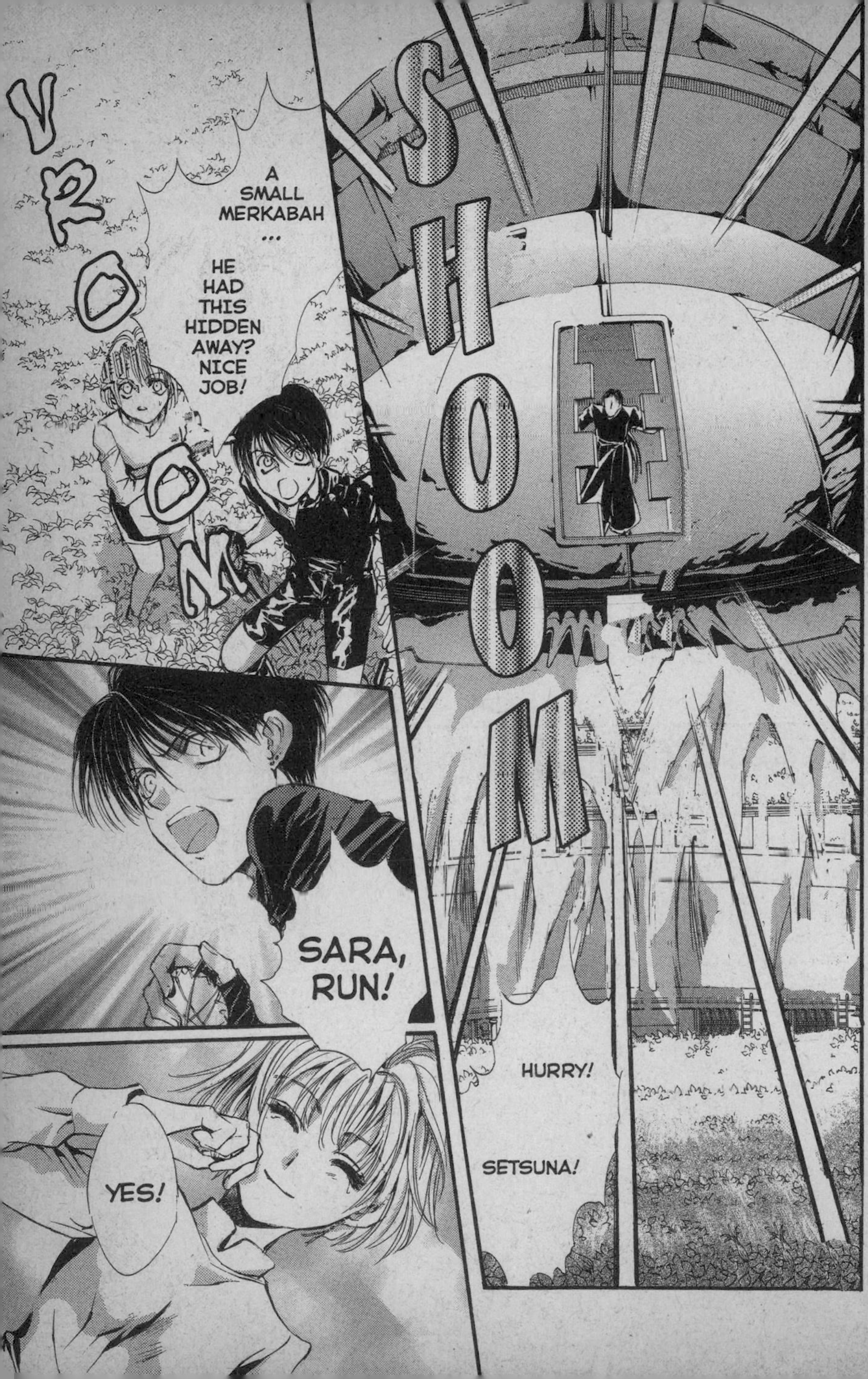
SHOOM
HURRY!
SETSUNA!
VROOM
A SMALL MERKABAH ...
HE HAD THIS HIDDEN AWAY? NICE JOB!
SARA, RUN!
YES!

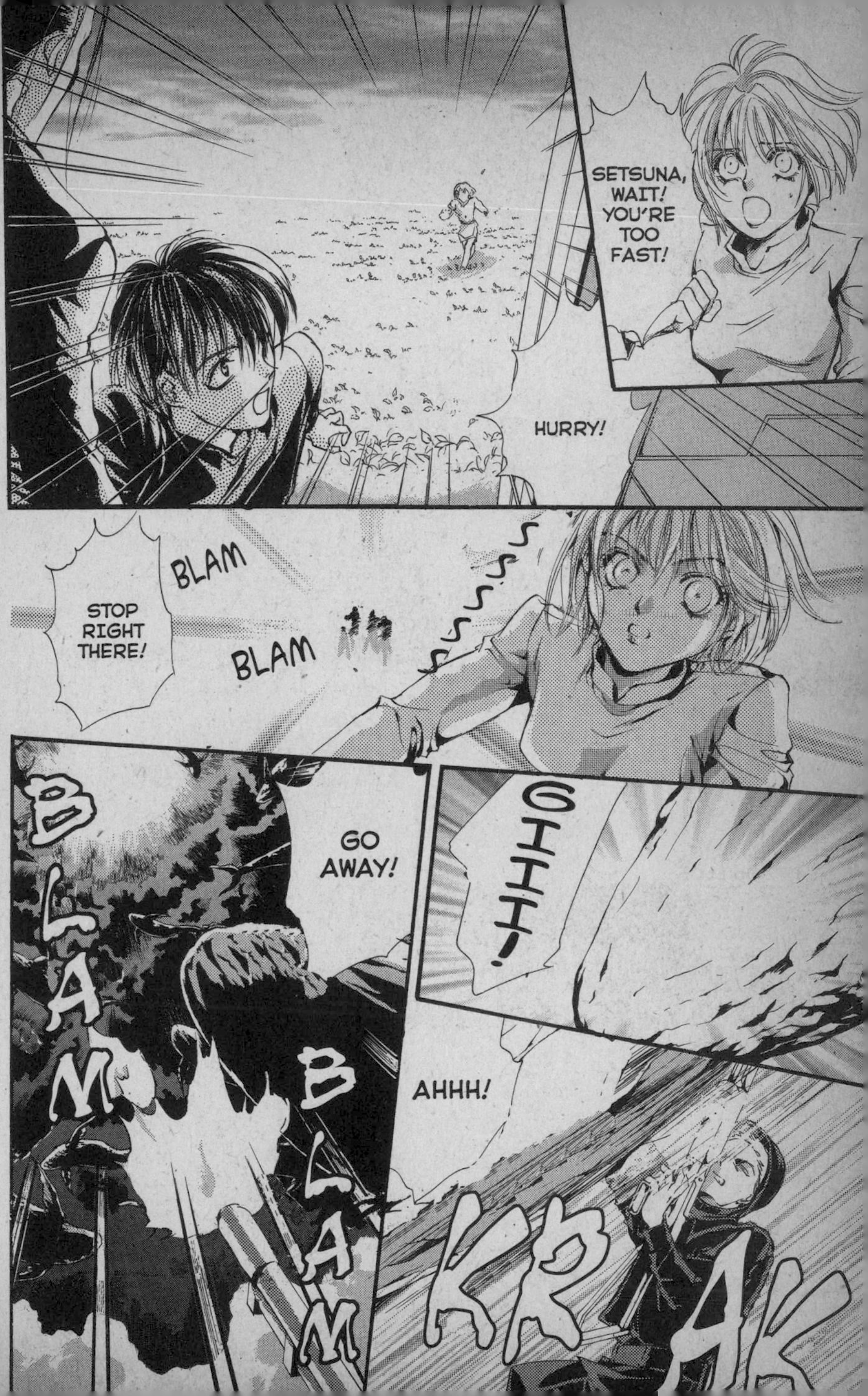
SETSUNA, WAIT! YOU'RE TOO FAST!
HURRY!
BLAM
BLAM
STOP RIGHT THERE!
GIIII!
AHHH!
KRAK
GO AWAY!
BLAM
BLAM

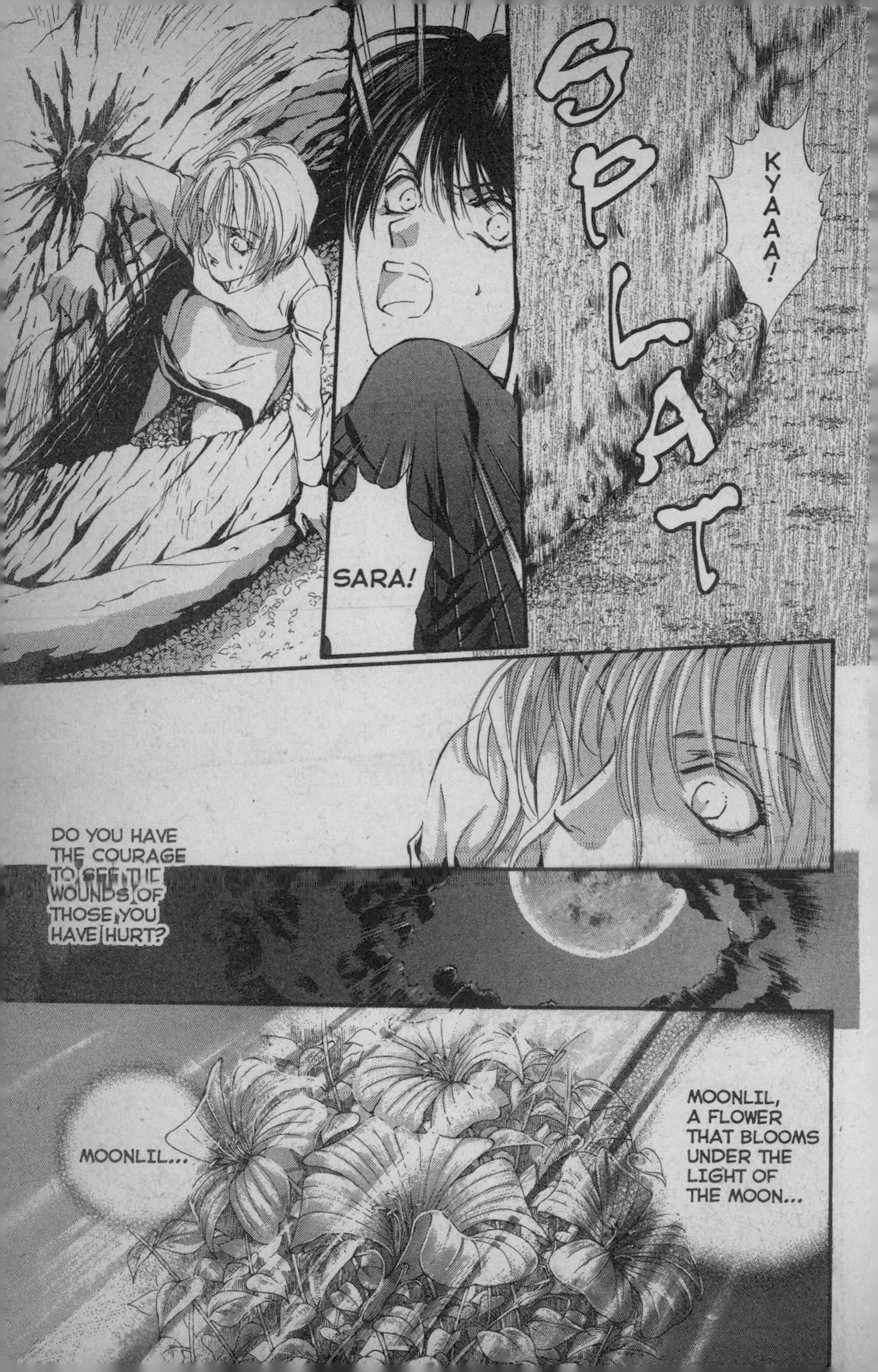
KYAAA!
SPLAT
SARA!
DO YOU HAVE THE COURAGE TO SEE THE WOUNDS OF THOSE YOU HAVE HURT?
MOONLIL, A FLOWER THAT BLOOMS UNDER THE LIGHT OF THE MOON...
MOONLIL...

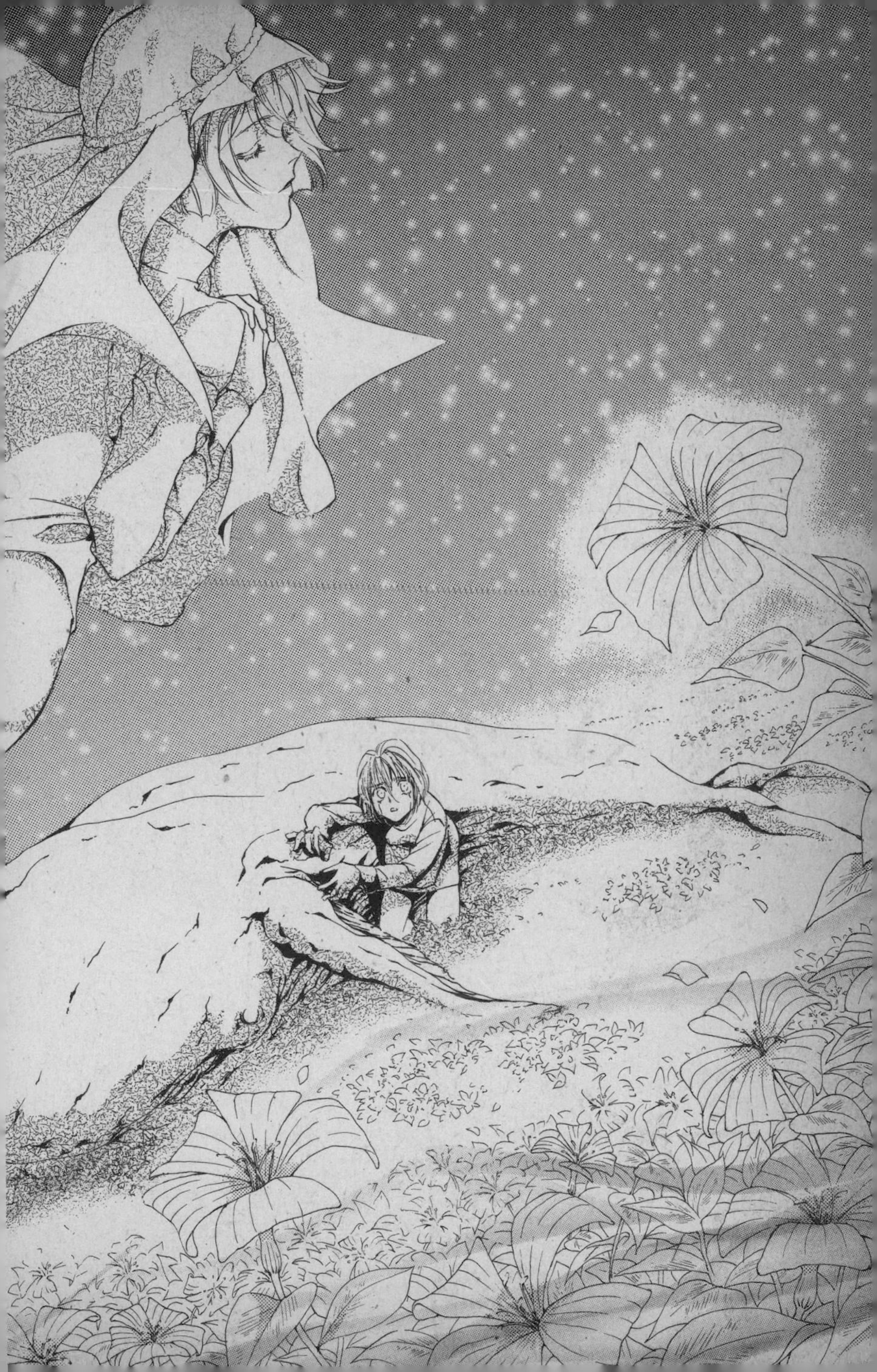

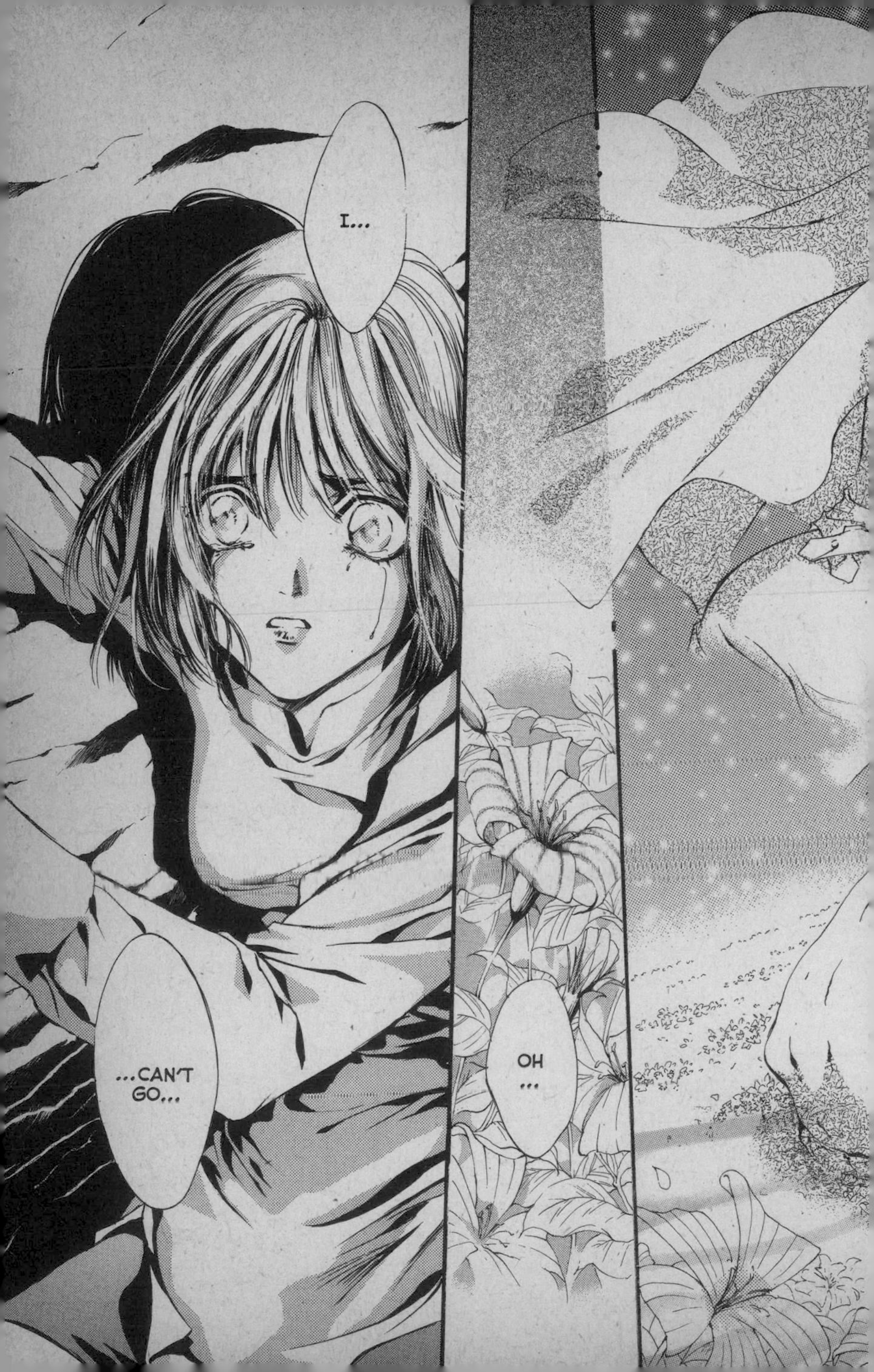
OH ...
I...
...CAN'T GO...

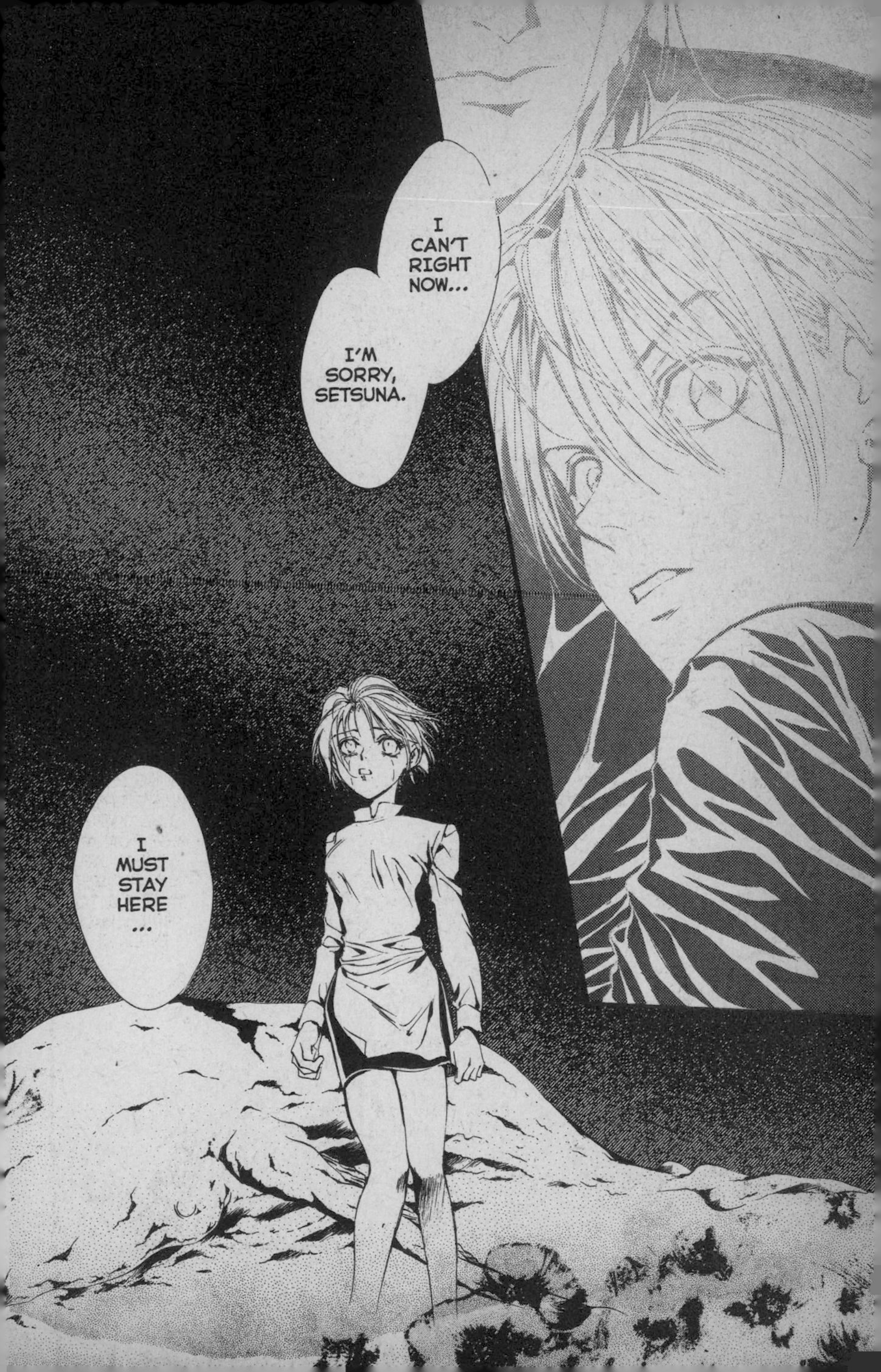
I CAN'T RIGHT NOW...
I'M SORRY, SETSUNA.
I MUST STAY HERE ...

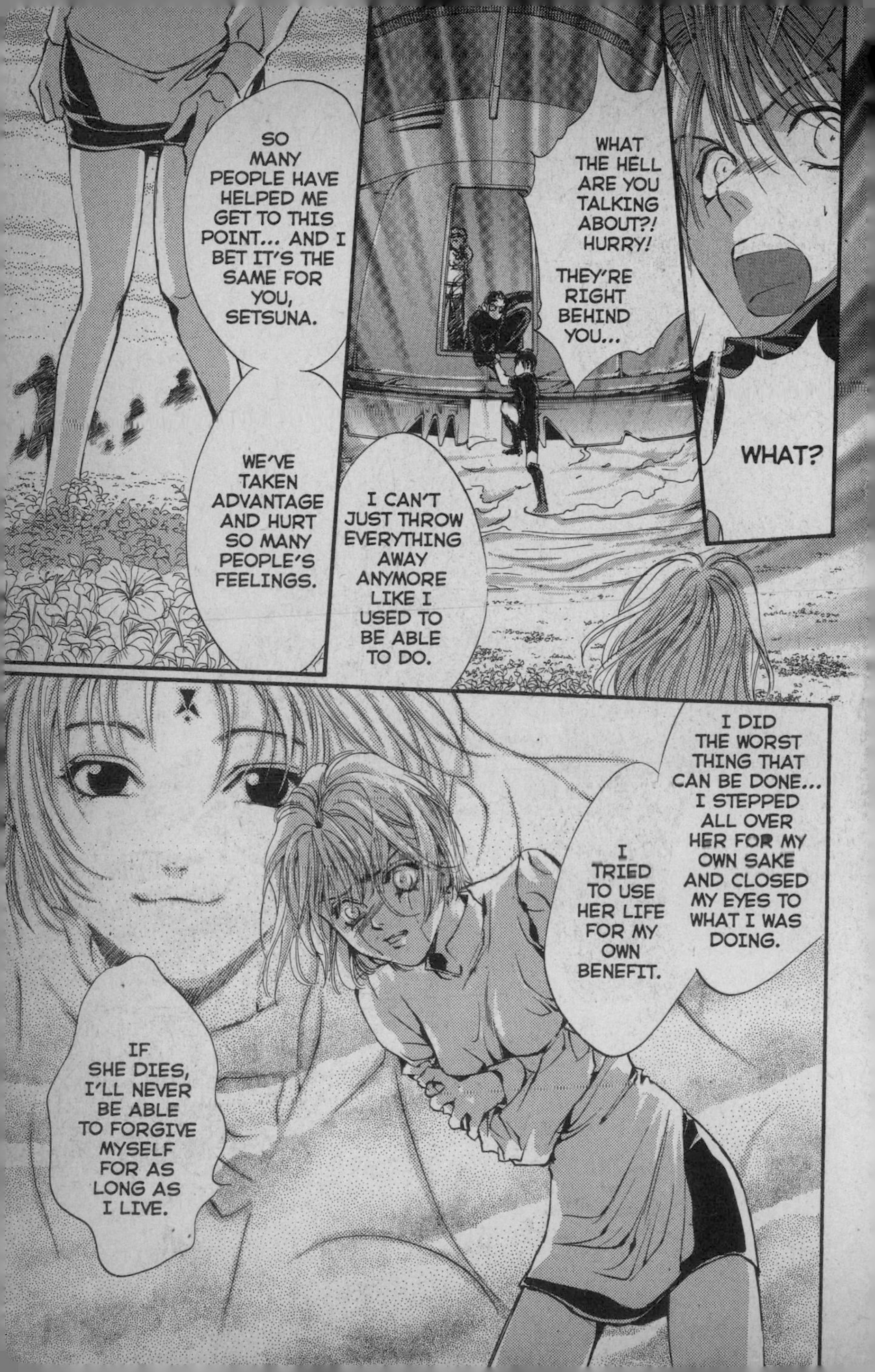
WHAT?
WHAT THE HELL ARE YOU TALKING ABOUT?! HURRY!
THEY'RE RIGHT BEHIND YOU...
SO MANY PEOPLE HAVE HELPED ME GET TO THIS POINT... AND I BET IT'S THE SAME FOR YOU, SETSUNA.
WE'VE TAKEN ADVANTAGE AND HURT SO MANY PEOPLE'S FEELINGS.
I CAN'T JUST THROW EVERYTHING AWAY ANYMORE LIKE I USED TO BE ABLE TO DO.
I DID THE WORST THING THAT CAN BE DONE... I STEPPED ALL OVER HER FOR MY OWN SAKE AND CLOSED MY EYES TO WHAT I WAS DOING.
I TRIED TO USE HER LIFE FOR MY OWN BENEFIT.
IF SHE DIES, I'LL NEVER BE ABLE TO FORGIVE MYSELF FOR AS LONG AS I LIVE.

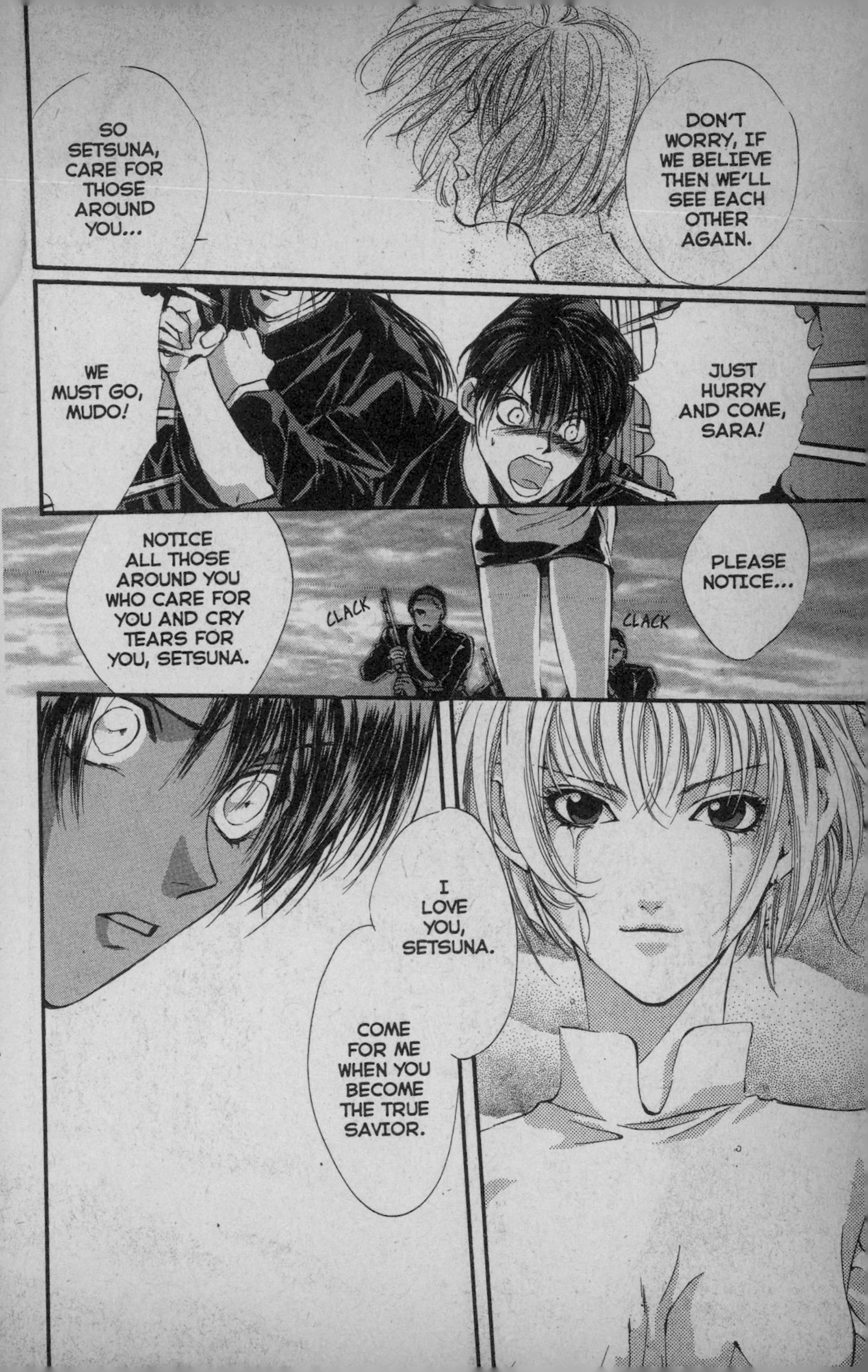
DON'T WORRY, IF WE BELIEVE THEN WE'LL SEE EACH OTHER AGAIN.
SO SETSUNA, CARE FOR THOSE AROUND YOU...
JUST HURRY AND COME, SARA!
WE MUST GO, MUDO!
PLEASE NOTICE...
CLACK
CLACK
NOTICE ALL THOSE AROUND YOU WHO CARE FOR YOU AND CRY TEARS FOR YOU, SETSUNA.
I LOVE YOU, SETSUNA.
COME FOR ME WHEN YOU BECOME THE TRUE SAVIOR.

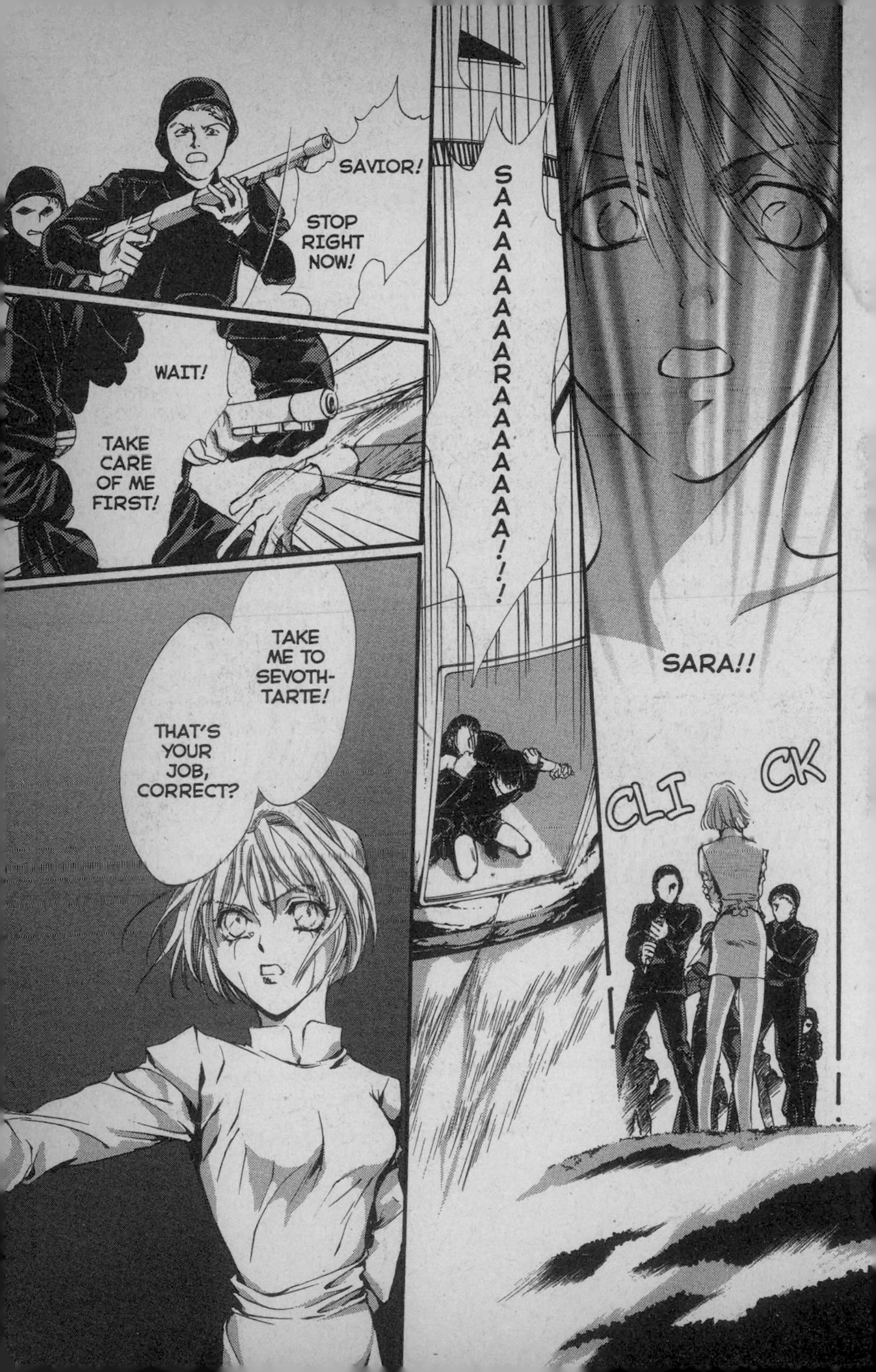
SARA!!
CLI CK
SAAAAAAARAAAAAAA!!!
SAVIOR!
STOP RIGHT NOW!
WAIT!
TAKE CARE OF ME FIRST!
TAKE ME TO SEVOTH-TARTE!
THAT'S YOUR JOB, CORRECT?

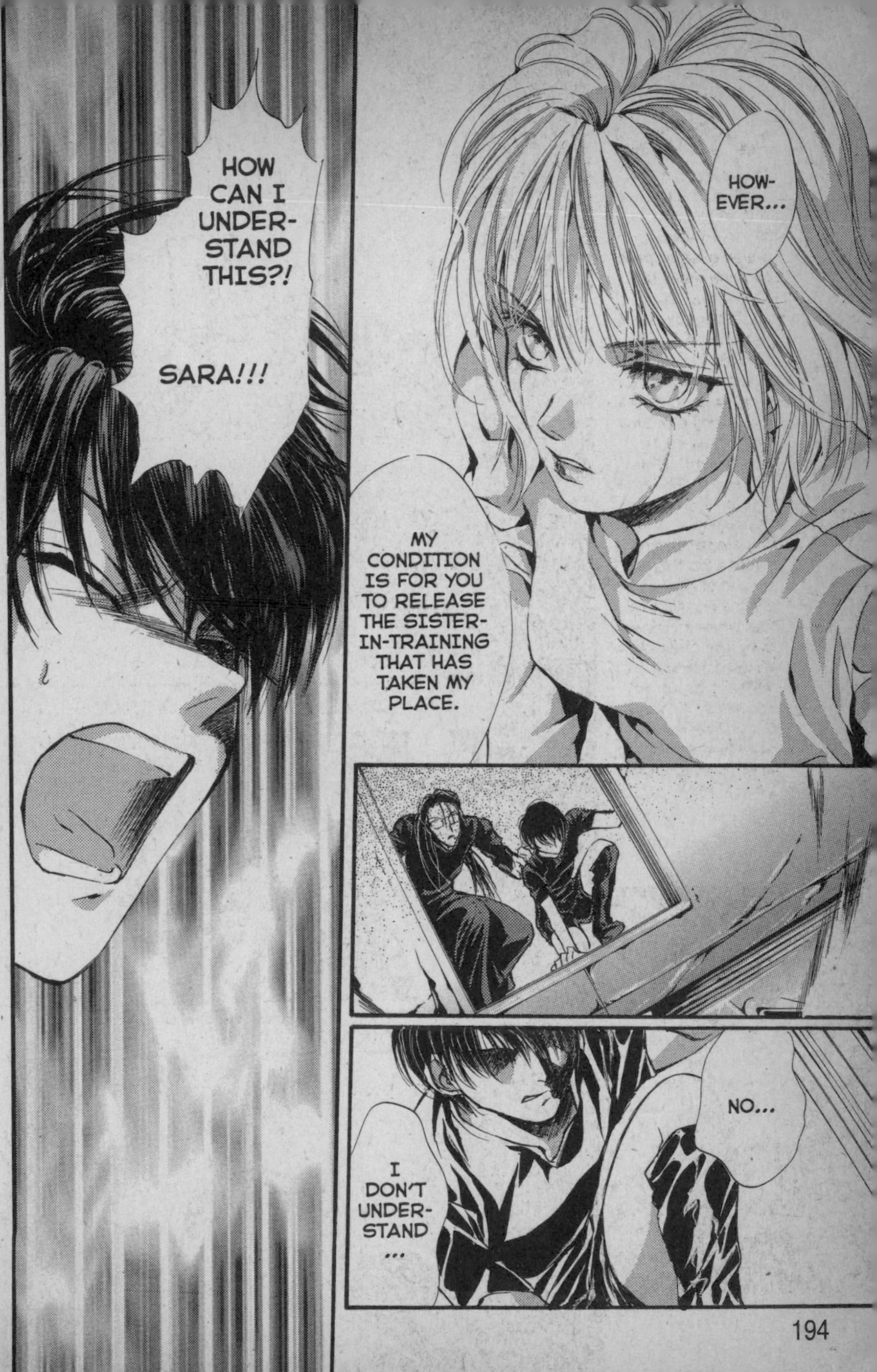
HOW-EVER...
MY CONDITION IS FOR YOU TO RELEASE THE SISTER-IN-TRAINING THAT HAS TAKEN MY PLACE.
NO...
I DON'T UNDERSTAND...
HOW CAN I UNDERSTAND THIS?!
SARA!!!

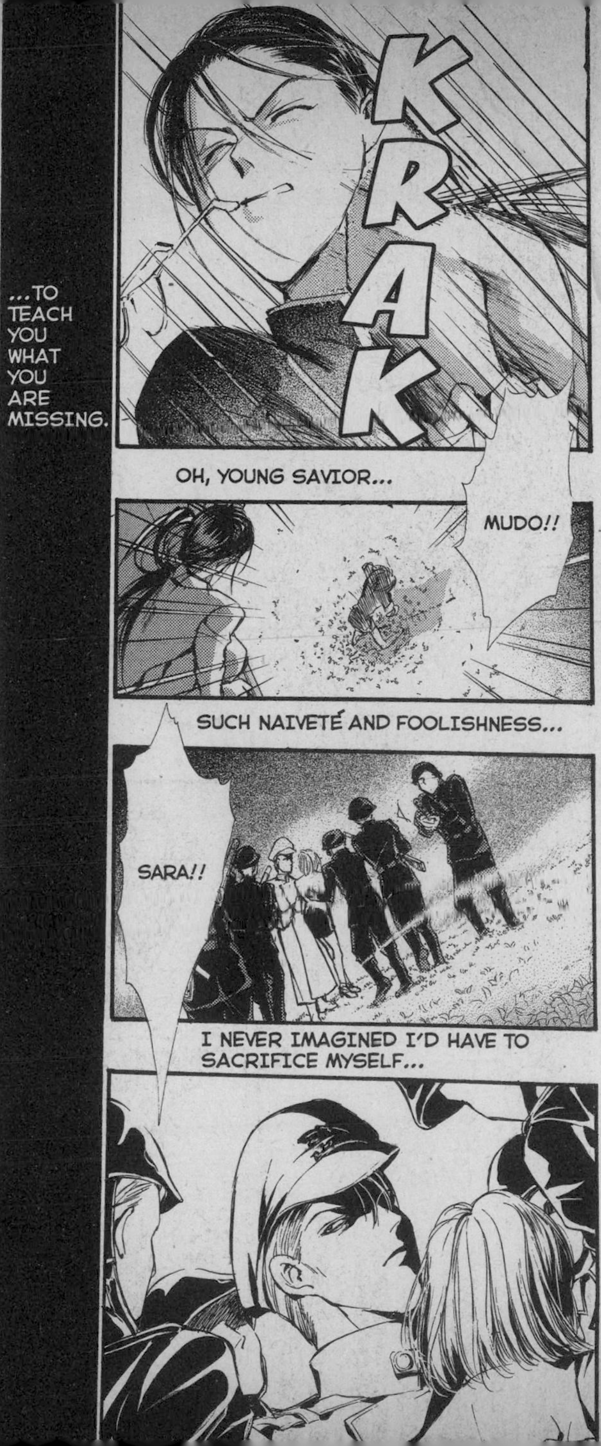
KRAK
...TO TEACH YOU WHAT YOU ARE MISSING.
OH, YOUNG SAVIOR...
MUDO!!
SUCH NAIVETÉ AND FOOLISHNESS...
SARA!!
I NEVER IMAGINED I'D HAVE TO SACRIFICE MYSELF...

The scene with the field of Moonlils was one of the climaxes of this chapter but it was a major pain to draw them. Not that I drew them all...Thank you, my assistants! I actually rarely have flowers appearing in my manga. Roses are seen from time to time, mostly for comedic value. Roses are so flashy, it's just funny when they appear. I mean, how embarrassing would it be to have a rose in your mouth? You can really see the artist's individuality when they draw flowers, since it's a difficult object to recreate. All those Cloud Whales were probably also really hard to draw... Thank you so much!

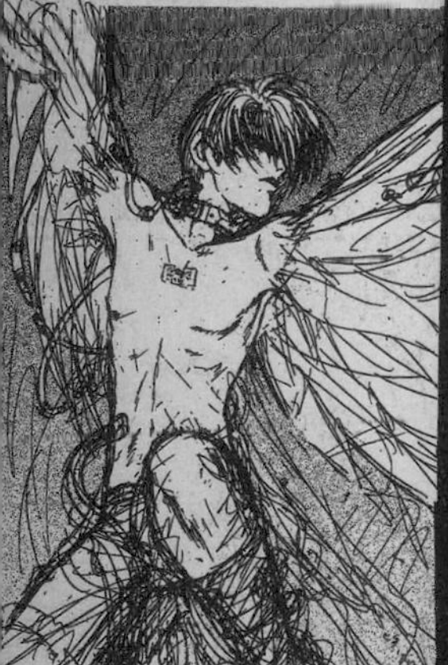

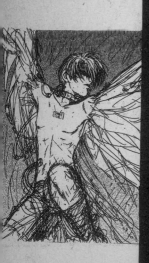

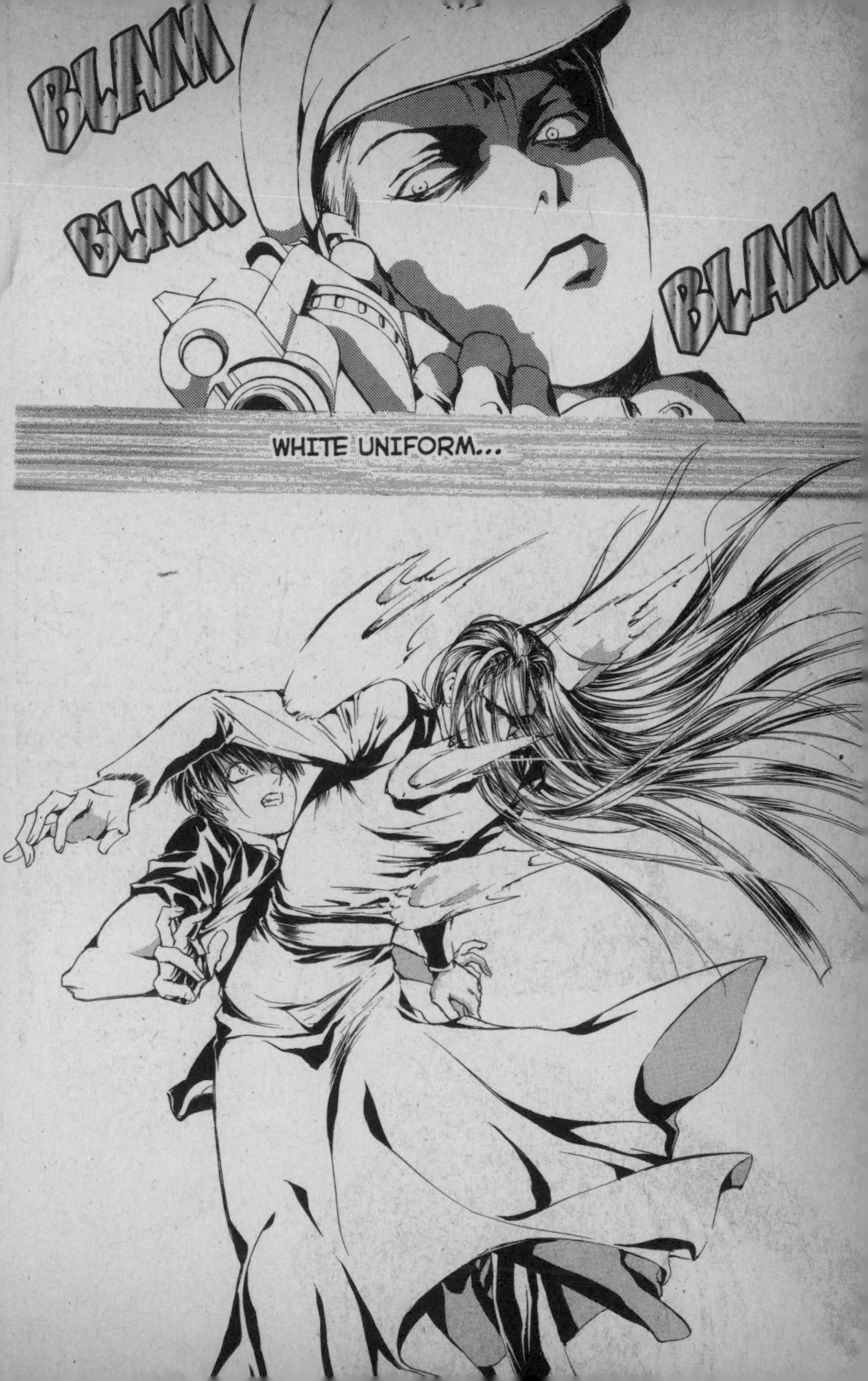
BLAM
BLAM
BLAM
WHITE UNIFORM...

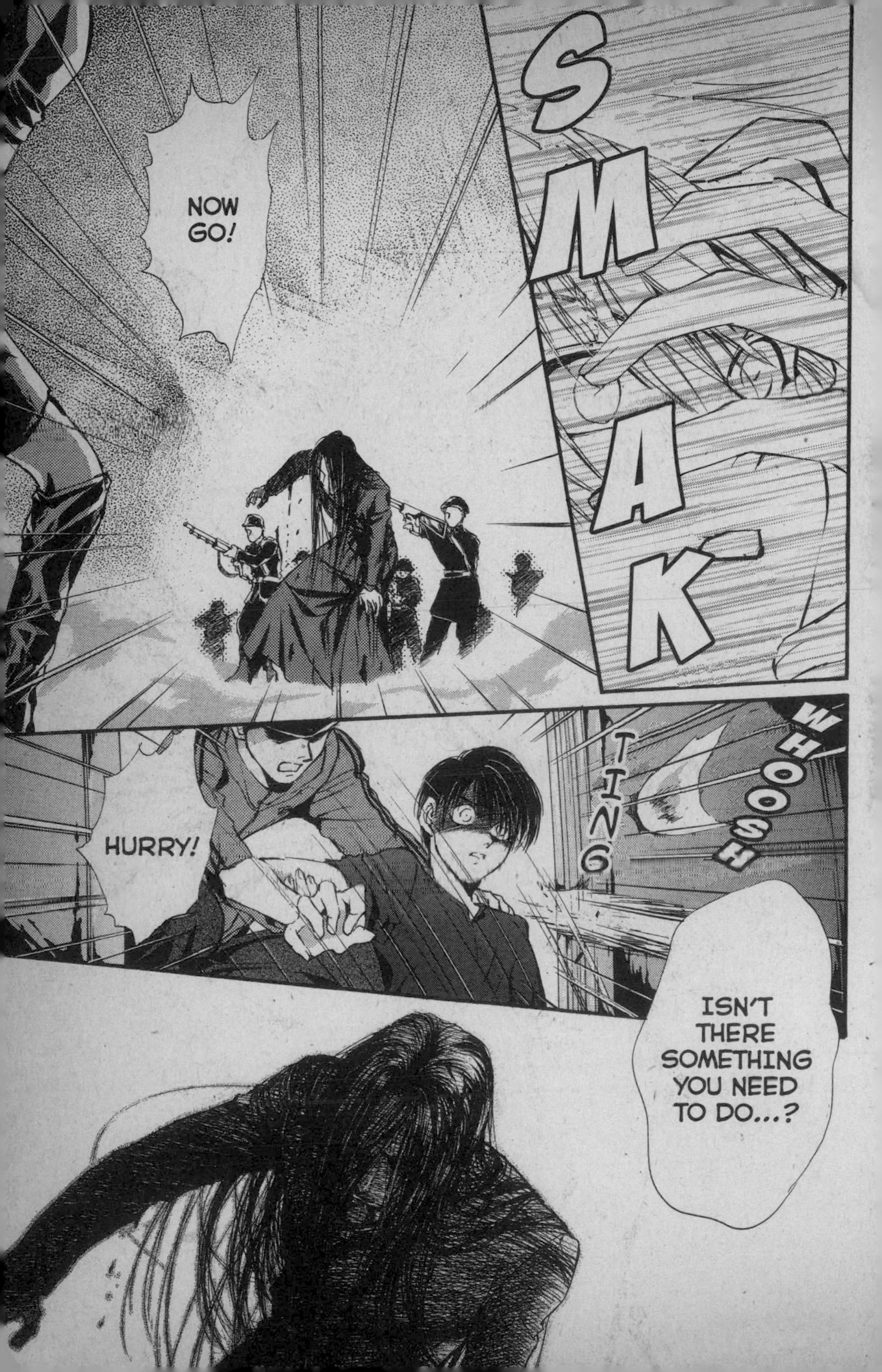
SMAK
NOW GO!
WHOOSH
TING
HURRY!
ISN'T THERE SOMETHING YOU NEED TO DO...?

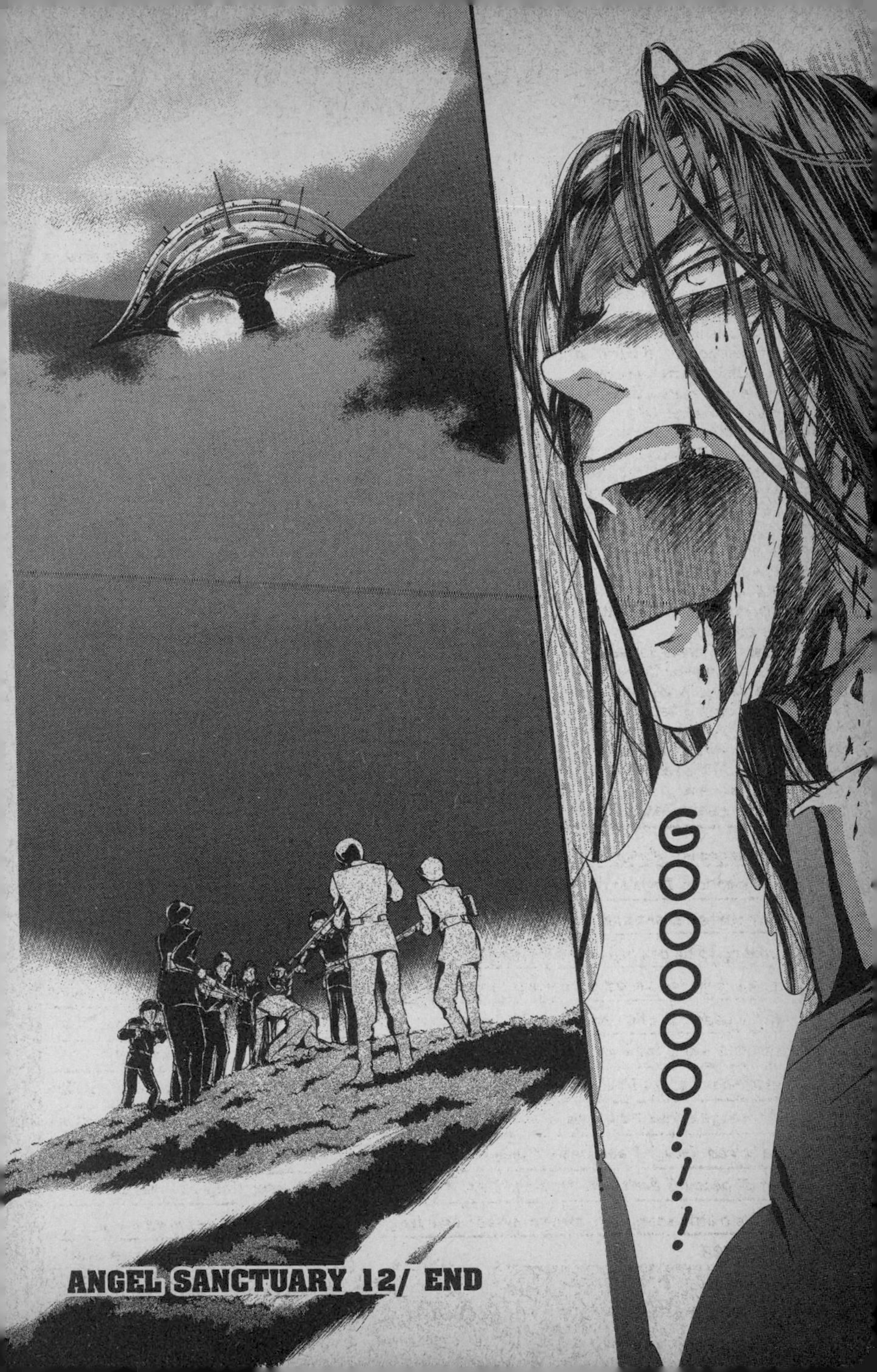
GOOOOO!!!
ANGEL SANCTUARY 12/ END

I like girls too!

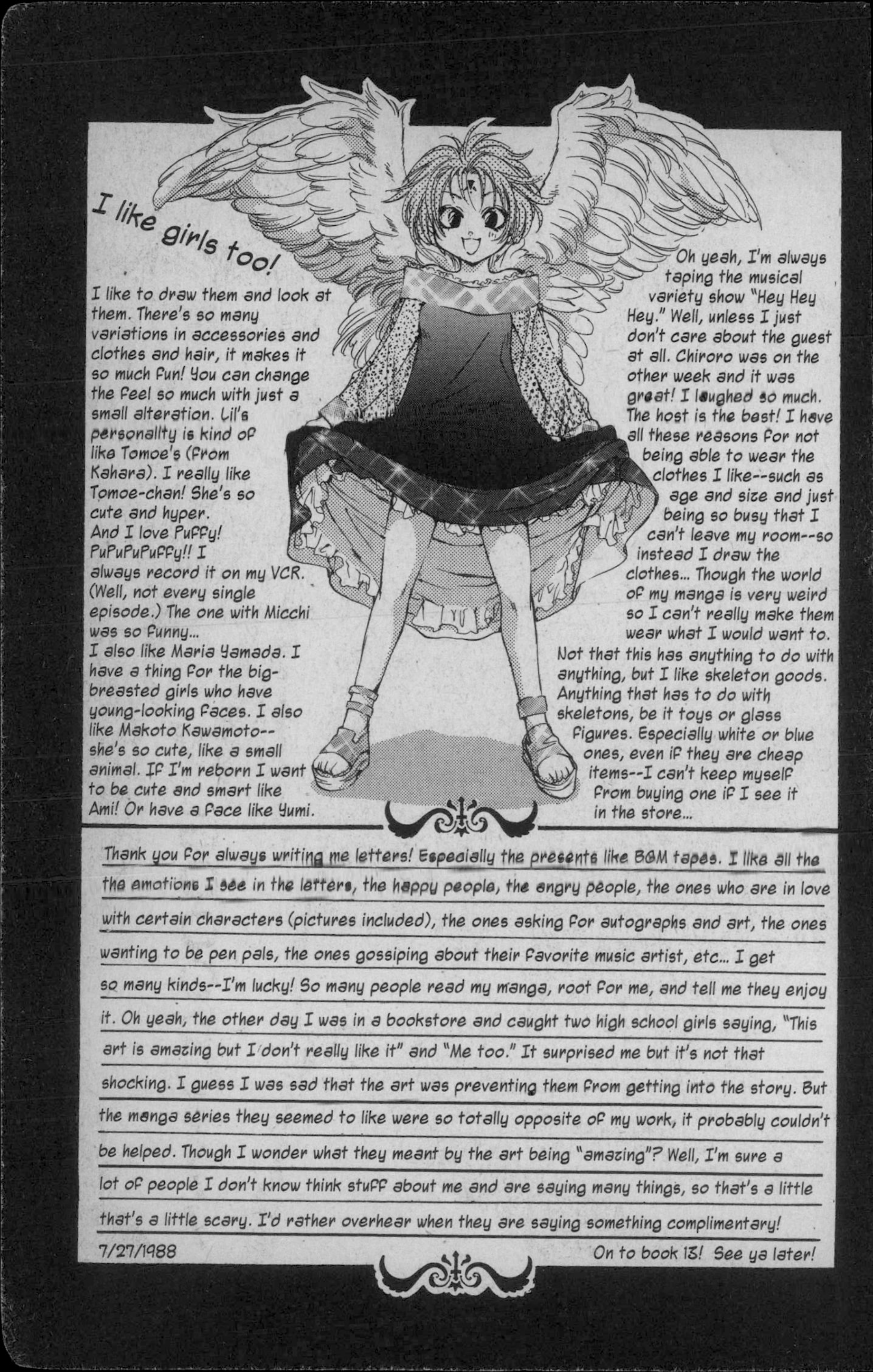

I like to draw them and look at them. There's so many variations in accessories and clothes and hair, it makes it so much fun! You can change the feel so much with just a small alteration. Lil's personality is kind of like Tomoe's (from Kahara). I really like Tomoe-chan! She's so cute and hyper. And I love Puffy! PuPuPuPuffy!! I always record it on my VCR. (Well, not every single episode.) The one with Micchi was so funny... I also like Maria Yamada. I have a thing for the big-breasted girls who have young-looking faces. I also like Makoto Kawamoto--she's so cute, like a small animal. If I'm reborn I want to be cute and smart like Ami! Or have a face like Yumi.

Oh yeah, I'm always taping the musical variety show "Hey Hey Hey." Well, unless I just don't care about the guest at all. Chiroro was on the other week and it was great! I laughed so much. The host is the best! I have all these reasons for not being able to wear the clothes I like--such as age and size and just being so busy that I can't leave my room--so instead I draw the clothes... Though the world of my manga is very weird so I can't really make them wear what I would want to. Not that this has anything to do with anything, but I like skeleton goods. Anything that has to do with skeletons, be it toys or glass figures. Especially white or blue ones, even if they are cheap items--I can't keep myself from buying one if I see it in the store...

Thank you for always writing me letters! Especially the presents like BGM tapes. I like all the the emotions I see in the letters, the happy people, the angry people, the ones who are in love with certain characters (pictures included), the ones asking for autographs and art, the ones wanting to be pen pals, the ones gossiping about their favorite music artist, etc... I get so many kinds--I'm lucky! So many people read my manga, root for me, and tell me they enjoy it. Oh yeah, the other day I was in a bookstore and caught two high school girls saying, "This art is amazing but I don't really like it" and "Me too." It surprised me but it's not that shocking. I guess I was sad that the art was preventing them from getting into the story. But the manga series they seemed to like were so totally opposite of my work, it probably couldn't be helped. Though I wonder what they meant by the art being "amazing"? Well, I'm sure a lot of people I don't know think stuff about me and are saying many things, so that's a little that's a little scary. I'd rather overhear when they are saying something complimentary!

7/27/1988

On to book 13! See ya later!

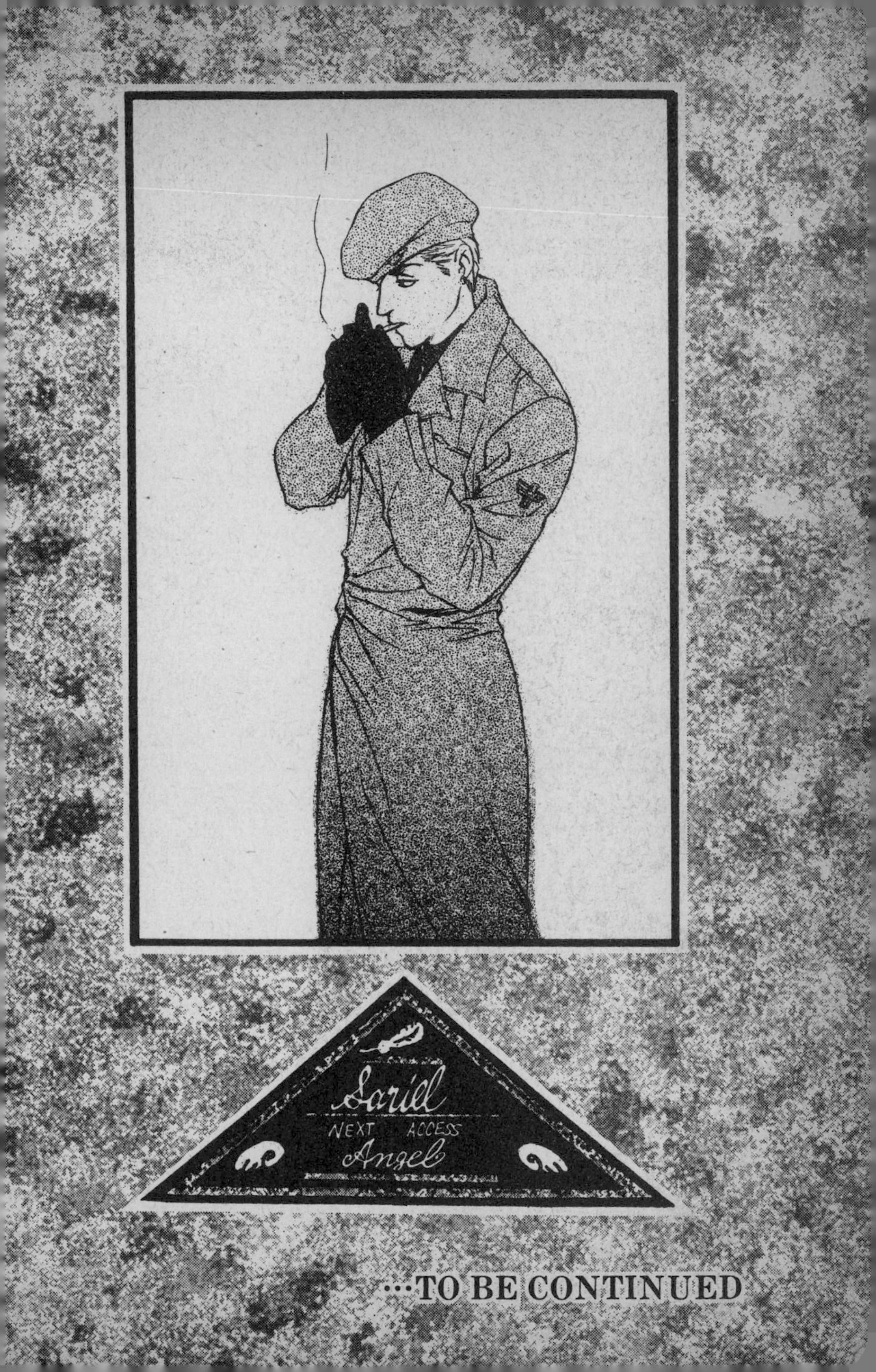
Sariel
NEXT ACCESS
Angel
...TO BE CONTINUED

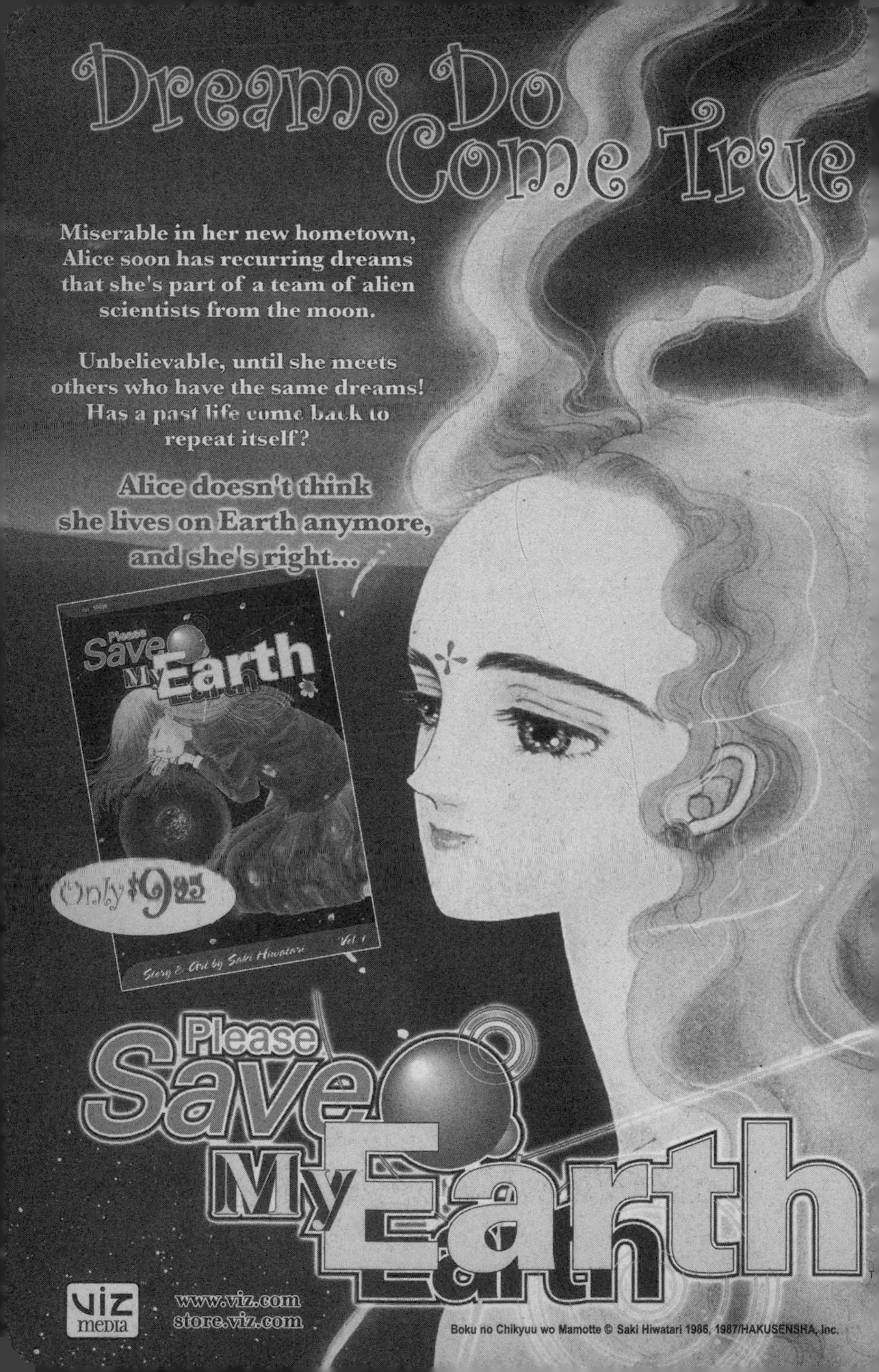

Dreams Do Come True
Miserable in her new hometown, Alice soon has recurring dreams that she's part of a team of alien scientists from the moon.
Unbelievable, until she meets others who have the same dreams! Has a past life come back to repeat itself?
Alice doesn't think she lives on Earth anymore, and she's right...
Please Save My Earth
Only $9.95
Vol. 1
Story & Art by Saki Hiwatari
Please Save My Earth
viz media
www.viz.com
store.viz.com
Boku no Chikyuu wo Mamotte © Saki Hiwatari 1986, 1987/HAKUSENSHA, Inc.

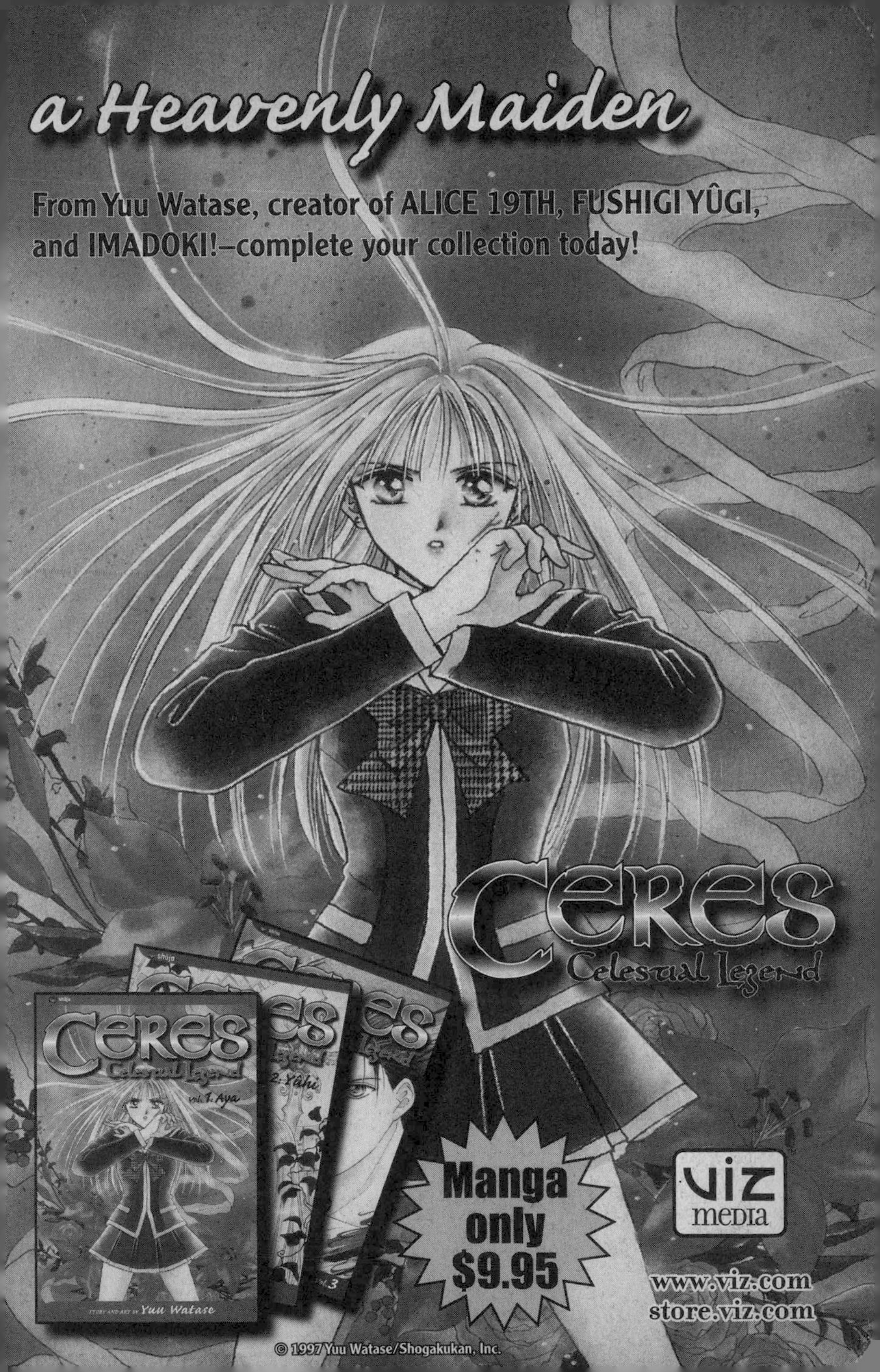
a Heavenly Maiden
From Yuu Watase, creator of ALICE 19TH, FUSHIGI YÛGI, and IMADOKI!—complete your collection today!
Ceres
Celestial Legend
Ceres
Celestial Legend
Yuu Watase
Manga only $9.95
viz media
www.viz.com
store.viz.com
© 1997 Yuu Watase/Shogakukan, Inc.

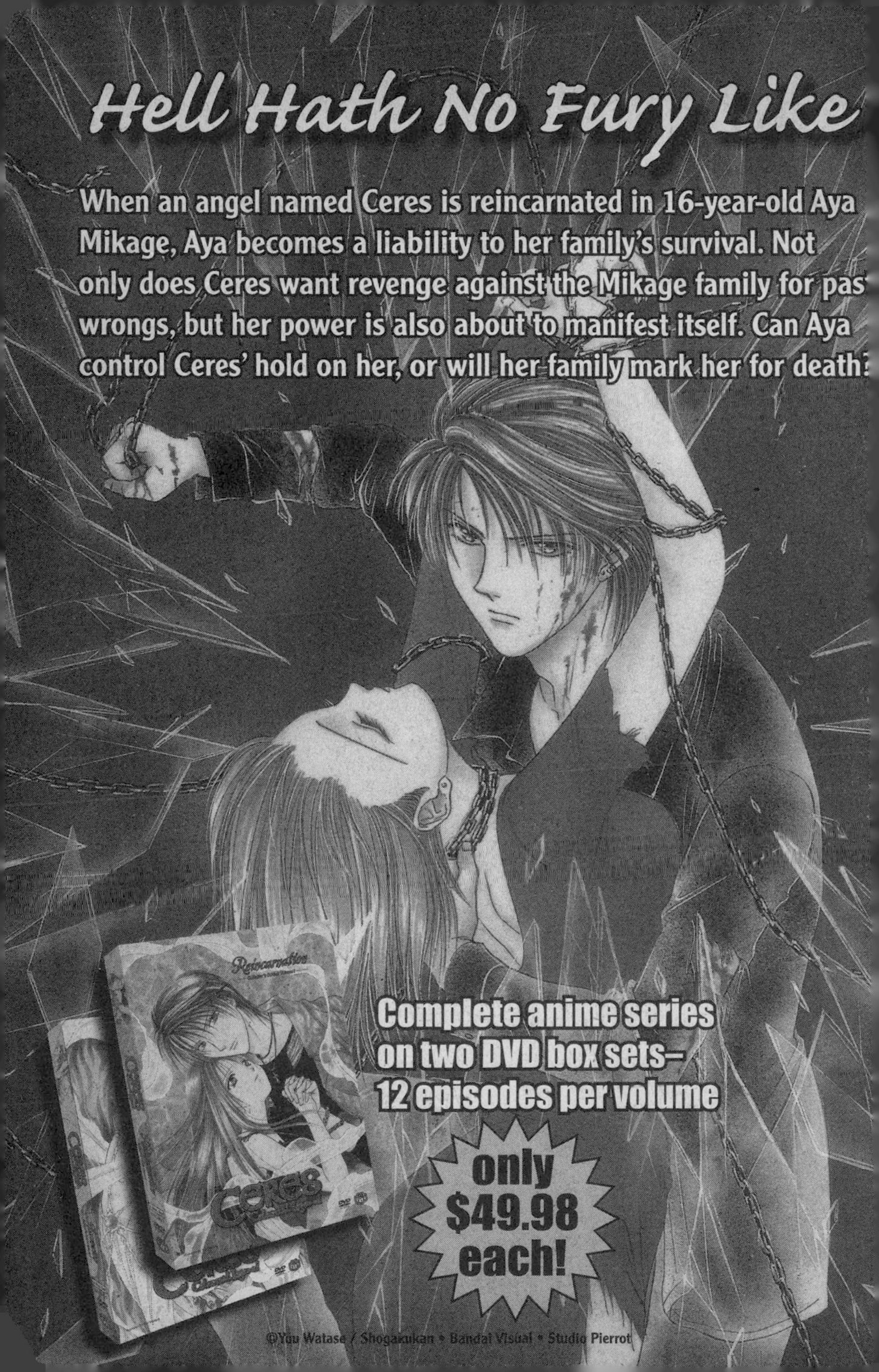
Hell Hath No Fury Like
When an angel named Ceres is reincarnated in 16-year-old Aya Mikage, Aya becomes a liability to her family's survival. Not only does Ceres want revenge against the Mikage family for pas wrongs, but her power is also about to manifest itself. Can Aya control Ceres' hold on her, or will her family mark her for death
Complete anime series on two DVD box sets– 12 episodes per volume
only $49.98 each!
©Yuu Watase / Shogakukan • Bandai Visual • Studio Pierrot

From Far Away

Trapped in a strange land, Noriko learns she holds a prophetic power – a power that could destroy the world. Befriended by the handsome and courageous Izark, Noriko realizes she must keep her power a secret, or risk her own death. But Izark also has secrets… could his spell her end?

Only $9.99!

From Far Away
STORY AND ART BY
KYOKO HIKAWA   Vol. 1

Start Your Graphic Novel Collection Today!

www.viz.com
store.viz.com

Kanatakara © Kyoko Hikawa 1991, 1992/HAKUSENSHA, Inc.